What Did You Do in the War, Dad?

WHAT DID YOU DO IN THE WAR, DAD?

Bob Sheridan

The Book Guild Ltd.
Sussex, England

The Book Guild Ltd
25 High Street,
Lewes, Sussex

First published 1993
Reprinted 1995
© Bob Sheridan 1993
Set in Baskerville
Typesetting by Ashford Setting & Design,
Ashford, Middlesex.
Printed in Great Britain by
Anthony Rowe Ltd.
Chippenham, Wiltshire.

A catalogue record for this book is
available from the British Library

ISBN 0 86332 804 0

TO

LESLEY RUTH
JILL SUSAN
PAUL ROBERT
SALLY ANNE

CONTENTS

List of Centre Section Photographs   9
List of Maps   10

Chapter 1: The Territorial Army — 1938/39   11
     Mobilization and the Old Bailey   19
     Stationers Hall   26
     Northolt   35
     Langley, Bucks   39

Chapter 2: 168 Officer Cadet Training Unit   45

Chapter 3: The Royal Ulster Rifles — 1940/44   56
     The Regimental Depot, Ballymena   56
     The Officers' Mess   61
     Stage Manager   67
     Draft Conducting Officer   71

Chapter 4: 1st Battalion — RUR   85
     Harpenden   85
     Hereford   91
     The Mules   94
     Carmarthen   99
     Newbury   106
     Dublin and the Bourke Family   108
     Under Close Arrest   114

Chapter 5: 1st Airborne Division   119
     Bulford Fields Camp   119
     Flying Experience   124
     Attachments to the RAF   131

Leave Travel by Glider   157
Air Observation Officer   161

Chapter 6: 6th Airborne Division   167
Chilton Foliat, Hungerford   168
Parachuting   170
The Death of Ian Aylmer-Jones   180
Kiwi Barracks   185
Events Leading up to D-Day   193
D-Day — 6 June 1944   206

Chapter 7: The Battle in Normandy   212
Longueval   212
7 June, 1940   217
8 June, 1940   226
9 June, 1940   228
10-11 June, 1940   234
13 June, 1940   236
Breville   239
Le Mesnil   247
Château St Come   258
Return to A Company   263

Chapter 8: Operation Paddle and Advance to the
                River Seine   265

Chapter 9: The Last Grip   299

Chapter 10: Return to England and Ireland   301

Chapter 11: The Parachute Regiment 2nd Battalion   328

Chapter 12: Liaison Officer with the Belgian Army   342

Chapter 13: Germany and Demobilization   348

LIST OF CENTRE SECTION PHOTOGRAPHS

Rifleman R.E.H. Sheridan, 1939

'E' Company, 2nd Battalion, The London Rifle Brigade, September 1939

Ballymena Castle. The Royal Ulster Rifles Regimental Depot Officers' Mess, 1940

Aerial Photography Recognition Course, Royal Air Force Experimental Establishment, Farnborough, September 1942

Major E.F. 'Killer' Johnson and Captain Huw Wheldon at Weston-Super-Mare, 1943

Colonel 'Rosie' Campbell, Commanding Officer, 1st Royal Ulster Rifles, 1941-1943

Officers of the 1st Battalion Royal Ulster Rifles, 1944

CSM Cunningham and Sergeant McCully

Captain R 'Dickie' Martin

Captain Ken Donnelly

Major E.F. 'Killer' Johnson

Lieutenants R.M. Burke, G.A. Maginnis and M.M. Archdale

One of our attachments from 82nd Airborne Division (USA)

Lieutenant Derek Boustead and his wife Lalergie

Major Paddie Liddle

Monty's message conveyed to all troops on 5 June, 1944

Monty's message of 10 June, 1944

Some of the gliders in Normandy

Battalion headquarters at Breville — after restoration

Breville Church . . .

. . . Used by the Germans as an ammunition store

Battalion Headquarters, Longueval

Our 'hosts' six years later

The café in Longueval. The lady in the middle is Mme Sheridan
Château St Come near Breville
We were well entertained by the present owners
The doorway where George Maginnis was killed by a mortar
  bomb
Battalion Headquarters at Le Mesnil
The German bunker at Touques near Deauville
The military cemetery near Deauville
The cross on the grave of Major E.F. 'Killer' Johnson
The Last Grip
2nd Battalion, The Parachute Regiment — Officers, November
  1944
'C' Company, 2nd Battalion, The Parachute Regiment,
  December 1944
Lochailort Hotel

LIST OF MAPS

Assault and Operations on D-Day of the Second
  British Army   211
Area of operations, 6th Airborne Division, 6 June
  to 17 August, 1944   214
Operation 'Paddle', 17 August to 1 September, 1944   292

1

The Territorial Army — 1938/39

One evening around the time of the Munich Agreement of September 1938 — when the Prime Minister, Neville Chamberlain, had arrived back at Croydon Airport after his meeting with Hitler, waving his piece of paper declaring 'Peace in our time', a group of about twenty Old Dunstonians (former pupils of St Dunstan's College, Catford) were in the bar of their sports club pavilion on Beckenham Hill, discussing the pros and cons of joining the Territorial Army. Because of the deteriorating political situation in Europe, the Government had announced that the strength of the Territorials would be doubled and had appealed to men between, I think, eighteen and twenty-five years of age to volunteer for military training in this way so that they would be better prepared to serve their country if the worst was to happen and war was to break out. Much the same happened, I think, with the Royal Navy and the Royal Air Force.

I don't think it could be said that young people of about my age at that time were particularly militaristic in outlook; in fact we probably had good reasons for not being so. Most of us had been born during the First World War and therefore had no recollections of it, but our parents' memories were very clear and many fathers, uncles and other relations had served in the forces and been subjected to the miseries of Flanders Fields, bombings and rationing. The tales they told of all that had happened only twenty years earlier were far from pleasant. However, despite being brought up on horrible stories about Paschendale, the Somme, Gallipoli and the like, we were undoubtedly very patriotic, having been nurtured on a diet of Empire Days, Anzac Days, St George's Days, and above all

11

perhaps, Armistice Days, when woe betide anyone, vehicle drivers as well as pedestrians, who didn't stop whatever they were doing at eleven am on the eleventh day of the eleventh month and remove their hats by way of tribute to the many thousands who had given their lives during World War One. To be in a busy area like Trafalgar Square in London at the time was a very moving experience when the busy hum of traffic would cease and all noise and movement would stop except only for the sound of gunfire salutes and the swish of wings as hundreds of pigeons, frightened by the silence, zoomed around Nelson's column and the steeple of St Martin's Church. Our family and other Irish families even celebrated St Patrick's Day. We would always receive a parcel of shamrock from Ireland and would each wear a sprig on our lapels to mark the occasion.

Our discussion that evening at Beckenham was not so much concerned with whether or not we would join the TA, but which particular unit would best serve our interests — and those of our country, of course. The only one of our number who was against joining was Rex Curtice, our rugger fullback and fast bowler. Rex was a journalist and had decided that he wasn't going to volunteer for anything. As fate would have it, Rex was conscripted soon after the outbreak of war, posted to the Royal Tank Regiment, sent out to Africa and was one of the first Old Dunstonians to be killed in action.

Our discussion, or argument might be a more appropriate term, centred mainly around three possible alternatives. First, there were those in favour of the 34th Ack-Ack Battalion, Royal Engineers, based at Holly Hedge House, Blackheath. This unit was the successor to the 20th London Regiment in which many Old Dunstonians had served during World War One. Others were advocating the 60th County of London (AA) Regiment which was located in a new drill hall at Bromley Road, Catford. This would have been very convenient for many of us living in the area, and a number of Old Boys had already joined that unit. The third main possibility was the 91st Field Regiment, Royal Artillery, based at Ennersdale Road, Hither Green, again fairly convenient for those living in the Catford district and which had the added attraction of being commanded by an Old Dunstonian who we all knew, Colonel — later Brigadier Bill Buffey. One of the attractions offered by the supporters of the 60th was that they were a searchlight unit and would therefore be employed on Home Defence and not sent overseas. As it subsequently turned out, they were despatched to France in the early days of the war with the British Expeditionary Force.

However, there was also a fourth possibility which a small group, including myself, favoured, namely, the London Rifle Brigade. In our opinion, the case for the LRB was unassailable. The headquarters was at Bunhill Row in the City of London where many of us were employed. Furthermore, the beer at Bunhill Row was known to be better and cheaper than anywhere else — we already had many friends including old boys in the regiment whose knowledge on that subject could be relied upon. Bunhill Row was also close to a pub on Ludgate Hill known as the Scotch House and much favoured by the Old Dunstonian Rugger Club at the time. Last but by no means least, the buttons and badges of rank of the Rifle Brigade were black, the same as we had worn in the OTC at school, and war or no war, there seemed to be no point in burdening ourselves with the task of cleaning brass buttons if this could be easily avoided.

The outcome of this debate and many others like it was that about twelve ODs, including myself, met one evening at the Scotch House, and after a beer or two to strengthen our resolve, drove round to Bunhill Row to sign up for King and Country. The only hiccup during the signing-up process which might have deprived the King and the LRB of our services, occurred during the somewhat perfunctory medical examination when the young medical officer announced that Bill Richard's eyesight was not up to the required standard. However, when it was explained to him that ours was a 'collective enlistment' — all for one and one for all — and on receiving our assurance that Bill would attend an optician the very next day to obtain a suitable pair of glasses, he relented and Bill was passed as medically fit. Little did the doctor know that it wasn't Bill's eyes that would create problems for the army but his abnormally large size fourteen feet.

So, in a couple of days the doubling up of the TA was realized with tremendous enthusiasm, despite horrific stories emanating from the Spanish Civil War about the ruthless efficiency of the German army and air force and bombs which destroyed all forms of life within forty miles of the point of impact! There were, of course, conflicting rumours — 'a friend of mine knows somebody who was driving in Germany and collided with a German tank which literally fell apart; it was only made of plywood.'

The OD contingent who joined the LRB at the time included Noel Balding (son of the founder of the United Friendly Insurance Society); John Jackson (the third of four brothers who had been at St Dunstans, and who was killed in Africa in 1943); David Beardshaw (who finished up the war as a staff captain on the British Military Staff in Washington, was demobbed in the USA and died in New York in 1949); Bill Richards, Leslie Lipsham (who is still going strong); Bob Clarke and Eric Scadeng (both of Lloyds Register. Bob, a fine rugger fullback and all-round cricketer died in the 60s); David Jones (the son of a prominent OD, E.B.T Jones, who lost an arm in World War One) and Reggie Albery (the youngest of the three Albery brothers). There were also a number of other ODs in the 1st Battalion of the LRB who we ran across from time to time, including Colin Watts, 'Johnie' Walker, Gordon Drucquer and John Childs.

We were all posted to Number 7 Platoon, E Company of the newly created 2nd Battalion. Our company commander was Captain James Wright and the platoon commander was a very tall and pugnacious looking Old Etonian, 2nd Lieutenant Harry Townsend. Our platoon also included a number of Bank of England staff we knew well from rugger visits to the bank sports ground at Roehampton; John Gore, Desmond Scaife, 'Porky' Cunliffe amongst others. The remainder of the platoon were a mixture from all walks of life; from the East End of London to the West; stockbrokers and barrow boys, accountants and engine drivers, and a first class bunch they all were.

The London Rifle Brigade, like its parent regiment, the Rifle Brigade, was very proud of its history, and 'encouraging' tales were told during periods of regimental history of the numbers slaughtered in historic battles around the world, such as the Somme and elsewhere whilst going over the top or holding fast to their trenches, all in strict obedience to the commands of general staff officers comfortably billeted in châteaux and villas many miles away from any risk — other than alcoholic poisoning.

Bunhill Row, our headquarters in the City of London, consisted of a large drill hall surrounded by armouries and stores and with a large bar ably run by 'old sweats', who, having been through the military training mill themselves, fully understood the thirst-making capabilities of drill sergeants in the drill hall below, and the thirst-quenching desires of large numbers of healthy young men on release from their labours. After every parade beer flowed in large quantities usually accompanied by the Bunhill Row speciality, a sausage and wad!

Membership of the TA at that time was not particularly onerous; two parades each week, in the evenings, involving an hour or so on foot and arms drill, including familiarization with various infantry weapons such as the Bren gun and two inch mortar.

Drill and related parades were conducted by NCOs; some regular soldiers, but mostly civilian part-timers but with longer service and who had transferred from the 1st Battalion. Some of the more junior NCOs were new recruits, like ourselves, but who had simply expressed a wish to be promoted. For some reason which I cannot explain, to volunteer for promotion in the TA was considered a bit queer, and in the case of quite a few of these NCOs, promotion was akin to being led like lambs to slaughter. The standard of discipline in the TA at that time was largely a measure of the respect one had for those in positions of authority and one had difficulty in respecting people who suffered from unjustified and exaggerated power complexes.

Anyway, there was very little these aspiring field marshals could do if their platoon or section decided to take the mickey. By prior arrangement, the order 'Left turn' would be followed by everyone turning to the right, 'shoulder arms' by a general stand at ease, and then a noisy debate as to whether the unfortunate victim had said what he thought he had said or what his tormentors had decided he meant to say. A general state of humorous chaos would then prevail until the hapless target would decide to revert to the ranks, or the RSM would arrive on the scene.

RSM Godbolt was aptly named. A regular soldier with many years service in the Rifle Brigade, he had what can best be described as a stentorian voice, a very discerning eye and although short in stature a very commanding presence, and there was no mickey-taking when he was on parade. Most of our platoon had spent several years in the school OTC, so we were reasonably efficient in foot and arms drill and were looked upon with some favour by the RSM who had no hesitation in attributing complaints about our inadequacy to the incompetence of our NCO volunteers.

Our twice weekly visits to Bunhill Row continued throughout the winter of 1938 and the spring of 1939 when orders were issued for the great event of the TA year, the annual camp, which was to be held in June at Burley in Hampshire.

Although there was no legal obligation for employers to release their employee Territorials for the annual camp, they were strongly encouraged to do so by the Government, the press and public opinion generally, particularly when the employee had obtained his employer's prior consent before joining up. Nor was there any obligation for the employer to continue to pay wages or salaries during the period of absence at camp although most did. This didn't apply in my case as an unpaid solicitor's articled clerk.

The camp was attended by all units in the London TA Division — several thousand troops, if we could be called such — and involved putting into practice in the field and on the ranges, all the military skills we had been taught at Bunhill Row and the other TA Centres. Section training, followed by platoon, company and battalion exercises, interspersed with route marches, demonstrations by regular army troops, and night training events. I wouldn't like to give the impression that we were overworked. Parades usually started around seven thirty am, by which time we had performed our necessary ablutions, had breakfast and laid our kits out in immaculate lines, with blanket folds facing front, in true military fashion and ready for inspection by our platoon commanders. On most days, parades finished in the early afternoon, after which we were free to do as we pleased subject to being back in camp by about ten pm, with lights out shortly after.

After 'dismissal' the routine most days for the OD contingent, plus a few hangers-on, was to head for Christchurch, a nearby seaside resort, where we could find good food and pleasant pubs in which to mull over the deteriorating political situation and our prospects as soldiers of His Majesty. Transport was no problem as several of us had brought cars to camp, so, after changing into suitable civilian clothes, our convoy would be seen heading off for the pleasures of the south coast.

Route marches always presented a problem because of the vastly different marching pace of light infantry and rifle regiments, from that of the 'ordinary' infantry of the line.

16

Whereas we, being a rifle regiment, marched at about 120 paces to the minute, with short strides, the London Scottish, for example, stepped out at a much more leisurely pace of about eighty, with the result that if we were the leading battalion, we were very soon out of sight from the rest of the column. When the Scottish were in the lead it was even more frustrating and comic with the riflemen trying unsuccessfully to match the long strides of those ahead or to ignore the skirl of pipes and drums and to set their own pace, with resultant concertina effect of the entire column. It was the usual practice for the senior officer or any brass hat from the War Office who happened to be around, to take the salute as the troops returned to camp after a march or a training exercise. When the LRB was in the lead, this presented no problem, other than a long gap between them and the following contingents. When the Scottish were in the lead, the riflemen were forced to halt some distance from the saluting base so that a suitable gap existed to enable them to march past at their accustomed speed.

Burley, in 1939, was the only TA camp I attended, but I had been to three OTC camps whilst still at school, and they followed much the same pattern except for the bar, of course. In addition to the military training and physical fitness aspects of those camps, they also provided an excellent opportunity for the officers, NCOs and men to get to know one another and to develop the necessary cohesion between the platoons, companies and Battalions not possible from a few hours a week at Bunhill Row and the other London TA centres. Our particular company was fortunate in that we needed no introduction to one another, but the camp also gave us the opportunity to get to know the other members of the battalion, including the officers, with whom, so far as we knew at that time, we would probably find ourselves in action before very long. We weren't to know of a decision of the War Office that in the event of war, Territorial units recruited in the same locality would not be sent into action as such, as had happened in the First World War when heavy casualties suffered by TA units had resulted in most of the menfolk of small villages and local districts being wiped out.

The food at the camp was very adequate and any quality deficiency was more than balanced by our healthy appetites. The quantity could always be supplemented in the evenings by a visit to the NAAFI tent for baked beans and bangers and

17

similar delicacies at very reasonable prices.

A feature of this particular TA camp, and no doubt of the many others around the country, was the bar, which, to the best of my recollection, served only beer and soft drinks. It consisted of a row of six foot wooden-top trestle tables, end-to-end, along the full length of a very large marquee, with numerous large wooden barrels laid out on the serving side, like a row of recumbent Buddhas. As the evening passed and the beer flowed, every song in the repertoire of the English, Welsh, Scottish and Irish would be sung with tremendous gusto, invariably ending with *Kiss me good night Sergeant Major*, after which, hoarse but happy, we would trip our way over guy ropes and latrine buckets back to our bell tents and palliasses largely anaesthetized from the temporary discomforts of military sleeping quarters.

The nocturnal latrine bucket is a feature of all military camps. This recognizes the natural consequence of consuming large quantities of beer before retiring, and the equally natural reluctance of common soldiery to make their way in darkness and bare feet, and sometimes rain, maybe several hundred yards to the nearest latrine in order to obtain relief, but rather to choose the easier course of simply raising the tent flap; an offence, of course, under King's Regulations. So, it was one of the duties of 'Dan, the sanitation man' — whoever he happened to be — to set down large buckets at the end of each line of tents at dusk to accommodate those who found themselves in need during the hours of darkness. A less attractive aspect of 'Dan's' job was carrying away the foaming buckets at first light!

There was no doubt, I think, in the minds of all those who attended Territorial camps in 1939, that the country would soon be at war with Germany, in fact at one stage there was a strong rumour that we would be mobilized at the camp and despatched to France without the opportunity to say farewell to our kith and kin. Whilst that possibility didn't worry us unduly, several of us were a little concerned as to what would happen to our parents' cars and the civilian impedimenta we had with us. However, this and other rumours came to nothing and the camp followed its scheduled two weeks' course without interruption.

Despite all we had read and been told of the horrors of the First World War, with the misery and discomfort of trench warfare and hand-to-hand combat, and the skill and ruthless efficiency of the German army, there was no despondency amongst the Territorials as to what might await them or that we wouldn't be able to give as much as we might be required to take. The camp had given us the opportunity to confirm our skills with our rifles, Bren guns and other weapons, not the least being the bayonet which required the simulation of a high degree of passion and a shriek of 'German bastard,' as we lunged forward to drive our piece of cold steel into the imaginary navel of a recumbent sack of straw. 'Now put the boot in,' our instructor would then roar as we stamped the heel of our boots into the imaginary genitals of the imaginary victim, withdrew our bayonets, dripping with imaginary blood and rushed on to repeat the slaughter of the next row of imaginary victims. After exhausting sessions of bayonet training I used to wonder what it would feel like if ever I happened to be at the receiving end, but quickly put such defeatist thoughts out of my mind.

To the best of my recollection, assault courses and field firing ranges hadn't been thought of at that time. Nevertheless, we were fit and strong and understood the principles of 'fire and movement.' We could crawl on our bellies over considerable distances to make use of cover and appreciated the importance of sections, platoons and companies working together as a team, and when the camp finished and we returned to our civilian lives we were a much more cohesive unit than we had been on our arrival.

Mobilization and the Old Bailey

On the evening of 28 August 1939 I arrived home about six thirty pm, switched on the radio and heard an announcement that the Territorial Army was being mobilized immediately, and that all ranks should report to their regimental headquarters without waiting for their formal mobilization notices. The announcement added that individuals should bring their own blankets for use until alternate arrangements could be made. Some weeks earlier we had received instructions that in the event of mobilization, we should report immediately to our Bunhill Row HQ in uniform, with our gas masks and kit bags. Uniforms, gas masks and kit bags had been issued, to be kept at our homes, and we were also fully instructed as to the personal clothing and items we should bring with us, but we hadn't contemplated the need to carry civilian blankets as we set off for war. I immediately telephoned Dave Beardshaw, and agreed that his sister would drive us both to Bunhill Row, picking me up at Beckenham in an hour or so.

When I was ready to leave, my mother was quite calm and simply bade me to look after myself and assured me of her prayers. Beneath the surface, I have no doubt, she was wondering whether she would see me again, but, as with millions of others at that time, and without any profound understanding of what was happening in Germany, she accepted that something had to be done about the Hitler menace; if that meant war, then it had to be faced. In any event she had great faith in the power of God to control events as he thought best and was content to rely on him in all things. On the other hand, Frances Stone, a cousin, who happened to be staying with us at the time, was in tears, being convinced that this was a last goodbye, influenced no doubt by thoughts of her brother who had been killed in France a little over twenty years earlier. Neither of them were to know that I would be back a few days later.

When we arrived, Bunhill Row was a hive of activity. Tables had been set up in the drill hall, one for each company, and manned by NCOs who had been called up a few days earlier and well drilled in mobilization procedure. We were directed to our respective company queues and, as our turn came, issued with our paybooks and mobilization shilling — or was it two?

Then, to other queues for our rifles, bayonets, belts, shoulder straps, pouches, haversacks, packs, steel helmets, ground sheets, boots, socks, pants, vests, shirts; at each distribution point stuffing the various articles into our sausage-like kit bags. When the size of garment was relevant the NCO in charge would take a quick look at his customer and bellow to his assistant, 'Small', 'Medium', or 'Large' as he thought appropriate. There was no option offered as we shuffled on, steel helmets dropping off as one bent to pick up a belt; something else clattering down as one bent to pick up the helmet, on and on until we reached the company assembly areas. I located E Company and dumped all my gear on the ground.

'Rifleman Sheridan, present and fully equipped, sir!'

Time was then available to sort ourselves out so that we could make some attempt at movement without dropping bits and pieces every second step. We knew by then that we had to march to wherever we were going to spend the night, and maybe other nights, but without knowing where that was to be. Webbing equipment had to be assembled so that it could be worn in the correct manner, all small items stuffed in the kitbag or pack, that most awkward of all items, the gas mask haversack, slung up on the chest, the bayonet in its holder and rifle sling adjusted, and last but by no means least, how to solve the problem of carrying two civilian blankets when both arms were required for a rifle and kitbag. Some unfortunates had also the temerity or stupidity to bring suitcases containing civilian clothes!

As time passed, the large drill hall became a mass of seething soldiery. Each of the four companies of the two battalions congregated in the areas allotted to them, standing, sitting, some fully dressed, others adjusting equipment, packing, smoking, and all without exception, in good humour until at last came the order: 'E Company, fall-in on the road, by platoons; Coy HQ 7, 8, 9, 10 platoon'.

The laughter changed to good humoured cursing with the necessity to prevent blankets trailing in the dust when carrying a rifle slung over one shoulder and kitbag over the other, but somehow E Company made its disorderly way out of the well-lit building into the darkness of Bunhill Row where the war-time blackout had already been partially introduced. Shouts, complaints, orders, advice, questions, answers could be heard from all directions: 'Where the hell is 7 Platoon?' 'Has anyone seen Sergeant Brown? He's got my steel helmet.' 'Where the hell are we going?' 'If this is war, I've had it,' 'Face this way,' 'Face that way.'

Gradually, the shambles took some form of order and as eyes became accustomed to the darkness the company sergeant major could be recognized as he moved up and down the line attempting to exert his authority on his disorderly flock. And then, horror of horrors, it began to rain. 'All those who wish to put on their capes may do so,' shouted the sergeant major, 'but hurry because we must be on the move.'

At last E Company trailed off behind him, leaving individuals still trying to adjust their capes, or repacking their kit bags, and trailing their blankets along the wet ground. The blackout then was by no means as effective as it was to become later, and some dim lights were visible from windows and the occasional lamp post. Despite this partial illumination, even those of us who were reasonably familiar with the area were soon 'lost' as we turned first one way and then the other, concentrating all our efforts on retaining a hold on our 'baggage'; not always with success, as indicated by a continuous flow of profanity from those unfortunate enough to drop something or to fall over someone else's fallen gear.

After about thirty minutes we concertinaed to an unmilitary halt. A small doorway opened near the head of the column, casting a shaft of light across the road and hurried consultations could be heard. 'Lead on in single file,' came the order and we moved forward, through the small eye of the needle gateway into the prison yard at the back of the Old Bailey — the Central Criminal Court!

This was the first time many of us had been in any form of prison, and it was with considerable interest that we were led down an iron stairway to a lower floor where there were rows of solid wooden doors, each provided with a small grill through which warders could keep an eye on their charges. To the best of my memory each cell was unfurnished except for a wooden seat on which, in normal times, the unfortunate occupant could rest himself. They were just about large enough to take a palliasse and were to be for most of us bedrooms for about two weeks. Scratched on the walls of the cells by previous occupants were brief records of the results of their trials or appeals — 'Jol Smith, ten years reduced on appeal to seven' — 'Tom Jones, five years hard — the bastards'. One of our number, Leslie Lipsham, achieved some notoriety by claiming, as he still does, that he slept for those two weeks in the cell reserved for unfortunates sentenced to death. Not all of us were privileged to have a cell to ourselves. Some were accommodated in interview and other rooms in the building, with four or five to a room and actual courts were set aside for use for reading, writing and relaxation. I'm sure that the High Court judges and leading silks of the day would have been greatly disturbed if they had seen the irreverent manner in which their seats on and below the bench were used for poker and other gambling sessions, bawdy sing-songs and other rowdy goings-on.

We were very fortunate in two particular respects. One of the riflemen in E Company happened to be the son of the owner of a large vegetable and fruit wholesaling business in Covent Garden market, only a short distance from the Old Bailey. After the implications of this had been explained to James Wright, our company commander, the company truck would set off for Covent Garden early each morning, returning an hour or so later with fresh vegetables and fruits of every description. If recruitment posters could have shown the riflemen, NCOs, and officers of E Company 2nd Battalion LRB gorging themselves on superb salads followed by unlimited supplies of apples, oranges, bananas, grapes, melons and other exotic fruits, the rate of enlistment would have greatly increased.

The other stroke of good fortune was that another father — that of Noel Balding, one of our OD group — was not only the wealthy chairman of a large insurance business but was also extremely generous. Opposite the rear entrance to the Old Bailey was a Pimm's House, which naturally became our unofficial or off-duty rendezvous, and regularly every night, or nearly so, Mr Balding Senior would join the party and would never fail to leave one or two large banknotes with the proprietor — 'to keep the boys going until I arrive tomorrow'.

Needless to say, we were not slow in taking advantage of this generosity. In fact some of our fellow riflemen from homes in the East End of London and less well endowed financially than ourselves, had never seen or experienced anything remotely like the life we led during those two or three weeks at the outbreak of war. Interestingly enough, although all the ranks of the company, and I am sure of the battalion, were drawn from all sections of society, upper, middle and so called lower classes, there was never any suggestion of snobbery, discrimination or resentment and all were at liberty to enjoy the fruits of Covent Garden and the mild and bitter provided from the resources of the United Friendly Insurance Company. The East Enders were just as proficient in their rendering of *Knock 'em in the Old Kent Road*, *Any Old Iron* and other cockney songs as we Old Dunstonians were of our repertoire of rugger songs.

I was an interested observer of a somewhat unique incident one evening when on my way to Charing Cross station, which reflected the friendly and easy-going relationships which existed in the Territorials at that time. I was approaching Ludgate Hill along Old Bailey when I saw our company commander, Captain James Wright, and our platoon commander, Harry Townsend, both immaculately turned out in their service dress, standing on the corner trying to attract the attention of a passing taxi.

Suddenly, a large and very opulent chauffeur-driven Rolls Royce drew up alongside them. A rear window was wound down and a head peered out which I instantly recognized. It was 'Dan,' our company sanitation man, also in uniform. He enquired, very politely but with no suggestion of deference, whether he could give them a lift to wherever they were going, an offer which they accepted with alacrity, and opening the door they climbed aboard. Incidentally, James and Harry were both Old Etonians whilst 'Dan' was an Old Harrovian. 'Dan' came from a very wealthy and aristocratic family. He had decided that the country had need of his services, but he had no ambition for promotion or to be commissioned and was quite content to remain as a permanent sanitation orderly. He continued in that lowly but nevertheless important capacity whilst I was with the battalion.

Our task whilst in residence at the Old Bailey was to guard it and one or two other buildings close by against unauthorized intrusion. We soon settled down to a daily routine. Every weekday morning — Sunday being a day of rest — all those not on guard duty or detailed for fatigues of one kind or another, were required to parade in 'shirt sleeve order,' with towel and soap and then to move off 'at the double' to a swimming bath somewhere around Farringdon Road, I think it was, for a daily bath. I can still recollect the regular clump-clump, clump-clump of our boots as we trotted around Snow Hill Police Station at about seven o'clock in the morning and the cheery waves of passers-by as they made their way to their work places.

Although our early morning swim was very refreshing, and we usually managed to combine it with a wash and shave to save congestion in the somewhat limited toilet facilities in the Old Bailey, we were always hot and sweaty by the time we trotted back, but with a hearty appetite for breakfast in the prison yard; usually smoky tea and cremated bacon. Then followed our daily duties.

Our first Sunday in the Old Bailey was 3 September 1939 — the day war broke out. Orders had been issued the previous day for a C of E parade in St Paul's Cathedral at ten thirty am. We duly paraded at nine am on 3 September for the usual preliminary inspection of the duty sergeant, followed by the inspection proper at nine thirty by Lieutenant MacKenzie, who was in command of the parade. Having overcome these two hurdles, we marched off smartly along Old Bailey to Ludgate

Hill, turned left and up the hill to the cathedral where, with appropriate reverence, we removed our headgear and filed into the cathedral and into pews immediately below the pulpit and in front of a fairly sparse civilian congregation.

The service proceeded in accordance with the Prayer Book ritual until, after the lusty singing of *Onward Christian Soldiers*, the Bishop of London slowly mounted the pulpit and the congregation settled down with the normal coughs, nose blowing and fidgeting in anticipation of a thirty minute or so sermon. At the precise moment when the silence was complete, and the bishop was poised to announce his text, a strange slapping noise commenced at what seemed to be some distance away at the back of the cathedral in the direction of the main entrance. The bishop looked up, opened his mouth, and then paused. The slapping noise gradually increased in intensity and the less disciplined amongst us could not resist a quick glance around to identify the cause. An elderly white haired verger, appropriately clad in a black gown and carrying his verger's wand-of-office and presumably wearing loose bedroom slippers which made the peculiar slap with each step, was making his way with great solemnity down the centre aisle. The bishop waited, obviously disconcerted by this unusual occurrence. The verger made his way around the front pews and slowly mounted the steps up to the pulpit where he halted, bowed his head in a gesture of subservience, and handed the bishop a piece of paper. The bishop nodded his head, presumably in a gesture of superiority, adjusted his glasses and read what was written on the paper. Meanwhile, the verger again bowed his head, turned and descended the steps and without the slightest trace of urgency or concern slapped his way back down the full length of the building until his steps died away in the distance.

Only when complete silence had returned did the bishop speak. 'I have just been informed', he said, as if pronouncing a death sentence, 'that in a broadcast just concluded, the Prime Minister has announced that as Germany has not complied with the Anglo-French ultimatum to cease hostilities in Poland, this country is in a state of war with Germany'.

The bishop paused for a moment, looking from left to right, as if expecting some response, then said, 'There will be no sermon. We will say a prayer and then all troops will return to their quarters'.

We bowed our heads, half expecting to hear the drone of German bombers overhead. The bishop said a prayer, then turned and descended from the pulpit while we all stood in respectful silence, then filed out of our pews and made our way down the aisle, fighting a strange urge to hurry. Since the end of the Spanish Civil War, the newspapers had resounded with stories about mass air raids by German bombers on towns and cities and fears were widespread that in the event of war with Germany, London would become the immediate target of similar raids. As we filed out of the cathedral, the air-raid sirens started the spine-chilling wail that was going to be heard so often in London in the years ahead.

Following the declaration of war, but not necessarily linked to that event, a system of short twenty-four hours passes was introduced which permitted us once every two or three weeks in groups of three or four, to stay away from the 'barracks' overnight: from six pm to six pm the following day. This was a great boon, as it meant that we could go home for a hot bath, home cooking and a night between clean sheets. Needless to say, when my turn came, my mother was delighted to see me so soon after my departure and I was able to catch up on all the family news. On one short leave I was able to drive to the then London Airport — Croydon — to see off my sister-in-law, Marjorie, and her two young sons John and Philip, who were flying off to stay with relations in neutral Ireland for what was then thought to be the three or four months' duration of the war, to escape the anticipated mass air raids, which didn't materialize until 1940.

When not involved on guard duties we were free on most evenings to come and go as we pleased, which usually meant visiting the Pimms House or some other local pub. From time to time we might go a little further afield, 'up West,' but with the intensification of the blackout regulations and the shortening evenings it was difficult to find one's way around, particularly when hurrying back to 'barracks' after closing time.

Stationers Hall

After about ten days in the Old Bailey and with the approach of the legal term when the courts and cells would be required for their normal purposes, we were moved a short distance to the splendour of the halls of two City livery companies, the Stationers Hall and the Cutlers Hall. Each of these halls normally accommodated a small administrative staff together with all the historic paraphernalia of these ancient societies: the banners, robes and insignia of the various officials over many centuries; records back to medieval times; glass, gold, silverware and cutlery used for banquets, receptions and similar splendid occasions, all irreplaceable and of incalculable value. The reception and banqueting rooms were superbly finished with wonderful antique furniture, luxurious carpeting and decorated with historic paintings and other works of art. Number 7 and 8 Platoons were allocated to Stationers Hall and when we arrived most of the valuable movables had been taken away, presumably to be stored in places of safety. However, there had been no time to remove or cover the carpets, so before making our way up the splendid stairways to the main reception rooms which were to serve as our dormitories, with palliasses laid out in four rows down the length of the room, we were required to remove and carry our boots. In the mornings it was a quaint sight to see the members of 7 and 8 Platoons tiptoeing down the stairs in their stocking feet before squatting around the hallway putting on their boots and gaiters. Invariably there was much cursing and swearing on the many occasions when, after doing up his boots, someone would remember some forgotten essential and have to rip them off before racing 'upstairs' to make good the deficiency. Fortunately, after a few days, fibre matting was procured from somewhere to cover the carpets and this irritation was discontinued.

By this time news was seeping through to the lower ranks and no doubt also to some higher ranks, that the reason the battalion was being held in the City was to protect vulnerable points (VPs) from attack by saboteurs. Who decided on the Points considered as vulnerable, and why, was never disclosed but it now became the important task of E Company to provide two sentries, twenty-four hours per day, at about four locations in the vicinity. Those not employed on guard duties continued to be occupied with weapon training, drill parades, filling sandbags and constructing anti-blast protection for nearby doors, windows and sentry posts. The other companies of the battalion were also quartered in various buildings in the City, including Unilever

House on the Embankment, performing similar tasks.

One morning, E Company in general, and Number 7 Platoon in particular, awoke to shattering news. During the night, two of our comrades-in-arms, John Jackson and Bill Richards, had been found smoking on sentry duty and placed under close arrest! This was the first time that we in E Company, and probably anyone else in the battalion, had come into serious conflict with the military discipline machine and its procedures, and we were uncertain and worried as to the possible consequences.

Up to that time and no doubt as with most other TA units, discipline had taken the form of a ready compliance with polite 'requests' by officers and NCOs to do this or that, provided always that whatever was required seemed reasonable and necessary in the prevailing circumstances. If any such requests seemed unreasonable or unnecessary we had little or no compunction about drawing attention to the reasons why compliance was inappropriate or indeed inconvenient. The emphasis given to any such objection naturally depended on the degree of respect in which the superior was held. As explained earlier, we had little respect for some of our volunteer 'upstart' NCOs; more for the NCOs with longer service who had transferred from the 1st Battalion and who in any event had the good sense to earn our cooperation by not being unduly bossy. Our officers also 'understood' the situation. They made a point of not pushing us around unnecessarily, so we had no hesitation in treating them with the respect their rank deserved. In other words, except for the little Hitlers amongst our ranks, we were all good friends, and willing to muck in and do our bit as circumstances and the good order and well-being of the company and country required.

Now, however, we were faced with an entirely new situation and we sensed, with much more foreboding, that the relaxed club-like existence we had enjoyed as TA volunteers was about to be disrupted and we were going to be required to conform, volunteers and conscripts alike.

Rumour had it that a retired general with staff experience in the Boer War had been called back to the colours to take command of the London TA Division. En route to assume his command, and whilst still clad in tweeds and brothel creepers he had been foolish enough to make a routine call at a battalion

HQ where he had been refused entry and addressed as 'old cock' by a relaxed solicitor's clerk in uniform. Clear orders had been issued that only persons known to have authorized business in the building and military personnel in uniform who could properly identify themselves, should be admitted, and the sentry, quite properly, did not consider an elderly gent in ancient Harris tweeds, complete with a hearing aid and requiring the support of a walking stick, fell into either category.

The general's first executive act on assuming his new command was to make it clear to his brigade commanders that the easy going ways of the TA would no longer be tolerated. Discipline would be brought into line with the regular army. The brigade commanders communicated this news to their battalion commanders, including our battalion commander, Lieutenant-Colonel Bignold-de-Cologan, who, in turn, informed his company commanders who, in their turn informed the platoon commanders. As fate would have it, Harry Townsend, our platoon commander, was informed of the general's edict by James Wright on the day that John and Bill accepted an invitation to go on twenty-four hour guard duty. This was a generous and patriotic gesture on their part because they could quite easily have persuaded — or perhaps bribed with the promise of a few pints of beer — a couple of other riflemen to take on the duty, which they certainly would have done if they had had any other plans for that evening.

And so it was that at four pm on the fateful evening John and Bill paraded with the new guard to take over the onerous responsibility for the protection of Stationers Hall and Cutlers Hall and the nearby VPs.

One of these VPs was an archway or covered precinct about ten yards long over the pavement of the roadway between the two halls and where we had built protective sandbag walls up to a height of about eight feet, thus converting an otherwise exposed and windswept archway into a fairly cosy strong point in the heart, as it were, of the British Empire. Naturally, as with all the VPs under our control, we accepted without question the importance of denying the enemy access to our archway, despite the fact that, for reasons of national security no doubt, the reasons were never explained to us. The two sentry posts were at either end of the covered area, about ten yards apart, and their duties were to watch out for and deal with any suspicious behaviour in the vicinity. Exactly what they were supposed to do if they observed any behaviour they deemed suspicious was left to their discretion. This was the preferred VP because it provided protection against both wind and rain during the two hour sentry stint, so John and Bill made it clear to the guard commander that this was where they would prefer to be posted for their spell of sentry duty in the early hours of the morning.

As fate would have it, on that very evening, Harry Townsend had a dinner date in the West End which ended in a night club in the early hours. As a taxi carried him back through the blackout to his room in Stationers Hall, he was feeling confident and self-satisfied. The evening had gone well and he knew that his tall, athletic, uniformed figure had cut quite a dash on the small night club dance floor. It was then that he remembered the stern admonition by James Wright that steps must be taken to ensure a higher level of discipline and efficiency in the performance of his platoon. Yes, he thought to himself, he would ensure that his platoon would be an example to the rest of the battalion, and this was a very suitable occasion to check that the sentries were alert and doing their duty. It would impress everybody to know that he was prepared to inspect the guard in the middle of the night, and this was an ideal opportunity.

He paid off his taxi a short distance from the Hall and walked towards the archway, expecting to receive the approved challenge of 'Who goes there?' It was a pitch dark night, but he was able to make out the entrance to the archway. No challenge was made. He continued cautiously through to the further end where he should have been confronted by the other sentry, but still no challenge. By now he was feeling a little apprehensive, and he recollected hearing of an inspecting officer who had not heard a sentry's challenge and had been run-through with a bayonet.

'Where are the sentries?' he said in a nervous whisper.

'Up here,' said a voice and looking up he saw a glow of a cigarette end appear over the top of one of the sandbag walls.

'What are you doing up there?' he demanded.

'Keeping watch,' came the reply.

'Come down immediately,' ordered Harry, and two figures clambered down and stood in front of him.

This was the first occasion that Harry had been confronted with such a situation and he was uncertain as to what he should do. He recognized John and Bill, with whom he had always been on most friendly terms, and he wasn't sure whether he should simply remind them that smoking on sentry duty was forbidden or whether he should take sterner action. He then remembered the general.

'You will both be charged with smoking on sentry duty,' he said, and turning, he walked away towards Stationers Hall where he summoned the guard commander, Corporal Godley, from the guard groom and ordered him to relieve Rifleman Jackson and Rifleman Richards immediately and place them under close arrest, charged with smoking on duty.

If the guard commander had been anyone other than Corporal Godley, the situation might have been saved, even at that late hour. A quiet man to man chat with Harry might have persuaded him to sleep on it and decide on a less drastic course of action in the cold light of day. After all, John and Bill were both very reasonable chaps and would accept whatever admonishment Harry decided to give them without the necessity of dragging 'Higher Command' into the act; and in any event, wasn't the good reputation of 7 Platoon and E Company at risk?

However, Corporal Godley — a rifleman on mobilization three weeks earlier — was ambitious and here was an ideal opportunity to exercise the authority vested in him. So, John and Bill were replaced by two other sleepy sentries and told that they were under arrest, whereupon they returned to their palliasses in the guard room having told Corporal Godley to have them called in time for breakfast at eight am.

Such was the story which spread through E Company the following morning, and much debate went on as to what would happen next. Reports filtered down that James Wright and Harry Townsend were closeted in the company office with the company sergeant major, pouring over King's Regulations. It was rumoured first that the charges would be withdrawn, then, later, that word of the event had reached Battalion HQ — no doubt through Corporal Godley — and the charges, and maybe others, would be pressed with the utmost severity. What might those other charges be? 'Sleeping on sentry duty whilst on active service?' — 'Exposing the lives of their comrades to risk?' Someone had the temerity to suggest that John and Bill would complete their military service before a firing squad at the Tower of London.

Through all this turmoil and debate, John and Bill were reclining on their palliasses in the guard room, apparently unaware or unconcerned about all the speculation as to their fate, until at ten am, they were formally charged and, because of the seriousness of their offence, remanded for trial by the battalion commander.

This gave rise to two possibilities. The first, the less fearsome of the two, was that the colonel would decide to deal with the matter himself, in which case there was a limit to the sentence he was permitted to impose: no firing squad or flogging for example. The second possibility was that the colonel would decide on a court martial, which conjured up all kinds of horrible consequences. Fortunately, the colonel was a wise old man.

An escort was detailed — a sergeant, corporal and rifleman — to ensure that the two accused were present at Battalion HQ at Unilever House by midday. The relationship between the accused and members of the escort was such as to dispense with too much military formality, and fortunately the time permitted the party and supporters to drop in at The Ludgate for a pint of beer to cheer them on the way.

From what John and Bill told us later, the case against them began to flounder when Harry Townsend gave his evidence. He was extremely nervous and became somewhat incoherent when the Colonel asked him why he had decided to inspect the sentries at three o'clock in the morning and whether he made a regular practice of doing so. Harry realized that he was in a fix. He had never got out of his warm bed to inspect sentries at any time and the only reason he had done so on this occasion was that he had been on his way back from a late party feeling very relaxed and had thought it a satisfying way of terminating an enjoyable evening. He found difficulty in explaining this to the colonel and mumbled something to the effect that he thought it a wise thing to do from time to time, and no, he didn't do it very often but he would in the future. The colonel caught on and turned his attention to the defendants. What had they to say?

Standing stiffly to attention and with his eyes fixed firmly on a knot-hole in the woodwork over the colonel's head, John quietly and clearly and presumably with some conviction, explained how it was that he and Rifleman Richards had found themselves reclining on a pile of sandbags, smoking cigarettes when on sentry duty. After careful deliberation as to the best means of ensuring that no stranger could approach without being observed, they had decided that the top of the sandbags was the most advantageous point to keep the full length of the archway under observation and to tackle any suspicious person should the need arise. To have remained at opposite ends of the archway where they had been posted would have increased the possibility of being surprised. As regards the cigarettes, John took the bull by the horns and said that he hadn't realized that on active service sentries were not permitted to smoke. He thought that the no-smoking regulation only applied to ceremonial sentries such as outside Buckingham Palace. They had lit cigarettes to help them keep alert and had been most careful to ensure that the glow didn't reveal their position.

John rested his case, as it were, and there were a few moments of silence. The colonel then looked up at Bill. 'Have you anything to add?' he said.

'No sir,' said Bill, emphatically.

The colonel turned to Harry Townsend. 'What have you to say about these two riflemen?' he asked.

Harry recognized the opportunity to restore the position and seized it. 'They have both been excellent riflemen,' he said, 'I am glad to have them in my platoon.'

The sentence was something of an anti-climax: fourteen days' confinement to barracks (CB), but this gave rise to further problems for Company HQ. What exactly did CB involve? There was a further study of King's Regulations from which it appeared that in addition to loss of leave-of-absence for the stipulated period, plus additional guard duties and cookhouse fatigues, the two prisoners must undergo two hours 'pack drill' each day. This involved separate hourly drill periods in full kit with packs filled with sand.

John and Bill suffered their punishment with appropriate stoicism and good humour, supported, it must be added, by their many friends, who turned up to watch and give them moral encouragement at the drill sessions which took place in a small enclosed garden near Cutlers Hall.

With the approach of winter, the TA or at least our part of it — suffered its greatest indignity. It was mid-October and no army greatcoats or gloves had been issued, which presented a particular problem for those on guard duty. This included at least three spells of sentry duty outside and around the two Halls, of which two spells could be during the night and very early in the morning. To have to stand more or less on the same spot in a London street for two hours was highly disagreeable in any circumstances. To have to do so on a cold autumn night clad only in battledress and carrying a rifle with bare hands, which one was expected to handle with precision, and generally to maintain an appropriate military bearing, was enough to dampen the ardour of the most enthusiastic soldier. And so it was; our enthusiasm was dampened.

Eventually, our plight was brought to the attention of 'Higher Authority' who, we decided, owned shares in one of the large ready-made men's clothing stores. An army truck arrived at the entrance to Stationers Hall and delivered about thirty civilian overcoats of a wide variety of patterns and designs. No two were the same. Herring bone and plain, wide striped and narrow stripes, wide lapels and narrow, double breasted and single, black, brown, blue and grey, all made with the eye for the spiv market rather than the bank manager; and it was in these monstrous garments that E Company, the cream of the British army, was required to mount guard in the capital city of the Empire. It was no wonder that Hitler thought the British army would be a push-over!

For the next few days we were a source of amazement and amusement to all passers by. 'Cor blimey, look at them pansies', shouted the messenger boys to one another. 'Call yourselves soldiers? — More like a bunch o'sissies'.

Young City secretaries would congregate on the other side of the narrow road, giggling nervously as they vied with one another in thinking up the most outrageous remarks. 'Oo, I like 'im in the plum colour' said one, 'I bet he could kill me, 'e don't 'arf look fierce'.

'Garn', said her neighbour, 'you'd kill 'im in five minutes'.

The hardest comments to bear were from the old soldier types. 'What's the bleedin' army coming to? If that's the army today we haven't got a hope', and so on, as we stood like statues, feeling and looking like freaks and wondering how long we would have to bear this abuse. Not so mute were the less inhibited East Enders amongst us. With a quick glance to either side to ensure that no officers or NCOs were within hearing — 'Fxxx off,' they would mouth at their tormenters, which only tended to aggravate ribaldry and ridicule.

34

Northolt

As the period of the 'cold war' progressed, it was decided, in the middle of November 1939, no doubt by someone in the War Office who had nothing better to decide, that the men of the 2nd Battalion of the London Rifle Brigade, and particularly E Company, were becoming far too comfortable in their City Livery accommodation, and should therefore be moved to more bleak surroundings. By sticking pins into a map of the outer London suburbs it was further decided that a number of electricity pylons near Northolt should be designated as Vulnerable Points in need of special protection against the IRA and Hitler's underground agents, and that we should be moved to that area for the purpose, away from the comforts of the Stationers and Cutlers Halls and the tempting fleshpots of the West End.

Northolt in 1939 was still 'in the country' but in the early stages of being engulfed by the greater London suburban spread. The area included the airport, which was then used mainly by the RAF, but was subsequently to become the main civilian airport for London during the construction of Heathrow after the war. Our new location was in a partially constructed housing estate, where E Company was allocated a number of three-bedroomed semi-detached houses which had reached or nearly reached the stage of structural completion and which included a roof, but which were otherwise far from ready for human habitation — if for no other reason than that they were completely surrounded by a sea of mud and contractor's rubble. The only practical means of access to or egress from the houses was over a network of planks laid between the front doors and the partly made-up road. Negotiating one's way over the planks wasn't too difficult by day, but extremely hazardous at night after returning from guard duty or, in a more relaxed frame of mind, from having a few pints in the local. To slip off a plank and find oneself sitting in six inches of cold wet mud was not only extremely uncomfortable but also particularly disastrous in that there were no black-out curtains and lights were forbidden, so cleaning-up was impossible before daylight. First parade in the morning was at the crack of dawn and many a muddy rifleman was disciplined for appearing in an untidy and dishevelled condition — another way of saying that their clothes and boots were caked with yellow clay-like mud. A few of us were fortunate enough to be billeted with local families. I was one of the lucky ones, and with David Beardshaw was allocated to a family a short distance away, where we lived, or at least slept, in relative comfort when not on guard duty.

Our stay at Northolt guarding electric pylons only lasted for about three or four uncomfortable weeks and was largely uneventful except for an amusing incident which lingers in my memory.

Harry Townsend had decided that for his bedroom he would use the rear upstairs room in the house designated as our platoon headquarters, and this was where his camp bed and gear were laid out. He only slept there when he was company duty officer and required to be in the vicinity overnight. Where he slept at other times I don't know. The guard room was established in the downstairs front room, no doubt now proudly used by the present occupants as their dining or sitting room. Each guard consisted of about ten riflemen and two NCOs and palliasses were laid out on the floor for the use of those not on duty at any particular time.

Following our mobilization, Harry had great difficulty locating and retaining a satisfactory batman from amongst the members of his platoon. One rifleman after another had been persuaded or pressurized into the job, only to be returned to normal duties after a few days for neglect of duty in one way or another. As I was to discover after I was commissioned, good batmen are born, not made, and it was a disaster for any officer to appoint a batman who didn't want the job. The batman's duties for a junior officer at this particular time were fairly simple. They consisted mainly of making-up his officer's bed and keeping his quarters clean and tidy; cleaning and polishing boots and shoes and Sam-Browne belt, and blanco-ing and polishing the brass fittings of his officer's webbing equipment. (We hadn't yet reached the state in the war when polishing brass was prohibited in case the glint gave one's position away to the enemy!) One other important duty in Harry's case was to call him at whatever time in the morning that he stipulated, with a large cup of hot sweet tea. In return for all these menial chores, the officer gave the batman some small payment each week; about 1s. This doesn't sound much but it has to be borne in mind that our pay at that time was around £1.2s. per week.Furthermore, if the batman was smart he could take advantage of his position in other ways. For example, it was the usual practice for the platoon sergeant or the platoon corporal to include the batman on rosters for guard duties or other fatigues and the standard reaction of the batman was, of course, to stipulate that this was impossible, as he had to be 'about his officer's business.' NCOs were generally unwilling to incur the wrath of an officer by interfering with his requirements, so, by playing one off against the other, the batman could avoid the more unpleasant aspects of army life. Occasionally an over-zealous NCO would approach an officer and ask whether the batman was available for other duties but this immediately created the impression in the officer's mind that his authority was being questioned and that he wasn't capable of running his own affairs. He also knew that if he didn't support his batman he would very soon be looking for a replacement so the usual terse response was that the batman should be excused other duties until the NCO was informed to the contrary. As a result, batmen were usually very unpopular with NCOs.

On this occasion, Harry Townsend had persuaded Rifleman Jimmy Davis to become his batman. Jimmy was a city gent in every sense of the term. He was somewhat older than the rest of us and had some difficulty keeping up on more energetic pastimes such as route marches and cross country runs. At the time of our weekly attendances at Bunhill Row before we were called up, Jimmy would arrived from his city office — I think he was in the insurance business — immaculately dressed in a dark pin-striped suit, stiff white collar, light grey silk tie, and with the cuffs of his shirt secured with large gold links which protruded an inch or so below the sleeves of his jacket. His bowler hat would be perched on the front of his head in the true city fashion. He was fastidious and somewhat foppish and was the last person one would think of as a potential batman. However, he took on the job and installed himself in the kitchen of the platoon HQ house.

As there were no cooking facilities, Harry had procured a brand new primus stove and a supply of paraffin and methylated spirits to enable his batman to make his morning cup of tea. Unfortunately, Jimmy had never seen a primus stove in his life and was given no guidance on its operation. From later investigations it appeared that Jimmy had consulted his predecessor on the question of operating the primus but the predecessor, being somewhat disgruntled at having lost his job, had not shown much interest and had simply informed Jimmy that all he had to do was to pour some methylated spirits around the burner, apply a match and when a hiss was heard to operate the pump.

On Jimmy's first morning as Harry Townsend's batman, I came off guard duty at around six am and after dumping my rifle and kit in the guard room, next to the kitchen, was instructed by the guard commander to go and call Jimmy. This I did and returned to the guard room for the comfort of my palliasse and a cigarette. After a few minutes I heard a shout from next door and went back to find out the cause of this commotion. As I opened the kitchen door I was met by a cloud of black smoke. I bent down and went in to see a large pool of burning paraffin surrounding the primus in the middle of the kitchen floor with Jimmy, clad only in his pyjama trousers, kneeling on the floor at the other side of the room and obviously in an advanced state of panic. In the few seconds I stood looking at this spectacle, the primus stove slowly collapsed like a dying animal. First, one of the three legs fell away, then another, then the third as the solder melted and what was left of Harry's new primus stove slowly rolled over in its death agony. I grabbed a couple of Jimmy's blankets from the corner of the room and flung them over the flaming paraffin and the flames were quickly extinguished.

A grimy looking Jimmy then had the harrowing experience of waking Harry Townsend up with the news that it was time to get up but that there was no tea available. How he subsequently explained the disintegrated primus stove was never known, but he resumed normal duties immediately, the first of which was to clean down the blackened walls and ceiling of the kitchen and to scrub the wooden floor in an effort to get rid of the paraffin oil and burn marks. To remove the burn marks entirely was, of course, impossible without replacing the boards, so probably in this pleasant semi-detached house of what is now, I am sure, an agreeable housing estate at Northolt, there is, to this day, a blackened patch in the middle of the kitchen floor, a lasting memorial to Jimmy Davis's short spell as Harry Townsend's batman.

Langley, Bucks

After a couple of weeks in the muddy misery of Northolt, we made another move which, as it turned out, was to be my last with the London Rifle Brigade. This was to Langley in Buckinghamshire where Number 7 Platoon was given the arduous responsibility of guarding a cricket pitch and two gateways to a large country house nearby. The house and its extensive grounds were surrounded by a high brick wall, beyond which we were forbidden to encroach, and despite our natural inquisitiveness we were never told what was behind the high brick wall but simply informed that it enclosed a most important building, and our function was to ensure that only authorized persons entered and left the property. This was all very well in the case of pedestrian traffic, which consisted only of a few RAF personnel billeted in the vicinity and who were willing to produce their identity cards when requested to do so, but was impossible with the motor cars which went in and out at great speed, ignoring our presence entirely. The two gateways, about a hundred yards apart, were not equipped with booms or any other form of construction which would require a vehicle to stop and submit to our inspection.

We were also given very precise instructions about saluting officers going in or coming out, and, in this connection, to distinguish between officers or general rank and below. The former merited a 'present arms' but the latter only a standard salute. The rank of the occupant, we were told, could be quickly observed by the small pennant flying on a little flagpole secured to the wing of the vehicle in question. Naturally we were anxious to uphold the honour of our regiment by carrying out these duties with alacrity and precision. However, more often than not the cars would come and go at great speed and by the time one had observed a pennant, sprung to attention, shouldered arms and presented arms the car and its distinguished passenger would be well out of sight and certainly not in a position to acknowledge our recognition of their exalted status. The tendency therefore, was to spring to attention and do nothing else. At night time the situation was even worse, particularly if it was raining, as was usually the case. We were not provided with sentry boxes, as at Buckingham Palace, so our usual practice was to get as much protection as we could under the trees inside the gateways leading up to this mysterious building. Some years later I read somewhere that the headquarters of Bomber Command were located at Langley and therefore presumed that this was the important establishment which we had helped to protect from enemy action during the early days of the war.

Our quarters at Langley were in an old pavilion alongside a cricket ground. The pavilion had a number of broken windows, missing floorboards and ill-fitting doors and as the weather at that time was bitterly cold, it was extremely uncomfortable. The only pleasing thing about Langley that I remember was a very pleasant pub about twenty minutes walk away from our pavilion, where we spent most of our off-duty time enjoying the excellent mild and bitter and the warmth of an open log fire and a congenial landlord. Even this pleasant memory is somewhat marred by an unfortunate incident which occurred on the last night before my departure from all my close friends in E Company.

One afternoon the battalion orderly corporal arrived at our platoon cricket pavilion and was fortunate to find me 'at home'. He instructed me to report at nine am the following morning to the company office at the nearby village for an interview with Captain Wright, our company commander. Despite my question as to the reason, he either couldn't or wasn't willing to disclose it, but it was quickly agreed by my colleagues in 7 Platoon that during the three months or so of our army life I had committed some serious offence which had just come to light and that I was for the high jump. However, in accordance with established practice, we all adjourned to the local to mull over the day's events and as the evening progressed, the reasons put forward for my summons to higher authority became more and more imaginative and lurid. Had I unwittingly disclosed any military secrets to the enemy? This suggestion was no doubt prompted by the national campaign going on at that time about the importance of security. 'Be like dad, keep mum,' warned the posters in railway stations, public houses and public toilets. I had no clear recollection of getting into conversation with any strangers, although admittedly I was inclined to get friendly with other occupants of the saloon bar at the end of the convivial evening, particularly if they were female and good looking.

Despite the general conclusion that my likely destination was the glasshouse at Aldershot, I slept well and the following morning made my way to Company Headquarters on the platoon bicycle. To my surprise I was received by the company sergeant major almost as a friend. He was waiting for me and I was invited, rather than marched under escort, to the company commander's office. The CSM knocked on the door, opened it and said in a somewhat enquiring tone as if upset that he hadn't been let into the secret, 'You asked to see Rifleman Sheridan, sir?' and withdrew, closing the door quietly behind him.

Obviously I wasn't going to be accused of some heinous crime but I was still a little apprehensive. James Wright was sitting behind his desk as I entered. He wasn't wearing his hat, a sign that the interview was informal.

'Good morning, Sheridan,' he said in a friendly tone. 'How are things in 7 Platoon?'

'Fine, thank you, sir,' I replied, standing stiffly to attention and rather taken aback by this unexpected civility.

'Stand easy,' he continued. 'Now, the reason I have sent for you is to find out whether you would like to take a commission. E Company has to submit the name of one suitable candidate to be posted to an officer cadet training unit and after talking to Mr Townsend, I have decided that your name should go forward — provided you are agreeable of course.'

He looked at me inquiringly and many thoughts were running through my mind. I hadn't given any thought to the possibility of becoming an officer and was somewhat surprised because it had never occurred to me that I had been particularly outstanding in the performance of my duties as a rifleman. Like all the OD contingent, I had had several years service in the OTC at school, eventually becoming drum major of the band, and no doubt this had made us all good TA material, but I hadn't joined the TA to cash in on that experience. On one or two occasions the possibility of getting commissions had cropped up but we had agreed that while we could stay together in 7 Platoon we were quite content, and as the war would probably be over in a couple of months, when we would all return to our respective civilian occupations, there seemed to be no point in having military aspirations. The question now exercising in my mind was, 'What would all the others say if I deserted?'

James Wright obviously sensed what was on my mind. 'I suppose you are bothered about leaving your friends,' he said.

I nodded in agreement. 'Well, let me assure you,' he continued, 'in a few months' time this battalion is going to be nothing like the TA battalion you joined. Naturally,' he continued, 'we would all like to stay together, but this war is going to last a long time so it just isn't possible. Before long most of the original members will be posted to OCTUs or NCO training units and we have already received our first draft of conscripts.'

This, for me, was the deciding factor. We had already met some of the conscripts, whose attitude to life in the army was totally different to ours — for better or worse — so my problem was solved, or partially so. 'Very well, sir,' I said, 'and I am grateful to you for the opportunity.'

He stood up and held out his hand, which I took. 'Good,' he said, 'and the best of luck. You will receive instructions in a day or so.'

I saluted, turned on my heel and left.

As I pedalled back to 7 Platoon pavilion my emotions were mixed. I felt pleased, even excited, at the prospect of becoming an officer, assuming of course that I survived the OCTU course, but at the same time, I was concerned as to how the rest of the platoon would react, particularly the OD element. We had served together now for nearly a year since joining the LRB, good times and not so good, though mostly the former, and now here was I, deserting the ship as it were. I needn't have worried.

When I reached the pavilion the only occupant was Lippy Lipsham, who was on cook-house fatigue which, for him at that moment, involved lying on his palliasse drinking a mug of tea and reading a newspaper. Lippy was and still is a very good friend. Quite a good few years older than the rest of us, he was physically small and unmilitary in appearance, particularly when wearing army denims, which always seemed and probably were too large for him. He had been a great supporter of Old Dunstonian activities; a great club man as they say. Not much good at cricket, but a keen cricketer. I don't think he ever played rugger but he came along as a supporter to all games, including Easter tours to Cornwall. He had been well established in business but hadn't hesitated to join up with the rest of us 'youngsters' after Munich and although we would never admit it, certainly not to him, he was something of a father figure and adviser.

As I walked in, he looked up from his newspaper and grinned.

'Well, you old sod,' he said, 'which OCTU are you going to?'

I was genuinely surprised and relieved. 'How did you know?' I said.

'Come off it, you silly bugger,' he responded, 'it was pretty obvious what Jimmy Wright wanted to see you about. Sit down and tell me about it.'

This I did and was further relieved when Lippy agreed that I had been quite right to accept, an opinion that was fully endorsed by all my other comrades-in-arms when they heard the news. The following day I received my instructions — to report to 168 OCTU at Ramillies Barracks, Queens Avenue, Aldershot within forty-eight hours.

And so it was that on a dark wet miserable evening we were all assembled once again in our local pub to celebrate my impending departure, and when, through a smoky and somewhat alcoholic haze, it was made clear to me by my many 'friends' first, that life in the OCTU was absolute hell; second, that I hadn't the remotest chance of successfully completing the course and of being commissioned, in which case I would come crawling back to ask for forgiveness, and lastly that if by some strange chance I was successful and met any of them again, in uniform, they would ignore me entirely.

After many last rounds for the road, someone realized we had a little under ten minutes to get back to barracks, a journey that normally took us at least twenty minutes, so there was no alternative but to proceed at the double. As we emerged into the fresh air, my powers of vision dropped to nil with a combination of mist and raindrops on the lenses of my glasses. However, I trotted off with David Butterfield, taking my course from his proximity and the thud of many boots both in front and behind us.

Suddenly I was brought to an absolute halt by someone hitting me in the face with a large sledge hammer, or so it seemed. I saw not only every star in the universe but also moons and suns, planets and comets, and sank to my knees under this terrible onslaught. As I gradually recovered my senses, my first thought was that I had somehow been transported to some dark place inhabited by gibbering idiots. I could make out about twelve shapes all holding their stomachs or staggering around in the darkness making strange noises. Then came realization; they were people I called friends convulsed with laughter that

I, an aspiring holder of the King's Commission, had run full tilt into a brick wall. Only those who have run full tilt into a brick wall without any semblance of warning, intuitive or otherwise, can understand how I felt. I stood up and felt a trickle of what turned out to be blood running down my forehead. My teeth felt as if they had cut through my lips. I felt my nose. Was it broken? It was certainly excruciatingly painful. My glasses were missing. I murmured something to that effect and bent down to feel for them on the ground. Someone, Bill Richards, stepped forward with a word of sympathy, to help. I heard a crunch and knew instinctively that my glasses were no more and swore, which sent my companions into further paroxysms of laughter. My eyes had now adjusted to the darkness and I was able to 'see' what had happened — even without my misted rain-obscured spectacles.

We had been running along a footpath in front of a short row of cottages at the end of which a high brick wall surrounding the garden of a large house jutted out, reducing the width of the footpath to about half. Unfortunately, I had been on the inside, running with my head down because of the rain and keeping pace with David on my right. He had edged out, he subsequently told me, to allow me to do the same and miss the wall, which I hadn't.

The following day, when I took my departure, I was a sorry sight. Two black eyes, swollen lips, loose teeth, very sore nose and forehead. Fortunately I had spare glasses. As I bade farewell to 7 Platoon, I little realized where we would next meet. It would be within a stone's throw of my home at Beckenham.

2

168 Officer Cadet Training Unit

I understand that Ramillies Barracks on Queens Avenue, Aldershot, were built during either the Crimea or Boer War. I don't know whether this is correct, but during the very severe winter of 1939 to 1940 it wasn't difficult to accept that they were built a very long time ago.

The troops, or 'cadets' as we were designated, were quartered in a row of single storey brick-built huts alongside a barrack square. Each hut was about thirty yards long with living space for about fifteen men at each end, separated by an enclosed area containing about eight wash basins and a row of toilets. There were no baths. At the time of our occupation, each man had an iron bedstead and palliasse and a metal locker. In the middle of each living area was the central heating system, which consisted of a cast iron tubular-like stove about three feet high with a metal flue running up through the roof. This, in some ways, placed a premium on securing a bed close to the stove, but with the great disadvantage that for the few hours a week that the meagre coal ration permitted a fire, everyone else in the hut came and sat or sprawled on the beds near the stove to get their ration of heat. When there was no more bed space available around the stove it became a source of minor irritation that latecomers would stand in a close circle around the stove with their backsides absorbing whatever warmth was available.

Over the period that I was there, the winter of 1939, the weather was so cold and the heating so inadequate, that before water would run from the taps in the ablutions first thing in the morning, it was necessary to break off the icicles under the spouts and then to breathe heavily on the tap to melt the ice clogging up the inner parts. Similarly, the cisterns in the lavatories frequently had to be dug out with a bayonet to permit the flow of water to flush the system. During the coldest nights of that winter it became the accepted practice to dress rather than undress to go to bed. One pulled on as many vests, cardigans and pullovers as one had been able to bring from home and then added bedsocks for good measure. In the morning, the edges of the blankets near one's nostrils were frequently frozen solid where one's breath had condensed and then turned to ice.

Our course at 168 OCTU consisted of about a hundred cadets, the majority from London Territorial regiments including three others from the LRB; Aalberg, Carter and Griffiths. There were others from the London Scottish, Queen Victoria Rifles and Queen's Westminsters. There were also a number of other rather strange people who had obviously had no previous military experience in a cadet force or the Territorials and who had come straight from university, destined, we understood, for the Intelligence Corps.

Following our arrival and the usual reception formalities we were addressed by the commanding officer of the OCTU, Colonel Bingham, an ex-guards officer called back from retirement, presumably, for that job. He was a most impressive man; a tall soldierly figure always immaculately turned out with several rows of decoration and campaign medals and with a black patch over one eye. He made it very clear from the outset that the four months' course would be very tough; that he expected a very high level of performance from us all and anticipated that some would not measure up to the required standards to be recommended for a commission. So it turned out, but it is also sad to relate that shortly after our course finished, Colonel Bingham was unwise enough to tell a newspaper reporter — the *Daily Mirror* I think — that in his opinion, the best potential officer-material posted to his OCTU were ex-public schoolboys. This was, of course, reported in the newspaper the following day and resulted in a socialist clamour in the House of Commons and Colonel Bingham was relieved of his command.

From now on we were officer cadets and would, said Bingham, 'behave and conduct yourselves as such'. We were required to wear a white band around our forage caps to indicate our enhanced status, which was a bit of an embarrassment until the public became aware of its significance, and I was asked on several occasions whether it meant that I was a conscientious objector.

The course itself followed much the same pattern as we had experienced at OTC and TA camps; arms drill, foot drill, squad drill, field training, map reading and so on, and in all of which we were expected to be already highly proficient. There was to be one important difference. Each day, cadets were nominated to act as company and platoon commanders and platoon NCOs and to perform all the duties those ranks entailed. It was difficult at times to respond in an appropriate fashion to orders and admonitions given by 'officers' and 'NCOs' who were, in fact, fellow cadets and who possibly slept in the next bed. It was an unwritten rule of the course however, that everyone co-operated fully in easing the path of the daily appointees, bearing in mind that the same support and assistance would be expected when one's own turn came around.

From first parade in the morning until the last at night, all movement to and from the barracks square and each place of work was at the double, which wasn't unduly burdensome in the winter but more so no doubt in the heat of the summer. I understand that a similar practice was followed at army prisons for penal reasons; in our case it was intended to promote mental alertness as well as physical fitness.

Our company commander was a Major Haslam, a member of the staff and commanding officer of the OTC of Campbell College, Belfast. Naturally, he was somewhat school-masterish but for reasons I will explain later, I was very grateful for his 'fatherly' understanding before I left OCTU. One of our platoon officers was a Bruce-Lockhart, a family well known in rugger circles. One evening he called me out as we came off parade and invited me to play the following Saturday for Aldershot Services. How he knew I played rugger I don't know, but I was very pleased to accept, with the result that once or twice a week from then on, I was regularly excused other duties for rugger matches often involving an enjoyable coach trip to various army and air force locations where the 'after rugger' hospitality left little to be desired.

I think it must have been my battered appearance on arrival that led someone to think that I was a boxer because one day, to my consternation, I read on the notice board that I would represent our platoon in the OCTU boxing competition. This was entirely voluntary of course, like many other army duties — 'Three volunteers are required, you, you and you' — so with the enthusiastic encouragement of the rest of the platoon, I resigned myself to the inevitable. I had done a little boxing at school where it had been recognized that my intuitive reaction to threatened assault was to shut my eyes and poke out my left hand as hard as possible, which is apparently one of the attributes of the successful boxer in the amateur field. One thing I was sure of, that three rounds of three minutes each, once and maybe even twice during the space of a few hours, required a higher level of fitness then existed even amongst officer cadets generally, so I recognized the necessity for some special training before the event.

The preliminary rounds progressed satisfactorily and much to my surprise I found myself in the final of my weight, drawn against a thick-set fellow cadet, an Old Haileyburian, who, at a guess, I felt weighed about twelve stone compared with my ten. Anyway, I proceeded according to plan, the only way I knew, and every time we closed in combat I pushed out my left hand. Unfortunately, he was far more skilful at the art of fisticuffs than me and his face was never where I thought it should be, with the result that I finished a very battered runner-up. However, I was not a complete loser. After the judges had announced the result, a foregone conclusion, and the applause had died down, Colonel Bingham at the ringside stood up and called for a round for 'a good loser.' I felt that maybe I had notched up a point towards my commission.

During the four months at the OCTU we were granted forty-eight hour leave passes once each month, when I invariably went home to Beckenham to see my mother. On the first of these trips, I rang David Beardshaw's home to find out if he was also on leave or whether E Company was still located at Langley. To my astonishment, his mother told me that the company had moved to Beckenham and that David was billeted somewhere in Copers Cope Road, a stone's throw from our home at Beckenham Place Park. I immediately took a walk down Copers Cope Road and discovered 7 Platoon in a large requisitioned house next door to John Jackson's home. Needless to say this was ideal for the OD contingent, most of whom lived in, or near Beckenham. The Railway Tavern opposite Beckenham Junction station (subsequently destroyed by a buzz bomb) became their local, and I was amused to hear that several of them went off to the comfort of their own homes and their own beds each evening, returning in time for parade in the morning. This was no problem for John, who simply walked into the adjoining house. Such was life for the TA during this 'cold war' period.

It was during one of these weekend trips to Beckenham in February or March 1940, that I experienced my first air raid. It had been arranged that I should drive my mother and a girlfriend from Ireland, Emmeline Deacon, who was staying with us, to Marsh Gibbon in Oxfordshire where my brother-in-law, and my sister were living. As we drove along the Upper Richmond Road, an air raid alert sounded, whereupon most traffic stopped and pedestrians and vehicle passengers alike took shelter in shop fronts and doorways. I remember stepping out to look up and saw a flight of about twelve German bombers directly overhead and not very high but with no opposition from anti-aircraft guns or fighters. We watched as they droned their way across South London and disappeared, and soon the 'all clear' sounded and we continued on our way. The following day I read that some bombs had been dropped on London docks, causing very little damage, but could not help wondering why there had been so little defensive action. It seemed to be generally accepted that the Germans would not bomb civilian targets so the public were not unduly concerned and if one happened to be in some place of strategic importance such as the docks area at the wrong time that was just hard luck. A few months later things were going to change with a vengeance.

And so we approached the conclusion of our OCTU course and our expectation of emergency commissions as second lieutenants. We were all required to complete a form giving our first, second and third choices of regiments into which we would like to be commissioned. I decided, as my first choice, to elect for the Royal Ulster Rifles, my reasons being very simple. I was Irish by parentage so an Irish regiment was appropriate. That narrowed the field to three choices; the Rifles, the Skins (Inniskilling Fusiliers) and the Faughs (Irish Fusiliers). Having served in the LRB I liked the idea of continuing in a rifle regiment but felt disinclined to go back to the Rifle Brigade. In addition, I liked the idea of retaining my black buttons as opposed to brass. I never regretted my first choice, which was accepted, and I was notified that I should report to the Regimental Depot of the Royal Ulster Rifles at Ballymena in County Antrim. However, I was to undergo a somewhat harrowing experience beforehand.

For the final night an exercise involving the entire OCTU was to take place on Laffans Plain, a training area at Aldershot familiar to many generations of British soldiers; an extensive area of scrubby undulating chalk land, littered and pockmarked with relics of bygone training 'battles': empty cartridge cases, ammunition boxes, rusty iron pickets with strands of barbed wire and half dug or collapsed trenches, all criss-crossed with the track marks of tanks and other army vehicles. It was recognized by all concerned, or at least by the cadets, that the main object of this parting 'fling' on Laffans Plain was not to put the final seal on our training for commissioned rank but rather to reduce the time available for valedictory sessions in the NAAFI. For this reason there was a strong tendency to treat the evening rather lightly and to hope that we would be back in camp in time for at least one pint or maybe two before the NAAFI shutters went up.

Rifles and bayonets had been thoroughly cleaned ready for handing in the following morning and thus facilitate a quick getaway. It was therefore with great consternation that we heard that for this final 'battle' blank ammunition was to be used which would necessitate the recleaning our rifles before our departure. Blank ammunition is designed for use in the same way as live ammunition, but contains no bullets. It can therefore be used to simulate the real thing; to create the impression of rifle fire without the lethal implications, and is useful for adding some realism to military exercises. When one is shooting at the 'enemy' the sound of rifle fire with blanks is more effective than calling out 'Bang bang bang — you're dead,' or shaking a rattle to simulate machine gun fire. However, blanks do contain wadding which is ejected for a metre or so when the round is fired and this can be dangerous at short range, as I was to discover that night, and again a year or so later.

When we heard that blanks were to be used it was quickly agreed that they should all be collected by one or maybe two people in each squad who, at the appropriate times, would engage in rapid fire and thereby create the required illusion of a number of rifles but, by this manoeuvre only those rifles actually used would require cleaning, the time for which would thus be considerably reduced by the combined efforts of all concerned.

Such was the plan. When we arrived at the starting point all was pitch dark, and strict silence was ordered to avoid disclosing our presence to the 'enemy'. Whispered instructions were received from somewhere in the darkness for sections leaders to collect blanks for their sections. All the blanks for my section were then passed surreptitiously to me and I quickly stuffed them into my pouches. It was then my job, at the appropriate moment, to faithfully fulfil the task imposed on me by my fellow cadets for sounding like ten members of our force all firing at the same time. I therefore proceeded to load up in the accepted fashion by canting my rifle up to the 'port' position and pressing two clips each of five rounds into the magazine. Now, I thought, with one round 'up the spout' I shall be set. I pushed a single round into the breech, closed the bolt and — bang! Immediately there was an agonized shriek — 'I'm blind, I'm blind,' and Ted Alberg staggered back, his hands over his eyes, into the arms of the platoon sergeant. I realized immediately what had happened. When closing the breech of my rifle after charging the magazine I had inadvertently overlooked the fact that I had also pushed a round into the breech and instinctively squeezed the trigger. My enthusiasm to represent as much 'fire power' as possible nearly ended in disaster and was a salutary lesson I have never forgotten.

For a few minutes there was consternation. Up rushed the sergeant major. 'Who fired the shot?' he demanded out of the darkness.

'I did,' I replied.

'Who are you?'

'Cadet Sheridan.'

'Consider yourself under arrest,' he hissed and strode over to where Ted was explaining that he wasn't blind but his eyes were extremely painful from the peppering they had received from the wadding in my blank cartridge.

Up came the platoon commander. 'What's happened, Sergeant Major?' he asked.

'Some damn fool fired a round of blank accidentally and this man caught the blast in his eyes,' replied the sergeant major. 'I think he'd better go back to camp and have his eyes checked.'

Despite his protestations, Ted was packed off in a truck back to camp and the exercise proceeded. I was full of misgivings; to have come so far and now no doubt to be returned to the LRB — in the ranks. The thought was unbearable. I would have to apply for a transfer to some other regiment, the French Foreign Legion perhaps. My anticipation of joining the Royal Ulster Rifles at Ballymena was shattered.

My misery was so great that I certainly couldn't bring myself to fire off any more rounds of blanks that evening and I quietly returned my supplies to their original owners. They, of course, were doing their best to cheer me up by pointing out that Ted was OK so no-one would want to upset the postings already authorized at this late stage. However, to me this sounded like wishful thinking. I was not reassured and my mortification was complete when, in the darkness and completely engrossed in my misfortune, I stepped straight into a deep trench left over from some previous military manoeuvrings, an experience reminiscent in many ways to running into a brick wall at Langley. To be walking across uneven ground in pitch darkness, in extended order with one's neighbours only shadowy figures six feet or so on either side, and to step forward anticipating solid ground to take one's weight and then to step on nothing is certainly a big surprise. I simply found myself very dazed at the bottom of a deep black hole. My comrades continued on their way, not even noticing that I had disappeared. After pulling myself together I scrambled out, still clutching my rifle, and more by luck than skill managed to catch up with the members of my section who had just noticed my mysterious disappearance, My explanation that I had fallen into a hole was received with vulgar expressions of disbelief most unfitting for young men on the brink of receiving the King's Commission.

As we made our way back to barracks I couldn't help but reflect that the only round of blank ammunition fired during the exercise was my round accidentally discharged in direction of Ted Alberg. Following our dismissal on the barracks square I went to the company office with a rather vague idea of finding out from the sergeant major what was to be the next step as regards my arrest. When he came in he ignored me for a few minutes while he spoke to one of the NCOs, then turned to me and said, 'That was an unfortunate incident tonight, Sheridan. What happened?'

I explained how I had charged a magazine, not mentioning that I was to be the sole source of the platoon fire power. 'Well,' he said, 'you have to report to the company commander, Major Haslam, at twelve o'clock tomorrow morning after the final parade.'

My morale was at a very low ebb as I returned to my barrack room where I found most of my fellow cadets, including Ted Alberg, had gone off to the NAAFI for a final OCTU drink in the few minutes that remained before closing time. With a black cloud of uncertainty about the following day's interview with Major Haslam hanging over me I didn't feel in the mood for end of term hilarity and set about cleaning my rifle without the promised assistance of my fellow conspirators. When they all arrived back full of the joys of spring and beer their united sympathy for my predicament was no consolation. Ted was extremely apologetic at his noisy reaction to receiving a round of blank ammunition in the face and aggravating the situation, but obviously he was in no way to blame. It was indeed very fortunate that he had suffered nothing more than bloodshot eyes for a day or so. I spent a very sleepless night wondering what the following day held in store, and imagining the worst.

The next morning spring was in the air but I didn't notice it. There was much to be done. Lockers to be cleared out and kitbags packed. Blankets and sheets to be handed in to one store, rifles and bayonets to another. Barrack rooms to be cleaned out and inspected; leave passes and travel warrants to be collected from the company office. Then our passing out parade taken by Colonel Bingham. 'Good luck to you all, and remember all you have been taught — mens lives will depend on you etc., etc.'

I went through all the motions without enthusiasm, I still had my twelve o'clock appointment with Major Haslam.

After the dismissal there was a rush to change into officer's service dress, final packing, and a hundred or so very smart second lieutenants clambered into trucks heading for Aldershot and North Camp station. All except for me.

At midday I made my way over to the company office and reported my presence to the company clerk. He explained that Major Haslam wasn't available and suggested that I should come back in fifteen minutes. I therefore returned to my barrack room and smoked another cigarette. I repeated the procedure every fifteen minutes for the next two hours by which time my spirits were at an even lower ebb. At two o'clock I was told that Major Haslam was free and would see me. I knocked on his door, entered and saluted. He was sitting behind his desk leaning back in his chair holding a document in his hand. He looked up. 'Ah Sheridan, I understand you wish to see me?' he said. He was a tall man with pleasant rubbery features and a quiet voice with a touch of Ulster accent and I thought I noticed a twinkle in his blue eyes as he looked at me. For a moment I was perplexed; he was the last person I wanted to see but obviously I couldn't tell him so.

'I thought you wished to see me, sir,' I replied.

'Oh yes,' he said and looked down at the document he was holding. 'I see you're going to the Royal Ulster Rifles. First class regiment. Well you'd better be off and the best of luck to you for the future.'

He stood up and held out his hand which I clasped. I stepped back, saluted and left in a daze. I couldn't believe that the cloud which had been hanging over me had lifted and felt like a condemned man after hearing of his reprieve. I no longer had to worry about what I had to tell my mother and brothers and sisters and many friends as to why I had failed to get my commission. I noticed that the sun was bright and warm as I went back to my barrack room for the last time. The only relic of the past four months was my kitbag lying on the floor with a large brown cardboard box containing my new service dress uniform. I sat on my bed for a few minutes to reflect. Had it all been a bad dream? No, I had been lucky and the episode could have had a much more unfortunate ending, particularly if Ted's sight had been damaged. I had been careless, there was no doubt about that. Why had I been let off so lightly? I shall never know. Was it to avoid a lot of administrative inconvenience at the end of the course which would have involved Major Haslam and a number of others and interfered with their plans to get away for a few days, or did an understanding heart beat somewhere that recognized that incidents will happen even in the best regulated circles? I suspected the latter and that the heart in question was Major Haslam's.

I roused myself and decided to get away while the going was good. I knew there would be no truck to take me to the station, so with my kitbag over my shoulder and my cardboard box under my arm I headed for the nearest bus stop in Queen's Avenue.

My luck was in, or was it pre-arranged? A car pulled up beside me, driven by my platoon commander. He leant over, opened the window and asked if he could give me a lift. I bundled myself in and off we set to North Camp station chatting about the course and where I had been posted with never a mention of blank ammunition or Ted Alberg.

About fifteen years later I was leaving my office in Waterloo Place when I came face to face with a very prosperous looking Ted. We chatted a few minutes about where we had been and what we had done during the war and he explained that he had been living in Brussels for several years and would get in touch with me the next time he was over. After a further ten years I was sitting with the British Consul in Brussels, having moved to that city, and called at the Consulate to pay my respects. At the end of our conversation I remarked, 'Have you ever come across a chap called Ted Alberg?'

'Ted Alberg!' he exclaimed. 'He is the life and soul of the British community in Brussels.' ·

He picked up the phone and seconds later I was talking to Ted who arranged to pick me up and take me to lunch and subsequently introduced me to everyone in Brussels who could assist in education, banking, insurance and other problems. We remained in frequent contact until he retired some years later and returned to the UK.

Ted was the only member of our OCTU company that I ever met or heard of after leaving Aldershot.

3

The Royal Ulster Rifles — 1940/44

Ballymena — The Regimental Depot

My commission as a 2nd Lieutenant in the Royal Ulster Rifles was published in the *London Gazette* on 27 April, 1940 when I was twenty-three. Two other commissions to the RUR were published at the same time, 2nd Lieutenants G. Tynan and I.R. Aylmer-Jones. We were required to report to the RUR Depot at St Patricks Barracks, Ballymena on or about 1 May, and it was on the platform at Euston Station, waiting for the train to depart for Heysham, that I first met 'Tiny' and Ian. Tiny Tynan was a very cheerful, enthusiastic extrovert, and we became very good friends. London Irish and with 'front-row-forward' physique, red hair and ruddy freckled complexion with a bristly military moustache, he had joined the London Irish Rifles, a territorial battalion of the RUR at the same time that I had joined the LRB. After a period of frustration at the depot and then with a Home Defence battalion, he volunteered to join the newly formed Airborne Forces Experimental Unit at Sherborne-in-Elmet, Yorkshire, where he found an appropriate outlet for his energy, trying out new designs of parachutes and new techniques for jumping from planes and gliders. A year or so later he was accidentally killed on a field training exercise when a mortar bomb fell short of its target.

Ian Jones was the son of a well known actor, Felix Aylmer-Jones, and before the war had been following in his father's footsteps with the Windsor Repertory Company. He was also to die in an unfortunate accident at Chilton Foliat in Berkshire some years later.

Ballymena, County Antrim was and probably still is a small and prosperous country town about thirty miles north of Belfast and about twenty miles inland from the beautiful glens and coastline of the county. The town had been chosen as the new location for the Regimental Depot of the Royal Ulster Rifles which was in the process of being moved from Armagh, and when we arrived the new depot buildings were only partially completed. There was a large new barrack block, the Sandhurst Block, complete with central heating, baths, showers, drying and recreation rooms and many other refinements, which compared more than favourably with the quarters I had previously occupied at Aldershot. The Sandhurst Block faced a large barrack square surrounded by lawns and flower beds, and beyond which were a number of private houses for married officers and their families. All this had obviously been planned and designed to meet the peace time requirements of the regiment, but because of the emergency and to provide facilities for housing a much larger inflow of recruits, a large number of smaller buildings and second barrack square were in course of construction nearby. The officer's mess was in 'the castle', so named I suspect, not because of its antiquity, but because of its high turreted tower at one end of the building which, from a distance, gave the impression of being a medieval castle. I imagine it was built by some wealthy local textile merchant as a home early in the century and who had been only too pleased to sell his estate to the army or whoever buys land for regimental depots — when the bottom fell out of the flax business.

The function of the regimental depot, as I understand it, is twofold. First, to take in 'raw materials' in the form of recruits from 'civvy street' and to process them into finished products or trained soldiers, ready to be shipped out to the consumer — the regimental battalions, wherever they might be located. Secondly, to provide a home for all those officers and other ranks of the regiment who, for one reason or another, became detached from the battalions and then find themselves with nowhere else to go; plus, of course, newly commissioned subalterns, like Tiny, Ian and me.

When we arrived at Ballymena, only the advance party had moved from Armagh, consisting of three or four officers, a warrant officer and about twenty NCOs and riflemen who were busy taking over and setting-up-shop as it were, in the new

57

regimental depot. The advance party was commanded by a very genial major, R.F.A. Cruickshank — affectionately known as Crooky. The warrant officer was Company Sergeant Major 'Ben' Matthews, a regular soldier with many years' experience and who seemed to me to exude military efficiency from every pore. He became a tower of strength to us young subalterns whenever confronted with any situation with which we were unfamiliar, and during confidential chats over a cup of 'char' in his office he would recount amusing stories of the idiosyncrasies and past escapades of one-time subalterns in the regiment who now held exalted ranks of colonels and generals.

Our arrival coincided with the arrival of a draft of conscripts from England which, together with a group of volunteers from Ireland, both North and South, became A Company, based in the Sandhurst Block, to which we were attached.

A daily routine was quickly established. After a hearty breakfast of eggs and bacon of which there was no shortage, we would leave the officers' mess at about eight am and make our way to the Sandhurst Block where the NCOs would be chasing their squads out into the square and carrying out the first inspection of the day. While this was going on we, the subalterns, would march up and down the length of the square as if totally disinterested in what was going on but in fact watching closely to be sure we were in the right spot at the right time. When the preliminary inspection had been completed and numbers checked, Sergeant Major Matthews would march over and report to me, as senior subaltern, informing me of the precise numbers on parade, by warrant officers, NCOs and men. It was then my task to hand over the parade to Major Cruickshank.

The house occupied by Crooky and his wife was close to the barrack square, and I imagine that he used to watch what was going on while he finished his breakfast. Anyway, at the appropriate moment, he would leave his front door and saunter down the garden path, slapping his leg with the short cane he always carried and gazing around at the surrounding countryside as if the last thing that interested him was the body of men drawn up for his attention. As soon as he reached the edge of the square I would take this as my cue to march up, halt, salute and pass on the parade statistics as previously conveyed to me by the sergeant major. I could never remember the exact numbers of NCOs and men given to me by the sergeant major but this didn't seem to matter as Crooky largely ignored my presence. Finding me in his path he would slow down slightly, then, without stopping, he would return my immaculate salute with a wave of his cane as if brushing off an offending fly from his brow, and deviating around me would continue his gentle amble to where the sergeant major was standing and enquire, 'What have you in mind for the lads today, Sergeant Major?'

'Ben' Matthews would respond with brief details of the day's training programme, whereupon Crooky would signify his approval by a nod of his head, a wave of his hand and then depart for the bank of the nearest trout stream. We emergency commissioned subalterns, standing, as it were, in the wings, were ignored. Fortunately, the company sergeant major was not so disdainful of civilian subalterns as Crooky and was only too anxious to make maximum use of our availability to ensure that in the time allotted, the recruits in A Company were fully prepared to take their places in the two regular battalions of the Regiment and in additional battalions then in the process of formation.

Weapon training and square bashing was largely left to the company NCOs, all regular soldiers, whilst we became more involved in subjects such as map reading, field craft, and last but not least, regimental history. It was important that recruits developed a knowledge of the past history of the regiment and of the many campaigns throughout the world in which it had been involved, so that they developed a sense of pride not only in their regiment but also in themselves, which would influence their behaviour, particularly when under stress in battle. Inter-squad competitions, covering every aspect of training from barrack-room cleanliness and individual turnout to weapon training and football, were initiated, adding enthusiasm and friendly rivalry to the daily activities, and woe betide the man who let his squad down through laziness or indifference. Later on, when basic training had been completed and men were awaiting posting, a special squad was formed of those who displayed potential officer or NCO qualities. These were then given the opportunity to carry out the duties of various ranks, much on the lines we had experienced at OCTU.

When the main body of the depot moved from Armagh to Ballymena, considerable changes took place, not the least being the arrival of the depot commanding officer, Lieutenant Colonel

Victor Cowley, D.S.O., M.C., etc., etc., and a number of other senior officers, including the quarter master Lieutenant Colonel Corrigan, with more medal ribbons on his chest than Colonel Cowley.

Colonel Cowley was a very large man; tall and very broad but with little sign of the surplus weight which usually goes with middle-age. He was around sixty, I imagine; with a nose that had obviously been broken and with twisted features which seemed appropriate for someone who in his younger days had been an army heavyweight boxing champion. He had commanded one or other of the two regular battalions, and his decorations and awards showed that he had a very good military record, but his job as commanding officer of the regimental depot suggested that he had reached the summit of his career. He was undoubtedly dedicated to the smooth and efficient running of the depot not only as regards the training of the young recruits, the primary function, but more particularly with those aspects of army life which might be considered more relevant to peacetime rather than wartime conditions. At that time, the impact of the war hadn't been felt in Northern Ireland.

Great emphasis was placed on the public relations aspect of depot life. The depot had a particularly strong soccer team, with 'Boy' Martin an Irish International and Ted Stringer the London Corinthians's goalkeeper as the stars, and local Derbys were arranged with our particular rivals, the Inniskillings and the Irish Fusiliers. These were staged at one or other of the large football stadiums in Belfast, and the entire depot was always commanded to attend. Special trains were arranged to carry us all to Belfast, followed by a march through the city centre with the pipe and bugle bands in full blast. Rugger matches, dances — other ranks, all ranks and officers — were held each week, usually in one of the gymnasia, to which the locals were invited. There also seemed to be a wealth of musical talent, and periodically, the depot pipe and bugle bands were reshaped as an orchestra for concerts, which were very popular.

The result of all this was that any officer who had any non-military talent or organizational ability which could be put to use for these activities could expect to remain at the depot for the duration of the war. This may have suited some of our number, but most were anxious to be posted to one of the battalions as soon as possible.

The Officers' Mess

For the first few weeks after our arrival, life in the officers' mess was relaxed and informal. There were only about six officers 'in residence' as Crooky and one or two other regulars were either living in the married quarters, or outside the barracks and only showed their faces in the anteroom when having a few quick pink gins after parades had finished and before returning to the bosoms of their respective families.

The procedure in the mess for buying drinks was by chitty. When the mess waiter delivered a drink the recipient was required to initial a small docket and the cost of the drink was later entered in the officers' mess account book which was kept in the anteroom where one could verify the state of one's indebtedness at any time, and which had to be settled each month. The president of the mess committee kept a close eye on each subaltern's mess account, and there would be a stern warning from him to any young officer whose account appeared to be excessive, suggesting that his consumption of alcohol was more than was good for him.

'Treating' or the purchase of rounds of more than two or three drinks was frowned upon, although perhaps not strictly forbidden, and this, with the chitty system, worked well in the ordinary course of events. However, it rather fell down on guest nights, when subalterns were permitted, if not actively encouraged to let their hair down, and when, the following lunch time, a check on the account book would reveal the shattering information that one had been charged with a vast number of pints of Guinness of which one had not the slightest recollection. The shock would be aggravated when, on cross-checking with one's fellow officers, one found that they had each, been similarly charged the same amount. Needless to say, the job of mess waiter on guest nights was very popular amongst the mess staff and batmen. During those first few weeks we hadn't been indoctrinated into the intricacies of regimental guest nights, and in the evenings a group of us would walk down into Ballymena to explore the local hostelries, bearing in mind that, as officers, we could only patronize the more affluent looking establishments where we would be unlikely to rub shoulders with 'other ranks'. A favourite haunt for an hour or two of relaxation was the Adair Arms, an ancient, somewhat dilapidated but nevertheless respectable hotel in the centre of town.

After the completion of the move of all the depot personnel from Armagh to Ballymena, the atmosphere in the officers' mess became much more formal and we became aware of various regimental traditions and practices not previously brought to our attention. First and foremost perhaps, that junior subalterns, particularly the emergency commissioned variety, were expected to be seen but not heard. At a meeting of subalterns convened by the PMC, certain rules or conventions were drawn to our attention. If seated in the mess anteroom when the commanding officer entered, all present would rise and not reseat themselves until the CO sat down or bade those present to do so. As Victor Cowley never sat in the anteroom and never bade anyone else to do so, this always caused a high degree of uncertainty and confusion. Furthermore, if the CO was speaking, no-one else should speak. If, of course, one was asked a question by the CO, then one should answer '. . . Sir!' But unfortunately, the CO never directed any of his questions to a subaltern, but only to the group of sycophantic majors and captains — all regular and TA officers — who would cluster around him, nodding their agreement to every crumb of wisdom that fell from his lips, and enquiring whether he would like another pink gin.

While all this was going on, we lowly subalterns were standing around the corners of the room, inhibited from sitting because Victor was standing and had presumably forgotten to tell us we could take it easy; inhibited about talking amongst ourselves because Victor was talking, and unable to get what we wanted, a glass or beer, because the mess waiter was fully occupied serving pink gins to the inner circle.

There was, however, one exception to this pattern of events, in the person of 'Beulah' Weatherilt. Beulah was a South African who had travelled to England on the outbreak of war, had joined the army, been sent to OCTU, and had asked to be commissioned in the RUR because his great grandmother's maiden name had been O'Shaughnessy. He had been commissioned the same day as Tiny, Ian Aylmer-Jones and me but had arrived at Ballymena a few days later. On his first night he had accompanied us down to the Adair Arms for a beer, and for some reason during the evening the subject of conversation had turned to hyenas — the South African variety, and he had informed us that the Afrikaner word for a hyena was 'beulah'.

From then on, for some reason, he became known as Beulah.

He was a most likeable young man, about my age, twenty-four, about six foot four inches tall, fifteen or sixteen stone in weight, as strong as an ox, and with a single-minded ambition, to fight the Germans whenever and wherever that could be arranged. He neither understood nor cared about mess etiquette which, so far as we conformists were concerned, was the saving grace of the officers' mess whilst he was with us. If Beulah was sitting in an armchair or reading a newspaper when the colonel walked into the anteroom everyone stood up, except Beulah, who went on reading. If given a gentle kick on the shin to draw his attention to Victor's presence, he would look up, then slowly stand up and say in his clipped South African accent, 'Sorry Colonel; didn't hear you come in'. His voice would then boom across the room to the white-coated mess waiter, about to take the order for those of higher rank: 'Wayder, bring us six beers'.

The looks of pained disgust on the faces of the PMC and the regular clique of officers at this blatant disregard of every unwritten rule of mess life would have been an ideal subject for a Bateman cartoon, but strangely enough, it never seemed to worry the colonel who, I suspect, accepted Beulah for what he was, a volunteer who had travelled many thousands of miles to join in the fight against the common enemy and who was first class officer material. Even more strangely perhaps, was that when Beulah ordered six or more beers, he usually got them, despite the PMCs whispered instructions to the waiter who would nevertheless return with a tray of beers. There's none so deaf as an Ulster rifleman who doesn't want to hear, and we knew where their sympathies lay — with us, the underdogs and delighted recipients of Beulah's hospitality.

For some time I shared a small room with Beulah at the top of the Castle Tower, and we became good friends, and after I bought a second hand motor cycle for £20 from a garage in Ballymena, we spent a number of very pleasant Sunday afternoons touring the delightful glens of Antrim through Cushendall and Cushendun and on up by the Giant's Causeway, returning to Ballymena through Portrush and Coleraine, towns which I didn't know at the time but with which I was to become very familiar ten years later. With me in the driving seat, and Beulah's fifteen stone on the pillion, motoring along quiet country roads in warm sunshine was very pleasant. But on occasions we would be caught in heavy rain and despite periodic stops for shelter and refreshment I would find motor cycling with rain-obscured glasses and with Beulah urging me to get a move on, somewhat hazardous. However, we managed to survive some hair-raising trips, and I often wonder what happened to my motor cycle when I eventually departed for the 1st Battalion and which I left leaning sadly against the wall of the 'castle'.

Although he didn't say much about his family and home life, I gathered that he was the baby in a large family of wealthy farmers, with several older brothers. If reference to himself as the baby of the family had any physical implications, I couldn't imagine what his elder brothers must have been like. He had decided to break loose, and the outbreak of war in Europe had provided him with an ideal opportunity. One quaint habit was to take a large slug of whisky first thing each morning. Our batman would call us with a cup of tea, which he would set down beside our beds. After a few minutes, Beulah would heave himself out of bed, take the cup to the window, pour the contents onto the gravel driveway, then return to his bed where he would reach underneath for his bottle of whisky, pour himself a good measure, which he would swallow in one gulp, shake his head, give a few grunts of apparent satisfaction and pronounce himself as ready for the day ahead.

The last I saw of Beulah was when he departed for one of the newly formed battalions in England from where he was posted to a battalion of the London Irish in Africa and I heard later that he was killed in action.

One particular eccentric character in the mess at that time was a Major Yeo, a middle-aged regular officer who had served with the regiment in Flanders during the First World War and who had been recalled from retirement. He was a schoolmasterish type who let it be widely known that he had made a study of military campaigns throughout history and had a clear understanding of the strategy of the Allied Command for the defeat of Nazi Germany. Shortly after his arrival, large maps were displayed in the anteroom, and before lunch every day, it became the practice for all subalterns to group themselves around these maps and the nearby radio to hear the latest news from the war front and to listen to Major Yeo explain the military significance of whatever was happening. On his maps, Major

Yeo had indicated the various fronts by pins with large coloured heads connected with strands of wool. During the period of the so-called 'Cold War' there wasn't much to be said, and Major Yeo would confine himself to comments on the impregnability of the Maginot Line and of the steps being taken by Lord Gort, the Commander in Chief of the British Expeditionary Force, to raise the standards of efficiency of his army to levels which matched or exceeded those of the Germans. This conflicted somewhat with the reports we had heard from people home on leave who spoke of spending their time digging holes and then filling them up again, and being perpetually badgered by staff officers who didn't appear to know one end of a rifle from the other.

At that time, the BEF, including the 2nd Battalion RUR, was in the vicinity of Lille, near the Franco-Belgian border. Belgium and Holland were maintaining a policy of neutrality, and although it was planned for the BEF to move into Belgium in the event of the Germans invading that country, the British and French were not permitted to reconnoitre any of the areas which they would be expected to occupy.

When the Germans invaded Holland and Belgium early in May 1940, Major Yeo deftly switched all his pins and strands of wool to the new front east of Brussels, with a firm assurance to his youthful audience that with the right flank of the Allied armies firmly fixed on the Maginot Line and after the initial German assault had been blunted by the combined Allied armies in Belgium and Holland, we could expect a major drive up to the Rhine and thence into the heart of Germany. To Major Yeo's extreme discomfort, the daily radio news bulletins indicated a very different pattern of events. 'German armoured columns', it said, had broken through the Ardennes, and as one day followed another, towns and cities far behind Major Yeo's strands of wool were reported as being in enemy hands. Initially, he was undaunted, and gave us his assurance that the radio news readers had obviously misread or misquoted their bulletins and would shortly be corrected.

As the days passed, and the bulges on his maps began to assume alarming proportions, he continued to assure us that this was all in accordance with the Allied Plan. The German armoured columns were being 'sucked' into a situation where they would be annihilated by French and British armoured

65

pincers from north and south which would cut the German supply lines so that their armoured columns could be destroyed, after which the Allied Master Plan for moving up to the Rhine could be restored.

I was away from the depot during the period immediately preceding the Dunkirk evacuation, but I was told that it was only when the full extent of the disaster was made known, that Major Yeo admitted that something had gone wrong with the Master Plan, whereupon he took down his maps and returned to retirement.

Despite the evacuation of the BEF from Dunkirk, the atmosphere in the depot seemed unreal. Everyone was aware of the seriousness of the allied defeat in France and Belgium, with the British and French armies smashed and disorganized on all fronts, but there was a general view that the evacuation had been a success — which in some way I suppose it was — and that the Royal Navy and Royal Air Force could be relied upon to prevent an invasion of England. For a brief spell, even Major Yeo recovered his poise and was confident that any invasion attempt would be repulsed, but by this time his opinion was viewed with suspicion. However, most people appeared to take the view that 'it would be all right in the end', so we continued to eat, drink and be merry and not let those German barbarians interfere with our regimental traditions. There was no shortage of food and drink in the Ballymena area, but for many of us with homes and families in the South of England, this was a most anxious time and the one thing we wanted was to get away from the artificial atmosphere of the depot and to feel that we were making a contribution to meeting the crisis.

The North of Ireland had its own problems, of course: the threat of the IRA. But this was small by comparison with the major threat. Attempts and threats of sabotage against vital installations such as bridges and power lines were regularly reported, and 'flying columns' from the depot were organized to move at short notice to help the Ulster Constabulary deal with incidents of this type. A hotspot of Republicanism was the Toomebridge area and on several occasions lorry loads of troops would be called out in the early hours to provide guards and patrols against such eventualities. For me, and many of my colleagues, this was our first experience of coming under the threat of enemy action. Not that we were ever shot at on those occasions, but it was much more realistic than standing on guard outside Stationers Hall in the City of London, in a civilian overcoat.

Stage Manager

There was a lively thespian group at the depot centred around Jack Allen and his wife, Ruth Dunning, both well known on the English stage before and after the war. They, together with Ian Aylmer-Jones and his wife, Anne, Lieutenant H.H. Beamish of the BBC, and several other aspiring actors, who spent most of their time acting but with little or no success behind the footlights, formed a Depot Dramatic Society, and decided as their first venture to put on a performance of *French Without Tears* — I think it was! Jack Allen was convinced that I had some theatrical connections, and persuaded me to take on the job of stage manager, which I did, with considerable reluctance. During rehearsals over the next several weeks I was to gain an insight into the highly volatile disposition of actors and actresses. Hysterical outbursts, tears, recriminations, resignations were the order of the day, with me as an amused and sometimes embarrassed onlooker, but all this seemed part of the scene, and gradually the play began to take shape as we approached the date for the first night. The play was to be put on in the new town hall in Ballymena, and would run for several nights.

During one of the scenes, the noises off included the sound of a motor car driving away from the front of the house in which the scene was set. Noises off being my responsibility, and having no appropriate sound effects to meet this particular requirement, I had thought up what I decided was a bright idea of bringing my motor cycle onto the wings at the side of the stage, and starting up at the crucial moment to give the required effect. I recognized that a motor cycle engine doesn't sound much like a motor car, but it seemed adequate to create the illusion that the actor concerned had mounted some form of transport and driven away, and Jack Allen seemed quite satisfied with the plan. I persuaded the depot transport sergeant to have the ignition system, carburettor and everything else tuned up so that the engine would roar into life at the slightest push of the kick-start, and arranged for the machine to be transported onto the appropriate side of the stage from where the noise was to emanate.

On the night of the dress rehearsal, it worked like a dream, and although the audience — troops from the depot who had naturally been given free seats and ordered to be in them by seven thirty pm — were probably not the most receptive for a light-hearted sophisticated comedy, they nevertheless appeared to enjoy the show, so we were all encouraged to look forward to the first night. Tickets had sold well and we anticipated a full house, including most of the local civic dignitaries and their families, together with senior officers of army units and Royal Air Force stations for miles around.

On the day in question — I think it was a Friday — I received instructions from Depot Adjutant — Captain (later General) Norman Wheeler that I was to be draft conducting officer for fifty men posted to the 2nd Battalion, and leaving the following day. Obviously someone in the orderly room had overlooked the fact that I was a vital cog in the dramatic society machine, already geared up for a major social event, or maybe they had got their priorities mixed up. It occurred to me later that they may have been aware of the catastrophic chain of events just beginning in Belgium and France, the implications of which hadn't then been fully appreciated in Ballymena and that a depot dramatic show was of less importance. When I consulted with Jack Allen about my assignment, he threw one of his artistic tantrums and wanted to rush off and complain to Colonel Cowley. However, my preference was for the draft and I managed to dissuade him from being too hasty, pointing out that the colonel might cancel the show and in any event I would be there for the first night and I could find someone who could be with me that evening to learn what had to be done and who could then stand-in for the remaining nights. He asked me who I had in mind and I replied 'Eric May,' to which he agreed. At lunch time I explained the problem to Eric who was more than delighted to help out, so that evening we set off together for the town hall.

I had given Eric a copy of the stage management cues for lighting, curtains, scene changes and other details, and for an hour or so before curtain-up we went through this so that he could familiarize himself with everything. With regard to the motor cycle I explained that after the actor — Ian Aylmer-Jones,

I think it was — had made his exit from the stage, Eric, who would be astride the machine, would allow a couple of seconds as the time required for Ian to get into his imaginary motor car before kicking down the starter. We even gave this a trial run before the town hall doors were opened, and all went according to plan, and we had time for a snifter or two before curtain-up.

Through a convenient gap in the stage curtain I could see the auditorium filling up, with groups being ushered to their places and much fussing around as to who sat where and beside whom, particularly amongst the front row of the stalls where the more exalted had their reserved seats. I got the impression from the noisy chatter, kissing, embracing and hand-shaking amongst those who probably hadn't seen one another since the night before, that all the pre-show dinner and cocktail parties had gone according to plan.

Behind the curtain the nervous tension and histrionics were increasing even amongst the more seasoned members of the cast. Most of them were on the stage, checking on whatever props might concern them; moving a chair a little to one side, then putting it back; pleading with one another for assurance that they looked the part — 'Darling, how do I look?' 'Dearest, you look positively divine.' 'Have you got your cigarette case?' 'Darling, DO remember this and don't forget that.' Meanwhile, the stage manager, with support and encouragement from his deputy, was having another snifter.

At last we were ready to go. With a nod from me, Eric pressed a button which sounded a loud bell which I suspected was originally intended as a fire alarm. Fifteen seconds of bell, we had agreed, followed by two minutes to allow the audience to settle themselves, have a last second nose-blow and whatever else; the surplus actors and actresses scuttled off the stage to the wings as the hubbub beyond the curtain gradually subsided, up went the stage curtain, and we were away.

The first couple of scenes went ahead without a hitch, although the thought went through my mind that the audience was strangely unresponsive. There were a few lines which were supposed to produce a laugh but only caused a somewhat stifled snigger. Then came the third scene when the heartbroken lover would make his dramatic exit through the French windows, leap into his car and vanish into the night. The motor cycle was a couple of yards away from the French windows with its rear wheel raised off the ground on its stand, with Eric astride the saddle, one foot on a foot rest and the other resting on the kick-start, poised for action. Out came Ian with a magnificent gesture of despair; I could see Eric counting to himself — 'a thousand and one', 'a thousand and two', and 'a thousand and . . .' down went his left foot on the kick-start and BANG! There was an ear splitting blast as the engine back-fired and an enormous cloud of smoke billowed through the French windows onto the stage and mushroomed upwards illuminated by the foot lights.

There was a moment of complete silence. I could see the actor-players on stage looking at me, but I couldn't see the audience. I heard one or two loud guffaws and was told later that several females in the audience looked a little anxious. My eyes turned to Eric just as his foot went down for a second time, and there was another almighty bang and a further cloud of blue smoke surged on stage. This time there was a derisory cheer from the common soldiery in the audience and several females stood up, gathering their skirts about their knees ready to make a quick get-away, convinced that the IRA were making a surprise attack. I think that Eric panicked a little and fiddled with one of the small levers on the handle bars. Down went his foot for the third time. Immediately the engine roared into life at full throttle. Either the vibration or Eric jolted the machine from its stand and although it shouldn't have been in gear it took off like a demented stallion sighting a broody mare with Eric still in the saddle. Fortunately, it could only move about six feet before coming to rest with a crash against the brick wall of the town hall.

I have no clear recollection of the next few minutes, during which I was helping Eric get out from under my motor cycle and get it back on its stand. However, it appeared that the audience were most impressed with the Effects Department and responded with a mixture of cheers, claps and laughter and for a few moments Jack Allen was unable to get the plot going again. When he did, with the next line of the script — 'That's the last we shall see of him' — it confirmed the audience's view that they had just witnessed a very well conceived and carried out assassination, and once again burst into loud applause.

The remainder of the play went off without further distraction, and I am sure that if nothing else the incident caused the audience to sit up and take more notice than might otherwise have been the case. Our stars, Jack Allen and Ruth Dunning, must have had difficulty keeping calm at the time, but with several curtain calls and an enthusiastic reception at the end they were more than mollified, the only outstanding question as we later stood around the offending motor cycle re-living the incident, being what would happen the next night. It was agreed that Eric would get the motor transport expert in the following morning to check the engine again.

I was off into the unknown the following day, and when I got back, Eric told me with obvious pleasure that on the second and third nights everything had gone like clockwork with no backfires — much to his disappointment.

Draft Conducting Officer

IN May 1940, I think it was, I received a note from the orderly room that I had been appointed as draft conducting officer for a draft of fifty men posted to the 2nd Battalion. It was common knowledge at the depot, and possibly everywhere else, that, after the German invasion of Belgium and Holland on 10 May, the 2nd Battalion had moved from France to somewhere near Louvain, to assist in throwing the Germans back across the Rhine, but it was also widely appreciated that this information was highly secret!

This was something new so far as I was concerned, but discreet enquiries from an orderly room clerk put my mind at ease. He assured me that all the necessary arrangements and reservations for the journey would be made 'through the usual channels', and all I had to do was to collect various documents before departure, and ensure that the men arrived at their destination in one piece. Details of the route and timings were decided, by someone somewhere, and I had to report to the various transport officers at each stage of the journey, who would then direct me as to the next stage.

On the day of the move I collected the necessary documentation from the orderly room, including my warrant for the return journey, and made my way to the barrack square where the men were formed up ready for my inspection. To my surprise, although I should perhaps have expected it, the commanding officer, Colonel Cowley, together with most of the other officers, NCOs and men were there to see us off, and the depot band was on parade to play us down to Ballymena railway station. After inspecting the draft, making sure they were all correctly dressed and equipped, including their haversack rations to cover at least part of the journey, I then had the wit to march up to the colonel and ask for permission to move off. This was all very new to me, and I had received no advice on the correct procedure. However, Colonel Cowley then addressed the draft, telling them what a privilege it was to serve with the 2nd Battalion and stressing the importance of upholding the honour of the regiment. He then gave me permission to move off, and with the band leading the way, we marched off to Ballymena station.

The movement of all troops at that time was classified as secret, but there appeared to be little secrecy about this move, as most of Ballymena was out in the streets to wave goodbye. As we marched down the hill I had visions of clandestine radios flashing messages to U-boats in wait for our boat from Larne to Stranraer. I also felt a bit of a fraud being part of this fervent display of patriotism, as my job was simply to deliver my draft to the front line, like lambs to the slaughter, and then to return to the peace and comfort of the depot. We entrained at Ballymena and with the band on the platform, playing the regimental march, and to the waving of many damp handkerchiefs, we moved off to Larne.

When we reached Larne Harbour it was dark, very windy and raining. We clambered down onto the platform where we were met by a lance corporal from the Harbour Transport Office who expressed his regret for the absence of the transport officer who had gone home with a cold. An hour later, still standing on the platform in the dark, wind and rain, I felt no sympathy for the TO, no doubt warm and snug in bed. For some reason the transport corporal had been told not to move the draft down to the ship until it was ready to sail, so we stayed on the exposed platform, but in accordance with army practice the reason for keeping us hanging around was kept secret. At long last and after many visits to the boat on my urging, the corporal announced that we could go on board, and with the aid of a very dim torch, he led us, stumbling and sloshing in the pitch dark, around bollards, over hawsers, through pools of water to the gangplank where the troops filed onto the deck, carefully counted by me as they passed, and were then led below. The counting of heads at every stage of the journey was a very necessary part of my responsibility to ensure that no-one was left behind, by accident or design.

I had no idea, and wasn't particularly concerned as to which ship we were on but had assumed it would be one of the ferries normally on the Larne/Stranraer run. My assumption was wrong and we found ourselves not in a nice warm carpeted passenger lounge, such as one might expect on a Channel crossing, but in a very dimly lit ship's hold without seating or any other comfort other than the solid wooden deck on which we stood. However, it was at least warm and the men were still reasonably cheerful, so with much good-humoured banter and profanity they soon had their equipment and coats off and were settling down for a smoke, cards and their haversack rations. At this point I was wondering where I should relax for the next two hours or so. Would it be considered unbecoming for an 'officer and a gentleman' to be seated on the deck with his men or would it be more fitting for me to demonstrate my superior stamina and sense of responsibility by simply remaining on my feet and, as it were, keeping watch over my charges?

My uncertainty was soon resolved. There was a loud clang as the metal door slammed shut behind a sailor clad in heavy oilskins and rubber boots. He wore a peaked cap so presumably was an officer or petty officer. He approached me and said, rather brusquely, 'DCO?'

I nodded.

'All ranks must collect their life jackets which must be worn throughout the voyage,' he said. 'Follow me and I'll show you where to get them,' and he moved towards the doorway.

'On your feet, lads,' I ordered. 'Cigarettes out.'

And with more good-humoured curses and swearing they heaved themselves up and made for the doorway where the sailor was holding the heavy door open. 'Single file, follow me,' he said and moved along a passageway where he opened a large chest and directed each man to pick out a lifebelt.

I had visualized dossing down in a corner of the hold where I would at least be on hand and able to keep an eye on my draft, and now, to my surprise, I was offered the comfort of a cabin. I opened the door and stepped inside. There was a dim light on and I could make out a small cabin with two bunk beds and a wash basin in one corner. Then I saw a pair of black shoes on the floor beside a suitcase. I looked around and on a hook behind the door saw a battledress jacket with major's crown on the shoulder lapels and a row of medal ribbons.

'Hello, old chap,' said a voice, 'I hope you don't mind me sharing your cabin.'

Looking down I saw, again to my surprise, a khaki clad figure in shirt sleeves and braces lying on the lower bunk with his hands clasped behind his head. I hadn't noticed him as I walked in because the lower bunk was hidden in shadow. Before I had a chance to reply, the voice went on, 'My name's Johnson, from NID. I couldn't get a cabin tonight and thought you wouldn't mind sharing.'

I opened my mouth to reply but it was too late. 'Taking a draft to the 2nd Battalion I suppose, I doubt if you'll ever get there.'

I didn't know what to say but several questions flashed through my mind. Had the cabin been set aside for my personal use? Could I, a 2nd lieutenant, ask a major to leave? How did he know I was conducting a draft to the 2nd Battalion? The only thing I knew was that the NID was an abbreviation for the Army Command of the North Ireland District which I understood was based at Lisburn.

I think my unwanted cabin mate realized what was going through my mind. He swung his legs over and sat up on the lower bunk. He was a genial looking person, about fifty, balding on top with signs of middle age spread. I remembered the medal buttons on his jacket; presumably from the First World War. Holding out his hand he said, 'Charlie Johnson.'

I took it and replied, 'Bob Sheridan.'

He continued, 'Sorry I barged in but I often do this trip and couldn't get a cabin tonight. I tried to find you first but couldn't. Do you mind?'

I relaxed, feeling that for a major to introduce himself and explain his intrusion to me in such a friendly way, he must be a good type, so I assured him that he was very welcome.

A couple of hours later we arrived at Stranraer after a choppy but otherwise uneventful crossing. I wasn't sure what time we would be required to disembark, so as we steamed up the smooth waters of Lough Ryan I went below with the intention, as I thought, of rousing the men and making sure they were just as ready as I was; I found them dressed, clean and tidy, some even with their equipment on, and their life jackets stacked by the door. By then it was about three am, but even at that hour their sense of humour was undiminished.

Within minutes of the ship tying up alongside the quay at Stranraer, the local transport officer appeared on the scene with instructions that we must disembark immediately. Fortunately we were ready to move but it soon became apparent that the sole reason for the hurry was to enable him to get back to the comfort of his office. Once again, rifles were slung and kitbags were shouldered, and with much profanity the men stumbled their way up several layers of steps to the open air where it was still dark, wet and windy. Across the gangplank, railway tracks, goods yards and several platforms, the TO striding along at the head of the column as if pursued by a pack of wolves, me at the rear urging the laggards to get a move on and feeling guilty about it. Unlike the men, I had no encumbrances other than the haversack slung over my shoulder. Eventually we arrived at a solitary passenger carriage standing in what appeared to be an otherwise completely deserted siding.

To all appearances in fact, the whole of Stranraer Harbour station was deserted. I had noticed a train pulling out presumably carrying the civilian passengers off the boat, including my cabin companion, but now it seemed that all the station staff had gone home to bed. Then I heard faint sounds of music coming from across the lines and decided to follow that trail to locate the Transport Office. I was near the end of the platform and couldn't make out where the subway between platforms was located, and although I realized there must be one somewhere, I decided to follow the practice of railway employees and cross over the lines on the wooden sleepers provided for the movement of trolleys between platforms. I had just reached the top of the slope at the end of the platform, when a bright light suddenly shone straight into my face and a broad Scottish voice said, 'Who the bleeding hell are you?'

To say that I was startled is a considerable understatement. I nearly fell off the platform onto the lines. I put up my arm to protect my eyes from the glare and replied, rather demurely, 'I'm in charge of a draft and I'm looking for the transport office.'

'You're in charge of what?' came the reply.

'A draft,' I said, 'a draft of men,' still trying to make out who was behind the light.

'Oh, you mean a drraft,' said the voice. 'I thought you were a saboteur.'

The light moved up and down as if to make sure I wasn't carrying any weapons. 'OK, come on, I'll show you,' and he waved his torch up the platform indicating that I was to go ahead. I decided by this time that he must be a member of the local defence force protecting Stranraer Harbour against subversive attack, but whether he was in uniform or carried any weapon I couldn't tell. His torch pointed the way as we walked up across the railway lines and up the platform but he kept a yard or so behind me as if suspicious that I might make a break for it or attack him. We continued along the platform behind a block of what appeared to be waiting rooms until the voice behind me said, 'Here we are then,' and I discovered the source of the music; a doorway which had been concealed from my view from the opposite platform.

The transport officer was sitting behind a bare wooden table at the far end from the door, in his shirt sleeves, smoking a cigarette, and reading what appeared to be a paper back novel. He looked up as I entered and seemed taken aback when I saluted. 'Oh there you are,' he said, 'take a pew.' He nodded in the direction of a chair on the opposite side of his table. I undid the buttons of my greatcoat, took off my hat and sat down.

By this time I was tired, hot, hungry and irritable — largely because, having come from the cold into a very warm room, my glasses kept misting up and I had to wipe the inside of the lenses with my finger to distinguish the figure opposite to me. He picked up a clip board of papers, turned over the top sheets and appeared to be reading the text. At the same time he reached forward and fumbled for a cigarette from a packet on his desk, which he lit from the stub of the one he was already smoking. I also lit a cigarette and waited. After a few minutes I decided to break the silence. 'What time are we likely to leave?' I asked.

He looked up and stared at me for a moment. 'Leave where?' he replied, as if the though that we might be going somewhere had never occurred to him.

'Leave here, Stranraer,' I said, restraining my growing irritation. I was beginning to think I was dealing with an idiot.

He put down the clip board and sat back in his chair. 'You were going to London with the boat train but your movement order was cancelled last night,' he said. He leant forward and stubbed out his cigarette in his already over-full makeshift ashtray as if to wash his hands of the whole affair.

I looked at him in disbelief. 'Cancelled?' I said. 'Well, what do we do now?'

'Wait for further orders.' He made it sound as if I was an imbecile. What else does one do in the army if an order is cancelled? Sit back and wait for something new. I had a momentary vision of spending the rest of the war with my fifty men in a carriage at a siding at Stranraer Harbour.

'Can we get some heating in the carriage?' I asked.

'There's no heating without an engine,' he replied with a touch of sarcasm, 'and by the way, make sure your chaps don't use the toilets, they'll have to use the station cloakrooms.'

This confirmed my impression that we were in for a long stay and as I got up to leave I was about to ask what we should do about food and drink. He anticipated the question and said, 'We'll see what we can do about some hot drinks later on.'

I thanked him, saluted, rather casually, because for one reason or another neither the transport office nor the TO seemed to justify barrack square discipline, and departed.

When I stepped out of the office it was still pitch dark and I paused for a minute to let my eyes become adjusted. A few yards down the platform stood a figure holding a lit torch who, I assumed was my earlier acquaintance, although this time he wasn't treating me as a suspect saboteur, and kept his torch away from my eyes. I turned towards him deciding that I would return to my carriage by the orthodox route.

'Where's the subway?' I asked, and he flashed his torch along the platform.

'This way sir, I'll show you,' he said and accompanied me along the platform to where I could see steps leading down into the gloom. 'Everything all right sir?' he said, as we walked down the steps.

'More or less,' I replied 'except that I don't know how long we are going to sit here.'

'Oh well, maybe it's a good thing. It doesn't look so good on the other side,' he responded, and I couldn't help reflecting that even this station guard at Stranraer seemed to know that we were destined for the BEF.

As we walked through the subway I could make out by a dim

77

gas lamp that he was an elderly man in a heavy tweed suit with thick woollen cardigan up to his neck, a wide webbing belt around his waist, a forage cap on his head, a brassard on his left arm, and a rifle hanging by the sling over his shoulder. 'How often are you on this job?' I asked him.

'It depends, normally every second night,' he replied, 'but if the others don't turn up they call me out on my night off but I don't mind that. We're here from dusk to dawn. Four of us, two hours on and two off.'

I was going to ask him who 'they' were, but he went on, 'I'd like to have got back into the army — I was in the last time — but I'm a bit too old now. Still, this is better than doing nothing.'

'Are you retired?' I queried.

He turned his head and looked at me but with the glimmering lamp behind us I couldn't see his face. 'Retired,' he said. 'Why now, how old do you think I am?'

'Oh about sixty I suppose,' I replied.

'I was seventy last birthday,' he said, 'old enough to be your grandfather.'

He turned and walked up the steps from the subway to the platform, my seventy year old companion lighting the way for me with his torch. I was astounded. Seventy years old and a volunteer to guard Stranraer station every second night and, when necessary, more often. It seemed unbelievable, and the thought came into my mind that there were probably hundreds, if not thousands of others like him — although maybe not in their seventies — doing the same thing all round the country, whilst I, in my early twenties and thousands like me, felt hard done by if we didn't get a couple of nights off-duty each week.

When we got to the top of the steps my thoughts were interrupted. As far as I could see, there was no carriage alongside the platform. It had been towed away in my absence! I was speechless with a sudden feeling of panic. What do I do now? My sense of shock was quickly relieved.

'This way,' his quiet voice said, and as I turned I realized that we had come up from the subway in the opposite direction to that which I had absent-mindedly anticipated. My carriage was still where I had left it and as we approached I could see no sign of life, so presumably the men were all asleep. We stopped beside my compartment and I turned to my guide and held out my hand. 'Many thanks and good luck,' I said, although I really felt he justified a salute.

'Good luck to you and the lads,' he replied, as he grasped my hand, 'I wish I was coming with you!'

Seventy years of age and here was this Scotsman wishing he could come with us. As he turned away I recollected the MTOs instruction about the toilets. 'By the way,' I called, 'where's the men's cloakroom?'

'By the transport office on the other platform,' he called back and walked off.

I have often had occasion to think of the qualities of the young-old man on the station at Stranraer.

As I clambered up into my cold compartment I was bothered by a problem. If I lay down, I would probably fall asleep. The men would wake up and would almost certainly start using the two toilets at either end of the carriage. I looked at my watch; it was nearly four o'clock; a couple of hours at least to daybreak. Should I go along and wake them up, compartment by compartment, and issue the necessary instructions, or should I remain alert for the first signs of activity and then tell them where to perform their morning ablutions? I lit a cigarette and pondered on the problem. An officer's first duty is the welfare of his men — they should be allowed to sleep on. However, I also needed sleep. I stubbed out my cigarette in the ashtray and leant back against the corner seat. The answer to my problem was clear; I would have to stay awake.

'Do you want some tea, sorr?' said a voice. I opened my eyes and in a flash realized that my problem had solved itself — for better or worse. I had fallen asleep and it was now broad daylight. I had an immediate vision of what the track would look like after we pulled out — if ever we did. I stood up with a poor attempt to look as if I had been wide awake when so suddenly interrupted.

'Tea,' I said, 'where's the tea?'

'Outside sorr, there's tea and wads on the platform.'

I stood up and walked over to the door. Outside was a large trolley bearing a tea urn with two well wrapped up ladies, one filling mess tins held out by riflemen with steaming hot tea, the other handing out packets which presumably held sandwiches. I looked at my watch; it was eight o'clock. I had slept soundly for at least three hours.

I opened the door of the compartment and stepping down onto the platform, walked up to the group surrounding the trolley.

'Good morning, sorr,' said several voices and before I had time to open my mouth I was handed a large mug of tea and a package. I noticed that I had been given the only mug available.

'This is very good of you,' I said to the two ladies.

'Not at all, sir,' replied one of them in a soft Scottish voice, 'Captain McKenzie telephoned first thing this morning and told us you were here and would welcome some breakfast.'

I wondered what time 'first thing' had been to enable them to prepare sandwiches and tea for fifty-one, and deliver them to the platform by eight o'clock. I took a sip of my tea; it was hot and sweet, exactly to my liking, and my opinion of Captain McKenzie, the TO, rose several points. Putting my mug down on the trolley, I opened my package to find two excellent spam sandwiches and as I munched them I took stock of the situation.

All the men on the platform, about half of the draft, had obviously washed and shaved and were looking clean and tidy. Again I wondered what the toilets in the train were looking like. Just then I heard the clatter of voices along the platform, and turning, saw another group of men from the draft walking towards us in shirt sleeves and carrying towels and washing gear and all looking spruce and fresh. Obviously they had all found and used the station cloakroom and my suspicions that they would disregard the well known regulation of the railway companies about not using the toilets when the train is standing in a station, were unfounded. I decided to take a look and sure enough, the toilets did not appear to have been used. Why, I asked myself, had I assumed that unless I had given clear instructions that they should not do so these men would ignore the obvious need not to foul a public place like this, knowing as they did, that they would soon be miles away, and that in any event, there was very little I could do if they chose to disregard the railway companies' regulations or exhortations? As with my former friends in the London Rifle Brigade, it was taking time for me to recognize that a rough and tough exterior and a propensity for profane and foul language did not necessarily indicate a lack of pride and personal dignity.

It suddenly dawned on me that I was probably the only one

of the group who had not washed and shaved, so I collected my haversack and made my way to the cloakroom to remedy the situation. When I got back the tea trolley had gone and a number of the men were standing around talking and smoking while others were walking up and down in small groups, obviously intent on keeping out the morning chill. I decided to explain the situation as given to me by the transport officer, so told one man to pass the message along that the draft should fall-in on the platform without equipment or arms. As usual I heard the curses and groans as the word went round.

'On parade you lazy bastards,' called my messenger as he walked along the corridor, obviously enjoying his temporary status as the conveyor of bad news.

As soon as the men were formed up and I had inspected them, confirming that all were washed and shaved, I told them the reason for the delay in our journey and the present uncertainty as to our destination. The possibility that they might not be joining the 2nd Battalion on the other side of the English Channel was received with genuine dismay and I was unable to offer any answers to numerous questions as to what the other possibilities might be. A partial answer was provided with the arrival of a corporal from the transport office who came marching up the platform, obviously intent on ending our uncertainty. He approached me, saluted, and said in a loud voice, 'Your draft will be leaving with the eleven o'clock train for London, sir.'

I was reluctant to question him in front of the draft as to what further instructions we might have received as to our movements, but did ask, 'and what happens when we get to London?'

He seemed to anticipate the question and simply replied, 'You'll get further instructions in London, sir,' saluted and walked away.

I decided to dismiss the men, telling them that they were to be sure to remain in the station and to be in the carriage at ten thirty. It was now about nine thirty.

The men fell out, and as they climbed back into the railway carriage there was much good humoured cross-talk about the possibilities of the many British Army stations around the world. One man was partially right; he volunteered the thought that we'd finish up with the 1st Battalion which, so far as we knew, was in India.

Our journey to London was uneventful except for the fact that it took nearly twenty-four hours, which I think was twice as long as the usual time. Whether or to what extent this was due to the rapidly deteriorating military situation in France and Belgium, and to air raids and threats of air raids en route, I don't know, but at various places down the line we just stopped and sat, moved a few miles and stopped again. Fortunately, at main stations we were well supplied with tea and wads, so no great hardship was involved, but it was a weary draft which eventually formed up on a platform at Euston the following morning.

We were met by a very smart military police sergeant wearing the usual MTO armband, and in no time kitbags were loaded onto trolleys and we marched off to an adjoining road where two coaches were waiting. All the sergeant could or would tell me was that we were heading for Ashford in Kent via Victoria station but no mention was made of what unit we were joining. The journey across London was of considerable interest to many of the men, particularly those who had never been in the city before, and I was able to point out the landmarks we passed. There were few signs of wartime activity other than heavily sandbagged windows and doorways, particularly in the Whitehall area.

At Victoria station we were switched from the coaches to a reserved carriage on a normal passenger train, and were soon rattling our way through the south-east suburbs of London, an area I knew well, and out into the Kentish countryside. I wasn't sure whether we were on a fast or slow train or how long the journey would take but I suspected not much more than an hour or so, and I wanted to be sure that when we pulled into Ashford we would be able to de-train quickly and with everyone properly dressed and equipped. It was obvious that we were nearing the end of our journey and that we would be met by someone from the unit to which the draft had now been redirected and it was important that we should create a good impression. I therefore made my way along the carriage, warning each compartment to that effect. It was fortunate that I did so because when we pulled into Ashford station we were met by someone who I subsequently came to know as the archetype of all battalion adjutants, Captain Terence Otway.

More of Terence later, perhaps, but on this occasion, there

was this army captain, immaculately turned out in battle dress and wearing, to my surprise, the green forage cap and badge of the Royal Ulster Rifles. I ordered the men to get their kitbags out of the luggage van — urged on by the shouts of a station guard anxious to get the train on the move — and to fall in on the platform. While this was going on, the captain and the warrant officer by his side just stood and watched and I assumed that in view of their obvious interest they must be somehow involved, so I approached the captain, saluted and said something to the effect that I was in charge of a draft of fifty men from Ballymena and was he expecting us? He returned my salute and looked at me for a few seconds as if wondering how anyone could be stupid as to arrive with a draft at Ashford station and find him waiting on the platform and then ask whether he was expecting us.

'What's your name?' he asked.

'Sheridan,' I replied.

'I'm Otway, battalion adjutant, you'd better come with me; the Sergeant Major will look after the draft. Where's the posting list?'

He spoke in a very terse, abrupt way as if words were expensive or indicative of inefficiency. I rummaged in my haversack and produced my several lists of names and handed them to him. 'Which battalion, did you say?' I asked.

Again he looked at me as if I was an imbecile. 'The 1st Battalion, of course,' he said.

'The 1st Battalion of what?'

'The 1st Battalion, the Royal Ulster Rifles.' He spelled it out as if teaching a child the alphabet.

'Oh,' I said, 'I thought the 1st Battalion was in India; the draft was posted to the 2nd Battalion.'

He looked through the list of names and handed them to the sergeant major and said to me, 'Yes, you'd probably have difficulty finding the 2nd Battalion.'

The sergeant major was a short, stocky man; good looking with bright blue eyes underneath heavy dark eyebrows and with open friendly features. He took the papers from Captain Otway saying, 'Right, sir, I'll get the draft up to A Company.'

He turned to me and said, 'When did the men last have a hot meal, sir?'

'Not since they left Ballymena two nights ago,' I replied, and he saluted and moved over to where the draft had fallen in on the platform. I didn't know it at the time, but the CSM's name was Cunningham and I was to get to know him well later on.

4

1st Battalion — RUR

Harpenden

Early in December, 1940, I was posted, together with Eric May, to the 1st Battalion. We were both delighted with the news. I had been at the depot for nearly eight months, and Eric almost as long, and whilst life there had been very comfortable it was most frustrating and demoralizing to be living in the peacetime-like atmosphere of the officers' mess with formal guest nights and a regular round of parties at a time when the German armies were more or less poised to land in England.

The instruction issued for Eric and me was to join the 1st Battalion immediately. No reference was made to the location of the 1st Battalion but we were told by the adjutant that it was located at Harpenden in Hertfordshire, not far from London. It appeared that there was no time to be lost. When we visited the orderly room to collect our travel warrants and other papers we were told that arrangements had been made for us to catch the Larne to Stranraer steamer the following night.

Eric and I were delighted with the news but our pleasure was not matched by the reaction of Ikey May, Eric's older brother. One of Ikey's objectives in life was to keep an eye on Eric, the black sheep of the family, and it wasn't in line with his wishes that they would be separated, and that evening in the mess during our farewell celebrations, he made it clear that he would aim to join us in the 1st Battalion as soon as possible which, in fact, is what he did a month or so later.

On our final evening there was an all ranks dance in one of the depot gymnasiums which provided a very suitable opportunity to say farewell to many of our friends at Ballymena, one of whom was an ATS girl called Sally Kellett. Sally and I had been on friendly terms following my discovery that she was a member of the Kellett family in Dublin, in whose shop in Grafton Street my mother had served her apprenticeship. Naturally, I promised Sally that I would write on every opportunity but on later reflection I decided that the future was too uncertain to justify the maintenance of any such relationships. At that dance I also met a very disgruntled young officer who had just arrived at the depot. His name was J.D.A. Boustead — Derek — and he was extremely upset at having been commissioned into an Irish regiment, not having the remotest connection with Ireland or the Irish and having given as his preference an English county regiment. He told me that his sole objective that night, his first at Ballymena, was to get very drunk in the hope of being sent back to England without delay and whether in disgrace or not; he didn't mind. As it turned out, he joined the 1st Battalion a few weeks later and in due time became more Irish than the Irish. Some months before D-Day in 1944, he married a charming ATS girl — Lalergie — but tragically he was the first officer to be killed in Normandy and never saw his son born later that year.

The following day was spent packing our gear, paying our bills and handing in our bits and pieces and that evening we were collected by a truck and set off for Larne Harbour. A subaltern's luggage, in those days, consisted of a bedroll and a large black metal kit box. The thing I couldn't take with me, of course, was my motor cycle which I left leaning up against the Ballymena 'castle' wall with clear instructions to a fellow subaltern to sell it for the best price he could obtain and to remit the proceeds to me. I subsequently heard that it was never sold but left outside the officers' mess for the use of anyone who was willing to provide it with petrol and oil. This news came from my cousin, Harry Hatton, who arrived in Ballymena the day after I left and who later joined the 2nd Battalion, serving with them in France and Germany up to the end of the war.

Our journey to Stranraer was quite uneventful and after a good breakfast we made our way to the train destined for London, which was standing at the dockside. As we made our way along the corridor of the first class carriage, we noticed a young officer with RUR shoulder badges sitting in a corner of a compartment on his own, and decided to join him. He introduced himself as Ronnie Wilson, on his way back to the 1st Battalion after a short spell of leave at his home in Portadown. Ronnie and I have been good friends since that day and we have visited him and his wife at their home outside Portadown on several occasions.

Ronnie was a solicitor and prior to joining the army had worked at the Crown Solicitor's office in Portadown. He was an attractive personality with dark wavy hair, bright blue twinkling eyes and a soft Ulster accent and it became the accepted practice in the battalion that if one wanted to meet the best looking girls one always went out with Ronnie Wilson and watched him at work. The first thing we noticed was that he was wearing a narrow piece of red ribbon on the epaulettes of his battledress jacket, and he explained that in the 1st Battalion everybody wore a coloured ribbon in this way to designate the company to which he belonged. The theory was that the identification of individuals in this way as belonging to particular companies promoted loyalty and pride and with the added advantage that individuals misbehaving in some way on the one hand or exhibiting efficiency and keenness on the other, could be more easily identified and followed up by a commanding officer's rocket or commendation to the company commander concerned as the circumstances required.

After a long and tedious train journey, we arrived in London very late at night so Eric and I decided that it would not be appropriate to report to the battalion at such a late hour and that we should find a hotel and continue our journey the following morning. Ronnie continued on his way.

The battalion at that time was stationed in Harpenden, a pleasant residential town twenty or so miles north of London, where we arrived the following morning and by some means or other located and made our way to the battalion headquarters. There I was instructed to join A Company. At that time, the battalion was commanded by Lieutenant Colonel Gerald Brunskill — later Major General — but we seldom met him, as the battalion was widely spread in billets around the town, and there was no central officers' mess. The company commanders included Charles Vickery, Gerald Going and Christie Miller.

The battalion was accommodated in requisitioned property

around Harpenden, including church halls and empty residential houses, and conditions were much the same as I had experienced with the LRB at Northolt about a year earlier. There was one major difference, however. I was now with a highly trained and disciplined regular army battalion which was very different to the somewhat carefree atmosphere of the TA unit.

On the outbreak of war, the 1st Battalion had been on operational duty on the north west frontier of India, keeping the road over the frontier open and providing protection for the movement of civilian convoys against attack by tribesmen in the area. Around the end of 1939 the battalion had been reinforced with a draft of officers and other ranks from the regiment's TA unit, the London Irish Rifles. These were mainly Londoners but many with Irish connections who, like me, had been in civilian jobs and who had joined the TA at the time of Munich.

After moving back from the Indian frontier to Rawalpindi the battalion went through a period of intense training and shortly after the Dunkirk evacuation were shipped back to England with a number of other regular army battalions to provide some regular forces for the defence of England should the Germans invade.

Before the departure from India three company sergeant majors had been granted commissions and promoted to the rank of captain. They were Charles Vickery, Bob Hynds and Tom Warner, all of whom had many years' regular service in the ranks and who were to demonstrate their respective capabilities with the regiment during the coming years. One warrant officer who refused a commission was Company Sergeant Major Cunningham — probably the most suitable of the four for commissioned rank — and who I had met at Ashford station with Terence Otway a few months earlier, and with whom I would be closely involved over the next three years.

When the battalion had arrived back in the United Kingdom it became part of the 31st Independent Brigade Group with two other regular battalions; the 2nd Battalion of the South Staffordshire Regiment and the 2nd Battalion of the Oxford and Buckinghamshire Light Infantry. The role of the brigade group was as a mobile reserve force to be used for the counter-attack against German invasion forces in the South East of England and intensive training took place to that end with particular emphasis on rapid deployment to wherever their efforts might be required. For a short period they had been moved to Ashford in Kent, where I first made the battalion's acquaintance, and where they formed a link in the 'thin red line,' the only defence against the anticipated German invasion. The battalion then moved back to Harpenden where I joined them in December 1940.

The majority of officers and men were either Irish born and bred, or with close Irish connections. The majority were from the North of Ireland with a fair number from the south, and with a sprinkling of cockneys, including the London Irish contingent; all made a very good mixture. The Ulster men were mainly Protestant, whilst the southerners were, in the main, Roman Catholics, but throughout the four years I served with the battalion I never came across any suggestion of serious religious dispute. The battalion padre was usually a Protestant but there was always a Roman Catholic priest on the brigade strength and both were equally welcome, not only in the officers' mess but also amongst the NCOs and men.

On arrival at Battalion HQ, a truck was provided to convey me and my kit to the A Company HQ which was located in a very run-down and unfurnished semi-detached three-bedroomed house not far from the High street. It was here that I first met my company commander, Charles Vickery, and renewed my acquaintance with CSM Cunningham. Charles instructed me to take command of Number 7 Platoon, and on Cunningham's recommendation I appointed an old soldier, Rifleman Gillanders, as my batman.

Our time at Harpenden was largely spent improving the skills of our men; weapon training, fieldcraft, map reading, movement etc; interspersed with company and battalion training aimed at getting on the move quickly should our services be called for, which was often the case with reports of enemy spies dropping by parachute in the surrounding countryside. On one occasion, there was a report that an enemy spy had been captured but whether this was true, I don't know.

I quickly settled into life with the battalion and, in particular, with the platoon which had been entrusted to my command. I quickly realized that commanding thirty men, the majority of whom were hardened soldiers who had seen service in many parts of the world, was going to be totally different to handling a group of new recruits at the depot. They were a discerning bunch and to earn their confidence and respect I had to demonstrate that they could rely on me to the same extent as I relied on them.

At that time, whilst the threat had receded, it still appeared possible that the Germans would attempt an invasion, in which case we would be in the middle of the battle whether the attack came over the beaches in the South of England or by air-borne landings such as had taken place in Belgium and Holland, and in which case every man had to be confident of the skill and courage of those next to him, including his platoon commander and platoon NCOs. With the full support of our company commander, Charles Vickery, we developed a strong sense of friendly rivalry between the platoons as to which was best at all the skills required of the infantry soldier. To this end I had to demonstrate that I was just as skilled at handling a rifle or a Sten gun or a two inch mortar or crawling on my belly through muddy ditches or taking part in long cross-country marches as the rest of my platoon. General discipline in matters of turn-out and behaviour were largely the responsibility of the NCOs but the platoon commander had to ensure that the highest possible standards were maintained at all times. Particularly when in billets, this involved a certain amount of nitpicking, such as checking that each man's blankets were correctly folded for kit inspection in the mornings, but in this connection it was of great benefit to be with a regular battalion in which all these requirements had been strongly inculcated for many years.

However, life had its lighter moments. Many opportunities arose for chatting informally with both the NCOs and the men, and there were many occasions when those of us who had little in the way of active service experience would listen to no doubt exaggerated tales of what life was like in the army in such places as Palestine, Hong Kong, Singapore and various Indian stations.

Whilst we were in Harpenden there was no central battalion officers' mess where one would normally meet and get to know one's fellow officers. However, a popular meeting place in the evenings was the Cock Inn, in Harpenden High Street and it was there that I got to know most of my fellow subalterns from other companies and some of the more senior battalion officers, who were, however, inclined to avoid getting mixed up in junior officers' sessions in the public bar.

My main recollection of Harpenden is of a cold and miserable winter spent in cold and miserable billets, or out in the cold and miserable countryside, taking part in battalion and brigade training exercises in which the main objective of 'Higher Command' appeared to be to keep the troops and junior officers as little informed as possible as to what was going on, or supposed to be going on, and at the same time creating imaginary military situations which would result in maximum discomfort and irritation for all those involved. All this was overshadowed by the heavy bombing of London which was going on at this time, and the extent of which was brought home to us by the glow in the sky from the extensive fires which raged in the city.

I knew that my mother and sister had evacuated themselves down to the farm at Marsh Gibbon near Bicester owned by my brother-in-law and my sister, but it was a perpetual worry as to how my brothers and their families and many other friends in Beckenham were faring in this terrible situation.

Hereford

Early in January 1941, the brigade was moved to the area of Abergavenny/Brecon/Hereford and shortly after this Lieutenant Colonel 'Rosie' Campbell replaced Lieutenant Colonel Brunskill as commanding officer of the battalion. About the same time, Terence Otway was promoted and transferred to another job outside the battalion and was succeeded as adjutant by Signals Officer Paddy Liddle.

For the first few weeks at Hereford life followed much the same pattern of events as in Harpenden. A period of platoon training, followed by company, battalion and brigade exercises all designed, we thought, to develop and improve our role as a mobile counter invasion force. Many of these exercises involved long route marches taking two or three days to and from places such as Hay, Brecon, Llandovery and over the surrounding countryside, including the Brecon Beacons and the Black Mountains. We always marched in open formation with sections staggered on either side of the road. From time to time someone up-front or at the rear of the long column would blow a series of short blasts on a whistle to indicate an imaginary air attack, whereupon everyone would dive for cover into the ditches, and

91

open imaginary fire at the imaginary attacking aircraft. When the men were reasonably fresh, during the first hour or so of a march, the response to these practice alarms was quick and decisive. As the hours passed, however, and legs and feet became increasingly tired and weary, imaginations became less and less responsive and the spontaneous dive for cover on the sounding of the alarm was accompanied by a stream of invective directed against imaginary enemy aircraft and their pilots.

Initially, these long marches took place in daylight, and along country roads; marching for fifty-five minutes and covering about three miles, and then resting for five minutes when all the troops would be seen sitting with their feet up, raised in some way or another, the theory being that this relieved the aches and pains resulting from marching on hard roads, but to my mind it always made it much more painful when we were required to get on the move again. We were very fit and enjoyed the strenuous exercise, and there was always the pleasant thought of a couple of days of relative ease when we arrived back at our billets. As the weeks passed, these marches began to assume a somewhat different flavour. We were required to march only at night-time and across country, making control and direction-finding much more difficult. The reason for this change was soon to become apparent.

Our battalion was located in the outskirts of Hereford City with the troops of A Company accommodated in an old disused brick field, using well-built brick huts for sleeping accommodation, and surrounded by old brick kilns and tall silent chimneys. The officers of the company were accommodated in an empty requisitioned house a short distance away and very close to a pub called the Bear where there was a very accommodating proprietor and where we made many friends amongst the locals. In the evenings, when 'home' from a strenuous training session, most of the subalterns in the battalion would congregate in the public bar of the Bear where we would organize a kitty and a continuous flow of very good draught beer, and as the evenings progressed the customary sing-song would develop, with emphasis on Irish songs and with the full approbation and vocal support of the locals.

There is one song which will always remind me of the enjoyable time we spent at Hereford; the Irish ballad *Father O'Flynn* and the singer, John McFaul, whose party piece it was.

John was from Carlow in Southern Ireland and had been at school with my cousin, Harry Hatton, at Kilkenny. He was a delightful person in every respect, about twenty-five, big and strong, with a very pronounced Southern Irish accent and a great sense of humour, and it was a great shock to us when he was killed one Sunday afternoon as the result of a motorcycle accident.

The battalion had received a batch of new motor cycles and after our midday meal on this particular Sunday, Ronnie Wilson and John asked the battalion transport officer if they could take two of the motor cycles on a trial run around the Hereford area. Later that evening, after we had gone over to the Bear, Ronnie walked in looking very distraught. He simply walked up to our group and said, 'John McFaul is dead.'

With some difficulty we got the full story from him, which was that he had gone on ahead and had waited at a particular road junction for John to catch him up. When John didn't arrive he rode back along the route they had followed and found some civilians lifting John off spiked railings beside the road, on which he was impaled. The subsequent investigation indicated that as John banked his cycle to follow a left turn in the road, the stand on which the cycle could be supported when it was not in use had dropped out of its clip and lodged in the road surface, swinging John around and throwing him over the handlebars onto the railings. John was buried at Hereford and the only member of his family who could attend the funeral was a younger brother, an RAF pilot who was killed a few months later. In my mind's eye I can still see John sitting back in his customary chair in the Bear, a pint of Guinness in one hand and his pipe in the other, leading the chorus:

> 'Here's a health to you, Father O'Flynn,
> Slainthe and slainthe and slainthe Agin,
> Powerfulest preacher and
> Tinderest teacher, and
> Kindliest craythure
> In old Donegal.'

The Mules

During its period of duty on the north west frontier of India and up to the time of return to the United Kingdom, the only form of transport available to the battalion had been mules, of which the battalion had considerable experience. Following its return to the UK and the adoption of motorized transport, much effort had been expended in training NCOs and men to ride motorcycles and drive trucks and Bren gun carriers.

In a relatively short time, and despite a fair degree of chaos, that problem had been overcome, and the use of animal transport was looked upon as very much a thing of the past. It was therefore with considerable astonishment that at a meeting of the officers of the battalion we heard the news from the commanding officer, Rosie Campbell, that the entire 31st Independent Brigade Group was to be trained in the use of animal transport, for which purpose a company of the Royal Indian Army Service Corps, (RIASC), was to be attached to the brigade with all its attendant mules and, as it turned out, other species of four footed animals. The first objective, said Rosie, was to develop the necessary load tables and methods so that the equipment and supplies with which the brigade was now provided could be carried on mules instead of motor vehicles. This was no easy task, as we soon discovered.

By the time this announcement had been made, the RIASC company was already encamped on Hereford racecourse, and we were soon to make the acquaintance of our new-found dumb friends and the Indian Army personnel concerned. We understood that a considerable Indian Army contingent, including service corps units, with their mules, had been shipped from India to France early in 1940 but, like the 1st Battalion, had arrived after the Dunkirk evacuation and had therefore finished up in England.

It has often been said that 'The War Office moves in a mysterious way its wonders to perform,' but what was behind the idea of training one of the very few fully equipped motorized divisions in the use of mule transport was difficult to understand. Naturally, rumours as to the reason for this dramatic switch were rife, the most commonly accepted being that we were destined to take on the Germans in the mountains of Norway. However, ours was not to reason why but simply to get on with whatever we were asked to do, and all ranks entered into this rather strange period of training with considerable gusto. If, for whatever reason, British troops in England at that time had to be trained for mule transportation, then maybe there was good reason for selecting the 31st Independent Brigade Group, each of the battalions of which had recently returned from service in India and many of the officers, NCOs and men were familiar with this form of transport, but, of course, in a very different environment. At least it made a change from what we had been doing over the past twelve months or so.

I was perhaps fortunate to miss the initial phase of the 'IRUR versus the Mules' saga as I was despatched with my platoon to Ludlow for four weeks to act as demonstration platoon at a Home Guard training centre, a very pleasant interlude, living in comparative luxury in an old coaching inn, which I would have appreciated even more if I had know what was going on back in Hereford.

No doubt Hereford racecourse has been the scene of many exciting events since it was created, but I doubt whether it had ever witnessed, or is likely to witness again, many of the scenes which occurred in the late summer of 1941.

One of the problems arose from the unfortunate fact that the mule company hadn't got enough mules. Whether this was due to an error on the part of whoever ordered the mules from India or whether a number were lost overboard, or died during the journey, will never be known, but after arrival in England when the shortage of mules became apparent, more or less anything resembling a mule was conscripted to make up the deficiency. The result was that 'our mules' included a large number of horses of one variety or another, from enormous and fairly placid cart horses to fine looking but somewhat temperamental hunting and showjumping specimens who certainly did not take kindly to the tasks now required of them or to the rather coarse treatment to which they were subjected.

We were provided with a plentiful supply of harness-like contraptions together with straps and ropes to devise ways and means of securing our various bits and pieces of equipment on the animals' backs in such a way that they could be transported over considerable distances without becoming loose and falling off, but this was no easy task. When a particular load appeared to be secure the mule or horse would be led off around the racecourse, alternately walking and trotting to ascertain whether the load would remain secure which, certainly in the early days, it never did.

The mules were not so difficult to work with as the horses, being more placid and docile than their better-bred companions. However, they appeared to be endowed with a high degree of cunning as to how they could make life as difficult as possible for their new masters. The technique for loading the animals was to have one man holding the animal's bit while other men would approach from the rear carrying the appropriate load with the intention of lifting it over the hind quarters and lowering it gently onto the animal's back. By turning their heads, the mules could see what was going on and at the crucial moment the animal would either move backwards or forwards a few paces, thus frustrating the intentions of the loaders, already sweating from their exertions. The load would be dumped on the ground to allow the men to wipe their brows; the mule meantime would appear to smile in a self-satisfied way, and a stream of Ulster profanity about mules and their parentage would flow between all involved. Eventually, the mule would appear to give in — until the next time!

Young horses, on the other hand, took fright on feeling the weight of a three-inch mortar barrel or a hamper full of ammunition on their backs, and would rear up, break loose and career off down the track scattering ammunition and equipment in all directions, accompanied by shouts of derision and ridicule from those not directly involved. As luck would have it, these sort of events frequently occurred when the brigade commander or some other 'brass hats' had come along to check on progress.

In due time, the brigade appeared to be ready to put its efforts and results to the test. The load tables for all equipment and supplies had been established; techniques for loading, securing and unloading had been developed and learned by all concerned, and even the mules appeared to be reconciled to the need for compliance with the orders of strange little men who spoke neither Hindustani nor English. Throughout all this experimental and training activity, the Indian troops or grooms — for such is what they were presumably supposed to be — had remained distinctly aloof; squatting on their haunches, a short distance away from the scene of activity and with an air of indifference to what was going on. There were also several

RIASC officers with the mule company — 'subahdars' — but their attitude seemed to be, 'You've asked for it and now you've got it.' The fact of the matter was that we hadn't asked for mules or horses, but we certainly had to put up with their eccentricities.

The next stage of the programme was a series of company and battalion exercises building up to a crescendo when the entire brigade was required to make a forced march across the Black Mountains to the Brecon Beacons in order to destroy an 'enemy' force which had landed on the Welsh coast and was making its way towards Abergavenny. We were informed that the exercise would last for eight or nine days.

The first three days were spent winding our way at night along narrow country roads, and bivouacking in woodland areas where we could remain concealed during daylight. Secondary roads, lanes and tracks were chosen so that our long column of mules, horses and troops would minimize the dislocation of normal road traffic. At intervals along the column, men would be carrying red hurricane lamps to warn approaching traffic of our presence, but from time to time when a noisy vehicle or motor cycle would pass the column, it usually resulted in many of the animals taking fright and stampeding in all directions, at the same time shedding their loads of arms, ammunition and equipment, all of which, of course, when the animals had been recaptured, had to be collected and reloaded before we could again get on the move; no easy task in the darkness. A most unpleasant aspect of a column of mules is the propensity of those animals to pass wind at every second step so that at the rear of the column one had the impression of walking through an endless sewage farm!

When it came to the trek over the Brecon Beacons, the brigade was led by Hugh McGuire, our battalion IO, who was acting brigade intelligence officer and who, it appeared, hadn't had adequate opportunity to reconnoitre the route but who nevertheless had great faith in his map-reading ability. It was fortunate that this part of the march took place in daylight. The head of the long column began to wind its way up a narrow path gradually climbing towards the highest part of the mountains, but unfortunately at some crucial point Hugh's map-reading failed and he took the wrong track. This also wound up the mountainside with a long grassy slope on one side and an almost vertical rock face on the other, and in about a mile the track disappeared entirely. The only possible course was for the entire column to turn around. In such tight conditions, whilst no problem for the mules, this was almost impossible for the more ponderous and heavily laden carthorses and it was a most extraordinary and indeed horrible sight to see a number of them lose their footing and go sliding and rolling over the hillside to the valley below, scattering their loads in the process. Fortunately, they didn't drag any of the men with them, but sadly, we heard later, that several animals had to be destroyed.

During one of the many prolonged and unexplained halts on this exercise, I was sitting with one or two others beside a mountain track enjoying the warm sunshine and the marvellous scenery when I noticed that one of the subahdars had dismounted nearby, and was following our example, wishing, no doubt, that he could be transported from the Brecon Beacons back to his native Himalayas. Fancying my ability as a horseman, I decided to borrow his mount which was happily grazing nearby, and ride up to the head of the column to find out the reason for the hold-up. Calling on my batman, Gillanders, to give me a leg up, I swung myself into the saddle and to the accompaniment of cries of 'Ride 'im, cowboy' I cantered off. In a short time, I saw Major Jeffries, the second in command and Paddy Liddle, the adjutant, sitting beside the track, and pulled up to have a word with them. I decided to dismount, and, in the accepted manner, removed my feet from the stirrups and began to swing myself to the ground. Suddenly, I found myself suspended under the belly of the horse. For a few seconds I didn't know where I was and then I heard the voice of Major Jeffries saying, very loudly, 'That's not the way to get off a horse,' followed by loud laughter from everyone around. As I disengaged myself and scrambled to my feet, I realized what had happened,. After dismounting near our company HQ, the subahdar had obviously loosened the saddle girth, and when I had taken over I had failed to check that it was properly fastened. Maybe I wasn't such a complete horseman as I had imagined.

Eventually we reached our objective where the news seeped through that the 'enemy force' had surrendered and that the exercise was over. All we then had to do was to make our way back to Hereford by a somewhat circuitous route of about thirty miles which took us two full days, emcumbered as we were by our four-footed beasts of burden.

That was the last we saw of the mules, and we never heard

whether our efforts and the trials and tribulations involved had been considered worthwhile. When viewed in the context of the role assigned to us a couple of weeks later, our period of training with mules confirmed the general opinion that the War Office was staffed by an efficient team of mental defectives!

Carmarthen

In September 1941, shortly after completing the series of exercises using mule transport, the brigade was moved to the area of Carmarthen in South Wales. Our battalion was located in a tented camp laid out in the grounds of a large country house on the western outskirts of the town and quite close to the main road from Carmarthen to St Clears. Battalion headquarters and the officers' mess were established in the house, but all officers and other ranks were accommodated under canvas in the grounds, which wasn't particularly welcome bearing in mind we were getting into the autumn and the weather was cold and wet. We were at least pleased that the RIASC company with their mules and horses did not accompany us, and I often wondered whether they ever found their way back to India.

At about this time, an Army Council Instruction (ACI) was published to the effect that a number of officers were required for posting to the Indian Army, and anybody interested was instructed to submit their name to battalion headquarters. At the Boar's Head at Carmarthen that evening the desirability or otherwise of going out to India was discussed at some length and as a result about eight, including me, decided to submit our names to the adjutant the following morning. The main reason for our decision was that we were bored with the interminable round of training exercises with little or no likelihood of real active service in the foreseeable future. This, together with the knowledge that British troops were fighting fierce defensive actions in Africa and holding the fort against a probably Japanese involvement in the Far East, added to our frustration.

There was a lot of talk even at that time, in 1941, of opening up a second front in Europe, but it was apparent that this could not take place for a very long time, and pleasant as it was to be enjoying the warmth and comfort of many pubs around South

Wales, this wasn't what we had joined the army for and we didn't relish the thought of it continuing much longer. We recognized, of course, that a considerable military garrison had to be maintained at home in the British Isles, but by that time the threat of a German invasion had receded completely and we felt that whatever duties were required at home could be adequately provided for by troops older and less active than ourselves.

The following morning one or two subalterns had changed their minds, but Eric May and his brother Ikey (who had joined the battalion by this time), myself and about five others, whose names I forget, duly submitted our applications to Paddy Liddle the adjutant. In the mess, that evening there was much banter between the volunteers and the rest, but Rosie Campbell, our CO, was somewhat put out, I think, by the number who had volunteered, although he appeared to understand and sympathized with our reasons. A few days later the volunteers were ordered to attend an army selection board at Chester, so off we went. This involved a series of interviews with Indian Army Officers, medical examinations and fitness tests, after which we were told to return to our units where we would be notified of acceptance or otherwise within a short time.

The day we returned to the dampness and misery of our tented camp at Carmarthen the news broke that the 31st Independent Brigade group, of which we formed part, was to become the 1st Air Landing Brigade in the 1st Airborne Division. Naturally we had very little idea of what this would involve, but the eight 'volunteers' for India immediately descended on the adjutant to ask that their applications should be withdrawn. A few days later a notification came through to the effect that all the volunteers had been accepted, but for some reason which I never knew, and never will know, I was the only one of the eight who was permitted to withdraw and to stay with the battalion, and it was with some sadness that a few days later we said farewell to our good friends, Eric and Ikey May and the others as they left us for India.

Although we had very little information as to precisely what would be involved, the news that the brigade was to assume an airborne role was greeted with great enthusiasm and did much to restore morale, which had flagged somewhat with the continuous round of training programmes and mock exercises

100

over the previous two years — in particular with the extraordinary switch from motor to mule transport. There may have been some rational explanation of that strange episode, but if there was it was never communicated to us.

We had read about and seen many pictures of operations by German airborne troops, both parachutists and glider-borne infantry, in Belgium and Crete. We also knew that volunteers from the British Army were being trained as parachutists, so it was not difficult to deduce that as air-landing troops we would be expected to travel into battle in gliders. The big question, of course, was what those gliders would be like. There was speculation as to whether officers and NCOs would be trained as glider pilots, as to the hazards of flying into battle and how much danger money we would receive, if any; but interestingly enough there was little adverse comment on the additional risks which might be involved compared with normal foot slogging operations. Some of our queries were soon to be answered.

Shortly after receiving news of our new role, the CO and adjutant were invited to a nearby airfield for an introductory glider flight. They were then introduced to the only gliders available at that time which were called Hotspur gliders. They were entirely of wooden construction and shaped like a large cigar with pointed nose and tail and, of course, wings. In the nose, under the perspex cover, were two seats, in tandem, for the pilot or pilots, with dual controls and simple instruments. The main body of the aircraft was rather like a large coffin about fifteen feet long and with room for six or seven men sitting side by side at the widest part along a narrow wooden bench. An average size person could sit with his torso more or less upright, but anyone of more than average height sitting towards the tail of the aircraft had to remain in a permanently hunched position, which raised serious questions as to the discomfort which might be experienced during a long flight. There were several very small windows along each side of the body of the glider which gave a very restricted view of what was going on outside.

It was explained to the assembled group that, on this occasion, and indeed for training purposes, the Hotspur glider could be towed aloft by a small powered plane such as a Tiger Moth, but it was envisaged that for longer flights which active operations would involve, it would be towed by a larger aircraft such as a Whitley bomber, which could, in fact, tow two

Hotspurs at the same time. It was also explained that, for operational purposes, the small undercarriage with which the gliders were fitted could be jettisoned after take-off in which case the glider would land on reinforced skids, thereby considerably reducing the landing distance required. The skids, however, could only be used once, so for training purposes around an airfield the wheeled undercarriage was left in position to permit frequent flights.

Accompanied by words of encouragement from their respective adjutants, the three commanding officers and three others from brigade HQ clambered through the small door in the side of the aircraft and prepared themselves for their initial glider flight, during which it was intended that they would be towed to a height of about 2,000 feet when the pilot, a young RAF sergeant pilot, would release the tow rope, thus permitting the glider to make its descent to the airfield. The glider was fitted with an altimeter and one or two other instruments necessary for control purposes, but there was no means of communication between the glider and the towing aircraft, so before take-off the route and intended landing area had to be agreed between the two pilots and it was up to the glider pilot to 'cast off' when he felt it appropriate to do so.

Following a thumbs-up visual sign from the glider pilot to one of the ground staff, which was then passed on to the towing pilot, the engine of the Tiger Moth roared into life as it took the strain of the glider on the tow rope and the two aircraft accelerated down the runway. The technique, with which we were to become very familiar, was for the glider to lift-off before the tug and to maintain a position above the towing aircraft in order to avoid the slipstream and a sudden drop in height which might pull the tail of the towing aircraft down and cause a stall.

On this occasion the two aircraft climbed to a height of about 200 feet when suddenly, to the consternation of the onlookers and, no doubt, the glider passengers, the tow rope broke and the glider went into a nose-dive near the edge of the airfield. Fortunately the pilot was able to level out and there were no obstructions to prevent an emergency landing and our three commanding officers ended their glider indoctrination with nothing worse than a few bruises and a recommendation that stronger tow ropes should be used in future.

Shortly before we left Carmarthen, Hugh McGuire, the

battalion IO, was transferred to brigade headquarters as brigade intelligence officer and I was appointed battalion IO in his place. I had very little idea of the precise duties of an intelligence officer but I was fortunate to inherit from Hugh a very capable group who took me under their wing as it were, and made it their business to educate me on that particular area of responsibility. The group was about five or six strong with a sergeant whose name I forget and who didn't stay very long in the section; a Corporal White and three riflemen I will long remember. Their names were Weighall, Lickfold and Henry.

White, Weighall and Lickfold had all been civilians in London before the war and had joined the London Irish Rifles, and after mobilization in 1939 they had been sent out with a draft to the 1st Battalion in India. In civilian life White had been working in the advertising field and was, to my mind, a brilliant artist. In a matter of minutes he could produce a panoramic sketch of a landscape not only from any vantage point from which he could actually see the contours of the land and prominent features, but he also had the knack of being able to do this almost as well in the case of countryside which he had never seen, using only the contour markings and other features normally seen on the Ordnance Survey Map. He was a quiet, unassuming man despite his artistic talents, and in no way forceful, as one might expect in an army NCO, but in his job in the intelligence section, results were not achieved by normal barrack square discipline but by example, close cooperation and team effort, characteristics for which White was particularly well suited, and he made a considerable contribution to the battalion effectiveness.

Rifleman Weighall, another key member of the section, was undoubtedly the most unmilitary person in the battalion. He was, and looked like, a son of a university professor. Well over six feet tall with an ungainly body which never seemed to bend in the right place, and whether dressed for fatigues or ceremonial occasions, he always looked untidy with his forage cap sitting squarely on his ears instead of being balanced slightly on one side of his head. His battledress always appeared to be too small, which it probably was by reason of his size; his equipment never seemed to fit his body despite whatever adjustments were made, and he never seemed to be able to stand up straight. Weighall was involved in an amusing incident when the battalion was being inspected by General 'Boy' Browning at our camp at

Bulford Fields.

After inspecting the rifle companies, the general was led across to battalion headquarters where he followed the usual practice of an inspecting officer, speaking to every third or fourth man as he walked along the ranks. He came to Rifleman Weighall and stopped and looked him for a few seconds. 'What is your name?' he said to Weighall.

Weighall leant forward slightly and replied, 'Charles Weighall, sir,' quietly, as if imparting some secret information to the general which was not for other ears. The normal military practice on such an occasion is for the soldier addressed by the general to remain absolutely motionless and not to look at or focus his eyes on the inspecting officer, but to continue to stare into space as he responded with his rank and surname. General Browning was obviously somewhat taken aback by Weighall's unconventional response and then asked him, 'What do you do?'

'In civilian life sir or in the army?' he responded, again as if chatting with a friend over a cup of tea or glass of beer.

'In the army, in the battalion,' said the general.

'Ah I see,' said Weighall, with a nod of his head, 'I'm in the intelligence section, sir,' again with a faint smile as if that information should have been clear to the general from the outset.

By this time General Browning obviously felt it was time to break off this friendly chat, which, to his mind, and no doubt those of his high ranking entourage, was unusual for such a formal occasion. Weighall had meanwhile assumed a very relaxed posture, his rifle sagging forward and his somewhat ungainly form resembling a reversed letter 'S' rather than the ramrod rigidity of those on either side of him. 'That's no reason why you shouldn't stand up straight,' said the general, tapping Weighall's protruding stomach with his cane. 'Get your stomach in lad,' he said, whereupon the shape of Weighall's body reversed itself as he pulled his stomach back as far as it would go, hunching his shoulders with the effort, which at least prevented his belt and pouches dropping down to his hips. General Browning moved on and was later reputed to have said to Colonel Campbell that he must have a very effective intelligence section, which I personally think was very true.

The intelligence section had a wide range of responsibilities, the most important of which was to receive and collate information received at battalion headquarters and to maintain an operations map for the use of the commanding officer, clearly indicating all aspects of the 'battle' with which we might be involved. In addition they needed to be knowledgeable on all aspects of not only our own forces but also those of the 'enemy', including identification of formations, tanks, guns and other weapons, vehicles, badges of rank, aircraft etc., and to assist in imparting much of this information to the remainder of the battalion. As intelligence officer I was fortunate to inherit such a small but nevertheless efficient and dedicated group.

Shortly after being appointed battalion intelligence officer I was sent off on what was known as an aerial photography course at the Royal Experimental Establishment at Farnborough in Hampshire. This course was confined to all the intelligence officers in the division, with the object of teaching us how to interpret and make use of aerial photographs provided by the RAF. For this purpose, the RAF used cameras which took double photographs which, when examined under an epidiascope, provided a three-dimensional picture of the area covered. The course was run by an army officer, Captain Mole, who was most impressed one day when I correctly identified some minute crosses in the bottom corner of a photograph he had circulated, as a glider training school. Before announcing the accuracy of my answer, he asked how I had come to that conclusion and there was much misplaced laughter when I replied to the effect that the small crosses could be aeroplanes but as I couldn't make out any engines, they must be gliders. Obviously, I had gliders on the brain at the time. Part of the time was spent on aircraft recognition, identifying the main features of all Allied and enemy planes flying then. We were required to study black and white silhouettes of all these aircraft, viewed from every angle. The object of developing our skills on aerial photography and aircraft recognition was to enable us to go back to our units and impart those skills to our colleagues, and I feel that this was achieved in the case of aircraft recognition, but not so successful as regards aerial photography because of a lack of epidiascopes.

Following the aerial photography course, I was sent off on an attachment to an army cooperation squadron of the RAF at Hooton Park, near Liverpool where I spent two weeks having the living daylights scared out of me flying as an observer in the rear-facing seat of a Lysander, usually at 'zero' level along the mudbanks of the River Clyde. The Lysander, a single engine, high wing, fixed undercarriage mono-plane with a very low landing and take off speed was used for carrying agents in and out of occupied territory, and the pilots seemed to spend most of their time practising the skill of locating obscure landing places from vague instructions such as 'proceed to church tower at X, turn left for 500 yards to electricity pylon, etc.' Seated, as I was, facing the tailplane in the observer's cockpit I at least had the comfort of knowing that when we wrapped ourselves around a telegraph pole or similar obstruction, it would be all over before I knew anything about it.

In December 1941, and much to our relief, we were on the move again, this time to Newbury, in Berkshire.

Newbury

Of all the locations of the battalion during the years leading up to D-Day in 1944, I think that Newbury was the most enjoyable. We were not billeted in the town but near the small village of Highclere a few miles south west on the road to Andover. Battalion headquarters was again established in a large country house, from which all the furniture had been removed, at a place called Woolton Hill. Two of our companies were billeted nearby in requisitioned buildings, including a racehorse training stable, and the two remaining companies were accommodated in huts and tents on the Highclere Castle estate; the ancestral home of the Earl of Caernarvon.

The knowledge that we were going to form part of the 1st Airborne Division did a lot to boost the morale of our Battalion and of the other battalions in the brigade. However, there was a feeling amongst some officers and men that although we were well trained and fit there was little likelihood of putting our skills to the test whilst we remained stationed in the UK. In addition to the 'Indian volunteers,' several officers left to join the Parachute Regiment or the Commandos, whose exploits in operations such as Bruneval, the Channel Islands and around the Normandy and Brittany coasts were widely reported in the newspapers.

There was much demand, voiced in the press and elsewhere,

for a quick return to Europe, but it was quite obvious to us that this could not take place in either 1942 or 1943. Much as we enjoyed swilling beer in delightful country pubs, there was a sense of guilt and frustration that whilst we were enjoying ourselves, the major part of the British Army plus the Navy and Air Force were fighting battles and enduring considerable hardship around the world. Moreover, the civilian population, particularly in the big cities such as London and elsewhere, were suffering tremendous hardship from bombing and food shortages, which had little impact on our daily activities.

The problem of maintaining the morale of the army units retained in England was, no doubt, recognized by 'Higher Command', and in addition to periodic morale boosting lectures on the progress of the war by visiting generals and politicians, we were also sent on 'holiday' on two occasions, each for a month, the first being to Ilfracombe and the second to Weston-Super-Mare. At both places particular attention was paid to teaching non-swimmers to swim, and as much sport as possible was arranged.

It wasn't long before we met our new division commander, General 'Boy' Browning, a most impressive Guards officer with an aura of military perfection in his appearance and demeanour. Despite several rows of First World War decorations and service medals on his chest he was a youngish, handsome, athletic-looking man with aquiline features, and it quickly became apparent that he was completely dedicated to the task of ensuring that the Airborne Division was an elite force, not only as regards fighting ability but also in terms of discipline, turn-out and all other respects on which military units can be judged. The fact that he was the husband of Daphne Du Maurier, the romantic novelist, added a touch of glamour.

One of General Browning's first stipulations was that no rifleman could remain in the division whose conduct record was assessed at less than 'good'. This assessment was based on a man's 'conduct sheet' on which disciplinary offences of which he had been found guilty were recorded and which could only be erased by subsequent periods of good conduct. Being a regular battalion, many of our men had several years' service around the world. They were a tough lot and prone to periodic lapses in conduct by drunkenness and other forms of misbehaviour, and the general's edict meant that he would lose a number of riflemen who might be considered very good risks in battle if not at other times. However, the ruling had to be enforced on the grounds that if a man could not discipline himself off the battlefield then he would not do so on the battlefield, and as a result we had to send away over a hundred men who were almost all regular army volunteers. There was no conscription in the North of Ireland.

One day the CO, Rosie Campbell, received an invitation for himself and three other officers to have dinner with Sir William and Lady Roote at Stype Manor, their nearby home, and Rosie designated Paddy Liddle, Ronnie and me to accompany him on that occasion. There were four other couples present, in black ties and long dresses and we had a most civilized and enjoyable evening, not the least of which was an excellent meal, supervised by the butler and served up by appropriately attired waitresses. The thought came into my mind at one point that it was difficult to realize that there was a war in progress. At the end of the meal Lady Roote indicated to the other ladies present that it was time for them to withdraw — a delightful aristocratic practice which my wife was never willing to accept — the males, standing up as the ladies withdrew, then congregating around Sir William at the head of the table. A decanter of port wine was placed in front of Sir William and then passed around while he regaled us with information about the fantastic steps being taken by him and his company to meet the demands of the services for vehicles of one sort or another. Sir William was obviously a very dynamic man and very interesting to listen to, but what impressed me most was not his stories but the quality of his port wine, the like of which I have never tasted previously and certainly have not done since. It's so long ago now that my recollection may be largely imaginary but whenever I have drunk a glass of port subsequent to that dinner, I have always felt disappointed.

Dublin and the Bourke Family

After the threat of enemy invasion had receded, it was the practice in the army to allow all personnel stationed in the UK ten days' leave every three months or thereabouts, but with not more than ten per cent of the total strength of any unit away on leave at any particular time. For us this mean that every sub-unit — section, platoon, company — and the specialist groups, were always about ten per cent below strength, which was a serious hindrance to effective training. It was generally welcomed, therefore, when instructions were received that complete units would all go on leave at the same time, leaving only small groups of men to provide necessary security duties. This meant that instead of being ten per cent below strength all the time, the brigade would be non-operational for ten days in each three months but fully effective for the rest of the time; a much more efficient arrangement. This news was received with considerable enthusiasm by all those with homes or connections in Ireland because it meant that a number of us could meet for a few days in Dublin and enjoy the delights of that 'fair city' where there was no blackout or food rationing. The South of Ireland being neutral it was necessary to wear civilian clothes. This was no problem so far as the officers were concerned, who all had civvies available, and in the case of 'other ranks', civilian clothes were provided.

Groups of about ten or twelve of us met on several occasions in Dublin for three or four days of our periodic leave entitlement. Despite the country's official neutrality, with a German Embassy in the city, the sympathies of the vast majority of the Southern Irish was undoubtedly with the Allies, and wherever we happened to be and as soon as it was known that we were British Army officers on leave, the hospitality and friendship shown to us was unlimited. To a large extent this was attributable to the Bourke family.

Lorcan Bourke was the managing director of the branch of the Strand Electric Engineering Company which my father had established in Dublin, in which capacity he was ably assisted by his younger brother Kevin. They were also involved in the management of the Olympia Theatre, and appeared to have close connections with most of the other Dublin theatres, and the family owned or operated the Four Provinces dance hall, and a firm of theatrical costumiers. Lorcan was a remarkable man, who appeared to know and to be known by everyone in Dublin. He was a sort of godfather of the large Bourke family, but nevertheless under the critical eye of his elderly widowed mother. In addition to Lorcan and his wife, Kathleen, and Kevin and his wife, Eileen, there were other brothers: Patrick, Billy and Rick and sisters Kathleen, Peggy and Maureen. Last, but by no means least of all the members of the family we met, was Lorcan's daughter, Grace — or Grainne — a member of the delightful team of young Irish dancers who we watched on several occasions, and who later became Mrs Eammon Andrews.

As a family, the Bourkes had a strong nationalistic and republican background, and could recount many a tale of how members of the family had assisted the republican movement during the years of conflict with the British. I gathered that in the 'Troubles' of 1922, this consisted largely of carrying messages between the various strong points set up by the rebels throughout Dublin. They were all devout Roman Catholics, with the possible exception of Lorcan, who didn't appear to be quite as devout as the remainder. And there were we, a group of British Army officers, mostly Protestants, and several with Orange connections from the 'Black North.' Why did they put themselves out to do so much for us? And not only the Bourkes themselves, but also the many other Dublin people we met through them? When a few of us visited Dublin after our return from Normandy in 1944 and they learned of the deaths of George Maginnis, Dicky Quinn, Reggie Morgan, Dan Woods and the others who had been with us on earlier trips, their grief was unmistakably real and profound.

I often asked myself and indeed discussed with Ronnie and the others why the Bourkes should make such an effort to ensure that we had an enjoyable time whenever we managed to spend a few days in Dublin.

There were several reasons, I think. Firstly, they realized that Nazi Germany was the common enemy, and despite all the propaganda that was being put out by the Germans as to the benefits which would result for the Irish from continued neutrality, when the war against the British was won — including the unification of North and South — they knew that if Britain came under totalitarian domination the new Irish Republic would go the same way. Second, like many other Southern Irish — but not enough perhaps — they believed that their destiny as a nation was irretrievably linked to that of the British, and whatever their history books told them of the atrocities of Cromwell and the Black and Tans, they were too intelligent to want to live permanently in the past. They didn't like partition, but accepted that for the time being it was a fact of life which had to be lived with, and they were prepared to work and develop relationships with the people of Ulster until such time as mutual confidence was established and both sides reached the inevitable conclusion that the division of a small country like Ireland made no sense, and was of no benefit to anybody, whether North or South of the border. Lastly, perhaps, the Bourkes and their friends in the theatrical world had known, respected and indeed loved my father, 'Pip' Sheridan, who had died only a few years earlier (in 1936), and anyone who was a friend of Pip Sheridan's son was a friend of theirs.

On our visits to Dublin during the war most of us usually stayed at the Hibernian Hotel in Dawson Street; some perhaps in Jury's or the Wicklow Hotel, but wherever we were staying, the initial rendezvous was invariably the best known pub in Dublin, Davy Byrnes, just around the corner from the Hibernian, in Duke Street. Davy Byrnes at that time was a very unpretentious, spit and sawdust sort of pub which was patronized by people from all walks of life; from politicians to paper boys, priests and playwrights, wealthy race horse owners, trainers and jockeys, and who all appeared to be long lost friends of everybody else, and where every current topic and historic event was discussed and where everybody was free to join in with whatever views he might have on any discussion which he might overhear.

As the evening progressed, the long bar would become more and more crowded and the hubbub of animated conversation and laughter would increase until it was impossible to hear what one's closest neighbour was saying, which didn't really matter all that much anyway, provided the flow of empty glasses to the sweating bartenders and the return of the foam topped refills of Guinness was maintained across the heads of the serried ranks of those fortunate to be close to the bar.

For each of the two or three days of our short stay in Dublin, our routine would follow much the same pattern. First, a substantial breakfast of eggs and bacon, largely unheard of in England at that time, even in the army, followed by an hour or so with the morning newspapers. Then, for those still below par from the night before, a couple of prairie oysters in the Hibernian Buttery. Following restoration to robust health, we would ramble off to visit the many places of interest in Dublin, those in the know ending up in Jammet's marble-topped oyster bar near the junction of Grafton Street and Nassau Street, unfortunately no longer existing. A dozen oysters, brown bread and butter and a pint or so of Guinness followed by another gentle walk, ending in the comfortable armchairs of the Hibernian lounge, would then prepare us for whatever the evening held in store.

By the time we had all assembled in Davy Byrnes, I would have phoned Lorcan or Kevin to let them know that we were in town, and from then on our evenings were more or less in their hands. They would specify some meeting place, usually the Four Provinces or one of the Dublin theatres. This would be communicated to all who had a 'need-to-know', and from then on it was up to each man to proceed as he thought fit, which meant that most of the party would arrive at the rendezvous some time during the evening, with or without new-found friends or hangers-on as fate might decree.

If we joined the Bourkes at the Four Provinces, some were tempted to take a turn around the floor with one of the many charming Irish colleens present, but without, so far as I can recollect, any dallying which might interfere with whatever other entertainment had been planned. This was usually a row of seats in one or other of the theatres in the neighbourhood, the Olympia, the Gaiety, the Queens, where we could either watch the show or swap yarns with whoever might be in the bar at the time.

The final 'event' each evening, after the show or whatever, was to meet at Costello's on the Quay. This was an optician's shop alongside the River Liffey, known, obviously, to Lorcan, which had a large room upstairs which could accommodate not only our party and the Bourkes, but also a number of others who, I assumed, were friends of the Bourkes, and friends of the Bourkes were friends of ours, and our friends were their friends. Lorcan would have arranged for a large boiled ham to be on the table with vast quantities of bread and butter, and ample supplies of Guinness and light ale. We would then sing ourselves hoarse, alternating between our regimental repertoire and Irish songs, interspersed with solo efforts from whoever felt so inclined. Molly, who was a trained singer and had a lovely voice would always render *I dreamt that I dwelt in Marble Halls*, despite Peggy's whispered aside to me that it was a very unlucky song! These parties would invariably end with everybody standing to attention and singing *God Save the King*, followed by the Irish national anthem, *The Soldiers Song*, after which the party would disperse, somewhat wearily perhaps. We would, of course, lie on in bed in the morning whilst all the Bourkes had to be about their business at an early hour.

Robin Rigby, a regular supporter of these Dublin reunions, despite his Manchester background, was a man of considerable sartorial elegance and invariably wore a green pork pie hat with his civilian clothes. He must have dug up an Irish ancestor to get a leave pass to Dublin. Very late one night we were making our way down O'Connell Street back towards our hotel when someone, in a moment of exuberance, took Robin's hat from his head and skated it up in the air where it landed on the glass awning extending over the pavement in front of the Gresham Hotel. Robin appeared to shrug off the loss of his hat with indifference, and we continued on our way. The following morning, at about eleven o'clock, a small group of us were meandering our way up O'Connell Street when we arrived outside the Gresham Hotel and the outline of Robin's hat could be clearly seen through the glass awning. On the pavement at that point was a somewhat ornate lamp-posts with a lot of decorative iron work around its base and extending up to a height of about twelve feet. Without saying a word to anybody, Robin walked up to the lamp-post and, with the assistance of the decorative iron work, began to shin his way up the pole until he was level with the awning. Retaining his hold on the pole with one hand he was able to reach across and secure his hat, which he placed on his head and then slid down the pole to the ground. He then bent down and dusted his trousers with his hands and proceeded on his way as if climbing lamp-posts in broad daylight in O'Connell Street was a matter of daily routine. There were many people in the vicinity at the time, most of whom had stopped to witness Robin's efforts, who also continued on their way as if accepting that if one's hat were lodged on the awning over the hotel entrance then it was perfectly natural to climb a lamp-post for the purpose of recovery. A civic guard who happened to be standing nearby was heard to remark to Robin as he walked away, 'That's a strange place to leave your hat, sorr!'

Under Close Arrest

On the last day of one of our Dublin trips, everybody had departed on their various ways, except 'Hoppy' Cassidy, our battalion medical officer and me. We planned to remain for one more night at the Hibernian Hotel and to catch the early morning train from Westland Row station to Dunlaoghaire to catch the boat back to Holyhead. We were due back at Newbury by midnight the following day at the end of our leave.

That evening, after a quiet meal in the hotel, we decided to take a walk around the area before turning in for an early night. At our first port-of-call, Davy Byrnes, we got into conversation with a pleasant middle-aged man who happened to be standing near us. Friendliness being the hallmark of all Dublin pubs, I offered our new-found friend a drink and a short time afterwards Hoppy did the same, after which we left to go somewhere else, I think the Wicklow Hotel. We had been in there for a few minutes when, turning around, and somewhat to my surprise, I noticed our friend from Davy Byrnes again standing nearby. He turned and saw us and expressed great delight at running into us again, whereupon the same course of events followed. When buying one another a drink we offered him a drink. We gathered he was a 'horsey' man as he claimed to know most of the likely winners at the Phoenix Park races the following day and expressed considerable regret that as we were leaving Dublin the following morning, we would not be able to take advantage of his tips. He made no offer to buy us a drink but we didn't resent this in any way, being quite content to accept his friendship as a quid pro quo for our hospitality.

When we again met at our third port-of-call it was like a reunion of long lost brothers. Hoppy and I continued to include him in our orders until we decided it was time for us to call it a night and the three of us walked arm in arm back to the Hibernian where our new-found friend bade us a warm good night and departed. We arranged with the night porter to have an early call with a cup of tea and retired to our rooms.

Very early the following morning everything went according to plan and with a warm farewell from the night porter, who had become a good friend over the course of our several visits, we clambered into a taxi and were on our way to the station. When we arrived at the station I put my hand in my back trousers-pocket to take out my wallet and to my somewhat befuddled consternation found that it wasn't there. A quick search through my other pockets and my bag was fruitless, and the chill realization gradually dawned on me that here was I, in a neutral country with no money, no ticket, no travelling warrant, no pass and no identification card. It took me a little time to appreciate the full extent of my predicament and it was Hoppy who suggested that we should return quickly to the hotel to see if I'd left my wallet in my room, although we both realized that even if we found the wallet this might well mean missing the boat-train. On arriving back at the Hibernian we quickly explained the situation to the night porter, whereupon he said, 'Could the gentleman who came back to see you last night know anything about it?'

I had no recollection of a 'gentleman' coming back to see me after we had returned the night before, and quickly told him so. We ran up the stairs to my room and under the bed up against the wall was my wallet with all my essential papers intact except my money, which I recollected had been about £20.

From the night porter's description of the 'gentleman' who had called back to the hotel about thirty minutes after we had gone to bed and explained that he wanted a quick word with his very dear friend and who had been directed to my room, it didn't take very long to identify the cause of my misfortune. However, there was no time to lose as we had already missed our train, the vital question being whether we had enough money between us, which meant the money in Hoppy's wallet, to take the taxi all the way to Dunlaoghaire and the boat. Fortunately, Hoppy's reserves were sufficient, and we again departed from the Hibernian with a great feeling of relief on my part. Although I had no money at least my documents were in order and I wouldn't have to defer my departure pending assistance from the British Embassy in Dublin.

Needless to say, the perfidious action of someone we had befriended was the sole subject of our conversation whilst ploughing our way across the Irish Sea and with no thought of submarines or bombers which had recently sunk the cross-Channel steamer between Rosslare and Fishguard. However, I had a sneaking regard for the cunning of this trickster who had taught me a lesson I wouldn't easily forget, and had at least had the decency to run the risk of returning my moneyless wallet even if he had been motivated by a desire to speed my departure and thereby lessen the likelihood of the police getting on his trail. As was often the case, I remembered my mother's word: 'A fool and his money are soon parted.' Unfortunately there was further misfortune in store for us that day.

As was often the case with train journeys in England at that time due to bombing raids and other wartime dislocation, we arrived in London very late and when, eventually, we reached Waterloo station we discovered that we had missed the last train to Newbury. However, we just managed to scramble on board the last train to Reading with the thought in mind that we would then telephone our battalion headquarters and ask them to send a truck from Newbury to pick us up. Bearing in mind that our leave passes expired at midnight, this meant that we would still be a little late, but there had never been any suggestion that officers were necessarily obliged to be back precisely on time, provided they were ready to resume their duties first thing the following morning. So, as we rattled our way through the London suburbs in a dimly lit compartment we felt no anxiety or urgency but only relief that a long and tiring journey would soon be over.

At Reading, the station transport officer was very accommodating and permitted us to use his telephone to call battalion headquarters at Highclere, where I spoke to Tim Dooley, who happened to be duty officer. I explained our predicament and asked him to get onto the transport officer and have a truck sent to Reading station, not thinking that there would be any difficulty about his doing so.

However, Tim appeared to be uncertain as to whether such a request lay within his powers and asked me to hold on while he spoke to Paddy Liddle, the adjutant. After what seemed like an unnecessarily long delay, he came back with the news that he had not been able to get hold of the adjutant but had spoken to Major Jeffries, the second in command, who had told him not to send a truck but that we must make our own way back. I was somewhat put out on hearing this and told Tim, that the only thing we could do was stay the night in Reading and catch the first train the following morning and I asked him to leave a message with the adjutant to that effect. With some difficulty,

Hoppy and I found rooms in a Reading hotel and after catching an early train arrived back to Newbury station at about eight thirty am where, rather to our surprise, Robin Rigby was waiting for us in a truck in the station forecourt, and with the news that we were both to consider ourselves under close arrest!

During the drive from Newbury to Highclere I don't think that Hoppy or I really knew what to make of the situation and Robin Rigby seemed reluctant to express any opinion. He told us that all the battalion officers with the exception of himself had gone off on a Brigade TEWT (Tactical Exercise Without Troops) and would not be returning until the evening. As battalion signals officer he hadn't been involved and before leaving, the adjutant, Paddy Liddle, had instructed him to meet us at the station, to place us under arrest and return to battalion headquarters. He wasn't sure what offence we would be charged with, but knew that Major Jeffries had been instrumental in this strange development. Robin obviously felt extremely embarrassed because only two days before he had been enjoying himself with us in Dublin, but now had no alternative but to comply with the orders he had received. We could only assume that our 'offence' was arriving back late from leave, but bearing in mind the efforts we had made to get back on time and the fact that we had communicated our predicament to the adjutant through the duty officer, we were reasonably justified in assuming that he agreed with out decision to stay overnight in Reading and return the following morning.

At about six o'clock we heard trucks arriving outside bringing the officers back from the TEWT, some going direct to their rooms, others coming into the anteroom. For a short time Hoppy and I were a little uncertain as to how officers under arrest should behave in the anteroom but it was quickly apparent that none of the others were aware of the situation and in a short time were joining in wisecracks about our Dublin visit and how fortunate we had been to miss the cold winds on Salisbury Plain where the TEWT had been conducted.

It was then that I suggested to Robin that we should search out Paddy Liddle and find out exactly what the situation was with regard to our 'arrest'. Fortunately, Paddy was in his office reading some papers and looked up as we entered his room. Robin saluted and said, rather nervously, 'Excuse me sir, what are your instructions as to the prisoners?'

117

Paddy looked up and in a somewhat offhand way replied, 'Oh, yes, I've had a word with Colonel Campbell, so forget it,' and lowered his gaze to continue reading whatever was in front of him on his desk. 'Very good, sir,' said Robin and we all saluted, turned about and left.

That was the end of the matter, except to add that a few days later Major Jeffries left to take up command of a battalion of the London Irish in Africa and about a week later I was promoted captain and appointed adjutant in place of Paddy Liddle who took command of HQ Company. When interviewing me prior to my appointment as adjutant, Rosie Campbell, the CO, made no mention of the incident, but when briefing me on my new duties Paddy Liddle did make a point of reminding me of my responsibilities for ensuring a high standard of discipline, particularly as regards junior officers, and of the desirability of avoiding situations which might cause embarrassment in this respect.

5

1st Airborne Division

Bulford Fields Camp

Unfortunately, our stay in the Newbury area was all too short. In addition to very comfortable accommodation we had made many friends amongst the local people and there was, of course, the rich diet provided, unknowingly perhaps, by Lord Caernarvon. It was therefore with some disappointment that we heard that we were moving to Bulford Fields Camp near Amesbury on the edge of Salisbury Plain. Bulford Camp is, I suppose, what is called a military garrison town, consisting of several different barracks and barrack lines, surrounding a garrison church and post office. Some of these barracks were brick-built and fairly new, whereas others consisted of rather ramshackle huts erected as temporary accommodation for troops during the First World War and which had somehow managed to survive the intervening period up to the Second World War. Each barracks had its own barrack square, motor transport sheds, gymnasiums, and living accommodation for troops and officers. Although it was never officially announced, we knew by this time that Bulford Camp was to become the base for the entire 1st Airborne Division. The camp was very convenient not only for military training on the adjoining expanse of Salisbury Plain, but more particularly because of its proximity to Netheravon airfield which was to become the scene of much gliding and parachuting over the next few years.

However, we were not to be located in Bulford Camp itself but in a newly erected hutted camp nearby, on the Bulford-Tidworth road. This turned out to be one of our less comfortable locations. The huts themselves were of wooden construction with doors and windows designed to aggravate draughts, and with heating facilities limited to single, round, cast-iron stoves similar to those with which I had become familiar at Aldershot. Their ineffectiveness for heating purposes was accentuated by the fact that there was a considerable shortage of coal. Another major disadvantage of the location was that there was no convenient pub where we could forgather from time to time. Official outings in our own transport were arranged to places like Salisbury and Andover, but, in general, relaxation was confined to the somewhat limited facilities in our own officers' mess hut.

The overall inadequacy of Bulford Field Camp gave Rosie Campbell further cause for complaint to brigade headquarters. We were the only non-English county regiment in the brigade and, rightly or wrongly, Rosie always took the view that at brigade and divisional headquarters we were treated as the poor relation. This certainly didn't give our officers any cause for concern as there was no doubt in our minds that, as a group, the officers in our battalion were far superior to those in the other battalions of the brigade. Similarly, our men didn't suffer from any inferiority complex as was demonstrated on many occasions when slight disturbances were caused in pubs and dance halls and it became necessary for the 'stickies' to demonstrate their superiority over other troops in the Airborne Division and indeed in other divisions and services. If anything, we had a feeling of superiority over lesser units which was amply justified by our performance on training exercises as well as in rugger, soccer, boxing and other divisional competitions.

During our stay at Bulford Fields Camp we lost one officer who was transferred because of poor health, and Rosie put in a request to Brigade headquarters to have a replacement officer transferred from our Regimental Depot at Ballymena. One morning shortly after this, I was sitting in the office which I shared with Rosie when he came back from a conference at brigade headquarters in an absolute fury. 'That bloody man Hopkinson,' he said to me — referring somewhat disrespectfully to our brigade commander, General Hopkinson, 'he's sending us some bloody Welshman to fill our vacancy and there's damn all that I can do about it.'

After he had cooled down a little he told me that Brigadier Hopkinson had arranged that the gap in our officer ranks should be filled by a captain from the Royal Welsh Fusiliers who was, at present, instructing in some army training school and who had applied for a transfer to the Airborne Division. Rosie was quite convinced that this was another indication of the brigadier's animosity towards him and his battalion. I asked him if he knew the officer's name and when he would be arriving, but he replied to the effect that he was so disgusted with the brigadier's action that he didn't care, and picking up his hat and stick he departed.

About half an hour later there was a knock at my door and in walked an officer in service dress and wearing the badges of rank and insignia of the Royal Welsh Fulisiers. He saluted smartly and said, 'Captain Wheldon reporting for duty, sir.' I don't recollect what I said to him or what else he said to me but after a brief chat I offered to take him to the officers' mess hut and introduce him to the mess sergeant. What else he did I don't remember except that by the time we went to bed that night, Huw Wheldon (later, Sir Huw, managing director of BBC television) had already established himself as a leading personality amongst the officers of the battalion.

It was also at Bulford Fields that we made the acquaintance of a somewhat mysterious character called 'Jock' Pearson. One evening Rosie Campbell walked into the anteroom together with a shortish, thickset companion about fifty years of age, dressed in battledress uniform with Airborne badges on his sleeves and the three pips of a captain on his shoulders, pilot's wings on his breast, over two rows of First World War medal ribbons. His cheerful but somewhat florid countenance was largely concealed behind a large bushy moustache. Over the next few weeks, Jock was a regular visitor to our mess and it became clear that the common bond between him and Rosie was their mutual dislike for the pomposity of staff officers in general and those in our brigade and divisional headquarters in particular. Exactly what Jock's status was at division HQ remained a mystery but from remarks he made about his friend 'Boy' we gained the impression that he had the ear of the division commander, General 'Boy' Browning.

One day, whilst sitting in our office, Rosie Campbell gave me some very strange instructions. I was to arrange for a jeep together with a driver/batman to be made available for Jock immediately. Moreover, the jeep had to be in 'mint' condition, and the driver/batman had not only to be the best I could select, but the individual concerned had to be given the temporary rank of corporal. The jeep and the driver/batman would be at Jock's disposal for an indefinite period. Naturally, I asked what authority we had for this strange assignment which would leave us a man and jeep short, and he simply said that we would have no written authority but that the arrangement had been authorized by the division commander.

So, with some difficulty I extracted a brand new jeep from Captain Fithian Franks, our transport officer at the time. The driver/batman I selected was an 'old soldier' rifleman employed as a mess waiter. He was a Belfast man with a great sense of humour and a unique ability to indulge in respectful repartee to suit whatever occasion might arise. Although content to serve out his time in the comfortable atmosphere of the officers' mess, the thought of an indefinite period on corporal's pay and two new suits of battledress was sufficient to persuade him to accept the assignment with 'yon Captain Pearson, sorr,' to whom he had served numerous pink gins by this time. So, off went Jock, jeep and driver/batman into the unknown.

About two months later, our driver/batman returned, by train, with no Jock and no jeep. To me he simply reported that he had spent his time on 'special duties' driving Jock the length and breadth of the country calling at factories, airfields, army camps, offices and other indeterminate locations, staying the night or nights at hotels or in services accommodation wherever they happened to be. Jock had always been most considerate of his needs, but had never mentioned what he was doing or why. They had eventually arrived back in London where Jock had taken over the jeep and told him to make his way back to the battalion. From what I heard later through my own batman, Gillanders, I was only given a bare outline of their journey, and it seemed that Jock had been a most convivial travelling companion.

Some weeks later, Rosie Campbell laid a thick document in front of me and suggested that I might like to read it, but I was to make sure that it was returned to him personally. The document was marked Top Secret, and was a feasibility study by Jock Pearson on the formation of an 'Airborne Armoured Division.' I spent the rest of that evening engrossed in this detailed analysis of the possibility of building heavy tanks with detachable wings and modified undercarriages and which could be towed into action like gliders, and of the implications of such a force being available in the context of an Allied invasion of Europe.

What happened to Jock's report I have no idea, and it may still be collecting dust in some military archives. Nor do I recollect seeing Jock again, but several years later, after the war, I discovered by chance that he was a director of Bowring Brothers, the London insurance brokers. I intended to make contact with him if only to find out what happened to the jeep, but sadly I failed to do so.

Throughout the period of our stay at Newbury in 1942 and subsequently at Bulford Fields, the cycle of military training which we had followed over the previous two years continued on much the same lines but with increased realism, including gliders and aeroplanes instead of mules. Individual small arms training, shooting practice on the ranges at Bulford, field craft, section, platoon, company, battalion and brigade exercises, including training in street fighting at a deserted village in Dorset. Much of this training now took place on field firing ranges using live ammunition under strictly controlled conditions, but unavoidably, accidents would happen and men killed or wounded. It was on one of these street fighting battles that Victor Silvester junior, the son of the well known dance band leader and a subaltern in the battalion, was blinded in one eye due to an unfortunate accident with a '69' grenade. On another occasion, another subaltern who had joined us only a few weeks earlier took his platoon to the range on Salisbury Plain for field firing practice. The two inch mortar was part of each platoon's armoury for firing either smoke or explosive bombs over distances of about 200 yards. It consisted of a simple barrel, about two feet long and two inches in diameter, secured to a base plate and with a simple firing mechanism at the bottom of a barrel.

The technique was to insert the bomb, fin first, down the barrel so that the propellant cartridge in its base was resting against the firing pin. The man operating the weapon then turned a small handle which caused the firing pin to strike the cartridge and eject the bomb which would explode on reaching its target. Unfortunately, on this occasion, one of the bombs did not eject immediately when fired. Whether due to absent mindedness or carelessness, the subaltern looked down into the

123

barrel just when the cartridge did go off, with disastrous effects to his head. Fortunately it was a smoke bomb; otherwise others in the team would also have been killed, or wounded.

Flying Experience

After we became 'airborne' as part of the 1st Air Landing Brigade, every opportunity was taken by division HQ to give us flying experience, presumably with the idea that this would help to eradicate any nervousness which the personnel of the division might otherwise have at this unusual mode of travel. This made sense, I suppose, because very few had any experience of flying, and if we were to be expected to go into battle by air it was obviously desirable that we should be familiar with all that this involved. Unfortunately, at that time, the Air Landing Brigade, or Glider Troops, had no gliders. However, this shortage in no way deterred the enthusiasts at division and brigade HQs. Both General Boy Browning and Brigadier Hoppy Hopkinson sported pilot's wings on their respective breasts, relics, I imagine, from days with the Royal Flying Corps in the First World War, and I have little doubt that if they could have had their way, all the troops under their command would have been trained as pilots against the possibility of a glider pilot or plane pilot being incapacitated during a flight and having a number of 'spares' behind ready to take over.

Three means whereby Airborne troops could be given flying experience were devised, although there was a strong body of opinion that it would be better to send airborne troops into battle without any previous flying experience on the premise that they would be so glad to get out of their gliders or troop transports that the risk of being hit by an enemy bullet would seem of little consequence.

The first of these three means of torture involved the procurement of one of the first bombers designed and manufactured for use in 1914, but which had then been classified as 'unsafe' and consigned to a museum. The story was soon circulating around the Brigade that Boy Browning had approached 'Bomber' Harris, AOC Bomber Command for the loan of a bomber. Bomber Harris, being convinced that the Germans would be bombed into submission without the aid of the army or navy or anyone else, had refused. Boy Browning then appealed to Lord Louis Mountbatten, recently appointed Head of Combined Operations, who persuaded Winston Churchill to instruct Bomber Harris to accede to Browning's request. Not unnaturally perhaps, Harris had taken umbrage and told one of his subordinates to locate the oldest bomber in existence and make a present of it to airborne forces with his compliments and sincere regret that he was unable to provide any air crew. Harris's subordinate carried out his mission to the letter, with the result that there appeared on Netheravon airfield a flying machine the likes of which had seldom been seen since the Wright brothers began their experiments in aviation in the early 1900s.

It was a large, twin-engined bi-plane, the most prominent feature perhaps being an observer's seat in the nose of the fuselage and about five yards ahead of anyone else who might be on board at the time. The engines were slung between the wings on either side of the fuselage, with what appeared to be electric cables and fuel pipes loosely attached to the struts and wires and leading back into the body of the plane. The box-like fuselage was about ten feet high and fifty or sixty feet long and closely resembled a large pantechnicon with the frame consisting of scaffolding covered with a rather loose tarpaulin. The floor was made of holes through which, no doubt, the designer had intended that bombs should be dropped on the enemy, the holes being connected by a catwalk of loose boards. This was the flying machine in which personnel of the 1st Airborne Division were to be made familiar with their new means of going to battle. I have no recollection of its name — possibly a Vickers Vimy or something similar — but there is no doubt that it scared the living daylights out of everyone who flew in it, except possibly the crew.

The crew consisted of two elderly gentlemen, dressed in well-worn civilian tweeds and suede shoes who, one could only assume, were the curators of the museum from which the machine had been resurrected. One, the pilot, always wore a tight fitting leather helmet with a flapping microphone on one cheek and a stethoscope-like tube hanging down his front. Their only other resemblance to one's mental picture of an aviator lay in the grubby white scarves they each knotted about their necks before take-off and which one associated with the open

125

cockpit flyers of the First World War. We never knew whether they were British because they never spoke to anyone, and seemed to be completely immersed in the task of cajoling their aircraft to lift off the ground and keep flying for hourly trips around Salisbury Plain.

The routine was for the plane to be allocated to each battalion and HQ group for a day once every week or ten days. During the course of the day, as many people as possible would be taken on a one hour flight. About twenty people could be accommodated on each flight, so each day a truck was earmarked to shuttle twenty somewhat apprehensive glider troops to Netheravon for their flight experience. Their apprehension stemmed partly from seeing this strange and very noisy flying contraption circling over the camp at Bulford, and partly from stories circulating from those who had preceded them. These included rumours of bodies seen falling out at various stages during each flight, particularly during take-off, and stressed the importance of finding somewhere to sit well away from the large holes in the floor and in close proximity to those parts of the frame where one could wedge oneself in and reduce the likelihood of being dislodged, even if sweaty palms lost their grip.

The long summer days of 1942 permitted an early start to the flying programme each morning, and as I was adjutant I felt that I should accompany the first group. I was also motivated by an instinctive feeling that if one has to undergo an unpleasant experience, such as having a tooth extracted or being shot at dawn, the sooner one got it over, the better.

Netheravon is, or was at that time, an unimpressive airfield used mainly for training, and located a few miles north of Bulford Camp. It has no wide concrete runway such as one associates with modern airports, and incoming and outgoing aircraft simply used the undulating grass expanse of the airfield in whichever direction the many wind-socks around the boundary indicated. We arrived at the crack of dawn, apparently before the RAF guards at the entrance gate had woken up, and drove up alongside the airport control tower, from where we could see the aircraft through the morning mist. It reminded me of a picture I had seen of Alcock and Brown standing by their crippled plane at Clifden in Galway in 1919 after being the first to fly the Atlantic. Our plane wasn't tilted onto its nose, but gave the impression that it might do so at any moment, and it occurred to me that perhaps this was the plane in which Alcock and Brown had performed their epic flight and that they had been called out of retirement to give us the flying experience we required. I later learned that Sir John Alcock, as he became, was killed in 1919.

In correct military fashion, I ordered the troops to de-bus and form-up beside the truck. For some strange reason, we always used the expression 'de-bus' whatever type of vehicle was involved, and this continued even when troop-carrying gliders became our mode of transport. I then marched the group over to the plane, halting them close to an opening where loading steps were already in position, and walked over to peer into the interior.

The first thing that struck me was the overpowering smell of aviation spirit, from which I deduced that re-fuelling had already been carried out and that there must be a leak somewhere. The second thing was the complete absence of any form of seating other than the partial floor, which was mainly concentrated around the sides of the fuselage. I didn't notice that the opening through which I was peering didn't have a door. What made me then look up I don't know, but I could discern two figures seated on canvas backed seats with their backs to me on a kind of platform about eight feet up in the front of the plane in what was, no doubt, the pilot's cockpit, or in modern parlance, the flight deck. With some hesitation I asked, 'Shall we come aboard?'

They ignored my question, and continued to fiddle with knobs and switches. Just at that moment I heard a shout and looking round saw someone running towards us from the cluster of buildings near the control tower. It was an RAF corporal waving a piece of paper and sounding somewhat irate. He skidded to a halt in front of me and demanded 'Why the hell didn't you report to the guard room?'

Presumably he hadn't grasped that I was an officer but I wasn't prepared to excuse his ignorance. I looked at him for a moment and then replied, 'Listen, Corporal. First, if you want to talk to me then you will salute and call me sir. Second, if you have a guard room then you should have a guard and if you have a guard he should be at the gateway, so I suggest you find out why he wasn't there when we arrived. Now, we are due to fly in this thing at eight o'clock. What do we do, climb aboard or wait for the RAF to wake up?'

He saluted and apologized, explaining that there should have been a guard at the gate to direct us to the guard room where our arrival would have been recorded. However, the plane was ready for take-off and we should get aboard. I thought it strange that he took it for granted that we were a properly authorized party and not a bunch of escaped prisoners of war, but decided not to pursue the point and ordered the party to embus.

My acquaintance with the private soldier up to that time had been largely limited to the cockneys of the London Rifle Brigade and their Belfast equivalent of the Royal Ulster Rifles, a regiment mainly recruited from that city, and one characteristic they had in common was their cheerful acceptance of the inevitable, however unpleasant the inevitable might appear to be. This resulted, I suppose, from the deprived circumstances in which most of them were reared: the city slums, where adversity of all kinds was the order of the day; where self-pity got you nowhere and if you wanted something, the only course was to go and get it — regardless or almost regardless of the consequences. Allied to this down-to-earth approach was a wonderful sense of humour.

Gillanders, my batman, was the first to reach the door of the aircraft where he blocked the entry of those behind him with his arms rigid against the sides and turning his head called, 'Shall I reserve a seat for you, sorr?'

'Yes,' I called back, having seen the seating arrangements or lack thereof, 'in first class,' I was the last to climb aboard and saw that there was no need to issue instructions about where to sit or where to hold on. Every usable area of floor space was occupied except a couple of square feet near the door, and it was then that I noticed that there was no door. Gillanders was sitting nearby and I was just about to tell him to move over so that I would at least have something to wedge my feet against, when the aircraft blew-up — or so it seemed. There was an earsplitting series of explosions followed by a roar which is impossible to describe and the plane began to vibrate and writhe as if seized by some gigantic monster determined to shake us out as if from a salt cellar. My first instinct was to jump out and hope for the best, but fortunately I looked at Gillanders. He was saying something which, of course, I couldn't hear, but I could see that he was highly amused by my discomfort. I turned and saw that Messrs Alcock and Brown, or whoever they were, had started the port engine which was about ten feet from me and which was backfiring with the noise of a battery of twenty-five pounders, accompanied by sheets of flame and dense clouds of black smoke from the exhausts. I looked up, half expecting to see Messrs A and B scrambling to get out before the whole contraption disintegrated. They were both gazing out at the agonizing engine as if anxious to alleviate its suffering, at the same time reaching for a knob here and a switch there, presumably to vary whatever one varies in aeroplane engines of 1914 vintage, and gradually the intermittent backfiring took on a more regular rhythm but with little abatement in the noise level.

I decided to sit back and prepare for take-off. No sooner had I done so than the noise level and the vibration doubled in intensity. They had started up the second engine. I looked out of the door and could see the RAF corporal standing about twenty yards away, holding his hat on with one hand and giving a thumbs-up sign towards the cockpit with the other. What qualifications did he have, I thought, to decide that it was safe for us to commence our journey into the unknown? He's probably never been in an areoplane. There was a thump as the brakes were released, and we began to roll forward. The creaks and jolts made it sound as if we were taxiing over a badly ploughed field instead of a reasonably level stretch of grassland. It was very obvious that our flying machine had been built long before the days of hydraulic and retractable undercarriages.

At the perimeter of the airfield we stopped for a few moments, as if to give the plane an opportunity to size-up the first hurdle it was going to encounter. Then, with one engine roaring its heart out, we swung round into the wind — and the noise of the engines died away. Ah, I thought, we've got engine trouble; the flight will be cancelled. Not a bit of it. The next instant both engines blasted into life, this time in apparent harmony, and we surged forward on our take-off run across the airfield.

I have mentioned that Netheravon airfield was a wide expanse of undulating grassland, and presumably, from whichever direction you arrive, or depart, by air, the 'ups' cancel out the 'downs'. Anyway, on this occasion we seemed to be labouring uphill one moment and then screaming down the next until I began to wonder if we would ever become unstuck from Mother

129

Earth. For a second or two the rattle and rumble of the undercarriage would cease as we became airborne. Then — crash — we would be back on an up-slope. Up again for a little longer then down again, and so it went on for what seemed an interminable time until at last we saw the perimeter fence slide away a few yards below and we knew there was now no turning back. Slowly but surely we clawed our way up into the morning sky, the engines labouring as if they knew that our lives as well as theirs depended on them putting forth their last ounce of strength to keep us in the air. On over Beacon Barracks where I could clearly see the troops in our battalion lines looking up and waving as we roared overhead, clearing Beacon Hill — but not by much — on over Amesbury, Stonehenge, Hungerford, Newbury, Andover, towns with which I would become very familiar and all looking very quiet and pleasant in the morning light.

I looked round to see how the others were enjoying the experience. To my surprise, some appeared to be asleep while others were admiring the view through the gaps in the floor of the fuselage. When we had reached what I assumed to be our cruising height of about 1,500 feet, the drivers up aloft had throttled back the apparently overworked engines which, for a time, seemed to be running in unison. Every few minutes however, one or other engine appeared to give a hiccup, and slow down. However, it would then roar back into life, whether or not assisted by some adjustment of the controls, and all would be in harmony for a few minutes when the same thing would happen again. For a while, I found this somewhat disturbing but comforted myself with the thought that if Messrs A and B were happy to follow this routine all day, then there was no cause for anxiety.

Suddenly, catastrophe! The engines stopped and I could see the four blades of the propeller on my side apparently idling and under no power as we began to drop like a stone towards the green fields below. Then I saw a windsock and realized that our one hour of flying experience was over as we sank down onto the green turf of the airfield and rumbled to a stop, before the engines roared back into life as we turned and taxied back to our starting point where I could see the next group waiting for their turn to undergo their indoctrination into airborne travel. Surprisingly, perhaps, these short flights became very popular with the majority of the troops, and there was never any difficulty in finding volunteers for repeat flights when the plane was at the battalion's disposal, and great disappointment if, as happened from time to time, flying time was cancelled for any reason. I think that they felt that at long last they were doing something to justify their airborne status and the red beret of Airborne Forces which had now been introduced.

It was about this time, the summer of 1942 I think, that division HQ announced a competition for a suitable design for a division sign or emblem. This gave rise to considerable interest, and a number of suggestions were submitted by our battalion and no doubt by other battalions. Those from our battalion revealed a wealth of artistic talent, orientated possibly towards alcohol and religion. One, I remember, portrayed the Pope and the Archbishop of Canterbury coming down to earth under the same parachute, whilst another consisted of a glider shaped like a bottle and bearing the sign 'GUINNESS IS GOOD FOR YOU.' The sign eventually chosen was that of Bellerophon, the Greek warrior, mounted on his winged horse, Pegasus — the proposal, we understood, of Lady Browning, or Daphne Du Maurier. The adoption of this sign may have caused confusion or perhaps consternation in the ranks of the German High Command who were no doubt fully aware of our exploits with mules in the mountains of Wales the previous year because it was reported that during one of his nightly broadcasts, Lord Haw-Haw poured scorn on the decision of 'that maniac Winston Churchill' to form an airborne cavalry division! What he would have said if he had heard of Jock Pearson's proposal for an airborne armoured division, I cannot imagine.

Attachments to the Royal Air Force

Another means whereby airborne troops were given flying experience during the period of shortage of aircraft and gliders was by attachment to operational units of the RAF. This was confined to officers and warrant officers. The attachments lasted for about a week and involved living with the RAF and flying on training exercises, and, if you were 'lucky,' on leaflet-dropping operations over northern France. Actual bombing raids were excluded, presumably because these required the coordinated concentration of all members of the air crew without the distraction of an inexperienced passenger, particularly in the event of an emergency. The timetables and other details for these attachments were circulated by brigade HQ, it being left to battalions to nominate the officers concerned. As adjutant of 1st RUR it was my responsibility to nominate our groups, so I decided to make up a group with Ronnie Wilson and Pat Giles to spend a week with a bomber squadron at Thruxton Airfield near Andover, so on the due date we set off for Thruxton.

When we turned in at the main entrance we were politely ignored by the sentry on the gate and drove past several buildings and hangars onto the perimeter road around the airfield. By this time it was late afternoon but we could see the outline of Nissen huts and parked aircraft on the far side of the airfield, but no signs of activity, so drove on around the perimeter to see what we might find. At the far corner away from the control tower and administrative buildings we came to a Nissen hut and I could just make out a sign at the entrance — 'A Flight'.

'This is me,' I said, 'hang on and I'll go and see what I can find.'

Ronnie stopped the truck and I got out and walked up the concrete pathway to the porch-like entrance at the end of the hut. There was another notice on the door — 'No entry to unauthorized personnel.'

This, I thought was RAF security at its best. I opened the door and went in. The hut was divided into two equal parts by a partition with a door into the far room from where I could hear the murmur of voices. There was nobody in the room I had entered, which appeared to be the flight office plus store room plus cafeteria plus communications centre plus planning department, all with central heating in the form of the usual round stove in the centre of the room with a long pipe-like chimney leading up through the roof. There were three six foot wooden-topped tables, two facing each other on either side of the stove, and one other up against the partition wall. On one was a typewriter and telephone, three dirty cups, a number of tins full of cigarette ends and a clip-board with papers attached, and alongside, a filing cabinet. On the table against the wall were other papers and a number of what seemed to me to be manuals of one sort of another. On the third table were two box-like field telephones and several other overflowing ashtrays. Everywhere were items of flying gear: flying boots, flying jackets, helmets, heavy pullovers and, to my surprise, a rolled-up umbrella. Pinned to the partition wall were several overlapping ordnance survey maps, and on the filing cabinet, a primus stove.

I walked quietly across to the door into the adjoining room, knocked, and walked in. On my left was another six foot wooden-top table under the window, lengthwise across the room. Seated facing each other across the table and both with their feet resting on the table were two RAF officers, both in battle dress, one, on the right as I entered, with the stripes of a flight lieutenant on his epaulets, the other a pilot officer. The flight lieutenant had pilots wings on his breast, the pilot officer the half-wing of an observer or navigator; I wasn't sure which. Neither of them even looked in my direction but simply continued their conversation. I waited, not knowing what to do.

'Excuse me,' I said, breaking into whatever they were discussing, 'I've been attached to A Flight. Am I in the right place?'

They stopped talking and the flight lieutenant turned his head and looked at me and said, in a quiet voice, 'Yes,' and turned back to his colleague. Despite the extreme brevity of his response, it wasn't said in an unfriendly or sarcastic tone, rather as if he spent his day telling army officers that this was the correct place to be if attached to A Flight.

I tried again. 'Can you tell me what's on — what I'm supposed to do?' I said.

After finishing what he was saying, he again turned his head and replied, again very quietly, 'We won't know until briefing in the morning,' again in a very matter-of-fact tone.

'Thanks,' I replied, 'I'll come back in the morning,' and left.

As I closed the door, I expected to hear them laugh and crack some joke about army types, but no, they seemed to carry on their quiet conversation as if I had never appeared. I reflected that if the situation had been reversed, I would at least have shaken hands and introduced myself to the intruder, however unwelcome. I was beginning to think that RAF types were a bit odd!

When I got outside I saw that Ronnie and Pat and our truck had disappeared. Thinking, presumably, that I was being made welcome, they had driven on to find their own flight offices.

I deliberated a few moments as to whether I should walk back the way we had come, or possibly cadge a lift from my new RAF mates, or continue around the perimeter road in the hope of catching up with Ronnie and Pat. Although it was now dark and starting to rain, I decided on the latter course, although I was somewhat apprehensive about the possibility that they had driven back to the main airport buildings, in which case I would be faced with a three mile tramp around the perimeter or a muddy trek across the airfield itself.

As I continued along, I could make out the shapes of various aircraft parked at the ends of spur roads around the perimeter. These were mainly Whitley bombers, with their black coffin-like shape, with an occasional Wellington, which reminded me of the story I had heard of the trial use of a Wellington for towing troop-carrying gliders. The Wellington has what I understand to be called 'geodetic' construction, which is rather like a piece of garden trellis work. After landing, following a glider towing exercise, this particular Wellington was found to be six feet longer than when it took off, which explained the pilot's complaint that when landing the controls 'were a bit ropey, as if everything was too tight.' Whether they were ever able to shrink the plane back to its normal length I never heard, but it was decided that Wellingtons were not suitable for towing gliders.

Suddenly, I made out the shape of another Nissen hut at the end of a narrow concrete path. No lights were visible, so more in hope than expectation I cautiously made my way along the path to the entrance. Striking a match I made out a sign at the doorway — B flight. This was Pat's flight, but the place was locked up with no sign of Pat, so I continued on my way, becoming reconciled to a long, long walk back to the warmth and comfort of wherever we were going to spend the night. I needn't have worried. After a few more minutes, and despite my rain-flecked glasses, I saw a small red light. This was either the wartime regulation rear light on a pick-up truck, or the reflected glow from the eye of a one-eyed guard dog which would, of course, attack me as a suspected intruder. I threw caution to the wind and approached until, to my intense relief I could distinguish our truck and Pat's voice said, 'Is that you, Bob?' He was sitting in the passenger seat of the truck, smoking his pipe.

'Am I glad to see you,' I said. 'Where's Ronnie?'

'Here he comes,' Pat replied, and looking round I saw Ronnie silhouetted against the light from the entrance to another Nissen hut.

'Good,' I said, 'let's get going,' and clambered into the back of the truck.

As we drove along, we agreed to make for the officers' mess which we knew was located at the far end of the group of buildings alongside the Bulford-Andover road. It was a large prefabricated building which we found without difficulty, and after parking our truck alongside the place reserved for 'Station Commander', we took our bags and went in. We hadn't noticed that a similar notice marked 'Station Adjutant' was lying flat on the ground at the end of the place where we were parked.

Inside the entrance, we found ourselves in a large, warm, well carpeted lobby, where a short thick-set man in blue battle dress trousers, blue shirt and black tie was pinning a piece of paper onto a notice board. As we entered, he looked over his shoulder, gave his pin a final push and came over to us.

'Good evening,' he said. 'You're from the Royal Ulster Rifles?'

We nodded our agreement.

'Fine,' he said, 'I was expecting you earlier. Anyway,' he continued, 'I've been told to tell you that there's no point in going to your flights this afternoon as there's no flying. They will expect you tomorrow morning about nine am.'

I looked at Ronnie and Pat and they looked at me. 'That's disappointing,' said Ronnie, with as much sincerity as his Irish blarney would muster, 'we were hoping for some night flying.'

'Yes, very disappointing,' said Pat. 'By the way, how do we get to the flight offices?'

'The flight trucks leave from outside the mess at nine am,' replied the mess sergeant, which is what we found our newly acquired friend to be, 'but you can, of course, take your own transport if you wish. If you'll come this way I'll show you your rooms.'

We picked up our bags and followed him along the corridors. 'Here we are,' he said, stopping and opening the door to a room clearly marked with my name and bearing the number 13. 'Captain Wilson and Captain Giles are in 14 and 15. The bathrooms and toilets are at the end of the corridor. When you are ready, if you come along to the bar I'll introduce you to the adjutant. By the way, gentlemen, will you be dining in tonight?'

We hesitated, all somewhat overcome by this unexpected civility, and the expression 'dining in' implied some degree of formality. 'Er ... is it customary to wear service dress at dinner?' I asked him. 'We have only brought battle dress.'

He smiled, 'Not at all, gentlemen, everything is quite informal, except on guest nights. I'll see you when you are ready,' and he turned and walked away.

We dumped our bags in our rooms and Ronnie and I joined Pat who, we knew, always carried a flask as an essential item in his toilet bag, and as this was passed around we agreed that perhaps our initial thoughts as to RAF efficiency had been somewhat hasty and that our week's attachment held out more prospect of enjoyment than had at first seemed likely. Further surprises were in store for us; mostly pleasant.

When we entered, the combined anteroom and bar was empty, but we managed to locate the mess sergeant in the adjoining store room. He took us into the dining room and outlined meal times, from which I gathered that one could eat or drink at more or less any time of the day or night. Drinks were signed for, and bills presented at the end of the month — in our case before we departed at the end of the week. 'Treating' was discouraged but not forbidden.

It was then that we were joined by the station adjutant who ordered himself a pint of beer, which gave us the cue to do the same. He appeared to be a quiet, friendly sort of character, aged about fifty and wearing First World War ribbons on his RAF service dress, but no wings, from which I assumed that he had signed on to do a necessary administrative job for the duration. He took a swig of beer, wiped his mouth and then looking at each of us in turn said, 'Who the bloody hell said you could put your blasted truck on my parking place?'

Pat and I looked at Ronnie for the answer. Ronnie immediately turned on his smoothest Irish charm and it was obvious that the adjutant didn't know whether Ronnie was pulling his leg or really being apologetic. 'I'm terribly sorry, Squadron Leader. I had no idea that I was parking in your place; that's the last thing I would have done. Please let me have your keys and I'll go and move them immediately,' etc., all with an air of serious concern, but with a twinkle in his blue eyes and the hint of a smile around his mouth. 'The last thing I would want to do would be to offend the station adjutant,' he finished up. 'Let me get you another beer, sir,' and he reached out for the adjutant's mug. Pat and I, who were well acquainted with Ronnie's ability to talk himself in or out of any situation, were obviously finding the situation amusing and fortunately the adjutant also had a sense of humour. He looked at Ronnie for a moment and then pulling a bunch of keys from his pocket handed them to Ronnie, saying, 'OK, you Irish bastard; the car's a blue Morris Oxford, it's parked at the far end of the parking area, and I'll have a large Scotch!'

Without a second of hesitation, Ronnie leaned across to the barman. 'Give the Squadron Leader a large Scotch please,' he said, and turning on his heel walked out, not knowing, he told us afterwards, whether the adjutant was really annoyed or not. In fact, once the ice had been broken, he couldn't have been more friendly.

Having asked us to join him for dinner he appeared to welcome the opportunity of swapping anecdotes about army and RAF life. He had served in the army for the last eighteen months of the First World War, finishing up as a lieutenant in France, and had subsequently found life with an insurance company such that the outbreak of another war was a blessing in disguise so far as he was concerned; and, although too old for flying duties, he thoroughly enjoyed his job with an operational squadron. He explained that we might get plenty of flying during the week but, on the other hand, we might get none. It all seemed to depend on the weather and the whims of 'Higher Command.' There would probably be cross country training flights, by day and night, and possibly leaflet raids, which we could go on if we felt so inclined, but we were under no obligation to do so.

After dinner we met a number of the other officers of the squadron, all of whom seemed to view their association with Airborne Forces with considerable trepidation. Parachutes, they contended, were invented for emergency use only, and why anyone should want to jump out of an aeroplane that wasn't on fire or about to crash for some other reason, was unimaginably stupid. They pointed out that nobody in the air force was trained to use a parachute or ever practised using a parachute. They were simply given a chute which they either sat on or strapped to their chests, and were told that it might help if a crash was otherwise certain, and then they might prefer taking their chance in a crash landing. As for being towed in a glider somewhere in enemy territory and then cast off without an engine to get back with, was beyond their comprehension. Most of the people we met had been on bombing raids, which they accepted as part of their function. The idea of flying parachutists into action, however, was a very different kettle of fish, and as for towing a load of glider troops — that hardly merited contemplation. It seemed to me that what they didn't really relish was the additional responsibility which parachutists and gliders placed on them as members of the air crews. For normal bombing operations each air crew was a self contained unit which worked together, lived together and, if fate decreed, died together. Their fate was largely in their own hands. To have a load of parachutists on board, or a cumbersome load of glider troops hanging on behind, whose lives were largely in their hands was a handicap for which they were unprepared and which they didn't relish. A formation of aircraft dropping parachutists or towing gliders had to stick rigidly to the stipulation height, route, speed and formation and there was no question of taking evasive action from ack-ack fire.

During our short stay at Thruxton we had several very enjoyable evenings arguing the pros and cons of airborne operations, all of which became less and less inhibited as the evenings progressed. If these attachments did nothing else, they certainly helped to create a better understanding between army and RAF officers of their respective contributions to the war effort. Our biggest handicap was, of course, that, at that time, we hadn't seen a parachute or a troop-carrying glider! Nevertheless, we were able to demonstrate our skill in landing when diving head first over the furniture piled high in the centre of the anteroom, which our new found RAF colleagues were unable to surpass.

Before going to bed on that first night we agreed that the first to wake up would call the others, and that we would use the flight trucks. As it turned out, I was the first to wake up, at nine o'clock, which resulted in a mad scramble for breakfast and the need to use our own truck for a breakneck race around the airfield perimeter just in time for Ronnie to deposit me outside A Flight office at nine twenty am, and fortunately just in time to follow the flight commander I had met the night before, into the outer office. Inside, about twenty aircrew were standing around, some officers, some sergeant pilots and navigators. Some short, some tall, some fat, some thin, but all looking fit and cheerful. The flight commander made no response to the murmured greetings of 'Morning, skip,' 'Hiya, skipper,' but walked through and entered his office.

To my surprise everyone followed him, apparently without invitation, so I squeezed through the door into the corner of the room. Everything was very informal. I could hear the flight commander talking but could make out very little of what he was saying. There were references to the importance of accurate navigation, day and night training flights, but nothing to give me a clue as to what I might be doing. After about twenty minutes I heard 'Any questions?' The only response giving rise to discussion was as to when two members of the flight could expect some leave, after which everybody filed out in a hubbub of animated conversation, leaving only the flight commander, the half-winged navigator or observer to whom I had not been introduced the previous night, and me, standing like an ornament in the corner. I decided to break the ice, so, lighting a cigarette, I stepped across the room towards the table, half inclined to make some jocular remark about me being permitted to fly one of the aircraft. I didn't get the opportunity. The flight commander looked up and said, 'You'll be flying with me. Give Nobby a shout and he'll get you some gear.' He spoke very quietly, as if the fact that I was flying with him was an every day occurrence, and that we had been buddies for years.

From that moment I almost felt at home. There wasn't the slightest suggestion that I was a nuisance who had to be fitted in somewhere, or that my presence was resented in any way. I thought I discerned a friendly look around his eyes as he spoke as if he understood my reluctance, as an army officer, to be in any way obtrusive in his domain, whilst he wasn't going to be patronizing or go out of his way to spoon-feed someone who should be quite capable of looking after himself. His name, I discovered from Nobby, was Stephenson, and he was considered the best pilot in the squadron. I was no judge of the technicalities of flying Whitley bombers, but certainly over the few days of my attachment to his flight and the few occasions I flew in his plane I developed a feeling of complete confidence in his skill,

which I also realized was shared by each member of his crew.
Shortly after our attachment had finished, the squadron took
part in the well publicized 1,000 bomber raid on Cologne from
which a large number of British planes didn't return and I often
wondered how Flight Lieutenant Stephenson and his crew had
fared.

Walking to the door, I stuck my head through and asked,
'Is Nobby around?'

A stocky, ginger haired cheerful looking figure in shirt sleeves
sitting behind the typewriter looked up. 'Will you come in?'
I said.

Nobby followed me back in to the room.

'Fit Captain Sheridan out with some gear,' said Stephenson,
'he'll be flying with me.'

The fact that he knew my name confirmed my feelings that
I was one of the team, despite his earlier reticence, and I followed
Nobby out, feeling much more relaxed than I had felt previously.

Nobby ferreted around in a large metal cabinet and produced
a heavy flying jacket and a pair of heavy fur-lined boots.

'These should do you, sir,' he said. 'Try them on while I
look for a harness.'

He disappeared, while I looked around for somewhere to sit
to change from shoes to flying boots. There were several others
in the room doing the same thing, and one stood up and
indicated that I could use his chair. 'Have you done much
flying?' he said, in an American accent.

'No,' I replied. 'The only flying I've done was a ten minutes'
flip with Alan Cobham's Circus at Yarmouth about ten years
ago.'

He gave a short laugh. 'That was a single engine biplane,
I suppose? I did a few of those trips in Canada. You'll find this
a lot more comfortable.'

By this time I had my boots on, which were a good fit, and
Nobby came in carrying a large package and a mass of webbing
and buckles. 'Here you are, sir,' he said dumping them at my
feet. 'One chute and harness.'

I zipped up my flying jacket while Nobby disentangled the
harness and held it up for me to put my arms through the correct
straps while he pulled two between my legs and clipped them
into a round box, which by this time was positioned somewhere
around the middle of my chest. 'There you are, sir,' he said,

'all you've got to do when you want to take it off is to turn this' — and he turned the centre piece of the box — 'and give it a tap.'

As he spoke, he punched the box with the side of his clenched fist, and sure enough, all the straps seemed to fall away, leaving the harness hanging loosely on my shoulders. 'Now,' he said,, 'all you've got to do when you're ordered to bale out is clip this on like this,' — he picked up the 'package', turned it round so that two large clips on the flat side were up against my chest and he clipped on to two spring clips on the harness — 'and you're ready to go.'

I concluded that Nobby wasn't a trained parachute instructor. 'What's this for?' I said pointing to a large D-shaped handle in the middle of the front of the package.

'Oh, that,' said Nobby, 'that's for opening the chute, but I've never met anyone who's pulled out of those so I can't guarantee what would happen.'

I decided not to continue with the discussion as the flight commander, followed by our mutual friend, the navigator, was then walking out of the hut, and I tagged on behind with my parachute still on my chest and feeling like Mae West on her way to the guillotine. At the end of the pathway a jeep was waiting. Stephenson climbed in beside the driver whilst the navigator and I clambered into the back. 'There's no need to wear that thing all the time,' said the navigator as we moved off and it was only then that I noticed that neither he nor the flight commander were even wearing a harness, and remembered a remark by a pilot in the mess the previous night, who had said that the last thing he would ever do was jump out of an aeroplane which wasn't on the ground, parachute or no parachute. Presumably I was a special case. Anyway, with some difficulty I managed to detach the package from my chest and dump it on the floor beside me.

After a short drive along the perimeter road, we turned off onto a spur road and drew up alongside a Whitley bomber. Clambering out of the truck with my parachute, I followed Stephenson and the navigator up the small movable steps through a small door into the aircraft. There were two or three men standing around on the tarmac, but little of anything in the way of conversation, and I was fast gaining the impression that in the RAF everything was so cut and dried that oral communication was unnecessary.

Inside the aircraft, to my immediate left and up a couple of steps was what I came to know as the flight deck. The pilot's seat was on the left with the control column surmounted by a horizontal figure-of-eight steering wheel, rudder bar and masses of gauges, dials and switches. The navigator's seat was on the right, set slightly back from the pilot's, with what appeared to be a chart table behind the seat. I looked back along the dark interior of the aircraft fuselage. Silhouetted against the light in the rear gunner's cockpit I could see a figure moving, from which it appeared that we also had a rear gunner aboard. Just then I heard the pilot speaking and realized he was addressing me. 'Stand there,' he said, pointing just in front of the navigator who was settling himself in his seat, 'for take-off, and then you can go down there.' He pointed to the nose of the aircraft.

I bent down and looked to where he was pointing. Access to 'there' was down underneath the dashboard via a deep step, and where there was just about room to lie with one's head in a perspex bubble in the nose of the aircraft, which obviously gave a glorious view of the countryside, but seemed a bit exposed. Anyway, for take-off I simply stood with my back up against the navigator's knees with very little to hold on to, and peering out of the narrow windows as if on the 36 bus from Catford to Victoria station.

A final series of checks, a switch up there and down there, a final word with someone somewhere as Stephenson held his microphone to his mouth. First one engine and then the other burst into life and we were off, turning slowly onto the perimeter road and bumping our way along to the end of the runway. Then the roar of the engines increased to a high pitched whine and we were away.

In later years, when flying in civil aircraft and the No Smoking and Fasten Seat-belts signs flashed on, I often thought of the first occasion I took off in a large aircraft, standing up and being pressed back against the navigator's knees by the acceleration of the plane and with at least an outwards appearance of nonchalance. Suddenly a drop in the noise level sent a thought through my mind that the engines had cut out, only to realize that our wheels were no longer rumbling down the concrete runway and that we had become 'unstuck' and were airborne. I watched, fascinated, as the fields and trees fell away beneath us. Suddenly I felt a thump on my back and turned, sharply sensing that a crash landing was imminent, only to see the navigator pointing forward and waving his hand for me to get forward into the bomb aimer's compartment. I picked up my parachute and gingerly clambered down into the nose of the aircraft and scrambled forward until I was lying with my head and shoulders in the perspex bubble from which the bomb aimer could identify his target. Immediately on my right was a box-like contraption containing a number of switches, by which I assumed the bomb load could be released at the crucial moment.

Lying on one's stomach on the hard floor of an aeroplane is not particularly comfortable, so after a short time gazing at the passing countryside and trying unsuccessfully to identify rivers, villages and towns, I began to shift myself into a more relaxed position. It was then that I noticed a small handle recessed into the floor immediately under my navel and beside which was stencilled in white paint, 'TURN TO OPEN' with an arrow indicating a clockwise direction. I then realized that I was lying across a trapdoor about two feet square which was an emergency escape hatch through which, if I had inadvertently caught my harness in the handle, I could have made a rapid descent to the fields below, without the benefit of an aeroplane or parachute. I heaved myself to one side, and as I did so I was reminded of an experience of another officer in the brigade — I think his name was Nankivell — during a leaflet raid on a town in Northern France.

After flying for a couple of hours on a cloudy moonless night he was dreaming pleasantly of the egg and bacon supper which would be ready for him on arrival back at Thruxton, when suddenly the plane began to vibrate violently and the steady hum of the engines which, up to then, had tended to increase his drowsiness was now punctuated by a series of rapid explosive bangs and crashes. Looking back over his shoulder he could see the navigator bending down and shouting to him through his hands cupped around his mouth. Through the din of the engines he couldn't hear what the navigator was shouting, but from the gesticulations which followed, he understood that he should bale-out. Without thinking of the implications, he put out a hand to grab his parachute and in the haste of the moment did so by the D-shaped ring which Ginger had drawn to his attention before take-off, and in a flash, the compartment was full of loose and flapping parachute silk. Undeterred, and with great presence of mind, he hooked the parachute clips to his harness turned the handle securing the escape hatch, which immediately disappeared, and swung his legs into the opening, gathering as much of the flapping silk as he could close to his chest, and dropped out.

Recounting the event later, he described how, to his utter astonishment and as if in a dream, he suddenly found himself floating in mid-air, in complete darkness except for flashes of flame from the exhausts of the plane engines which he saw gradually disappearing above him. He had no recollection of letting go of the parachute, which must have been ripped from his arms by the slipstream and opened above him despite the somewhat unorthodox method used. Up to that point he had had no sense of fear or panic, although, as he collected his wits, numerous doubts were crowding into his mind. He had no sensation of going up or down. He didn't appear to be in cloud but couldn't identify anything below or even stars above. The thing that concerned him most was whether they had crossed the French coast on their return journey and were over the Channel, in which case he was destined for a watery grave. His reflections came to a sudden end when his knees were driven up into his chin and he saw more stars than he thought existed. He had landed apparently in one piece, and no violent pains suggested a broken limb or other injury, but he lay for a few minutes completely devoid of any ideas as to what he should do next. He could make out the untidy shape of his parachute which had, like a dead monster, its task completed, collapsed a few yards away, the silken umbilical cord still connected to his shoulder harness.

He sat up and looked round to see if there was any sign of the crashed plane or of the other members of the crew but could see no flames or any signs of life. He was lying on soft muddy ground, presumably a ploughed field, and could make out a row of high trees about fifty yards away. He then thought of the instructions frequently repeated by his officer training unit, that it was the duty of every member of HM Forces to avoid falling into the hands of the enemy. He looked around again anxiously, half expecting to see the lights of an enemy column heading his way in response to a report of a crashing plane and descending parachutists. There was still nothing to be seen, but he should obviously get away from the area as quickly as possible. The problem of which direction he should take didn't bother him unduly. Instinctively, he thought that the plane, when he had last seen it, was heading in 'that' direction, to his right, in which case the Channel and England were in that direction whilst the Pyrenees and neutral Spain were straight ahead. His wrist watch told him that it was less than three hours since he had left the comfort of the Thruxton officers' mess, so it would be several hours before daylight when he could confirm his sense of direction from the sun rise. So, immediate action was required.

His spirits were beginning to rise and his sense of adventure to return. It would be tough going, he thought, and no doubt many difficulties, but he could imagine the astonishment of the faces of his fellow officers at Bulford when he arrived back by plane from Gibraltar after walking over the Pyrenees and Spain. He spoke quite good French and had a smattering of Spanish from his school days and as a boy had travelled in both countries with his parents, so there was a lot in his favour. The fact that Gibraltar was several hundred miles away was somewhat daunting, but he had seen many films and read many books portraying characters who could jump trains and lorries and find other ways of speeding travel, methods which he could emulate as the need arose, so, again following Ginger's instructions, he turned the disc on his chest. A quick twist and his harness fell away from his shoulders. He rolled up the parachute and harness, carried them to the trees which he found formed the boundary of the field where he had landed, and concealed them under some bracken, and set off for Gibraltar.

Ensuring that he maintained his predetermined direction was a problem because every field he crossed was bounded by a high impenetrable hedge or a wood, which necessitated a detour to find a gateway and there was insufficient light to pick up landmarks which he could follow. From time to time he came across narrow tracks and laneways which helped to speed up his progress, but when he was suddenly startled by a dog barking on the other side of a low hedge and realized that he was passing a group of farm buildings, he decided that his best course was to keep well away from roadways and to stick to a cross country route.

After several hours of steady, if slow progress, he began to feel confident that he had at least put several miles between himself and his hidden parachute, and even if his descent had been observed by unfriendly eyes it was becoming less and less likely that he would be discovered by any investigating patrol. Suddenly, and away to his right, he heard a faint clanking noise which resembled the start-up of machinery and which seemed to be increasing in intensity as he paused to try and identify its origin. Could he be near a factory preparing for the coming day's work? Was it an early rising farmer starting up his tractor? In a flash it dawned on him that it was a train, and as he waited, he could distinguish the familiar chuff of a steam engine only a few hundred yards from where he waited.

Trains in occupied France would almost certainly be carrying military guards, he thought, so continued to crouch down under cover until the sound of the train faded away in the distance. If he followed the railway line this might help to identify his exact whereabouts and enable him to plan his further progress. On the other hand, a train going in one direction indicated the probability of another going the opposite way; also, a busy line suggested signal boxes and maintenance workers, so he moved ahead with great caution, until he found himself peering through a wire fence into a cutting with double railway tracks stretching away to right and left. Walking alongside the lines, he reflected, would certainly enable him to cover the ground more quickly than across country, and might also help him in finding out where he was, but which direction should he take? His doubt was resolved by a sudden awareness of the chatter of birds in the nearby hedges and trees, and a perceptible lightening of the sky away to the right — to the east, in the direction of Germany. He slipped quickly through the fence, slid on his backside down the short embankment and turning left continued his walk alongside the railway.

He had decided that at least for the first few days of his journey he would aim to travel by night and lay-up during the day, well away from any signs of habitation, and with broad daylight not many minutes away he was becoming anxious about finding a suitable place to conceal himself. Luck was on his side when the ideal spot appeared: a railway tunnel into the side of a hill only a few hundred yards ahead. Soon he had found a recess well inside the tunnel, provided, no doubt, for the safety of workers on the line, and although it offered nothing in the way of comfort, it at least provided concealment, and it was with relief that he settled down to while away the twelve hours or so before he could again continue his journey.

He soon realized that the hide-out he had selected was not only going to be extremely uncomfortable but also not as safe as he would have liked. It was about four feet deep and three feet wide with just about enough space for two people standing upright, probably the purpose for which it had been provided. From his position, he could see both ends of the tunnel, which was about 400 yards long, and he was about 100 yards from where he had entered. If a German Army patrol or even a maintenance gang entered from one end, he couldn't possibly run to the other end without being seen. He was also anxious about the possibility of being spotted from a train passing through the tunnel, something which might occur at any moment. By this time, he was feeling very tired and footsore. If he lay down full length, his feet would protrude from the recess, which might give his position away, so the best thing was to squat down with his back against one wall and his feet against the other with his legs drawn up to his chest.

With a growing feeling that his decision to stay in the tunnel had been unwise and that he was somehow trapped, he thought about the possibility of moving out and finding concealment in a nearby wood, but realized that to attempt this in what was now broad daylight would probably be even more hazardous, so reconciling himself to the fact that there were going to be many worse risks to be faced up to over the following weeks or possibly months, he squatted down up against the inner wall to try and get some sleep. He had taken off his flying jacket which he pulled around his shoulders. The thought that worried him most was that he would be seen by the crew from the footplate of a passing engine. The carriages of a passenger train would be unlikely to have its lights on during daylight, and the wagons of a goods train presented no problem. However, he remembered the bright glow from the fire box of the engine that had gone through earlier which would make the sides of the tunnel very clear to the engine crew and he might be seen if they happened to be looking in his direction.

His fears were soon proved to be justified. A few minutes after he had settled himself down, hoping to get some sleep, he heard the distant whistle of an approaching engine followed a few moments later by the hiss of escaping steam and the clankity clank of a train approaching slowly from the direction he had been following. He realized that the train was moving very slowly, which heightened the chance that he would be seen, so pulling the flying jacket over his head and tucking his feet well up under his backside, he sat motionless, but extremely uncomfortable, as the noise increased in intensity. Suddenly, even under the heavy jacket, he could see the reflected glow from the cabin of the engine and felt that he must be as visible as if standing on the track waving his arms. And then the glow passed, but his agony was not yet over. Before the engine had reached the exit from the tunnel, there was a loud squealing of brakes on the lines and the train ground to a halt with the crashing of metal buffers as the wagons concertinaed one against another down the length of the train. He must have been seen, he thought, and the engine crew were coming back to investigate. He pulled the coat down from his head, and by the faint light. from the tunnel entrance could make out a large black wagon halted opposite where he sat. Should he make a run for it through the tunnel? He waited, expecting to hear the footsteps of the approaching engine crewman. Maybe he would be a friendly Frenchman and there was no German escort on the train. But the only sound was the faint hissing of the engine. No sounds of running feet; no shouts between the driver and the guard. He waited, his heart thumping in his chest, and then, relief. A short faint whistle, a louder burst of escaping steam, the race of metal wheels on the line and the train began to move forward with the resentful clank of metal links taking the strain of each wagon. He never had the opportunity to count the wagons, but was convinced that it was the longest train ever put together, and with the thought that there would be a guard's wagon at the end, again hid his head under his jacket until the noise faded away in the distance.

With a great sense of relief, he stood up to stretch his aching legs and back, and lit a cigarette, carefully shielding the flame of his lighter. As he did so, he suddenly thought that perhaps someone had got off when the train stopped, and was now waiting for him to show himself. Very cautiously he peered out to right and left but there was no-one to be seen against the light of the tunnel entrances. He leant back against the inside of his hide, and again reflected on his situation.

By this time he was feeling very hungry, but could see no

way of solving that problem until he could get on his way again, when he envisaged having to scavenge around for raw vegetables in fields, or whatever else he could find. He also needed to get out of his battle dress and the thought was in the back of his mind that he would be able to contact the Resistance or some other friendly group who would help to solve these problems. How he should go about doing this, he had no idea, so the possibility would have to wait. The first question to be solved was his location, so he resolved to remain where he was until darkness and then to continue along the railway line in the hope of seeing a sign post or some other evidence of his whereabouts. He realized that in England, all road and station signs had been removed so as not to help people 'on the run', like himself, but felt reasonably confident that the French would not have done the same, or certainly not with the same degree of thoroughness, unless, of course, under German direction, and he felt this was doubtful, as it would add to the problems of the army of occupation.

So, he again settled himself down to get as much rest as possible, reluctant to sleep, for fear of inadvertently exposing himself to passing traffic, but realizing the need for conserving his strength and energy for whatever lay ahead. The time passed very slowly and although the railway line didn't appear to be very busy, a train passed through the tunnel in one direction or another about every hour, possibly more frequently allowing for the short periods when he fell asleep. Whenever he heard a train approaching he made sure that his face and hands were full covered to enhance the possibility that even if he was seen he would not be identified as anything other than a pile of rubbish.

The main anxiety throughout the day was that a maintenance or inspection party would come through the tunnel on foot, in which case he would have little or no chance of avoiding detection. His only hope then would be that such a group would not include Germans or collaborators and might be willing to give him assistance. Fortunately or otherwise, this didn't happen and his spirits began to rise after hours of sitting and standing when he saw the light at the ends of the tunnel begin to fade, and he prepared to move off on the next stage of his journey.

He realized the need for great caution when making his way down the tunnel to avoid being exposed to a passing train when between recesses and thus unable to take cover quickly should the need arise. The pattern of traffic up and down the lines seemed to have been a train up — or in the direction he was taking — every hour, followed by a train down about ten minutes later. He therefore decided to make his move immediately after the next down train. He had considered the wisdom of climbing onto a train and concealing himself in one of the wagons if a suitable train should slow down sufficiently for him to do so, but having no idea of what lay ahead in the way of built-up areas or open country, decided against such a course, at least for the time being.

Settling himself down for what he hoped would be the last time, at least in this particular tunnel, he waited for the down train that would signal the time for departure. He was feeling well rested, and optimistic but increasingly thirsty. Despite having had no food he had lost his earlier feelings of hunger but would have happily exchanged his heavy flying jacket for a pint of draught beer, the thought of which he had to force out of his mind with the knowledge that it could be a very long time before he would again be able to enjoy such a luxury.

The expected down train passed and he stepped out and walked quickly along the side of the tunnel. This wasn't easy in the darkness and he stumbled frequently but reached the far end without incident. It was now dark but such visibility as there was, was better than in the tunnel and he paused for a moment, peering out to ensure that there was no signal box in the vicinity from which he might be spotted. There was nothing to be seen other than a slight sheen from the rails beside him, and the shapes of trees against the sky. He continued on his way, stumbling from time to time, but nevertheless making good progress and with a sense of relief from the sense of entrapment which he had felt during the day in the tunnel.

His feeling of relief was rudely interrupted. Some instinct rather than any warning noise prompted him to glance over his shoulder and for a fraction of a second he couldn't understand what he saw; two tiny lights like the eyes of a large cat, surrounded by a red halo. In a flash he realized that another train was emerging from the tunnel. He flung himself into the darkness alongside the track, without any thought as to whether he would drop one foot or fifty feet or find himself impaled on spiked railings or immersed in a muddy stream. Fortunately, fate was kind. He landed in a mass of weeds and brambles from which he subsequently had the greatest difficulty in disentangling himself, and lay still with his head buried in his arms and hoping that the engine crew would not be looking in his direction as they passed. In his mind's eye, he visualized the cab of the engine, with the driver operating the controls on one side with his attention directed ahead for approaching signals, whilst the stoker was shovelling coal into the fire box or going about whatever other tasks were required. If he was stoking the engine, the fire box would be open, lighting up the track on either side, but at least he would be concentrating on the job in hand and not taking any interest in bodies lying alongside the track. He could feel the ground trembling as the engine thumped its way towards him. Suddenly the spot where he lay was bathed in a bright red glow of the engine's fire box and he felt as if the heat of the red hot coals was burning into the back of his neck, and then the hiss of escaping steam was fading away down the line leaving only the regular clonkity-clonk of the wheels of a seemingly endless chain of good wagons.

He stumbled on, several times having to take evasive action because of passing trains, but he was now more alert to that risk and was able to conceal himself behind trees and shrubs without the discomfort he had suffered on the first occasion.

In the early hours of the morning he was feeling very tired and wondering if he would ever identify his whereabouts, when he suddenly realized that he must be approaching a village or town. He could make out another line to his left which he assumed was a railway siding and several pinpricks of light ahead. He continued, moving cautiously until he could make out the shapes of buildings across the tracks to his right and a high wall to his left. He paused for a few moments, uncertain as to whether he should continue and risk being seen or find some new place of concealment until daylight and then decide on his next move. He glanced at his wrist watch. It was nearly four o'clock so he had about an hour before dawn; time enough, he decided, to find some indication of the name of the station, and maybe some food and drink to see him through the day to come.

He moved across to the wall on his left and slowly made his way forward until he could make out a dimly lit and deserted platform between the siding and the double tracks along which

151

he had reached the station. On the far side was another platform, with a light shining through the glass top of a door. A booking office or waiting room, he thought, and paused again. There was still no sign of activity, although it was becoming obvious that it was a large station and there were bound to be night staff on duty somewhere. Still not being able to see any identifying signs, he stepped carefully over the rails to the edge of the platform. It was then that he sensed trouble. Something was wrong; he was being watched! He ducked down under the edge of the platform and waited, expecting to hear a challenge or approaching footsteps . . . but there was no sound. He realized he was trembling and had to restrain an urge to run back the way he had come. After a few moments he eased himself up and peered over the edge of the platform. Everything was still and silent. It was then that he saw a wooden seat about ten yards to his left and up against he wall of the platform building, and across the back of the seat he could just make out some lettering, presumably the name of the station. But in the dim light it was impossible to make out the letters. With a quick glance to left and right, he heaved himself up onto the platform and tiptoed across to the seat and peering down, read 'HAYWARDS HEATH'.

Strangely enough, his initial reaction when the significance of the situation sank in, was one of disappointment. He had keyed himself up to getting back to England and pitting his wits and stamina against he occupying Germans and perhaps the Spanish also, and now, instead of returning to his battalion at Bulford with a story of achievement which would be a credit to his regiment, he would be the laughing stock of the brigade, if not the entire army and air force once the story got around. He felt the strength drain from his legs and sat down heavily on the seat. He leant forward, his eyes closed, his head resting on his open palms, not knowing whether to laugh or cry. But his tribulation was not yet over.

'Are you coming quietly, lad?' said a gruff voice. He sat up, to be blinded by a bright light shining directly into his face, and raised his arm to shield his eyes. 'Steady now, lad,' said the same voice more abruptly, 'don't let's 'ave any trouble.' Still shading his eyes from the glare, he could make out three figures, two in khaki and one in blue, and the khaki clad figures were each holding rifles pointing at his chest!

152

'I'm an army officer,' he said rather lamely, and paused. Should he explain that he had been on a leaflet raid in France, had parachuted out on the way back and been hiding in a railway tunnel near Haywards Heath for the past twenty-four hours? Somehow or other the story didn't even seem true to him, and in a hazy way, he was convinced that he was having a nightmare.

The policeman turned and led him up the platform, followed, in turn, by the two Home Guards, each with a rifle pointing at his kidneys. Up the dimly lit steps, across the bridge and down to the station entrance. There wasn't a soul in sight as they stepped into the station forecourt where a small truck was standing. The policeman opened the nearside door and motioned him to get into the back seat. One of the Home Guards walked around and got in beside him from the far side while the other clambered in behind him.

The truck drew up in an unlit street, but Nankivell could see the unmistakable blue lamp of a police station. Still conscious of the guns at his back, he followed the policeman up the steps and into a well lit hallway, then left into the station office, a large room with a wall-to-wall counter parallel to the door. At the end of the counter to the right, was a hinged flap to permit access to the area behind, where there were several desks, cupboards and filing cabinets. There were two policemen in the room. The first, with sergeant's stripes on his arm, was seated at a desk behind a very antiquated looking typewriter. The second, a constable, was leaning on the counter flap with his back against the wall, holding a china mug in his hand. ''Ere 'e is Serg,' said the police escort as they filed into the room.

He was very tired, very hungry and very thirsty. He knew that in due course his identity would be established but in the meantime he wasn't going to be of any use to attempt to explain how he had got into his present predicament. Slowly, he emptied his pockets onto the counter.

'And your watch, lad,' said the constable, and he took off his watch and laid it by his few other bits and pieces.

'Put him in number 3,' said the sergeant. 'I'll call Command.'

The second constable raised the flap of the counter and stepping through into the outer part of the room, opened a door leading to the rear of the building. 'This way, lad,' said his escort, taking him by the arm, and directing him to follow. They entered a short passage with steps down at the end of the passage.

The second constable led the way down, flicking an electric switch when they got to the bottom, revealing another passage with a number of heavy doors, each with small aperture for viewing the interior without unlocking the door. They stopped outside the door on which the figure 3 was stencilled in white paint. The constable opened the door and stood aside. Nankivell walked in, followed by his escort.

The cell was about twelve feet long and slightly less wide and contained only an iron bedstead with a grubby looking mattress, a bucket beside the head of the bed, a small wooden table and a chair. There were no windows and no carpets. 'There you are lad,' said his escort. 'I don't suppose you'll be here for long.'

'Can I get a cup of tea?' asked Nankivell.

'Yes, I think we can fix that,' said his escort and turned to leave. Nankivell heard the key turn in the lock. He sat down on the bed, bent down and took off his shoes, swung his legs up and in a few moments was sound asleep. Whether anyone brought his tea, he never knew.

The next minute — it seemed at the time, although later he was to discover that it was three hours — he woke to find himself being shaken very vigorously.

'Wake up, John,' a voice was saying, and opening his eyes he saw his battalion adjutant, Dick Stokes, leaning over him. He swung his legs off the bed and sat up, stretching his arms and shaking his head as he tried to remember where he was.

'Where the hell have you been?' Dick was saying. 'Half the army has been out looking for you for the last thirty-six hours.'

Nankivell looked back at him, his mind gradually clearing. 'I've been hiding in a railway tunnel,' he said quietly as if his adjutant should understand that hiding in railway tunnels was a perfectly reasonable pastime for army subalterns.

Dick Stokes didn't understand and obviously thought that Nankivell was slightly deranged. He sat down on the bed and put a hand on Nankivell's shoulders. 'Why were you hiding in a railway tunnel?' he said.

Nankivell turned his head and replied quietly, 'I thought I was in France.'

Dick Stokes, a regular soldier, had known John Nankivell for some time and greatly admired his qualities, which he was sure would be a credit to the regiment of which Dick was so proud. He had been very worried about Nankivell's unexplained absence since the RAF had reported his bailing-out on the return from a leaflet raid. No clear explanation had been given. Apparently one engine had developed a defect, but the pilot had been able to coax the plane back to Thruxton with the crew intact but without their passenger, who, for some reason had decided to abandon ship over Sussex. The mystery was now solved and a great weight lifted from his mind. He began to smile and as the humour of the situation dawned on him he burst out laughing. His laugh was infectious, and John Nankivell, forgetting his discomfort, suddenly appreciated the comic side of what had happened and also roared with laughter until it seemed that their sides would burst.

The constable waiting at the door of the cell looked in at them both rolling about the bed holding their sides in apparent agony, then turned and walked up to the station office.

'Did he identify him?' asked the Sergeant.

'Yes,' the constable replied, 'and now they're both laughing their heads off. I can't see what's so funny.'

I was suddenly conscious of something prodding me in the back and I rolled over and sat up, startled. The observer had climbed down from his seat and was shouting something to me which I couldn't hear over the noise of the engines. He pointed forward and looking round through the perspex nose of the plane, I could see two parallel lines of lights shimmering a short distance ahead. We were coming in to land. I had slept for most of the run out and the entire journey back from my one and only operational flight and unlike John Nankivell had no story to tell. I hadn't even got a sample of the leaflets we had dropped over Rouen!

The remainder of our stay at Thruxton was largely uneventful except for an unfortunate mishap at the end of the week. I think it was the Friday. It was a wet and misty morning and as we ate our usual hearty breakfast we agreed that there was unlikely to be any flying unless, of course, conditions improved. However, having not received any instructions to the contrary, we made our way to our respective flight offices. After an hour or so sitting around drinking numerous cups of luke warm sweet tea, smoking cigarettes and yarning with the flight crews, Ginger arrived from somewhere with the news that all flying was cancelled for the rest of the day. I had no idea what flying personnel did when they weren't flying or getting ready to fly, but I got a lift back to the officers' mess and settled myself in the anteroom with the daily papers.

It wasn't long before Ronnie and Pat arrived, and over a cup of coffee we deliberated as to how we were going to spend the day — at least until the pubs opened in the evening. We decided on an early lunch and a visit to the cinema in Andover. After the usual good lunch, we drove to Andover and located the cinema. The problem then was to find somewhere convenient to park our truck which Ronnie duly managed, by crossing the pavement alongside a wide road and onto a vacant stretch which appeared to serve as a parking area. At this time, it was pouring with rain and as none of us had coats we jumped out and ran for the shelter of the cinema. Whether the others did or not, I don't know, but I certainly paid no attention to anything in the vicinity of where the truck was parked.

As with most cinemas in those days, the programme consisted of a main and secondary film and a newsreel, and ran continuously for about three hours, so we duly sat through until we reached the point where we had come in, and decided to leave. Outside, the light was fading; it was still raining heavily and the road and pavement surfaces were wet and shiny. We decided to run the 200 yards or so to where the truck was parked. I arrived first and tried to open the door by the driver's seat which, of course, Ronnie had locked. I knew he was close behind me so decided to nip round the other side to be ready to jump in out of the rain as soon as he opened the door on the passenger side. I darted to the front of the truck, stepped over a low wall onto what I thought was another stretch of wet glistening roadway, and fell about six feet into a river. Needless to say, the water was extremely cold and the shock considerable. However, the water was only about four feet deep, and I managed to flounder to my feet to see Ronnie and Pat looking down and convulsed with laughter. To this day, I just cannot understand how I mistook a river for a road, and as I shivered my way back to Thruxton, I could only console myself with the thought that if the river had been ten feet deep instead of only about four feet, I would have drowned long before my friends and colleagues had recovered their composure sufficiently to drag me back from a watery grave.

Leave Travel By Glider

It was around the middle of 1943 that we were first introduced to the troop carrying glider when a number of Hotspurs were delivered to Netheravon. These were the small version of troop carrying glider, designed to carry about eight men, and in which the commanding officers of the brigade had been taken on their initiating flight which had so nearly ended in disaster. Whether it was ever contemplated that the Hotspur should be used for operations, I don't know. Probably not because of its limited load capacity, and it was later superseded by the Horsa supplemented by the gigantic Hamilcar. Anyway, for the time being all we had were a number of Hotspurs to continue our flying and gliding experience.

By this time, the prehistoric 'bomber' in which we had received our initial flying experience had given up the ghost, and presumably returned to the museum whence it came, and from then on we would be glider-borne in the full sense of the term. Every day, from first light until nightfall, truck loads of troops from all units of the brigade were ferried between Bulford and Netheravon for what was now called 'glider experience', which amounted to a short flight of about twenty minutes around the neighbourhood, which, for most people, was twenty minutes too long and not to be repeated more often than military discipline required. It wasn't too unpleasant for the man sitting in tandem behind the pilot because he could see and enjoy the passing scenery in reasonable comfort. For those incarcerated in the cabin, however, it was very different. Once the sliding door was closed there was no means of communication with, nor could one see, the pilot or the Number Two behind him. The small porthole-like windows appeared to be made of opaque plastic which admitted light but prevented any view, so, for the duration of the flight, on a hard wooden seat in a cramped position, all one could do was sit and 'enjoy' the sinking and rising sensation and the swaying from side to side — *yawing* I think they called it in RAF and naval circles. There was very little noise, so one could converse quite freely with one's fellow sufferers if one wanted to do so, and as there was no fire risk, smoking was permitted — one cigarette after another.

With the gliders had come a number of tug aircraft, mainly Tiger Moths modified for the purpose with a tow rope attachment device, and both gliders and tugs were piloted by young RAF sergeant pilots. Rumour had it that all these pilots had demonstrated some inadequacy for piloting 'real' aeroplanes, so the RAF had welcomed the opportunity to keeping them employed tugging or piloting gliders with airborne forces. Later on, the RAF pilots were replaced by pilots from the Glider Pilot Regiment which was then being formed.

The routine at Netheravon became clock-like in its precision. The gliders would be drawn up along the perimeter, down wind of any wind there might be, with about forty yards of tow-rope attached to each and laid out on the ground in front. The tug aircraft would taxi along until level with its glider, then swing into the wind. The ground staff would attach the free end of the tow rope to its tail, thumbs-up signs would be exchanged between the pilots and the ground staff; the tug pilot would slowly pull away until the tow rope slack was taken up and would then open up his engine and the combination would rumble away across the grass airfield. The glider would always become airborne before the tug and would hold its position several feet above the powered plane to avoid getting into its slipstream.

As each combination of tug and glider took off, one after the other, they would climb to a height of about 2,000 feet and then head off on their prearranged circuit around the countryside, returning along a predetermined route across the airfield perimeter, when the glider pilot would pull a lever to release his tow rope and would then make a steep descent to the ground. Although the glider undercarriages were designed to be 'dropped' to facilitate landing in difficult enemy country, their use for training made this impracticable and the wheels were left in position, and the only means of braking was for the pilot to tip the glider up on its nose so that a wooden skid rubbed along the ground and acted as an effective braking system. The glider pilots became so adept at all this that they could bring their gliders to a halt at almost the precise spot from which they had started their flight.

While the gliders were landing, the tug aircraft would drop their tow ropes at a convenient spot and then land ready to taxi in for the next trip.

One morning, the brigade major rang me and asked whether we would welcome the possibility of sending troops on leave to Northern Ireland by glider. I told him that I was sure that this would be welcomed, so he undertook to follow up the idea with the RAF on the basis that leave parties would fly between Netheravon and Aldergrove, outside Belfast.

A few days later confirmation arrived and arrangements were made both for the first outgoing and return flights.

When the proposal was announced, there was no shortage of volunteers, qualms about flying for two hours or more in a Hotspur being overcome by the thought of an extra two days' leave; the time saved against travel by rail and boat. It was decided that each party would consist of an officer or NCO, and seven men, the 'spare' seat having to be occupied by an inflatable dinghy because part of the flight would be across open water — the Irish Sea. The first party consisted of Major Bob Hynds, the company commander of C Company, and seven of his men. Bob, a regular soldier of many years' service who had joined the regiment as a band boy and with a quaint turn of phrase for a fervent Presbyterian, expressed the view that 'If there's a sodding glider going to Belfast then I'm sodding well going to be on it.'

The day arrived for the inauguration flight of this novel service, and I accompanied Bob and his men to Netheravon to witness their historic departure. They were all in a cheerful mood as they clambered aboard, with Bob in the Number Two seat behind the young RAF pilot, and all wearing Mae West lifejackets as required by RAF regulations. The tug aircraft was a Whitley bomber and all went well as they trundled across the airfield and disappeared into the morning haze. I returned to Bulford thinking what an excellent idea it was that the men should be able to return to their native Belfast in a couple of hours compared with the tedious journey otherwise involved, plus, of course, the extra flying experience they would derive.

I was at my desk later that morning when I received a further call from brigade HQ with the news that the glider, for some reason then unknown, had ditched in the Irish Sea some fifteen miles off the Isle of Man. A rescue operation was underway, but for the time being the fate of the occupants was unknown. Several hours later I received another call to the effect that all had been rescued, but it wasn't until the next day, when the party arrived back at Netheravon, that we heard the full story.

All had gone well until after they crossed the coast south of Liverpool and headed out towards the Isle of Man, when they began to encounter severe turbulence and the pilot had difficulty maintaining the correct station behind the tug. He had no means of telling the pilot of the tug aircraft of his problems and told Bob that, unless conditions improved, when they reached the Isle of Man he was going to cast-off and make a forced landing.

'Suddenly,' said Bob later, 'there was a strange sort of silence and I saw the tug disappearing in the distance with the tow rope or part of it hanging on behind while we headed down towards the sodding sea.'

The tow rope had broken, but he had no means of telling the men in the rear to prepare for a watery grave!

Meanwhile, in the cabin, the seven riflemen had been having an uncomfortable time with the glider pitching and tossing and oscillating from side to side, and it was a considerable relief when suddenly it became stable and it appeared that they were descending, as they thought, to the airfield at Aldergrove, having reached their destination more quickly than anticipated. Their relief was short-lived, however, when the glider appeared to bounce a couple of times and then stop and water began gushing into the cabin around the edges of the door and they could make out water lapping against the portholes. Fortunately, before take off they had been given instructions with regard to the use of the inflatable dinghy and with great presence of mind and no panic, this was passed up to the man nearest the door. As he opened the sliding door water cascaded into the cabin until it was up to their waists but it was apparent that the glider was still floating, although partially submerged. With one man grimly hanging on to a connecting rope, the cumbersome package was pushed through the door where, to their intense relief, it seemed to come alive, gradually expanding and unfolding until it was fully inflated and sitting on the water beside them like a mother hen waiting for her brood of chicks to seek her protection. One by one the riflemen plunged through the door and hauled themselves into the dinghy. By this time, Bob Hynds and the pilot had climbed out of their cockpit and were sitting on the wing of the glider, and were quickly dragged to safety.

Subsequently, Bob was loud in his praise for the glider pilot who had brought the glider down onto the water without the craft breaking up; no easy task on a rough or choppy sea. The technique was, apparently, to land in a particular direction

160

relative to the movement of the waves, no easy task and requiring a lot of quick thinking when without power for manoeuvre other than from the speed of the glider itself.

While all this drama was taking place, the Whitley tug pilot had realized that there was nothing on the end of his tow rope, and had turned and was circling around sending out a distress call. After about forty minutes bobbing around in the choppy sea, a naval frigate appeared and they were soon scrambling up netting onto the deck and heading for the warmth and comfort of the ship's ward room. Despite Bob's protestations, the captain was adamant that he could not take them on to Belfast to continue their leave and they were landed at Birkenhead, I think it was, and flown back to Netheravon the next day — 'like a bunch of sodding Chinese,' commented Bob, explaining the yellow tint on their uniforms and skin from the marker dye given off from the lifesaving dinghy.

A few days later the same party set off again for Belfast, this time by rail and boat, and we heard nothing further from brigade headquarters about leave parties travelling by glider.

Air Observation Officer

In addition to towing Hotspur gliders, the Tiger Moth tug aircraft were used as observation aircraft during division and brigade field exercises. On one of these exercises the brigade was split into two units, two of the battalions being designated as 'the enemy' (the red force) the other two battalions 'the defenders' (the blue force). The imaginary scenario was that the red force had landed somewhere on the Bristol Channel and was advancing rapidly in the direction of Reading and it was the duty of the blue force to locate them and delay the enemy advance until reserve forces could be deployed to destroy or drive the enemy back into the sea. The exercise operating instructions issued by brigade HQ provided that each of the defending battalions would designate two officers to act as air observers and thereby assist in locating the enemy positions, using Tiger Moth aircraft from Netheravon. The instructions also stipulated that when carrying out their task, the observation aircraft would fly at not less than 2,000 feet. Ronnie Wilson and I were designated as the air observation officers.

161

The night before the exercise began, the four battalions marched out of Bulford to their locations from where the exercise would commence. That night Ronnie and I were given our orders as to the areas we were required to patrol and it was explained that, as the Tiger Moth had no radio equipment, in the event of us spotting the enemy or making any other observations which might be of value to the defending force we had to return to Netheravon and telephone the information through to brigade headquarters from where the exercise was being directed.

So, at first light the following morning, Ronnie and I were delivered to Netheravon where we had considerable difficulty in locating the officer in charge of flying, who apparently wasn't used to getting up at such an early hour in the morning. Furthermore, there was a heavy mist over the airfield which prevented an early take-off and this meant kicking our heels around the RAF officers' mess for an hour or so, but RAF officers' messes being much more comfortable than those of the army and with a plentiful supply of coffee, the delay caused us no undue anguish. In due course we were introduced to our pilots to whom we explained our mission and after being fitted out with a flying helmet, parachute harness and parachutes, we clambered on board our aircraft.

The Tiger Moth is a single engine two seater biplane with the two cockpits in tandem, both fitted out with a full set of controls and instruments. The only cautions given to us by the RAF pilots when flying in these aircraft was to avoid interfering with the rudder bar, the control column and the throttle control. On this occasion it did occur to me as being rather strange that the pilots suggested that we occupy the front seats whereas, whenever we had flown previously as passengers, we had gone in the rear seat, but I assumed at the time that this was to give us a better view of the countryside over which we would be flying. At the end of the day I wondered whether these two young pilots hadn't decided beforehand to give us a demonstration of the capability of the aircraft, and, more particularly, of their flying skills.

Although flying as 'observers', we were issued with 'pilot type' parachutes, which were attached to the harness and acted as a seat in the aircraft, but we were given no advice as to how the parachutes should be used in the unfortunate event of having to bale out. I suppose this conformed to the usual attitude of RAF flying personnel who took the view that despite having to carry parachutes with them at all times when flying, the last thing they wished to contemplate was having to use them, preferring the thought that, in the event of an emergency, they would chance their arms in a crash landing.

On the frequent occasions when I flew in a Tiger Moth, the thought always came into my mind that this was the type of aircraft in which Amy Johnson had flown to Australia and many other far distant places. She certainly must have had more than her share of courage and endurance.

So, the RAF having woken up and the morning mist have cleared, we strapped ourselves into our tiny cockpits and took off, gradually climbing to our allotted height of 2,000 feet and heading westward over 'enemy lines'. Looking back and giving a wave to Ronnie in his plane which took up station slightly behind and to the right of us, I was further reminded of films I had seen of intrepid pilots of the Royal Flying Corps in the First World War setting off on their 'dawn patrol'. Fortunately we were not likely to run into any enemy aircraft — or so I thought!

After flying around for about half an hour, with my folded ordnance survey map on my knee and peering over the side of the open cockpit trying to identify roads and railways and villages and rivers in an endeavour to pin-point out location, I was becoming extremely cold and hoping that my pilot would soon think it necessary to return to Netheravon to re-fuel the plane, and his passenger. Having been out in the open all the previous night, both Ronnie and I were well equipped with several layers of warm clothing and we hadn't thought it necessary to ask for flying jackets such as were worn by the pilots. This turned out to be a great mistake. It was also unfortunate that the only means of communication between the two cockpits in the model of Tiger Moth in which we found ourselves was by a voice tube such as was common in the Victorian era for passing orders from 'upstairs' or 'downstairs', but which was less than useless against the noise of the aircraft engine. If the person in the front seat wanted to communicate with the person in the rear seat it was necessary to half stand up in the front cockpit and, with the full blast of the slipstream in the back of one's neck, to turn and attract the attention of the man behind with shouts and signs, hoping to be heard or understood. Similarly, if the man in the rear seat wished to do the same he had to strain forward within the limits of his harness and tap his colleague on the head to attract his attention.

Suddenly, to my surprise and delight, I saw what appeared to be a body of troops making their way along a narrow country road slightly to our left. They were marching in open formation on either side of the roadway. Straining against my seat harness, I turned and lifted myself up to attract the attention of my pilot, at the same time pointing downwards over the side of the aircraft to indicate that I had seen something worth investigating. This was just the moment he had been waiting for. With a wave of his arm to attract the attention of the pilot of Ronnie's plane who was still flying slightly to our rear, he tipped the plane up on its left side, down went the nose and we were on our way to investigate.

For the next fifteen minutes or so I really learned what it was like to be in a flying circus. Sure enough, a body of troops was marching along the road and at times I felt as if I could reach out and shake them by the hand. We flew alongside hedges, around telegraph poles and under the wires, around trees and woods, with steep banking turns to left and right, climbing one minute and diving the next until I really felt that I was being flown by a lunatic, which was probably the case anyway. My greatest concern was that he, being in the back seat, and me being in the front seat he couldn't see what I could see, but that didn't seem to matter. Furthermore I had noted that the troops on the ground were not wearing steel helmets, which indicated that they were not the enemy force but 'the defenders', which rendered this dicing with death rather unnecessary anyway.

In due time my pilot appeared to be satisfied with the performance of the plane and himself, and with Ronnie in close pursuit we climbed back to our cruising altitude and headed back for Netheravon. It was at that moment that I noticed a third small plane flying in the same direction as ourselves but at a higher altitude. It stayed with us for a short time and then peeled away and went back about its business. I didn't give it any further thought at the time.

When we arrived back at Netheravon I clambered out, feeling cold and stiff and not a little relieved at being on firm ground once again, and walked across to greet Ronnie. Instinctively,

164

I think, we made no comment to the pilots, wishing to create the impression that flying under telephone wires and around telegraph poles was an everyday occurrence, and slipping out of our parachute harness, we made our way into the control building for a Jimmy Riddle and a cup of coffee before our next sortie after the planes had been re-fuelled. The same thought was in both our minds, namely, that we had transgressed the 2,000 feet ruling and we decided to make it clear to our pilots before taking off again that we were not to drop below that height on the second trip, which turned out to be uneventful and unsuccessful from the point of view of spotting the enemy force.

A couple of days later, when the exercise had finished, we attended, as was customary for all the officers who had taken part, a post mortem examination in the Bulford Garrison Theatre. Just before nine am on the day in question everybody was assembled with the exercise directing staff on the stage awaiting the arrival of Brigadier Hopkinson, who walked onto the stage promptly at nine o'clock. He was a short thick-set man with pilot's wings on his left breast over several rows of medal ribbons. He laid his hat on the table saying, into his microphone, 'Good morning, gentlemen,' and then after a long pause, 'Stand up, Captain Sheridan and Captain Wilson.'

There was a hush in the hall as if a drama was about to unfold and in complete silence I stood up. I assumed that Ronnie, who was several rows behind me, did the same. 'In the instructions for this exercise,' continued the brigadier, 'I stipulated that the observation planes at the disposal of the defending force would not fly below 2,000 feet.' He paused and then went on, 'There was nothing in those orders about descending to ground level to see the whites of the eyes of the enemy troops, however commendable that thought might be. Nor was there any reference to hazardous flying under telephone wires and similar obstructions in the area.'

There was a murmur of stifled laughter in the hall and I noticed that one or two of the directing staff on the platform were smiling, as if the incident had its humorous side, and I relaxed a little. Hoppy then went on. 'When flying over the exercise area this is exactly what I saw and the two observers in the planes were, I understand, Captain Sheridan and Captain Wilson. Have you anything to say?' I had been thinking fast. I could say that I wasn't piloting the plane; I had no control over what we did or alternatively that I couldn't communicate with the pilot, but all this sounded rather lame so I simply said, 'No, sir.' I heard Ronnie behind me, with his soft Ulster accent say the same thing.

The brigadier then went on to say, 'Let me make it clear that whenever officers of the brigade are assigned to observation duties like this, they are in command of the aircraft and must make that clear to the RAF pilots before take-off.'

Obviously Hoppy appreciated what had happened and was taking a lenient view of our breach of discipline but he wouldn't do so in the event of a further occurrence.

The doorway where George Maginnis was killed by a
mortar bomb.

Battalion Headquarters at Le Mesnil.

The German bunker at Touques near Deauville — now (1980) surrounded by a screen of trees. 'A' Company headquarters about 30 August 1944.

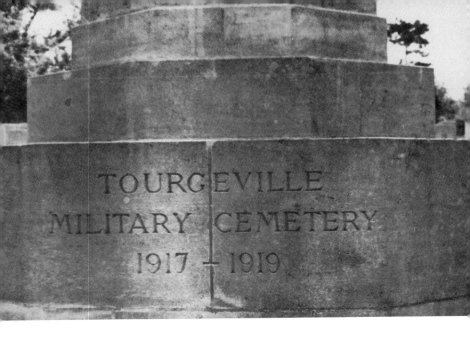

The military cemetery near Deauville where 'Killer' Johnson,
Corporal Southern and others are buried.

The cross on the grave of Major E.F. 'Killer' Johnson.

Lochailort Hotel.

6

6th Airborne Division

It was about this time, May 1943, that we heard of the proposed formation of a new airborne division to be known as the 6th and were a bit mystified as to the whereabouts of numbers 2, 3, 4 and 5. It had been decided, we were told, that the 1st Airlanding Brigade, which consisted of four battalions, would be split into two separate brigades, one continuing to be known as the 1st and forming part of the 1st Division and the second the 6th, part of the new 6th Division. Unfortunately, our battalion together with the 2nd Battalion, Ox and Bucks (the 52nd) were to be in the new 6th Air Landing Brigade which was to be bought up to full strength with a battalion of the Devonshire regiment. Naturally, we were somewhat put out about this because we considered ourselves to be the elite battalion of the brigade, if not of the division. However, it may well have been that our view was not shared by Brigadier Hopkinson, who was appointed division commander of the 1st Division and who may well have thought that life would be more pleasant without the somewhat unconventional attitudes and behaviour of the wild men from Ulster. Our resentment was even more pronounced when the news was leaked through the usual confidential channels that the 1st Division would shortly be moving to the North African sphere of operations. As it turned out, whoever decided that we would switch to the 6th Airborne Division in fact did us a good turn because it meant that we would ultimately spearhead probably the greatest military operation of all time when the allied forces returned to the continent of Europe.

Possibly in recognition of our disappointment at not going overseas with the 1st Division, somebody decided that we should be sent off on 'holiday at the seaside', so we departed from the very restrictive existence of Bulford Fields Camp for the fleshpots of Ilfracombe in North Devon where military training was forgotten and the entire battalion spent three or four weeks relaxing with sporting activities of one sort of another and a very good time was had by one and all. The officers' mess was established in a requisitioned hotel from which all 'comforts' had, of course, been removed, but nevertheless it was ideal for our purposes. In addition to rugger and soccer matches against nearby clubs and military establishments, a complete athletics programme was undertaken, culminating in a battalion sports day to which wives and girlfriends and local people were invited. The high point of the day's events was during the final of the pole vaulting competition, which, it was generally agreed, would be won by the regimental sergeant major, 'Scoop' Griffiths, a long serving regular soldier who had in his younger days been a great exponent of the art of pole vaulting. His nickname, Scoop, was derived from a strange habit of sucking air in through his pursed lips when about to make some pronouncement in his capacity as RSM.

The crucial moment in the competition was reached when Scoop was about to attempt a vault which would not only win him the competition but also break the regimental record for this event. He took up his stance at the end of the run-up with the pole poised in front of him, took his usual deep breath and raced towards the bar over which he was resolved to hurl himself. Reaching the point just in front of the stands holding the bar, he stuck the end of the pole into the ground and took a convulsive leap, whereupon there was a loud crack as the pole broke into two parts and Scoop dived head first under the bar into the sandpit on the far side leaving the bar completely undisturbed. Howls of delight and derision greeted this extraordinary sight and it was said that Scoop never again recovered his self-confidence and poise and remained convinced that someone had sawn partly through his pole in order to create his discomfiture.

Chilton Foliat, Hungerford

When the time came to leave Ilfracombe we were delighted to find that we were not going back to Bulford Fields Camp but to a new location at Chilton Foliat, near Hungerford in Berkshire, a county which we had come to know well and liked very much following our stay at Newbury only a few miles away. Our location at Chilton Foliat was a temporary wartime camp consisting of a number of Nissen huts in the parkland area adjoining Chilton Foliat house, a large attractive country house owned by a Lady Ward. The officers' mess and quarters were set up in one wing of this house whilst Lady Ward continued to reside in the main part of the building. She was most hospitable and each week entertained a group of officers to lunch or dinner.

The large room we used as an anteroom was festooned with what I think were relics of hunting and exploration trips to Africa, presumably by the master of the house — or his forebears — although I never discovered who he was. There were native spears, assegais and all manner of other lethal weapons together with witch doctors' masks and the heads of all manner of wild animals, all displayed with pictures of hunting parties grouped around the dead bodies of lions, tigers, elephants and other dead game. I remember standing at one end of the room during a particularly riotous mess night when suddenly an assegai flung from the other end of the room stuck and remained quivering in the wood panelling about a foot from my head. I looked up to see Ambrose Magonigal (later Justice Magonigal) debating with others as to how close he could get with a second throw.

Whilst we were at Chilton Foliat, all ranks were given flying experience in the new Horsa gliders which were then becoming available at Netheravon. The Horsa was much larger than the Hotspur, and could carry about twenty-five fully equipped men or, with modifications, other loads including jeeps and the small trollies we used for carrying heavy equipment. It was designed for two pilots side by side and with a tail unit which could be detached or swung on one side to facilitate the loading and unloading of jeeps and other equipment. At that time, the Horsa seemed enormous, with a wing span of nearly ninety feet, but later on it was dwarfed by the Hamilcar which could carry about forty men or other heavy equipment such as a light tank or an antitank gun. These gliders were made entirely of wood and not having any engines had very little fire risk and with little or no noise were very pleasant to fly in.

Soon after we arrived at Chilton Foliat it was decided to turn night into day to give all personnel more experience of night time operations. All our clocks were simply put on or back twelve hours so that we had breakfast at seven o'clock in the evening, worked a normal day with a 'midday' meal around midnight and 'dinner' at seven in the morning. All training was therefore carried out at night time, which I'm sure was beneficial, the only problem being that of getting enough sleep while it was daylight. However, after being up for a few 'nights' this problem was overcome. I missed a large part of this 'night training' because I had managed to fix up to go on a parachute training course.

Parachuting

Early in the summer of 1943 we had a change in commanding officer. For some months, Rosie Campbell had been experiencing difficulty in moving some of the fingers of one of his hands, and I knew that he had been extremely worried about the possibility of being medically 'downgraded', in which case his ambition to take the battalion into action would be unfulfilled. This is what happened, and despite a personal appeal to General Boy Browning, he was posted away from the battalion and replaced by Lieutenant Colonel J.C.H. (Hank) Carson. This was a shattering blow for Rosie and indeed we were all very sorry to see him go. He refused any form of farewell party and I was one of the very few present when he simply packed his bags, clambered into his jeep and drove off. Hank Carson was a very different personality; a quiet, pipe-smoking man who was inclined to remain aloof from our more lively mess parties but who we all came to like and respect.

I set off for my parachute course with a feeling of excited anticipation. I suppose I wanted to prove to myself that I could jump out of an aeroplane with a parachute strapped to my back which I hoped would float me gently back to the ground, and I didn't give much thought to the possibility that I might be one of the very few unlucky ones with a parachute which failed to provide that essential service. However, my immediate concern was whether or not I would pass whatever eyesight tests were required. By this time I was wearing the contact lenses I had acquired earlier throughout the day without any

170

discomfort, but I was uncertain as to what view the doctors might take if they knew that my eyesight without glasses was below standard. I recognized that losing a lens during training mishap would not be unduly serious, but when in action when good sight was essential, was a different matter. As my role involved gliding rather than jumping into action, I decided to wear my contact lenses for the medical examination and not to mention that I was doing so unless asked. I was encouraged in this by the frequent observations made to me when wearing my lenses as to why I wasn't wearing my glasses.

On the morning after our arrival at the Airborne Forces Depot, Hardwick, a notice was posted on the notice board indicating the times at which each man had to report to the medical centre for a check-up. Before my time arrived I had inserted my contact lenses and duly reported to the medical officer. He asked me a few questions and was obviously aware that I was already in the Air Landing Brigade and was not a raw recruit to the Parachute Regiment, and his examination suggested that he was quite prepared to take my physical fitness for granted. He did spot the fact that I had restricted movement in one shoulder which, I explained, followed a rugger injury, but obviously didn't think that this would inhibit my parachuting in any way. After going through the usual motions of deep breathing, tapping my chest, coughing and peering into my ears, he asked me if I could read the eyesight chart on the wall to which I was able to respond that I could read it quite clearly. All this time I avoided looking directly at him in case he might spot a strange glint in my eyes. He then completed his form, expressed himself as being satisfied and asked me to tell the next man to come in. That was a great load off my mind.

On conclusion of the Hardwick part of our training, we were transported to Chesterfield and then by train across the Pennines to Ringway Airport. Despite the variety of ranks in our group, from a captain down to several private soldiers, we had got to know one another very well at Hardwick and as we approached the time when our courage and determination were to be put to the ultimate test, it became a matter of pride in our group representing the 6th Air Landing Brigade, that no-one should drop out. We were determined to show that glider troops were equally capable of parachuting should the need arise. At Ringway the officers in our squad were permitted to use the officers' mess, which was of the usual very high standard associated with the RAF. Amongst the air crew personnel at the parachute training school were a number who had obviously been badly burned in air crashes and who, despite their terrible disfigurement, had retained their skill and desire to continue flying.

The outstanding feature of the parachute training school, to my mind, was the quality of the instructors. With these men there was never a dull moment. Our squad was divided into three 'sticks' each of ten men with an instructor for each and from the moment we paraded in the morning on the tarmac outside the main training hangar until we fell out exhausted in the evenings, it was all a matter of enthusiastic go-go-go. Inside the hangar was every form of equipment and device designed to teach us how to jump, control our parachutes, and land safely.

There were several mock-ups which resembled the central portion of an aircraft fuselage. In the middle of the floor was a hole about three foot in diameter with sides about twelve inches deep, all made to resemble the hole in the floor of the Whitley aircraft which were then being used for parachute training and operations. It was on the mock-ups that we were taught the correct techniques for 'jumping through the hole'. Jumping through the hole onto a mattress about five feet below may sound relatively simple. However, it wasn't so simple as it might sound. Our instructors pointed out that when jumping from an aeroplane we would each have a bulky parachute pack on our back and if we didn't eject through the centre of the hole the pack would strike the edge, tipping us forward and smashing our faces against the opposite side: known as 'ringing the bell.' Another hazard was that of ejecting with legs apart, in which case one would be thrown into a twist by the slipstream of the aircraft, which could result in becoming entangled with the rigging lines thus preventing the full development of the parachute. We were quick to learn that mistakes might have fatal results and that jumping out of an aeroplane, even with a parachute, was not quite so simple as it might sound. Jumping techniques had obviously been designed with a view to the ten men in the stick getting out as quickly as possible so that they all reached the ground in the closest possible proximity, notwithstanding that the plane was probably flying at around one hundred miles per hour. A precise drill had been worked out for the jumping procedure and this we had gone through during our training sessions time after time until it became automatic and only then had achieved the high standard required by our instructors.

One of the first techniques we had to learn, on the mock-ups was that of landing. Most if not all the training equipment involved landing, if only from a height of a few feet, when the risk of twisting an ankle or knee or shoulder was probably just as great as if landing by parachute from an aeroplane. We were all provided with special helmets with a thick band of rubber encasing the head to reduce the risk of head injury. The first session every day therefore consisted of landing practice; feet together, elbows well into the sides, head tucked down onto the chest, roll over on the left shoulder or the right shoulder.

We would jump off low, and sometimes not-so-low platforms, learning the technique and repeating it time after time under the encouraging but sometimes exasperated exhortation of our instructors, until the techniques became second nature. Day by day we progressed to more sophisticated equipment. One apparatus which I didn't like a bit was known as the fan. This took the form of a small platform about six feet square built high up on the wall of the hangar; I suppose about forty feet from the ground, which first of all had to be reached by ascending a vertical ladder up the side of the hangar wall and clambering through a hole onto the platform, itself a somewhat frightening experience. On one side of the platform was the fan from which the apparatus took its name. This consisted of a cylindrical drum connected to a wheel on which were mounted a number of flat blades — the 'fan' I refer to. Wound around the drum was a thin wire cable with the free end attached to a parachute harness which one was required to fit on without falling off the platform during the process. The next step was to sit on the edge of the platform in what seemed to be a most precarious position and then to launch oneself into space with no visible means of support, with the inevitable consequence of hitting the ground forty feet below and having one's knees driven out through one's shoulder blades. However, this device had been designed so that as one dropped the cable unwound from the drum. This in turn activated the fan, which developed sufficient air resistance when the victim was a few feet from the ground to check the fall to what might be called normal parachute dropping speed. This

173

was a fearsome contraption which, unlike most of the other equipment, I never relished putting to the test.

Suspended from the roof of the hangar were several parachute harnesses used for training recruits in techniques for controlling the parachute during descent. They were designed to simulate oscillation due to wind, and other conditions and could be dropped suddenly to give experience of landing which those conditions might require.

After seven days of training, which included watching demonstration films and a visit to the parachute packing building, the time arrived for our first balloon jump. There is no doubt, I suppose, that jumping from a small cage suspended under a barrage balloon from a height of about 600 feet was useful for putting into practice the lessons we had learned about jumping and landing techniques, and to develop our faith in the capabilities of the people who had designed the parachute and the girls who had packed them. Nevertheless, the sensation when jumping from a balloon was very different from the sensation when jumping from an aircraft. From a balloon one had no doubt that one was dropping like a stone but from an aircraft there was less sensation of dropping but more of floating in the aircraft slipstream.

All the training jumps took place at Tatton Park, about twenty minutes' drive from Ringway Airport, and although there were brave attempts by a few hardy souls to sing some of the parachuting songs we had learned, this wasn't very convincing and it was fairly obvious that there were many sweaty palms and dry lips as we made our way to the park for the initial test of our courage and determination. Just inside the entrance to Tatton Park was a large van such as might be used by a furniture remover and to which we were directed by one of the instructors to line up and collect our chutes. One by one we moved up, wondering whether the heavy bag dropped into our outstretched arms was the one in 500 which contained a 'gremlin.' The next step was to get into the harness and adjust the straps to suit one's build so that the parachute pack was well up on the back. This was achieved under the direction of our RAF instructors who gave each of our quick release boxes a tap to ensure that the four strap buckles were securely locked and then checked that the static line was correctly hanging over the shoulder and not inadvertently fouling the remainder of the harness. If this

174

happened, as the instructors reminded us, the wearer would be 'a dead duck,' adding the comforting observation that if a parachute failed to open we were at liberty to take it back and ask for a replacement!

When we were all ready and checked, we formed up and set off. As we marched out of the wooded area surrounding the park, there, ahead of us was the balloon. It was a normal type of barrage balloon as seen in the sky over London and other cities. It seemed to be under-filled with whatever gas was used and somewhat flappy in the slight breeze, but presumably this was to allow for expansion as it ascended into the sky, with us suspended underneath. The balloon was attached by a cable to a large winch mounted on the back of an RAF truck and which obviously controlled the ascent and descent. Suspended under the balloon and resting on the ground was a small box-like cage with a lone figure standing in the corner — the instructor — and into which four figures were clambering who, we knew, we would shortly be following. As we watched there was a shout from the cage 'Up 600 — four to jump.'

To one side of the dropping area was a small group of about six RAF officers and sergeant instructors, and parked beside them was an ambulance with a large red cross painted on its side. We marched up to this group and halted. Our sergeant instructor approached one of the officers, saluted and reported 'Number 7 squad; twenty-eight men present and correct, sir.'

The officer in charge acknowledged his salute and turned to look up at the balloon which I now saw had reached a considerable height. He was holding a microphone with a lead extending to a loudspeaker mounted on a tripod a few feet away. We all turned and gazed up and the noise of the winch on the truck suddenly stopped and almost immediately a small doll-like figure holding itself rigidly to attention dropped out of the middle of the floor of the cage. After falling about twenty feet a long cord with a bubble on the end appeared to snake out of the bag on the doll's back. Suddenly the bubble seemed to open and close and then open again like a large mushroom as the canopy of the parachute became fully developed. By this time another doll had dropped from the cage, then another, then another, until all four parachutes with their small doll-like figures suspended beneath them were slowly descending at intervals of about a hundred feet and close to where we were watching. As they descended, the officer with the microphone was giving instructions over the loudspeaker: 'Feet together, Number 1.' 'Elbows in, Number 2,' and so on, until the four figures had landed and were scrambling from their harness. Almost immediately after the last figure had appeared I heard the whining of the winch as it wound down the balloon for the next load — that was to be us.

Our squad had already been divided into groups of four, with me as number one in the first group, and on the word of command from our squad sergeant we moved off around the dropping area to where the balloon was descending, stopping about twenty yards short and getting our first close view of the rickety looking cage in which we were about to ascend — but not descend. The cage was about six foot square and consisted of a framework of tubular steel loosely covered with heavy canvas and with a 'doorway' on one side. The floor consisted mainly of a large hole about three feet in diameter leaving just sufficient floor space in each corner for the four occupants to sit with their legs extended along the sides of the cage. The hole was constructed with sides about eighteen inches deep and was in all respects similar to the hole in the floor of an aircraft through which we would be required to jump at a later stage.

'OK, fellows, all aboard the Skylark,' said our instructor cheerfully and led me and my three companions across to the cage from which the instructor of the previous squad was clambering. 'OK, it's all yours,' he said to our instructor who stepped into the cage and moved across so that his back was against the side opposite the narrow entrance. Across the top of the cage was a steel bar from which a number of straps each about two feet long were hanging, with heavy buckles at their free ends. As we climbed aboard he clipped these buckles to the static lines of our parachutes and we settled into our respective corners ready for our ascent.

It was at this crucial moment our instructor asked in a loud voice, 'Where did you get your parachutes?' We looked up at him, not understanding the question.

'From the van inside the park gates,' I said.

'Well, I hope they're not practice chutes, because they would only have blankets in them,' he responded rather off-handedly, and then, 'Up 600 — four to drop,' he shouted and we were left to reflect on the possibility that all that the bags on our backs

176

contained were army blankets, unlikely to check our descent from 600 feet. Fortunately we were all well aware of the techniques used by the instructors to weed out anyone who, for any reason, might be doubtful about jumping. Once committed to the parachuting role, one man refusing to jump could cause delay and confusion which might well result in the death of all his companions, so there were no holds barred in the techniques used to weed out possible waverers. I don't know what thoughts went through the minds of my fellow sufferers, but mine were to convince myself that the RAF were hardly likely to have practice parachutes containing blankets at the balloon jumping training area.

Suddenly I realized that there was a strange hush as the whine of the winch faded away beneath us. I was tempted to lean forward to peer down through the hole at the surrounding countryside but thought I might slip off my narrow ledge and fall out, which was a strange thought in the circumstances, so I pressed myself back and gripped more tightly on the bar of the cage. The thought came back into my mind that maybe the RAF did have some parachute bags packed with blankets. Again I forced the thought from my mind. Suddenly — 'Action stations Number 1.' That was me. I swung my legs into the hole. Thought for a fraction of a second that I might slip out. 'Go' — and I went. Pushing myself forward into the centre of the hole and stiffening my body, I dropped.

If I had had time to think about it during those last few seconds I probably wouldn't have gone at all, but the reaction to the instructor's command had become so instinctive that in that last second or so there was no thought that I was jumping into space about 500 feet above the ground. There was a feeling, perhaps, that I was about to do something unnatural, which my body didn't want to do but had to be done, but there was no time to think about it.

When jumping from a balloon it takes about four seconds for the parachute to fully develop, in which time one falls about 200 feet. During those four seconds, I remember looking up and seeing the cage which appeared to be going away from me rather than me going away from it. I saw the parachute cords snaking out behind me like an umbilical cord with the bubble at the end which suddenly expanded, closed and then fully developed with me swinging in mid air beneath it. I also remember seeing the next man leaving the cage after me. My first inclination was to seize the webbing harness above me in case it came undone, allowing me and my parachute to part company; then there was a tremendous sense of elation as I looked down on the surrounding countryside. But this was quickly dampened by a loud voice coming up from below over the loudspeaker: 'Number 1, get your feet together, elbows in, head down.'

Suddenly, the earth appeared to be coming up rather than me going down. I made a good landing, feet and knees pressed tightly together and rolling forward on my shoulder in the manner we had practised so often. Thumping the quick release box on my parachute harness I pulled myself free from the straps under my arms and legs and ran round to gather up the canopy of my parachute. There was little wind so this was no problem. I had made it.

No cup of tea ever tasted better than the tea we had at the YMCA hut at the entrance to Tatton Park after we had returned our bundled-up parachutes to a truck waiting to take them back to Ringway for re-packing. The atmosphere in the truck returning to Ringway was very different to the mood of apprehension that we felt on the outward journey. Nobody was bothered about the further jumps which would have to be made over the next few days and we sang all the rather bloodthirsty parachuting songs which we had learned over the past few weeks. It would have seemed like tempting providence to have sung those songs on the way out to Tatton Park. One of these was as follows:

'They scraped him off the tarmac like a piece of strawberry jam,
They scraped him off the tarmac like a piece of strawberry jam,
They scraped him off the tarmac like a piece of strawberry jam,
And he ain't going to jump no more.

Chorus
Glory Glory what a hell of a way to die,
Glory Glory what a hell of a way to die,
Glory Glory what a hell of a way to die,
And he ain't going to jump no more.'
(Sung to the tune of *John Brown's Body*)

178

Whilst we were at Ringway the first Dakota (DC3) arrived from the United States which was specially adapted for parachute jumping. The big advantage was that it would carry about twenty men in much more comfortable conditions than in the Whitley and the jump was made from a doorway in the side of the fuselage which was much more simple than through a hole in the floor.

Those responsible for establishing the parachute training school at Ringway had done a wonderful job in every respect, not the least being the requisitioning of a large pub on the boundary of the airport and quite close to the training school itself. I think it was known as the Airport Arms and is still there. There was a large bar in the pub which had been cleared of all furniture except for several old upright pianos. The object was to provided a convenient pub where newly trained parachutists could congregate and let off steam at the end of their training period, during which a high level of abstinence was insisted upon. This was also a rather subtle means of reducing the likelihood of all these young men, suddenly released from the strict disciplines of the training school, giving way to their pent-up emotions and pride of achievement at the rather less salubrious establishments in the area. On those nights, the beer flowed very freely, and every ballad and ditty known to the British Service men was sung with great gusto. They were also well attended by the training school instructors and many WAAFS, all of whom were assumed to be from the parachute packing department, and therefore heroines in everybody's eyes. Whereas drunkenness or unruly behaviour in a normal public bar would result in unpleasantness with the civilian police or the military police, the efficiency and foresight of the RAF was such that anyone who passed out or made a nuisance of himself at the Airport Arms simply woke up the following morning in his bed with nothing worse than a violent hangover.

And so I returned to Chilton Foliat the proud possessor of a small parachute badge on the bottom of my right sleeve, and with the personal satisfaction, I suppose, of having overcome the natural reluctance of throwing myself into the air from a balloon cage or from an aeroplane with a parachute on my back, which might not serve the purpose for which it was intended.

179

The Death of Ian Aylmer-Jones

A few days after I arrived back from my parachuting course, an accident occurred which resulted in the death of Ian Aylmer-Jones, causing great sadness not only amongst his fellow officers but amongst all other ranks. Ian was a tall, athletic, good looking young man of about twenty-four years of age and the only son of Felix Aylmer-Jones, an actor well known at that time and who achieved considerable prominence on the stage and television during the post war years. Both Ian and his wife, Anne, had entered the acting profession, and before the war were members of the Windsor Repertory Company. Ian had been in the Territorials and commissioned on the same day as me and Tiny Tynan. We had all reported to the regimental depot at Ballymena on the same day. There were several other professional actors amongst the officers at the depot at that time, including Jack Allen and his wife, Ruth Dunning who, with Ian and Anne, were the backbone of a very accomplished dramatic society. Ian had been kept back at the depot because of his acting ability and after joining the battalion he told me of the many attempts he had had to get away from Ballymena and Colonel Cowley. He turned out to be a very capable platoon commander and was very popular.

A few days after I returned we heard that Colonel Cowley had retired from command of our depot and was living at Newbury, only a few miles from Chilton Foliat and he sent a message inviting Hank and one or two other officers for sherry the following Saturday morning. Hank accepted the invitation and asked Dai Rees, our medical officer, and me to go with him and we had a pleasant hour or so chatting with Colonel and Mrs Cowley about regimental life.

We arrived back at the officers' mess in Chilton Foliat House somewhat late for lunch, after the other officers had finished. However, ours had been held back so when we sat down for lunch the dining room was otherwise empty. We had just started when one of the orderly room clerks came into the room and up to our table and said to me, 'Will you please come quickly to the orderly room. Lieutenant Jones has shot himself.'

For a moment or two I didn't appreciate what he was saying but then, realizing how agitated he was, said 'Come on Dai,' and we both made our way down the driveway to where the battalion headquarters hut was located. This was the first of a long row of Nissen huts which provided accommodation for the battalion personnel. The office of the CO and myself was at one end of the hut, the other end being partitioned off for battalion HQ clerks.

In the centre of the section of the hut which the CO and I used was the usual circular stove with a flue pipe leading up to the curved roof. The stove stood on a square concrete plinth, with a rim about three inches high. The only furniture was the wooden top table which I used as a desk, and two other tables; one alongside the partition wall and the other facing my desk and intended for the use of the CO.

As I opened the door and stepped in the first thing I saw was Ian sprawled across the concrete plinth beside the stove with his head resting partially on the floor and partially on his outstretched right arm. Near his right hand was his .45 calibre automatic pistol still attached to a lanyard connected over his right shoulder. I could see that one side of his head was badly shattered.

As I entered, with Dai Rees behind me, the medical sergeant, Hamilton, was standing over the body. He looked at me and said, 'He's dead, sir.'

Sitting at the end of the table, up against the partition wall, was Lieutenant Tommy Haughton, later to become ADC to General Gale, the division commander. As we entered, Tommy stood up looking very pale but otherwise appearing to be quite calm. Dai bent down and moved Ian's head and checked his eyes and looked up and said, 'There's no doubt about that.'

I looked across to Tommy and said, 'Were you here, Tommy?' He simply nodded and sat down. I indicated to Sergeant Hamilton and to Sergeant Birch who were standing in the connecting doorway to leave, then picked up the telephone and told the operator to get me Hungerford police station. Although we were on active service, all cases of death or serious injury resulting from violence other than military operations or enemy action had to be reported to and investigated by the civil police, and an inquest would have to be held. After a few moments a voice came on the line. I explained who I was and that an officer had been killed and would they please send somebody along as soon as possible. The voice at the other end simply said, 'Very good, sir,' and cut off.

Tommy then told me the story. He had come to my office after lunch to clarify some points about his posting to divisional headquarters as ADC to the general. Having knocked and entered my office and found it empty he walked across and opened the connecting door to the clerk's office and asked Sergeant Birch if he knew when I would return. Sergeant Birch had replied that I had just got back from Newbury and was having lunch and would be in my office in ten or fifteen minutes. Tommy had replied that he would wait for me. He had then closed the door and picked up a bundle of 'current affairs' pamphlets which were on the table and sat down to browse through them while he waited. After about two minutes there had been a knock at the door which had then opened and Ian had come in. Seeing my chair empty, he had asked Tommy if I was coming back fairly soon. Tommy had looked up and said, 'Yes, so I understand,' whereupon Ian came into the room and closed the door behind him. Tommy had turned to continue reading his pamphlets. He said he was aware of Ian being in the room, but that was all. He then heard Ian say, 'Shall I shoot myself, Tommy?'

Having no reason to think that Ian was other than play-acting, Tommy didn't even look up from his reading but simply replied, 'Yes, you might as well.'

Within a second or two he heard a loud bang and as he looked round saw Ian collapse on the floor beside the fireplace. He ended by saying that although he realized that someone had come in from the adjoining office, until I arrived he had a strange sensation that he was having a nightmare. I didn't take any notes and didn't question Tommy because I knew the police would require a full statement from him and would question him in considerable detail.

While listening to Tommy, and looking down at Ian's body on the floor, my thoughts kept switching to Anne, Ian's wife. Quite recently she had stayed for a few days in Hungerford and I had seen them together in the bar at their hotel. Having been commissioned on the same day and joined the regiment at Ballymena together we had become good friends. Although his background and interests were somewhat different to mine, we got along very well together and had, in fact, shared a room at the depot for several months. It was then that I had learned how badly he suffered from asthma. Quite often he would wake up in the middle of the night having terrible difficulty with his breathing, and it had occurred to me that if he had wanted to avoid active service he could certainly have done so, on the basis of his medical history. However, it didn't appear to interfere with his theatrical work, and in addition, he was an enthusiastic games player, having a particular interest in cricket. Anne had also lived for a time at Ballymena whilst we were at the depot where she had been very friendly with Ruth Dunning and Jack Allen and had been a leading performer with the dramatic society. I wondered what Anne was doing at the moment and how she would receive the dreadful news of Ian's death.

An obvious question which came into my mind was whether Ian had intended to kill himself, but I found it impossible to accept that this was so. I remembered him as a very happy, somewhat flamboyant character, mature but with a keen sense of humour and during relaxed times in the mess, inclined to indulge in play-acting and extravagant theatrical gestures when making conversation; but it just did not seem plausible that he could have intended suicide. The only explanation I could think of was that he had been indulging in the sort of theatrical play-acting we associated with him and that he had held the pistol to his head and squeezed the trigger without realizing that the pistol was loaded.

I remembered the occasion when a similar mishap had occurred to me when at my OCTU in 1940.

I was also told subsequently by Sergeant Major McCutcheon that Ian had planned to go on reconnaissance during the afternoon and had wanted to pay me a quick visit before setting out.

At the inquest on the Monday morning I did not see Ian's father in the coroner's court but he may have been represented. After the police sergeant had informed the coroner of his call to battalion headquarters at Chilton Foliat, the coroner adjourned the inquest to view the body which I was required to identify. We then each gave evidence to the coroner of our knowledge of the matter. There were tears running down the coroner's face as he said that he was quite sure from the evidence that there was no reason to think that Ian had fired the shot intentionally and that somehow he must have inadvertently overlooked the fact that there was a round in the chamber when he pressed the trigger. He then pronounced a verdict of accidental death.

Immediately after the inquest I arranged for Ian's coffin to be returned to the small church at Chilton Foliat where it would rest under the care of an officer's guard until arrangements about the funeral had been settled. The guard consisted of fellow subalterns on continuous duty around his coffin in groups of four for periods of two hours each. I also advised the War Office of the coroner's verdict and that the funeral service would take place at the church on the following Thursday, subject to any arrangements the family might request. We were subsequently advised that representatives of the family would attend the funeral service and that they would make private arrangements for the burial.

Anne, Ian's wife, together with his parents and other friends, attended the funeral service, after which the coffin was borne out of the church by a group of subalterns, placed in a hearse provided by the family and driven away.

A few days later, Colonel Carson told me that Ian's father, Felix Aylmer-Jones, had telephoned to say that he would be visiting the battalion to discuss the exact cause of Ian's death. Colonel Carson had explained that he had only recently joined the battalion and although he had been fully informed on the matter, he had not been directly involved so he would therefore prefer that Mr Aylmer-Jones should speak to me. Naturally, I was surprised about this because I had assumed that the coroner's verdict would be the end of the matter. A few days later, Mr Aylmer-Jones arrived by car outside my office, and I took him to a small room set aside for our use in Chilton Foliat House. He said nothing until we were seated together, and he declined coffee or other refreshment. He appeared to me to be very upset, which was of course understandable because Ian was his only son, and there was a long pause before he said anything. He then said, very clearly and precisely, 'I have seen the transcript of the evidence given at the inquest but I would like to know, now, the real reason for Ian's death. Was he in some trouble or difficulty which had not been disclosed?'

He appeared to be convinced that Ian's death had not been accidental and that he had in fact intended to shoot himself. I was convinced that this was not the case. I therefore replied to the effect that so far as I was concerned the coroner's verdict was correct. There was no reason to think that Ian's action was in any way premeditated and if he wished to question any of the other witnesses, then, with the commanding officer's approval, I thought that this could be arranged. He appeared to be reflecting on this for a few minutes and then stood up and said, 'I don't believe I have been told the full story and I therefore propose to put the matter into the hands of a friend at Scotland Yard and ask for a further and full investigation.'

That was the end of our brief conversation. I conducted him back to his car, feeling very sad but not knowing what else I could say or do, and he drove away. That was the last I ever heard of the matter but some years later I noticed in a newspaper a report that Anne, Ian's wife, had remarried.

After the war, Felix Aylmer achieved considerable prominence on the stage and on both radio and television, and whenever I heard or saw him I was reminded of the very enjoyable times I had spent with his son at the depot and subsequently with the battalion, and of the tragic events which had led to our last meeting at Chilton Foliat in 1943. Whether he consulted his friend at Scotland Yard with regard to the circumstances of Ian's death I do not know, but I hoped that when the initial shock of his loss had worn off he had reconciled himself to accepting the verdict of accidental death, despite the very unfortunate manner in which Ian had died.

Kiwi Barracks

At the end of the summer of 1943, the battalion moved back from Chilton Foliat to Bulford, but we were relieved to hear that we would not be returning to Bulford Fields Camp where we had been before, but this time to Kiwi Barracks. These barracks had been constructed in the First World War to accommodate troops from New Zealand; hence the name and the shape of a large Kiwi dug out of the chalk subsoil of Beacon Hill overlooking the camp. Bulford Camp itself consisted partly of somewhat antiquated accommodation, such as Kiwi Barracks, and partly of new modern brick-built barracks which had been allotted to the newly formed 3rd and 5th Parachute Brigades. However, this caused us no resentment. We rather preferred the freedom of being on the outskirts rather than in the centre of a highly militarized garrison town.

Our troops were accommodated in rows of corrugated iron huts lined internally with plaster board. They were warm and provided comfortable quarters fronting on to the barrack square. The officers' mess, a short distance away, consisted of two similar huts, end-on, and connected by an entrance hallway which incorporated toilets and washroom facilities. The hut to the left of the entrance was used as a dining room and to the right as an anteroom, to which an annex had been constructed which provided a very satisfactory bar. In no time after our arrival, the mess was comfortably furnished with not only standard type furniture — 'Officers' Mess for the use of' — issued at the camp, but also with pleasant carpets and easy chairs which somehow or other seemed to move with the officers' mess baggage. Where these had originated I cannot imagine. Opposite the officers' mess building which faced out onto the slopes of Beacon Hill, a number of semi-detached houses had been constructed as quarters for married officers and their families which now provided satisfactory accommodation for our officers without families. I shared a house with 'Killer' Johnson where we each had a room on the first floor with our batmen comfortably and conveniently installed on the ground floor. They were able to make full use of the domestic equipment installed in the kitchen. (Many years later when driving along the A303, I made a detour through Bulford and located our residential house, but the officers' mess hut had disappeared.)

Shortly after arriving back at Bulford we again went off on a month's 'vacation,' this time to Weston-Super-Mare in North Devon where we followed much the same pattern of activity as on our previous holiday trip to Ilfracombe. There must have been concern in high quarters that, when the time came to fly across the Channel, some gliders could be expected to land in the sea, because particular emphasis was placed on the importance of ensuring that all ranks could swim whilst still wearing their battle dress uniform. For this purpose we were given the exclusive use of the town swimming bath for several hours each day where many amusing incidents occurred with men and officers attempting to keep themselves afloat despite the dead weight of boots and other equipment. In addition to cross country runs in which everyone was required to take part, all forms of sporting activity were organized and ending in another athletics meeting.

Just before we departed from Weston-Super-Mare we were invited by the local Home Guard unit to visit their headquarters on the outskirts of the town. During our short stay we had from time to time at their request, provided the Home Guard with NCOs and officers to give instruction in weapon training and field craft, which was not unwelcome to our people because of the generous hospitality extended to them when each training session was over. It was therefore no surprise when we received an invitation for as many officers who cared to do so to visit them in their headquarters one Sunday afternoon. Their HQ was located in in a pleasant pub a little distance out of town. So, in the late afternoon of this particular Sunday, a truck load of us set off on what we thought was going to be a pleasant interlude casting our expert eye over their facilities before the pub opened in the evening. Having had a church parade in the morning, we were all smartly attired in our service dress with highly polished Sam-Browne belts and shoes, and ready to impress our newly found friends with our military knowledge and skills.

On our arrival, we were warmly welcomed by what appeared to be the entire Home Guard company. We were ushered into a large wooden hut where the company commander, a local farmer with a row of First World War medals on his chest, thanked us for coming and talked at some length about the organization and objectives of the Home Guard. He pointed out that their greatest strength was their detailed knowledge of the surrounding countryside, which would be put to good effect if they were ever called upon to harass or delay an enemy force or to capture enemy agents who might land by sea or air with the objective of damaging or disrupting local industry and essential services. His men obviously came from all walks of life, from farm labourers to bank clerks, and I couldn't help but reflect that they would certainly give a good account of themselves in an emergency if called upon to do so. But at the same time I couldn't help thinking that he was exaggerating somewhat when he compared the skill and enthusiasm of his own men to the qualities of the Red Devils who they were privileged to have with them that afternoon. On reflection, his remarks were obviously a prelude to what was to come later.

With the aid of a large map hung up at the end of the hut, he explained how his company's responsibilities fitted into those of the local Home Guard battalion and the areas for which he would be responsible, and when pointing these out on the map I noted that he made a passing reference to 'this area, where we have our assault course.' We fell into the trap, hook, line and sinker. When we had finished, he suggested that we might adjourn to the pub for refreshment, a proposal which we all accepted with enthusiasm.

We made our way out of the hut and down the road to the pub and into the little bar where the counter was almost completely covered with pint glasses filled with a yellow liquid which obviously wasn't beer. As we were handed our glasses, one or two of us mentioned that we normally drank beer, to which they responded with an assurance that we could of course have beer if we preferred it but 'Why not try some of our local cider? It's not very strong and after all it's very good for you.'

Little did we know. In no time there was a noisy hubbub of conversation and laughter and then someone, I think it was Dan Woods, made the big mistake. He said in a loud voice, 'Where's the assault course that the company commander mentioned in his talk?'

The bait had been truly taken, and the response was beautifully stage-managed. 'Oh that,' said one of the 'yokels,' 'it's up in the orchard behind this 'ere pub, but it's very simple and would be chicken feed to you chaps.'

'Yes,' said another. 'This is Charlie here,' pointing to one of the more weedy looking individuals present. 'He holds the record at the moment, three minutes fifteen seconds, I think it is.'

'Would you chaps like to take a look at it?' said another and with one voice we all exclaimed that we would be delighted to do so. So, out of the back door of the pub we went, through an orchard, over a small wooden bridge plus a narrow stream and into a field on the side of a fairly steep hill. There laid out before us, was the assault course.

We followed our leaders like lambs to the slaughter, along a track across the field and up the slope to the starting point from where we could survey the various obstacles laid out before us. It followed much the same pattern of many other obstacle courses we had experienced in the past. However, on those occasions, we had not been dressed in our best service dress and we had usually been quite sober.

188

I think it was one of the Home Guard platoon sergeants who continued to excite our sense of adventure. 'You start here,' he explained, 'then over that fence.' He pointed to a very solid looking eight foot high timbered fence with a number of ropes hanging from the top. 'Down the other side then over to that scaffolding with the rope ladder on either side; up the ladder, down the other side then onto that overhead rope . . .' And so he went on until, pointing down to the bottom of the field, he said, 'And that's the last obstacle. You just have to jump over the stream and run up to the finishing point alongside our hut.'

It was again Dan Woods who let his regimental pride, aided and abetted by several pints of rough cider, get the better of him. 'I'd like to have a go,' he said in a loud voice. 'What did you say the record time is?'

There was a loud cheer and shouts of encouragement from the large number of spectators now congregated around the start point. It was quite obvious that the trap had been baited and we had walked straight in, as anticipated by the local villagers, and they had turned out in force to support their Home Guard unit and to witness our discomfort.

Dan was a tall, thin man, well over six feet and although not particularly athletic, was full of determination. On the word 'Go' he set off and had no problems with the first four or five obstacles. He then came to a large tarpaulin pegged tightly to the ground on both sides, and beneath which he was required to crawl from front to back, a distance of about ten yards. His progress could be followed by the mole-like hump under the tarpaulin and all seemed to go well until about the midway stage when the hump stopped and muffled noises coming from under the tarpaulin suggested that he was being violently sick. Having got rid of several pints of cider seemed to give him new life because he then quickly emerged from under the tarpaulin and set off again with renewed vigour. Along a narrow line of planks mounted on brick piers, hand-over-hand by rope over a deep trench until he finally came to the penultimate obstacle, a row of concrete pipes about two feet in diameter through which he had to wriggle flat on his stomach until he emerged from the far end and turned to face the last hurdle, the water jump. This was a ditch or shallow stream about ten feet wide, with a bank of about two feet on either side and which Dan, or any of us, could have cleared quite easily in more propitious circumstances. Dragging himself out of the culvert, Dan turned for home with the look of a man heading towards certain death but wanting to get it over as soon as possible. He seemed to summon up his last reserves of energy as he tottered towards the stream but whether he never saw it or not I don't know. When he reached what might be considered the take-off point he made no attempt to jump but simply ran over the bank and flopped down on his stomach in the stream with arms and legs outstretched as if in supplication for someone to put him out of his misery, and although helping hands swiftly dragged him onto the bank he never in fact reached the finishing line, so was pronounced disqualified!

Honour now required that the remainder of us should follow the splendid example set by Dan, and one by one, to the enormous delight of the large crowd now gathered around, we shed our belts and jackets and at intervals of only a few seconds, set off on this test of our physical fitness on which might otherwise be called an orgy of self-immolation. Whether we would have done so if we hadn't been full of cider I very much doubt, but we were spurred on by the hope that one of our number would complete the course and take the record.

The greatest hazard was, of course, the final obstacle, the stream, the banks of which were slimy with wet mud, which necessitated a jump of about fifteen feet from the only dry take-off point. Most of us therefore simply jumped down into the stream and clambered up the other side before running on to the finishing line. Not so Ronnie Wilson who believed himself to be quite capable of clearing this simple obstruction. Sure enough, he made a very good leap landing with both feet on the far bank, but without the momentum to fall forward and establish himself on dry ground, and instead simply flopped back into the stream on his backside where he sat smiling broadly at the spectators convulsed with laughter on the bank and explaining forcibly that at least he had had a go.

Whether or not anybody had broken the record I don't know, but I'm sure that our host, the local Home Guard, appreciated our efforts. As we returned to the pub they lined up on either side and gave us a clap as if w were the victorious side leaving the pitch after a rugger match and that's exactly what we looked like.

After returning to the pub and cleaning ourselves up, plates of sandwiches and glasses of beer were produced, which demonstrated that so far as the Home Guard were concerned, the afternoon had gone according to plan. The lesson for us, I think, was that 'Pride comes before a fall.' However, despite our muddy clothes we sang our way back to our billet in Weston-Super-Mare where our dishevelled appearance was the subject of much critical comment by those who had pursued a more leisurely Sunday afternoon.

Following our return to Kiwi Barracks, nothing specific was said about the part which the division would play in the invasion plan but the training programme which was followed during the early months of 1944 left no doubt in anybody's mind that we would be taking an important part in that operation. Great emphasis was placed on all forms of communication; getting to know the personnel of units with which we would be involved; both in our division and other divisions, and including the organization of football matches, boxing and athletic competitions with commando units, which suggested that when the invasion took place we would be operating closely with them. We also received several visits from the 2nd Battalion of the regiment who, by that time, were located not so far away and who, as it ultimately transpired, would be landing across the beaches over which we would fly on the first day of the invasion. The Royal Ulster Rifles was the only regiment to provide two battalions for the D-Day landings.

Those last few busy weeks at Bulford were by no means a matter of all work and no play, which would have made Tommy or Paddy neglect our social life. Frequent all ranks dances were held in the large Bulford Camp gymnasium and were well supported by the contingents of ATS girls in the vicinity, and WAAFS from the RAF station at Netheravon. Parties were also held in the officers' mess of the various battalions and other units, including the RAF at Netheravon. Authority was given for the use of army transport to bring girls to these functions which, so far as we were concerned, included any girls we had befriended — or who had befriended us — from as far afield as Newbury and Hungerford, towns where we had been located and where we still had many contacts.

In our mess at Kiwi Barracks and earlier locations, these parties were always very lively occasions. They invariably started with a preliminary session in the bar before the lady guests arrived, when we would each have several pints to overcome the natural reluctance of young bachelors to fraternize freely with the members of the opposite sex. This was probably a good thing because when the girls did arrive, we had overcome our inhibitions and welcomed them with open arms. At one stage in our travels our transport officer was a Captain Fithian-Franks who, in his spare time in civilian life, had run a dance band and was without question incomparable when it came to playing appropriate dance music on the piano to fit in with our gyrations around the dance floor set-up in the anteroom. Frankie was undoubtedly a great asset. His favourite dance tune was something akin to *Tiger Rag* which we could all perform with great skill and which our female companions seemed to thoroughly enjoy. After he was medically downgraded and posted away from the battalion mess parties were never the same, and we were forced to fall back on a somewhat antiquated gramophone for our musical accompaniment. As the evenings wore on, singing sessions would commence when everybody would be required to offer their party piece, which usually consisted of some distortion of an Irish ballad interspersed with more gentlemanly songs from the good friends we always invited from the Ox and Bucks (52nd), a battalion in our brigade and with whom we were on very good terms.

With ample food, plenty of somewhat unconventional dancing, the consumption of considerable quantities of beer and a spontaneous and noisy 'sing-song' to finish, it might be thought that such parties, at such a time, would be the occasion for skulduggery of one sort or another. This was not the case. It was always made clear that transport for the ladies' homeward journeys would leave at midnight, and leave it did, and I have no recollection of seeing a girl the worse for drink, although I cannot say the same for some of my fellow officers, and maybe they couldn't say the same about me! Hank Carson, our CO, one of the few married officers in the mess, would slip off to bed fairly early in the evening, having dropped a gentle hint that the fun and games should be called to a halt at or around midnight when, wringing with perspiration and hoarse from our vocal efforts, we would see our lady guests out to the homeward-bound trucks.

Events Leading Up to D-Day

Our battalion — the Royal Ulster Rifles — was one of the three infantry battalions which made up the Air Landing Brigade of the 6th Airborne Division. The other two battalions were the 2nd Battalion Oxford and Buckinghamshire Light Infantry, and the 12th Battalion the Devonshire Regiment. The two other brigades of the division were the 3rd and 5th Parachute Brigades, consisting of the 7th, 8th, 9th, 12th ad 13th Battalions of the Parachute Regiment and the 1st Canadian Parachute Battalion. The division also included specialist supporting units such as medical, light artillery, anti-tank and anti-aircraft batteries, armoured reconnaissance and Royal Engineers.

The units of the Air Landing Brigade and certain other elements of the division, were organized, equipped and trained to go into battle by glider, which meant that they could take into battle with them heavier and more powerful arms and equipment than could be 'dropped' with their comrades in the parachute battalions. Again, glider-borne troops could not carry the same punch in the way of heavy arms, equipment and vehicles as did normal infantry units, which was the price which had to be paid to achieve the element of surprise associated with the use of airborne troops.

One of the ideas which prompted the creation of an airborne force was to support and assist conventional attack against enemy defensive positions by landing behind the enemy lines and seizing important features such as roads, bridges and high ground, thereby disrupting the enemy's supply lines and communications, and reducing his ability to withstand the main attack. Hopefully, the efforts of the airborne troops would be such that the main attack would be successful, when they would be relieved and withdrawn to prepare for their next airborne operation, but it had to be accepted that if everything didn't go according to plan, as it seldom does, the airborne troops would be expected to hang on to the last man and the last round. Bearing in mind the limits on the loads which could be carried in planes and gliders and also the need for maximum mobility of the troops once they were on the ground, close attention had to be paid to what was carried, and uncertainty as to the strength with which the enemy could and would react against an airborne landing once the initial surprise had been overcome meant that priority had to be given to arms and ammunition.

In addition to the tools of their particular trade — Bren gun, rifle, pistol, mortar, etc., each officer and man carried as much ammunition and grenades as he could fit into the pouches of his webbing equipment and the pockets of his camouflaged smock: on one hip a water bottle and the other an entrenching tool and on his back a small haversack containing a mess tin, 'compo pack', toilet gear, ground sheet, a spare pair of socks and whatever other small items could be fitted in.

The 'compo packs', or 'hard rations' were small cardboard boxes about six inches square and two inches deep which contained small blocks of concentrated meat, cubes of dried porridge, tea, sugar, very hard biscuits, and two small blocks of concentrated chocolate. Each man was also provided with a supply of concentrated fuel tablets and a small collapsible metal frame into which the fuel tablets could be fitted and ignited for heating water or whatever else he might be cooking in his mess tin. The pack was intended to keep a man going for at least forty-eight hours, by which time, hopefully, contact would be made with supporting troops. When crumbled, mixed with water and heated, the meat tablets made a very palatable stew and could also be used to soften the biscuits, which was about the only way they were edible. The porridge was prepared in the same way. It was very sweet and satisfying and by no means unpleasant. Although there were strict rules against any form of looting, with dire penalties promised for anyone found guilty of that offence, airborne troops, the same as any others, were very adept at scrounging additional food stuff from whatever sources happened to be available, particularly if it appeared that it would otherwise go to waste!

In addition to his 'compo pack,' each man was provided with an 'escape package.' This was a small fabric pack which could be sewn into the battle dress, or carried in the pocket. It contained a number of tablets, including Benzedrine tablets, which were only to be used in an emergency and which were understood to keep a man on his feet when otherwise near exhaustion. These packs also contained a small compass, a hacksaw and maps printed on a silk-like cloth, all intended to facilitate escape in the event of capture, or movement if lost in strange territory.

The army groundsheet consisted of a large piece of canvas,

about six feet by three feet, coated with rubber on one side to make it waterproof and with buttons and buttonholes along the long sides. It could be worn like a cape, or used to lie on or to lie under or suspended overhead in the form of a bivouac. It was an item of equipment which I had always disliked from my days in the OTC at school, but which I eventually came to appreciate.

A standard item of army equipment was, of course, the gas mask. This consisted of a small cylinder of charcoal or some other substance through which one breathed air along a corrugated tube attached to a rubber mask held over the face with elastic straps. I don't think the design had changed since the First World War, and when being worn it was impossible to see or do anything except gasp for air. This was all carried in a haversack which was normally worn on the chest, but which we found so cumbersome and restricting that its use was dispensed with. It was hardly likely that the Germans would use poisonous gas against us in the circumstances in which we were expecting to meet them.

By the end of 1943, the 6th Airborne Division was concentrated at Bulford Camp. We knew by this time, or deduced without being officially informed, that the division, together with two American airborne divisions which had arrived in England, would be used to spearhead the planned invasion of Europe. After four years of training, training, training, this prospect stimulated motivation and enthusiasm during the final period of preparation, and the awareness that one's life would shortly depend on the skill and courage of one's comrades demanded that there could be no tolerance of slackness and inefficiency. By this time, we were well trained, very fit and ready to go. General Gale, the division commander, had in fact introduced as the division motto — 'GO TO IT.' We were ready to go, but didn't know when or where.

As we moved into 1944, training effort was concentrated mainly on exercising the entire division as a complete unit, presumably with the object of developing the skills of the various staff and specialist groups and also to iron out the problems associated with mass formations of aircraft and gliders and getting these to the right place at the right time. These exercises culminated in 'MUSH' during which we flew half way across the Channel before turning back to our landing zones on home ground, and which must have given the German sentries along the French coast cause for some concern. Although not announced as such, this was obviously intended as a dress rehearsal for the division's task during the subsequent Normandy landings.

Exercise Mush involved parachute and glider landings in 'enemy territory' in the vicinity of Salisbury Plain where the 'enemy' consisted of units of the 1st Airborne Division which had by this time returned to the UK from Africa. For the purposes of the exercise we were fully operational with a complete range of equipment, ammunition and other battle necessities. We knew that the duration of the flight was to be approximately one and a half hours but we had not been told the actual flight path and there was some trepidation when we found ourselves heading out over the English Channel in the direction of the north coast of France. When the French coast was clearly in sight and the vast numbers of aircraft and gliders must have been clearly visible to the Germans manning the coastal defences, we turned down the Channel and subsequently back across the English coast to our designated landing zones. It seemed as if we were cocking a snoop at the Germans and saying, 'Watch our chums, we shall be along shortly,' and was made possible by the complete ascendancy in the air which had by then been established by the allied air forces over the Luftwaffe.

Attention to the importance of physical fitness was unflagging, with every officer, warrant officer, non-commissioned officer and man, including cooks and clerks, required to undertake a six mile cross-country run at least once each week, and returns to that effect having to be made to brigade HQ. Who checked on brigade HQ was not disclosed but presumably Monty himself. Close liaison with other units continued and short periods of attachment were arranged for both officers and other ranks with the American airborne divisions, and groups from those divisions joined us for short periods.

A high standard of discipline was insisted upon at all times. Any officer or man found guilty of anything other than a minor offence was immediately dispatched from the division, the justification for this being that if he couldn't be relied upon to observe the rules in what were peaceful conditions, he wouldn't be likely to do so in the stress of battle. This might have seemed a way out for the faint hearted, but there was never any evidence to that effect; the opposite in fact. Discipline was of a very high order, and serious crime, such as absence without leave, was almost non-existent.

The importance of health and medical care were not overlooked. All ranks were reminded again and again of the importance of good hygiene and personal cleanliness; never to miss an opportunity for a 'shit, shave and shampoo.' Repeated instruction was given on the use of the field dressing which every man carried, and in the application of tourniquets and splints. The regimental aid post of each battalion was commanded by a qualified medical officer, with trained medical orderlies and stretcher bearers, but their scope for medical attention was limited and the best they could hope to do for casualties was to administer painkilling drugs such as morphine and to keep casualties alive until they could be transported back to an advance dressing station where surgical operations and similar sophisticated treatment was available.

I have no recollections of guidance being given as regards sexual activity in strange places; maybe, as adjutant, I was left out. Condoms had always been made available at 2d. or 3d. a time, and were in high demand, particularly when troops were going off on leave and to catch a 'dose' was a military offence which could be serious for an officer or NCO, being looked upon as a 'self inflicted wound.' Catching a dose of 'crabs' was embarrassing perhaps, but not so serious, as it didn't involve any loss of duty time!

In addition to all these tasks, special refresher sessions were run for specialist groups in the use of radio codes which, hopefully, would prevent the enemy listening in to our radio communications and thereby finding out where we were, what we were doing, and intending to do. No doubt in certain circumstances this was of value, but in the situations in which we were to find ourselves, there was frequently too little time to bother about encoding and decoding messages when immediate action was called for, and in any event, German radio operators would have some difficulty understanding messages transmitted in broad Belfast or cockney accents.

The month of May was marked by a series of visits and inspections by top brass, including General Boy Browning, the Commander of the Airborne Forces; the 'colonel' of the regiment and previous colonels of the battalion who had moved on to higher rank in the War Office and elsewhere, and, ultimately, by HM King George together with Queen Elizabeth, Princess Elizabeth and Princess Margaret. The most impressive visit of all, however, was that by General Montgomery — as he then was — the Commander in Chief of all the D-Day landing forces.

After his tremendous military successes in Africa and Italy, it had given us considerable satisfaction to learn that Monty would be in command, but even that satisfaction was greatly enhanced by his visit one day in May, 1944. We were paraded in two ranks to form three sides of a square with each rank facing inwards about ten yards apart to form a laneway through which he walked, slowly looked at each man to the left and to the right as if to ensure that he knew us and we knew him. Instead of being dressed in the formal attire usually adopted by visiting generals, he appeared exactly as we had seen numerous pictures of him in the desert. Corduroy trousers, battle dress jacket, web belt around his waist and the airborne forces' maroon beret on his head bearing the Parachute Regiment badge. After walking through the ranks he went back up the hill, climbed onto the bonnet of a jeep and then waved to everybody to gather round to hear what he had to say. There was a mad rush to get as near the jeep as possible, and a complete lack of formality, but I am sure that there had never been such an informal assembly of the battalion with everybody so completely hushed to hear every word that came from his lips.

It was the usual speech which we knew he had made on numerous occasions to other battalions, but it suffered in no way from repetition. We were 'the cream of the British Army' and there was no doubt that we were going to 'hit the Germans for six' right out of France and occupied Europe. However, he warned that there was to be hard fighting ahead but that he had no intention of asking us or any other unit of the invasion force to take on anything which he was not completely confident we could achieve. The effect was electrifying. After three cheers called for by our commanding officer, Hank Carson, Monty departed with his entourage, leaving behind a battalion which was not only well trained and well equipped, but which was also quite confident of success under his command.

It was about this time, towards the end of May, that I, as adjutant of the battalion, received a thick official booklet, marked

'OPERATION OVERLORD' and 'TOP SECRET.' This set out all the administrative detail which had to be complied with before and for our move to the concentration areas. There was no indication as to the precise location of the areas, or when the move would take place, but all preparations had to be completed by, I think, 25 May. This particular booklet related only to the Air Landing Brigade, but it gave me a glimpse of the enormous administrative detail which had to be worked out, covering all the invasion forces then assembling in the South of England. After consultation with the commanding officer and the second in command it was my job to extract all the details applicable to our battalion which then had to be communicated by battalion orders to the company commanders and others responsible.

This was a particularly busy time for everybody, but as luck would have it, I suddenly developed a lump on the side of my face which became very inflamed and painful. I decided to pay an unofficial visit to our medical officer, Captain Dai Rees, to get him to take a look. He prodded my lump around a few times, then extracted a very sharp looking scalpel from his tool kit and told me to lay my head on the table, lump uppermost. This I did. A quick stab followed by a squeeze and a piece of plaster, and he pronounced me fit for the invasion! Several years later Dai Rees became a highly qualified surgeon, while I still carry the scar of one of his first operations.

All personal possessions not essential for operational purposes had to be packed, labelled and disposed of, either by consignment to one's home or to a hut specifically set aside for the purpose. It was unavoidable that after several years moving around various locations in England, individuals had accumulated numerous surplus items of clothing, electric heaters, primus stoves, small radios, bicycles, books and anything else which could be used during times of relaxation, which were going to be few and far between during the coming months.

One problem peculiar to an airborne unit is that a number of people such as the quartermasters' clerks and others do not fly on operations, but follow up later by whatever means available, in this instance, by sea. They would bring with them all clothing and equipment which we wouldn't carry with us but which we might need if our stay was longer than anticipated; and assuming that we were still alive and in need of it. All these items had to be packed into our army packs and consigned to our 'rear echelon'. So, we were then left with only the clothing, supplies and equipment we would take with us to our concentration area, or transit camp as it became known, and with us in our gliders and which we hoped would sustain us until our 'rear echelon' caught up with us, wherever.

There was, of course, no secrecy about the fact that an invasion of Europe by allied forces would shortly take place. For weeks, the roads around Bulford and the surrounding area had been choked with military traffic heading for the South and South West. All unit signs and emblems had been removed from uniforms and vehicles to reduce the risk of giving any information as to the allied order of battle. Forty years later, Huw Wheldon presented a TV programme about the allied counter-intelligence operation put into effect before D-Day to keep the German High Command guessing as to 'where and when' the invasion would take place. The same question was exercising our minds, but I'm sure that we weren't as worried about it as the Germans.

And so, the days passed quickly, until 25 May, when we were ready to go, and on that day we received our orders to implement the planned move to our transit camp. Our 'rear echelon', under our quartermaster, Captain Billie Beattie, who would be bringing along our reserves of clothing and other supplies, would be travelling by sea, and moved off to a camp on the South coast, while a very disconsolate E Company, under Major Gerald Rickord, was left behind at Bulford, ready to send out reinforcements when needed.

As we drove along the narrow roads of Wiltshire and Berkshire we gained some small appreciation of the immensity of the operation being put into motion. Columns of tanks of all shapes and sizes, troop-carrying vehicles, supply lorries, ambulances, artillery, all heading in the opposite direction to us, and enormous dumps of ammunition and supplies stacked up in woods and other areas where they were concealed from the air.

Our transit camps had been set up close to the airfields from which we would take off, and for the 6th Airlanding Brigade, were at Broadwell, Blakehill Farm and Down Ampney in Oxfordshire. Our battalion was split between Broadwell and Blakehill Farm, with the main body, including battalion headquarters, at Broadwell. The camp at Broadwell was located in a field close to Broadwell RAF station. The camp consisted of numerous rows of white bell tents, two or three large white marquees, and a line of semi-permanent ablution facilities including toilets and showers. At one end of the site was a large hut of solid construction which was kept under constant guard, and we were soon to learn the reason why. It contained a scale model of a stretch of coastline about twenty miles long and stretching about the same distance inland, and including, in miniature, every detail imaginable. Towns, villages, houses, churches, farms, roads, tracks, rivers and streams, canals, railways, telegraph poles, fields, hedges, tall trees and short trees, and all in their natural colours, exactly as would be seen from the air, which was the way we were going to see it. We were not informed of the area which the model portrayed until a day or so before D-Day, but I suppose that anyone who knew the area, which included the River Orne and the Orne Canal, could have identified it. Hence the need for strict security.

The camp was surrounded by a high chain link fence with a single gateway controlled by security guards, and we were told that once inside there was no going out without very good reason. The camp commandant and staff were from the Airborne Forces Depot, and the attention which had been paid to the administrative details and requirements of the camp and its occupants was first class in every respect. We had brought with us only essential supplies and equipment for the airborne assault operation, but all other requirements for an extended stay had been anticipated, including not only cooks, cooking equipment, food, beds, bedding, but also all manner of sports and recreational gear for use when we were not preoccupied with planning and other necessary preparations. The was a NAAFI tent with supplies of beer and cigarettes and other essentials, and although we knew that we were confined within the camp until 'OVERLORD' was launched, and this might be a matter of days or even weeks, there was never any sign of discontent or frustration. Fortunately, the weather was fine.

I'm not exactly sure when our commanding officer, Lieutenant Colonel Hank Carson received his orders, but shortly after our arrival at the camp all officers were called to a meeting around the model in the briefing hut and were given a broad outline of the objectives set for the division and how these fitted in to the overall plan for the invasion. At the same time, maps

201

were issued of the assault area and distributed to company commanders, but on these maps all actual place names had been replaced by imaginary English names so that the terrain could be studied without disclosing the names of the actual places involved. All these maps had to be kept in the briefing hut, and times were allocated when company commanders and their subordinates could make use of the hut, the model and the maps in order to familiarize themselves with the area without, at that time, knowing precisely what their objectives were going to be. Later, we were provided with aerial photographs which, when viewed through an epidiascope, provided an almost uncanny three-dimensional view of the countryside in which we would be operating, and in such detail that one had a sense of being on the ground and looking at the fields and hedges, gateways, trees, farm buildings and farm animals grazing in the fields from only a few yards away. The only difficulty that I, and I think that the others had, was to realize that in a short time all this peace and tranquillity would be rudely interrupted by us and that a knowledge of those fields and hedgerows might well become a matter of life or death for ourselves and many others.

Gradually, over the next few days, the broad outline of the total operation was explained, and followed by precise orders given as to the objectives of the battalion and each company, platoon and section, until every man knew what was expected of him and his comrades and how this fitted into the task assigned to the division. However, it was not until the day or so before 5 June — the date originally set for the invasion — that the picture was completed, and we were told where all this was going to take place and that the area we were required to seize and hold was the high ground to the east of the River Orne in Normandy. I'm quite sure that until that time, very few, if any of us, had ever heard of the River Orne or of a small village called Longueval with which we were going to become very familiar.

Our spell at Broadwell was marred by a tragic accident which caused the death of an officer and a sergeant, and injuries, some serious, to a company commander and a number of others. This happened on 1 June.

At the time, I was sitting in the briefing hut attending to some battalion headquarter business, when I heard a loud thump somewhere in the vicinity. I got up and walked to the door and looking out, saw a large cloud of black smoke rising above one of the tents about fifty yards from where I was standing. Obviously there had been some form of explosion, so I called out to Corporal Hooper, who was in the hut with me, not to leave the hut unattended, and hurried across to the lines of tents from where the smoke was still rising. As I approached I heard the regimental sergeant major, RSM Griffiths, shouting, 'Keep clear, keep clear,' and then saw a number of bodies lying near a tent which was badly torn and smoking in several places. Two of the recumbent bodies were obviously badly mutilated, but I recognized Lieutenant Theo Seale, a platoon commander, and his platoon sergeant, Sergeant Dwyer. Almost immediately Captain Rees, the medical officer, arrived, and despite the obvious risk to his own safety, walked up to the body of Sergeant Dwyer and kneeling down, placed his finger on Dwyer's neck to check his pulse. After a moment he walked the few paces to Theo Seale and did the same. He then called over two stretcher bearers who were being restrained by the RSM, and turning to me said that Dwyer was dead. Theo Seale was still alive but he didn't give much for his chances. By this time, several others who were wounded were being carried or helped away from the scene, and the RSM was leading a small group, combing the area for detonators.

A particular problem was the disposal of a number of grenades scattered near the point of the explosion and the uncertainty as to whether they had been primed, in which case probably made sensitive by the blast. Not without considerable risk to the men involved, these were collected and removed by the pioneer platoon for disposal by controlled explosion at a safe place and away from the tented area. The body of Sergeant Dwyer and all the injured personnel were taken by military ambulance to a special security wing established at a hospital, I believe in Oxford. The injured included Major Tom Warner, the commander of B Company, and the next day we heard that Theo Seale had died. The same day Gerald Rickord arrived to take command of B Company, together with replacements for all the other casualties. Although the deaths of two popular and capable members of the battalion were deeply regretted by everyone, particularly the circumstances of their deaths, the morale of the troops was in no way diminished; if anything, the opposite. The loss of friends had to be expected in the days ahead, but was something for which the Germans would have to pay a heavy price.

From statements made by witnesses, there was little doubt as to the cause of the accident. Theo Seale, together with Sergeant Dwyer and several other men of the platoon, had been priming their grenades. These were metal box-like weapons about the size of a brick, which were primed by sliding a detonator into an aperture on one side so that when pressure was applied, the detonator fired and exploded the grenade. Sergeant Dwyer had been squatting on his haunches at the time. After priming a grenade, he had pushed it behind himself, and reached for another. As he did so, he overbalanced and sat on the first grenade, causing it to explode, with fatal results for himself and his platoon commander. I felt particularly bad about Theo, who I had known since my time in the regimental depot at Ballymena in 1940. He had joined the regiment as a volunteer at that time and had quickly been identified as a potential officer and placed in the cadet platoon. His sister was an officer in the ATS at the depot, and I could only reflect sadly on the tragic telegram which his parents in Portadown would shortly receive.

On 4 June we were told that Operation Overlord had been put back from 5 June until 6 June because of adverse weather conditions in the Channel. I had no recollection that this caused any undue anxiety, although some of us realized that it would mean an uncomfortable twenty-four hours for those unfortunate enough to have put to sea before the deferment had been decided. Letters had been written, collected and censored, to be delivered after the operation was underway, so the time was spent sitting around in the sunshine we were still enjoying, playing games, and with final visits to the briefing hut for more familiarization around the model with the hedgerows and ditches we were shortly to occupy.

The morning of 5 June was bright and sunny, and it was with considerable relief that we heard that the operation was definitely on for the following day. Whilst a delay of twenty-four hours was acceptable, all ranks were undoubtedly anxious to get going and any further delay could have had an adverse effect on morale. By this time, all jeeps, trailers and trolleys had been packed, weapons and ammunition checked and rechecked, 'compo' rations and 'escape' packets issued, maps marked up with the latest information and an extra packet of cigarettes stowed away wherever space could be found.

The time passed very quickly, and in the evening a number of us were transported to the nearby Broadwell airfield to give our friends in the 9th Parachute Battalion a send off on their way to destroy the German gun battery at Merville. There was no lack of good cheer as we stood around chatting to the parachutists, looking like hunchbacks with their parachute packs on their backs, and I recollect shaking hands with Mike Dowling, who had left us to join the 9th Battalion only a few months earlier, and who was to be killed that night, only a matter of seconds after reporting to his commanding officer, Terence Otway, also an Ulster Rifleman, that the last gun in the Merville battery had been destroyed. Photographs of Mike and many others killed on that operation now hang in the museum established in one of the gun emplacements to commemorate their bravery and devotion to duty.

It was at Broadwell on that occasion that I first saw that all the aircraft had wide black and white stripes painted around the wings and fuselage. The same applied to the gliders we were to use and to all other allied aircraft, as an easy means of identifying friend from foe.

After we had seen the last plane roar down the runway we returned to the camp in a somewhat subdued mood. This was IT. The operation we had been training for and waiting for, was now underway. In a little over an hour, the *coup de main* glider parties of the 52nd — Sandy Smith, Dennis Fox, Dan Brotheridge, with whom we had spent many a convivial evening — would be swooping silently down to seize the vital bridges over the river and the canal, while thousands of parachutists would be dropping into the peaceful Normandy countryside, determined to capture and hold the objectives allotted to them. Would the landings be successful — at the right place and at the right time? We were well aware of the hazards of such an enormous night-time operation. Would the all important element of surprise be achieved, or would the Germans be waiting? What was in store for us the following afternoon? Our thoughts were also with the thousands of assault troops who would be storming up the Normandy beaches before sunrise the following morning and of the American airborne landings at the western end of the front.

I remember going to bed that night and thinking that I would have difficulty sleeping, but, to my surprise, when I woke up the following morning, I realized that I had had a very good night's sleep. This was just as well because the opportunity for anything more than a couple of hours' kip over the following weeks would be few and far between.

D-Day — 6 June 1944

The morning of 6 June was again bright and sunny, and began with a voluntary nondenominational service conducted by our padre, the Rev. McM. Taylor and attended by every officer and man in the battalion. There was no doubt that the hymn singing and the responses to the prayers he said were much more fervent than on a normal Sunday service. During the morning the few radios available were set up so that the troops could listen to the brief announcements that allied forces had landed on the Normandy coast, and that everything was going according to plan, news that was treated with some scepticism and the comment that 'they could hardly say anything else.' However, greater credulity was given to a message from our brigade headquarters that the airborne landings had been successful.

After an early midday meal, the glider-loading parties left for the airfield with our jeeps, trailers and trolleys. These were the people specially trained in the technique for loading and securing vehicles and heavy equipment in the gliders. Flights and landings could be bumpy and every precaution had to be taken against the risk of vehicles breaking loose. The rest of the battalion sat around in their shirt sleeves, smoking, chatting, playing cards and drinking the ample supplies of tea made available from the cookhouse: jackets, smocks, steel helmets — the peculiar inverted pot shape designed for airborne troops and covered with strips of hessian camouflage — equipment and personal weapons laid out ready to be struggled into as soon as the time came to move. Each man also had a small camouflage net, which was worn as a cravat or scarf and a yellow triangle of nylon to facilitate identification by friendly aircraft. Our maroon airborne berets were tucked away in our haversacks for use when circumstances permitted. In the early evening, I think about five pm, a column of troop-carrying vehicles arrived to convey the rest of the battalion from the transit camp to the airfield on the second stage of our journey to Normandy.

All the gliders, about fifty Horsas, each with its distinguishing black and white stripes around the wings and fuselage, were drawn up in two tightly packed lines at the extremity of the main runway, looking to me like a gigantic fishbone from which all the flesh had been removed. The tow ropes attached to the nose of each glider were laid out in perfect line in the centre of the runway. The procedure was for the tug aircraft to approach the gliders along the approach runways on either side of the main runway, then, in turn from left and right, to swing in onto the main runway. The next tow rope would be quickly attached to the tail of the tug aircraft, a signal given and away it would go, with the next tug swinging into position before its predecessor was fifty yards down the runway. It was important for the build-up and maintenance of tight formations in the air that the combinations of tug aircraft and glider be got away in the shortest possible time, and the RAF were to be congratulated on the skill with which this was achieved.

In a short time all the gliders were reported fully loaded and ready for take-off, after which we stood around drinking more tea provided by the local Women's Volunteer Service and similar organizations. Much use was made of the temporary latrines thoughtfully provided by the RAF until the order was given to emplane, and everyone climbed aboard his allotted glider. Each man wore a sort of makeshift Mae-West, always provided when a flight was to take place over the sea. This looked like the rubber inner tube of a motor cycle tyre with a few straps attached and was worn around the chest with instructions to blow hard into the valve to inflate the tube if a forced landing in water appeared imminent. To what extent these would have helped a fully laden man to stay afloat, I don't know.

In my glider we carried a jeep and trolley loaded in the centre of the fuselage. I was in the front immediately behind the partition between the main fuselage and the pilot's flight deck, together with my batman, Rifleman Gillanders, a signaller, Rifleman Martin, and two riflemen of the intelligence section. At the rear, behind the vehicles, were another five members of battalion HQ. I was able to watch the take-off procedure through the doorway into the flight deck. As soon as the preceding aircraft began to move away down the runway, I saw our tug aircraft swing into position in front of us. The free end of our tow-rope was quickly fixed to the attachment on its tail, and the slack was gradually taken up until with a slight jerk we were on our way. Quickly, we gathered speed, the characteristic rumble of the undercarriage on the tarmac increasing in intensity, and then a sudden hush, the only sound being the whistle of air past the fuselage as the pilot lifted the glider off the runway and we were airborne above our tug aircraft. I saw the tug then lift off slightly, then drop back, then begin to climb away in the wake of the long line of aircraft and gliders ahead.

It was a bright and sunny afternoon, but with a fair amount of scattered cloud. I don't know the route we took from Broadwell, but after about ten or fifteen minutes' flying we merged with other formations which had left from Blakehill Farm and Down Ampney until there were tugs and gliders ahead of us, to the right and left of us, and presumably, behind us, which must have been a most impressive sight from the ground. I have no personal recollections of fear or apprehension, but rather of excitement and exhilaration, and from time to time had to convince myself that within the hour we would be landing in enemy-held country. My fellow passengers seemed equally unconcerned with the momentous events taking place at the time, as we sat smoking and chatting on the hard wooden seats provided for our comfort. I have a very clear recollection of Gillanders, my batman, fast asleep with his chin on his chest and his arms folded for the entire journey. From time to time I stood in the doorway to the flight deck talking to the two pilots and admiring the skill with which they kept station behind the tug aircraft. Occasionally we passed through cloud which resulted in slight turbulence, particularly when the tug aircraft would disappear for a few seconds and then the glider would appear to be enveloped in cotton wool, and after emerging the pilot would have to adjust his position behind the tug, but this presented little or no problem. Soon, I could see below the coast as the great armada of aircraft headed south over the Channel, on the same lines as we had a few weeks earlier during Exercise Mush, but this time there was to be no turning back.

The time passed quickly. I saw the leading aircraft change direction to the west, down the Channel, and looking up saw and was much impressed by the sight of a large group of fighter aircraft obviously shepherding us on our way and keeping a sharp look-out for any enemy planes that might attempt to interfere with our progress. I saw no sign of enemy aircraft throughout the flight. I could see the French coast to our left, but as we were flying into the sun visibility was hazy, and it was quite startling when an incredible sight suddenly came into view; literally hundreds of ships spread out on the sea below. We had reached the main sea-borne landing force, and what a sight it was! Large ships and small ships, stretching as far as the eye could see; some moving at high speed and others apparently anchored with the small shapes of landing craft leaving a white wash behind them as they carried troops and supplies into the beaches. A series of dull thumps drew my gaze back to the pilot and then in the direction he was pointing and I realized that I had heard the guns of a large battleship almost immediately below.

It was then that we turned in towards the coast and in a few minutes I had no difficulty in recognizing the mouth of the River Orne and the nearby canal, a sight with which I had become familiar through the model back in Broadwell. We crossed the coast and flew along the line of the river, clearly visible to our left, and I recall being surprised and relieved that there was no sign of enemy anti-aircraft fire or other opposition to our progress. As I turned to remove my Mae-West, the pilot called out 'Five minutes to go.'

I relayed the message to the others in the rear of the glider, and we prepared ourselves for landing, opening the sliding door of the glider to facilitate quick exit and buckling-up our equipment and helmets and doing up our seat belts.

'Casting off,' called the pilot, and I heard the clonk as he pulled the tow rope release lever, and felt the nose go down as we began our glide into the landing zone. Leaning forward, I suddenly saw streaks of light flashing past the nose of the glider and I realized that this was ack-ack fire from the ground. We took up our landing positions, with arms around one another's necks to help cushion any impact, and waited — with a prayer for a safe landing. Suddenly, the familiar crunch and rumble as the landing gear touched the ground. On and on we seemed to go as the pilot fought to steer the glider away from the line required for following gliders and then we were still.

'Under fire,' shouted the pilot, and we all released our seatbelts and dived for the door, jumping the four or five feet to the ground and then taking up the defensive positions previously rehearsed so often. This was the normal drill to fight off any immediate attack. However, I could see no signs of the green-grey German uniform but only groups of khaki-clad men standing around nearby gliders and unloading their equipment, and realized that we were not under any immediate threat, so shouted to my men to start unloading and everybody sprang into action. This involved disconnecting the tail of the glider and pulling down the metal troughs so that we could run the trolley and jeep down to the ground. As usual, disconnecting the tail caused a little delay, but in no time we were ready to move off. We had arrived, and it was interesting later to hear that of the 145 gliders which took off from England that 6 June evening, all but two landed safely on the correct landing zones. One glider was hit by mortar fire after landing and was burned out.

Before we left our glider to make our way to the battalion rendezvous, I was able to shake hands with our pilots and to thank them for a 'happy landing' before they left for their RV to return to England to prepare for their next operation. I always regret not remembering their names. As I looked around I could see groups from other gliders making their way across to the narrow track leading to Ranville. So far as I could see and thanks to the parachutists who had preceded us, there had been little opposition to our landing and I assumed that the ack-ack fire I had seen had come from isolated German positions over which we had flown. Again, I had to shake myself a little to realize that we were now on French soil and the battle was about to begin. The only other thing I can remember is seeing a number of parachute canopies hanging in nearby trees and thinking to myself that I hoped the parachutists concerned had been able to climb down without injury. Our immediate rendezvous was the village of Ranville and I led our group across to join the others who were making their way in that direction.

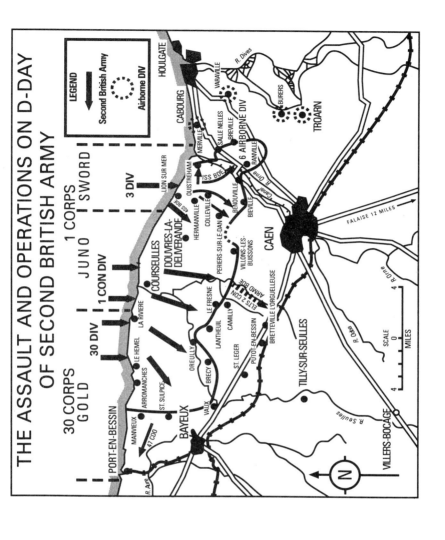

THE ASSAULT AND OPERATIONS ON D-DAY
OF SECOND BRITISH ARMY

LEGEND

Second British Army

Airborne DIV

30 CORPS
GOLD

1 CORPS

JUNO
SWORD

30 DIV   1 CON DIV   3 DIV

PORT-EN-BESSIN

MANVIEUX

47 CDO

ARROMANCHES

ST. SULPICE

LE HEMEL

LA RIVIERE

COURSEULLES

DOUVRES-LA-DELIVERANDE

LION SUR MER

OUISTREHAM

HERMANVILLE

COLLEVILLE

PERIERS-SUR-LE-DAN

VILLONS-LES-BUISSONS

LE FRESNE

ELLIS 2 CDN ARMD BDE

LANTHEUIL

CAMILLY

ST. LEGER

PUTOT-EN-BESSIN

BRETTEVILLE L'ORGUEILLEUSE

OREULLY

BRECY

VAUX

BAYEUX

R. Aure

VILLERS-BOCAGE

R. Seulles

TILLY-SUR-SEULLES

R. Odon

R. Orne

FALAISE 12 MILES

CAEN

Canal R. Orne

BENOUVILLE

BIEVILLE

RANVILLE

6 AIRBORNE DIV

ISS BDE

ASS BDE

3DE BDE

MERVILLE

SALLE NELLES

BREVILLE

CABOURG

HOULGATE

VARAVILLE

R. Dives

BURERS

TROARN

SCALE

MILES

4   0   4

N

7

The Battle in Normandy

Longueval

During our briefing, prior to leaving England, it had been explained that the task of the 6th Airborne Division was to seize and hold the bridges over the River Orne and the Caen Canal at Ranville and Benouville and the high ground to the east of the river, to secure the left flank of the invasion forces and thereby eliminate the risk of interference with the seaborne landings from that direction. We had to hold this ground, we were instructed, until relieved by the forces landing from the sea. If the high ground to the east of the Orne was available to the enemy it would have had disastrous results for the troops landing across the beaches west of the river; the 3rd British Division. Once these objectives had been secured there could be no question of withdrawal, once we were there we were there to stay, dead or alive, and naturally we preferred the latter possibility. A company of the Ox and Bucks would be landing during the night of 5-6 June by glider to seize the two bridges. This would be followed by the two parachute brigades, one of whose tasks would be to clear the areas on the east bank of the river where we would be landing on the evening of 6 June and where the Germans had erected obstructions to impede glider landings. The success of our operation was largely due to the efforts of the parachute battalions combined with the skill of the glider pilots of the Glider Pilot Regiment.

Our battalion's orders were to rendezvous after landing and then to move to the village of Ranville — by that time hopefully captured by our parachutists — and that our task then would probably be to move south and seize the villages of Longueval and St Honorine and to prevent any enemy forces moving up to the bridges from the south east. Longueval is a small village on the east bank of the river Orne, about eight miles inland from the coast. St Honorine was another small village about two miles due east of Longueval. A final decision about attacking and securing these two villages would depend on the situation on the ground after our arrival.

After landing and unloading our gliders our first task therefore was to rendezvous near the landing zone. We had landed in exactly the designated position and thanks to the excellence of the model we had studied back in England and to our aerial photographs and maps we had no difficulty in moving to the rendezvous area. Alongside our landing zone was a narrow roadway, not much more than a farm track and I well remember, as we moved towards Ranville, seeing my first German soldiers. They were lying in the long grass beside the track, both very dead, and lying in grotesque positions, presumably having been surprised by our comrades in one of the parachute battalions the previous night. After some delay near Ranville I managed to contact the CO, who informed me that he was going to brigade headquarters at Ranville Château and that battalion headquarters should be established in a farmhouse in the middle of the village with our four rifle companies and supporting troops deployed in the immediate vicinity. The battalion HQ personnel from other gliders had now joined us. Together with Dai Rees, the medical officer, we made our way to the village and into the yard of a large rambling farmhouse. There was no sign of the occupants so we set up battalion headquarters in the large farmhouse kitchen where our two radio operators, Rifleman Martin and Rifleman Flynn, made contact with each of the four companies who reported themselves as being in their required positions. The RSM had posted sentries in the immediate vicinity of our location, and we sat down to await further orders.

By this time it was dark and I remember being surprised at the complete lack of local inhabitants and assumed that they had all departed when the landings had started the previous night or were hiding away to await developments. In no time I appreciated the value of a good batman when Rifleman Gillanders provided me with a mess tin of hot sweet tea. In fact

213

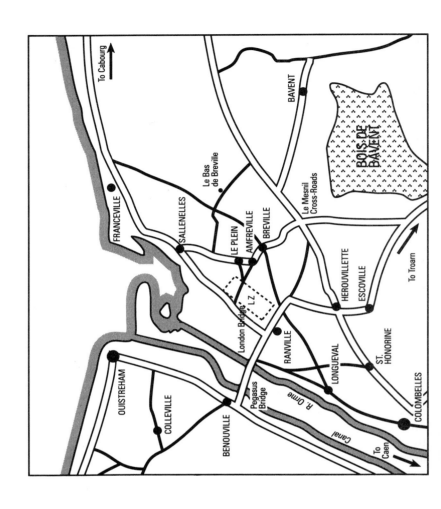

Area of operations
6th Airborne Division 6 June — 17 August 1944

214

the whole atmosphere was not dissimilar to the many exercises we had carried out over previous years, other than the thought that at any moment we might be subjected to an enemy attack which would be for real, and without impartial umpires. However, for the time being there was no sound of rifle fire, no shelling or mortaring; in fact all was peace and quiet and strangely unreal. I wondered what the Germans were doing and had a mental picture of Marshal Rommel and his bemedalled generals standing around his map table somewhere around, each deciding how we would be driven back into the sea the following day.

I suppose it was about eleven o'clock when the CO returned, accompanied by John Drummond, our second-in-command. John had had the extraordinary experience of taking off in a glider which was forced to land because of a broken tow rope before crossing the English coast. He managed to get back to the airfield, how I don't know, in time to thumb a lift in another glider which was more successful and delivered him safely, if somewhat later than intended.

At that time, our entire battalion was concentrated around a cluster of houses in the southern outskirts of Ranville — Le Bas de Ranville — and we had suffered only one casualty, a man having been wounded by mortar fire on the landing zone — far less than we had suffered from accidental causes during our many months of training in England. At battalion HQ in our farmhouse kitchen we were in touch by radio with each of the four company headquarters and immediately Hank and John arrived back all the company commanders, together with specialist platoon commanders (or O group as they were known), were called to battalion HQ to receive their orders. The atmosphere was very cheerful, with much hand shaking and cheerful banter about gliders and their eccentricities, and much praise for the skill of the members of the Glider Pilot Regiment who had delivered us to the right places and at the right time and in one piece. However, the atmosphere quickly became serious as the CO outlined the present situation of the division.

During D-Day and the preceding night everything had gone more or less according to plan, but there was no doubt that a very tough time lay ahead over the next few days. Units of the division were in position around the bridgehead protecting the crossings over the Caen river and canal, a position which had to be held at all costs until relieving troops arrived. The CO went on to explain that, according to the latest information, the Germans were in possession of both Longueval and St Honorine, and that the provisional plan for the battalion to attack and capture both these villages would probably be put into effect at daybreak. Further orders on this were expected from brigade later. In the meantime, C Company would move out of Ranville and would seize and occupy the high ground between Ranville and St Honorine, identified as Ring Contour 30. Sections of the machine gun platoon under Harry Morgan and of the mortar platoon under Lieutenant Hanna would be under their command.

The CO then reviewed the orders given in England with regard to the attack on these two villages with the added information that the battalion would be supported by some field artillery and naval gun support for the attack on St Honorine. Then followed a short session of question and answer from which it was obvious that minds were becoming quickly reconciled to the realities of the situation.

It was particularly important to know the precise location of the regimental aid post because casualties would no longer be designated by umpires, but would be men torn apart by red hot shrapnel or bleeding from gunshot wounds or with feet or legs shattered by antipersonnel mines and whose lives might well depend on immediate medical attention. All serious casualties would have to be evacuated to the division casualty station in Ranville where surgical relief might be possible, but in the circumstances in which we were to find ourselves, getting casualties back was no easy task, particularly at night in country where one was just as likely to run into enemy patrol as into our own troops. We had no ambulance of course, only jeeps which could carry two stretchers across the bonnets for the seriously wounded. Less time was spent in dealing with the problem of disposal of prisoners; a matter which was now a reality and not make-believe. I never really did discover what happened to our prisoners. After a quick interrogation when we thought we might gain some information which would be of immediate use, particularly in the case of captured warrant officers or NCOs, they were sent back to the POW cage, wherever that was, under arrangements made by the regimental sergeant major.

When the company commanders had left to return to their respective companies, the few of us left in our kitchen settled down to get whatever rest was possible. The only light we had was from two oil-fired hurricane lamps which the battalion HQ staff had somehow or other carried with them in their trolley, presumably filled with paraffin oil. These were certainly not itemized in our normal equipment but, as in many other ways, regular soldiers always seemed to be able to produce what was necessary at the right time, whether or not included in our official list of equipment and supplies.

In addition to the CO, Hank Carson and the second in command, John Drummond, there was myself and Tim Dooley, the signals officer, and Robin Crockett, the intelligence officer. Also with us were our batmen and the CO's driver, three battalion headquarter clerks, two signallers with their radio equipment and somewhere in the vicinity the six members of the intelligence section. On that and subsequent nights, Robin, Tim and I would take turns as duty officer to allow the others to get some rest whilst the batmen, intelligence section personnel, drivers and clerks took turns in providing sentries around the battalion HQ location.

In the early hours of the morning we heard from Bob Hynds that C Company was in position on Ring Contour 30 and at about the same time a message was received from brigade HQ that the attack on Longueval and St Honorine would go ahead at dawn.

7 June, 1940

Before dawn on 7 June, we were on the road ready to move off. The leading companies, A and B, had already moved out of Ranville to their start lines for the attack on Longueval. Battalion HQ was to move behind D Company, which had the task of supporting A Company to the initial attack, and then moving through A Company to secure the village, including the southern outskirts in the direction of Caen. The intention was that after securing Longueval A and B Companies would then swing east to attack St Honorine, supported by fire from C Company from Ring Contour 30. While it was still dark and we were on a clearly defined but narrow road we kept our vehicles and personnel close together.

Away to the right I could hear the rumble of gunfire coming from the beachhead area at Ouistreham but in our area there were no sounds of enemy activity whilst the darkness continued. However, as visibility gradually improved with the breaking of dawn there was a sudden burst of shell and mortar fire from our left where C Company were located. We subsequently learned that after digging themselves in during the night some of the positions selected were clearly visible from the direction of St Honorine and from where the Germans subjected them to heavy gun and mortar fire. It was at this time that Huw Wheldon won his MC by showing a complete disregard for his own safety when encouraging the men of C Company to relocate themselves in more secure positions despite the German fire.

Whilst it was dark our progress seemed to be slow but with increasing daylight D Company moved ahead very quickly and I suddenly found myself with battalion headquarters and elements of the antitank platoon completely separated and having to make our own way forward to the outskirts of Longueval.

By this time, the roadway we were following had deteriorated into a narrow track which veered away to the right and down towards the River Orne. We were on the brow of a hill with a very extensive view of the countryside to the west where, we hoped, the British 3rd Division either were, or would shortly be, in occupation. At that time there were no signs of activity of any sort and my anxiety was that we were very exposed to view from the far side if the Germans were still in occupation, as in fact they were.

Our little column consisted of two or three jeeps of the antitank platoon, each towing an antitank gun, followed by two battalion HQ jeeps and miscellaneous people on foot. I remember shouting to the leading vehicle to move more quickly to get away from the skyline when suddenly there was an almighty crash and the front of the leading jeep seemed to shoot up into the air and flop down on its axle with one wheel completely missing. I ran forward to find out what was happening and discovered that the jeep had run over a '75' antitank grenade buried on the pathway, obviously by the 13th Parachute Battalion who had penetrated as far as Longueval the previous night before being withdrawn. A quick check showed that there were several other grenades buried just below the surface of the track.

Fortunately we had some members of the pioneer platoon in our group and these grenades were quickly lifted.

We soon found ourselves on a better road which ran along the top of the steep bank running down to the river. The houses of Longueval were now well in view and it seemed odd to me that there was no sound of fighting in the village, nor was there any sight of D Company with whom I had completely lost touch.

My first glimpse of Longueval was of the corner of a seven or eight foot high wall with one arm running at a right angle up from the road over the brow of the hill to our left whilst the other arm continued alongside the left hand side of the road along which we were cautiously approaching. We could not see beyond the walled area because of a belt of high trees. Suddenly, and to my surprise, I saw and heard a motor cyclist coming towards us from the village and I recognized the rider as Lieutenant Peter Fogt of the Anti-Tank Platoon. He stopped beside me and smiling broadly said, 'There are no Germans in Longueval.' He then went on to tell me that A and B Companies had quickly passed through the village without meeting any opposition and had now swung round to the left and were preparing to attack St Honorine. I asked him where D Company were and he simply waved in the direction of Longueval and said, 'Somewhere down there.' He also told me that advance battalion HQ, including the CO and the intelligence officer were up on the start-line for the attack at St Honorine. He was going back to inform them of our whereabouts. I decided to move forward and set up our headquarters in the village. Little did I appreciate what awaited us.

We continued along our roadway for another couple of hundred yards or so to where the road swung to the left still parallel to the river and from where part of the village came into view. This consisted of a row of terraced cottages on the left hand side facing towards the river and with a low wall on the right hand side of the road at the top of the river bank. Standing in the doorways of most of these terraced cottages were the local inhabitants, all clapping and cheering and without exception, carrying bottles with glasses or mugs or other drinking receptacles which they proceeded to press on our men as we passed by. I thought at first that the drink they were offering was wine but in fact, of course, it turned out to be that Normandy speciality, Calvados. Whilst a nip of this fiery liquid on a chilly morning might be very welcome, I knew that several glasses on empty stomachs could be disastrous, and I had visions of a small group of drunken Irishmen attempting to repel a German attack up the road from Caen. In certain circumstances perhaps, it might be said that an Irishman fights better when he has had a drink or two but I didn't think that this was such an occasion, and shouting to the NCOs to do the same I ran down the road trying to persuade the locals to keep their liquor for a more appropriate time. They were so enthusiastic with their welcome that I was forced to literally push them back from offering trays of drinks to the men, only succeeding in knocking glasses to the ground and shouting, 'Non, non' which was about fifty per cent of my French vocabulary at the time. However I think they understood and we managed to extricate ourselves from what could have been a difficult situation and moved on down the only village street.

The first thing I wanted to do was to get our battalion HQ set up in some suitable place which was under cover from the far side of the river and so that our signallers could concentrate on getting in radio touch with our advance headquarters and the CO. I eventually decided on an old shed — a chicken house, I think — built on about the only flat spot on the river side of the road. This seemed suitable until we started to dig-in when we discovered that below about an inch of earth was solid rock. However I decided that this would at least do as a temporary base and got our group off the road and under cover. The thought did occur to me to break into one of the small cottages along the side of the road, which appeared to be unoccupied, but due perhaps to lack of battle experience and to typical British reserve, I decided that this wasn't appropriate, particularly as half the village was watching what we were doing.

After a quick word with Tim Dooley, the signals officer, who was still trying to unravel the mysteries of his wireless sets and make contact with advance HQ, I told him that I was going to take a look around the village and, calling my batman Gillanders to come with me, I set off cautiously down the road to the southern end of the village. At that time I had no contact with Tony Dyball commanding D Company, which I discovered later had passed through the village in the direction of Colombelles and Caen.

At any moment I expected to be confronted with the field-grey uniforms of German troops, but there was nobody in sight. At the far end of the village on the left was another high wall with a very wide and substantial looking metal gateway leading obviously to a large house. The gate was locked but peering through an iron grille I could see a driveway swinging away to the left up towards a large château-like building with well-maintained lawns but no other signs of habitation. Beyond the lawns was a low wall and beyond that a dense area of woodland sloping up to the top of the hill. This was to become Dai Rees's regimental aid post. Returning along the road the way we had come I could still see no signs of activity on the far side of the river and the canal.

On the right hand side as we returned there was a narrow lane at right angles to the river and running up into the wooded area on the crest of the hill. On the left of this lane was another high wall, the boundary of the grounds surrounding a pleasant, detached, chalet-type house which we had passed on our left on the way in. As I stood at the bottom of this lane I again heard the sound of a motor cycle and down the hill came Peter Fogt on his 'airborne' motor cycle. He stopped beside me and after switching off his engine said, 'The attack on St Honorine is not going too well.' I asked him if he found the CO and he said that he had just come from him and that he would be joining us in the village shortly, so I decided to return to our temporary headquarters.

Shortly after this Hank Carson came down the lane and along the road towards us in his jeep together with Robin Crockett, our intelligence officer. The first thing he told me was Derek Boustead had been killed. He then went on to say that although A and B Companies had got into St Honorine there had been an immediate strong counter-attack supported by tanks and he had ordered them to withdraw to Longueval. He wasn't sure about casualties but I later discovered that five officers and about sixty other ranks had been wounded and that Reggie Morgan and many others were still missing. He had ordered the four rifle companies to consolidate around Longueval. John Drummond then appeared and instructed me to move back to the chalet-type house at the north end of the village where battalion HQ would be established.

Longueval is situated on the lower slope of a hill overlooking the River Orne and the Caen Canal — only about fifty yards apart at that point — and the flat country beyond, over which we were anxiously awaiting the advance of the 3rd Division. The village is sandwiched between two narrow roads, roughly parallel and about 300 yards apart. One, the lower road along which we had arrived, more or less followed the line of the river, whilst the upper road ran along the higher ground at the top of the hill. Both roads linked Ranville with Colombelles and Caen. Along the river bank itself was a towpath which, on and off for a few days, provided our only link with Ranville and brigade HQ for sending back wounded and prisoners, and collecting supplies. The upper road overlooked to the east the open undulating country, leading down to St Honorine and beyond, and had formed the start line for our unsuccessful attack on that village on 7 June. Between the two roads and immediately above the village were several small fields and orchards and, above them, along the upper road was a strip of dense woods.

The village itself lies mainly along the lower road and at that time consisted of about 200 yards of small, solidly built but somewhat dilapidated looking houses, mixed up with farm buildings and sheds, all looking as if they had seen better times, which they probably had before the German occupation. Surprisingly perhaps, there was no chapel, but there was a small combined café and shop, where, on a visit shortly after the war with Huw Wheldon, I was introduced to an elderly lady called Madame Sheridan. After the First World War, she had married a British army officer of that name; no relation as far as I knew. At opposite ends of the village were two more affluent looking properties, sited in their own grounds. One, the biggest, was situated at the southern end in the direction of Colombelles and which I had peered into on my initial recce and was where Dai Rees established his first RAP in the area occupied by C Company.

The other house where we set up our HQ was at the northern end of the village. The entrance to the property was through heavy wrought iron gates mounted on tall brick pillars set at an angle to the narrow lower road, presumably to facilitate driving in and out. Inside the gates was a gravel driveway of about thirty yards up to the front door of the house, with pathways around each side connecting with a patio area at the rear. Beyond the patio was a pleasant lawn sloping up for about thirty yards to thick woods which extended back for a hundred yards or so to the top of the hill and the upper road. On the left of the lawn was a thick laurel hedge and beyond that more woods extending to one of the boundary walls of the property whilst on the right of the lawn were more trees and another wall alongside the laneway I had noticed earlier connecting the lower and upper roads. On the right of the gravel driveway was a group of sheds and stables where Support Company established its HQ, including elements of the anti-tank, mortar and pioneer platoons. One of these sheds was used as a mortuary during periods when burials were not possible.

When we moved back to this house I assumed that John had already told the occupants, an elderly man and his wife and son, of our intention to move in. Whether they had raised any objection I don't know but they disappeared down into the cellar and we only caught an occasional glimpse of them from time to time. The son was an invalid, and they were most grateful when Dai arranged for him to be evacuated back to England where he would receive the medical care he required. We set up our HQ in a large room in the front of the house, and the care with which we moved furniture and ornaments to make room for our wireless sets and other equipment was no doubt a reflection of our respect for our French allies and the unreality of the situation at that time. Although we had lost a number of officers and men killed, wounded or missing, the only Germans I had seen up to that time had been dead, and I hadn't heard a shot or gun fired in anger other than one of the jeeps running over one of our own grenades. However, this situation wasn't going to last much longer.

From the road in front of our HQ location and looking north or downstream towards the sea, we could see the canal bridge but not the river bridge which was obscured by trees. After watching a German bombing attack on the bridges on the evening of 7 June, we were much relieved to hear the following day that although hit, both were still intact for traffic. Looking south or upstream towards Caen, thick woods extended down to the banks of both the river and the canal, but over the tops of the trees we could clearly see the tall chimneys of the brick factory at Colombelles where, we were to learn later, the Germans had established observation posts more or less looking down into our 'backyard.' Longueval was about eight miles inland from the coast, and the lack of activity on the far side of the river and the canal indicated that the advance inland by the seaborne assault troops had been slower than planned, so our situation was somewhat precarious. It was difficult to understand why the Germans had withdrawn from Longueval without a fight as it turned out to be a key position for the defence of Ranville and the bridgehead.

Digging in was the first priority, as we had no illusions as to what would happen as soon as the Germans appreciated our position. Appropriate sites having been selected to provide the all-round protection we required, all set-to working in pairs, all wielding their entrenching tools with great vigour to provide themselves with below-ground-level cover while the going was good and we didn't know how long that would be. We knew that the enemy was in St Honorine in strength, with tanks, and we had no doubt that a major attack towards the bridges would not be long delayed in an effort to eliminate the bridgehead secured by the division before support arrived from the beaches.

By early evening our companies were in position around the village with the exception of part of C Company who had not yet arrived from Ring Contour 30. We heard later that they had been held up by heavy mortar fire on the towpath between us and Ranville. With our backs to the river, we had B Company on our left with forwards positions up to the upper road. In the woods on our immediate front was the Recce Platoon, under Robin Rigby, linking up with A Company to the right of the laneway dividing the battalion area, and with C Company securing the right flank including the lower road where the regimental aid post was established, and the river bank. D Company was in reserve in the village. Our position seemed reasonably secure that night, but we recognized that in daylight we could be observed from the west bank whilst it was still held by the enemy. This danger became more apparent the next day, but from an unexpected quarter, when we found ourselves being shelled from the west bank somewhere well back towards the beaches. This shelling suddenly stopped but it wasn't until Robin Rigby arrived at battalion HQ a couple of hours later, in his underpants, that we learned the reason. Robin had been along the towpath returning from a patrol towards Ranville when he had seen guns shelling our position from the west bank. He had suspected that these were forward elements of the allied forces so he stripped to his underpants and swam both the river and the canal to get word through to the offending artillery. On his return he had to avoid an enemy patrol and was unable to recover his clothing and was forced to spend the following few weeks in the uniform of the German Todt organization. Exactly where he got that uniform from I don't know.

Our anticipation of the German reaction when they realized we were consolidating in Longueval was well justified. From that evening of 7 June, we were subjected to mortar and shell fire which continued, on and off, in varying intensity, for the next seven days and nights. To the uninitiated, like ourselves, mortar fire can be most demoralizing. At one instant all can seem relatively quiet and peaceful with troops in the open digging or improving their slit trenches or brewing tea when suddenly, whoosh-bang, and the area can be full of red hot shrapnel, causing instant death or terrible lacerations to those unfortunate enough to be in the vicinity. However, we quickly developed a technique for minimizing the effects. The sound of the enemy mortars and guns being fired could be heard several seconds before the bombs arrived, so 'mortar sentries' were established with orders to concentrate on listening for the noise of mortars or guns being fired and to shout a warning — 'Mortars!' — which gave everybody time to dive under cover before the bombs arrived.

The sound we found most bloodcurdling was that of the German multi-barrel mortar, or 'Minnenwurfur' I think it was called. This fired about eight bombs in quick succession and did so with what sounded like the agonized groan of a prehistoric monster in labour! An added hazard of mortar fire was that many of our men dug-in in wooded areas and if, as was often the case, the mortar bombs exploded on hitting the tree tops, the shrapnel would rain down and penetrate even the deepest slit trench. The men were quick to learn to avoid digging-in under heavy overhead cover or, if this could not be avoided, to develop cover which provided some degree of protection. We were thus able to minimize the effect of this continual bombardment. But despite our efforts, the cry of 'Stretcher bearer!' was heard all too frequently.

Notwithstanding these trials and tribulations, including the losses we had suffered in the attack on St Honorine and subsequently, the morale of the men remained extraordinarily high, and as the days passed they seemed to positively welcome the arrival of groups of enemy infantry attempting to penetrate the battalion area. This at least meant some temporary respite from mortar fire.

On the far side of the hill fronting the battalion position and away from the wooded areas and the river bank where we were located, the country was open and undulating down to St Honorine and beyond, and it was up through this area that the Germans put in successive attacks with increasing intensity towards Ranville and the bridges beyond. They made no progress into our area, which was on their left flank, but further north, towards Ranville, succeeded several times in reaching the river and the towpath, which provided our only means of communication with brigade HQ. However, these attacks were all repulsed with the Germans pulling back to the St Honorine area and leaving many dead behind them. At one point early on we were worried about a small patrol under Robin Crockett, which had been sent back along the towpath to guide the group which had been located on the Ring Contour 30 position and it was with considerable relief that they eventually found their way back to the battalion.

From a tactical standpoint our location was very secure. We occupied a semicircular position with our backs to the river and on the reverse side of a hill from which an enemy attack was most likely to materialize. Despite the heavy mortar and shell fire to which we were subjected, the Germans never appeared to accurately register our positions and the slope on which we were located resulted in a lot of their shell fire falling harmlessly behind us. Furthermore the wooded nature of the area provided the best protection against what we feared most, enemy tanks and self propelled guns.

8 June, 1940

On the morning of 8 June, following a particularly severe stonk of mortar fire, a group of enemy infantry infiltrated between the recce platoon and A Company's positions, and battalion HQ was subjected to heavy small arms fire from the woods at the top of the lawn in front of the house, but we had considerable difficulty in locating exactly where this was coming from. I went up into the attic of the house with the RSM and after knocking out a tile in the roof took up my binoculars to try and locate the precise positions from which this fire was coming. As I traversed the hedge on the left hand side of the lawns, somewhat to my consternation, I suddenly found myself looking straight into the eyes of a face under a typical square German helmet, as if we were standing talking to one another. The head turned to one side and said something, whereupon another square helmet appeared and a brief conversation took place between them as they peered down on our position. They both then ducked down and moved away and immediately afterwards I could make out a number of other figures moving down the far side of the hedge towards B Company's position. I estimated that I had seen about ten figures but was mystified as to how they had got through the recce platoon's positions without a warning having been given. I told the RSM to go down and warn the battalion HQ personnel behind the building and also went down myself and out of the front entrance across to warn B Company what I had seen. Amidst all the racket that was going on I found Gerald Rickord and shouted to him that an enemy patrol was moving into his company's position. Gerald shouted back, somewhat hoarsely, 'We are well aware of that. What the hell do you think we are doing?' And waved me away.

I went through the front door and into the corridor at the back of the building which had large glass windows from floor to ceiling, at that stage unbroken. Just at that moment I saw a group of four Germans burst through the hedge on the left of the lawn and about twenty yards from where I was standing. There was an immediate burst of firing from the battalion HQ defence and intelligence sections, dug in at the rear of the house. Before covering five yards, two of the group simply crumpled up and collapsed. A few yards further on a third man fell and lay still. The one survivor appeared to stumble over his comrade but continued to run across the lawn and then fell into a partially dug slit trench. Despite the heavy fire directed at him he leapt out of the trench and continued to run across the lawn and disappeared into the woods. How he had escaped being riddled with bullets like his comrades I don't know.

After a short time the firing died down and we were able to remove the bodies from the lawn and identify them as four 21st Panzer Division which we knew was in the Caen area. The next day I had occasion to go up the laneway to the right of the battalion HQ and saw a dead German NCO hanging across the wall with his head and arms down one side and his legs the other. I assumed that he was the NCO who had miraculously escaped death the previous morning but whether he had died from wounds received at that time or had been spotted by A Company personnel on the far side of the laneway, I don't know. Anyway he had to be collected and buried.

We had established a temporary burial area on the lawn behind the house with our men on one side and Germans on the other. Shallow graves were dug by the pioneer platoon whenever circumstances permitted, and our padre, the Reverend Jim MacMurray-Taylor, was very faithful in carrying out a brief ceremony for the dead of both sides, despite frequent interruptions by cries of 'Mortar!' from our sentries, whereupon those present, including the padre, would run for the nearest cover. These burials were, of course, only temporary and the bodies were subsequently removed to official war graves when these were established. Jim Taylor was always most conscientious in carrying out his duties. However many times a short burial service might be interrupted he would always complete a ceremony at the first opportunity, whether over our dead or German dead, and it was fortunate perhaps that one didn't have too much time to reflect on the death of a close friend. When we buried Derek Boustead I remember thinking of Lalerge, his wife of only a couple of months, who would shortly receive the standard telegram: 'The War Office regrets etc . . . ' I thought of the first time I had met Derek at the all ranks dance at Ballymena and of his irritation at being posted to an Irish regiment with which he had no territorial or other connections, and how he had become one of our most enthusiastic and popular officers. I thought of Derek's party song, *One Meat Ball*, and wondered who would be the next to join him. Then the cry of 'Mortar!' and that was the end of that until the next time.

9 June, 1940

This was an exciting day. Early in the morning one of four patrols reported that St Honorine had been vacated by the Germans, and later, Division decided that we should occupy the village, with one of the parachute battalions taking over in Longueval. This was to be achieved by two platoons of D Company under the company commander, Tony Dyball, moving up river to Colombelles which had also been reported clear of enemy troops. This would secure our right flank, while the remainder of the battalion moved across to occupy St Honorine.

When the two platoons of D Company reached Colombelles they were informed by the local civilians that a large group of enemy troops were at that time approaching Colombelles from St Honorine. An ambush was laid and almost the entire enemy party was destroyed which, apparently, caused the enemy considerable annoyance and a desire for retribution. All the patrol returned safely with the exception of one rifleman reported missing. In the meantime, it was also reported that enemy troops had reoccupied St Honorine, so the attack on that village was cancelled. Shortly afterwards a heavy and prolonged concentration of mortar fire was directed on Longueval, causing a number of casualties, following which, groups of German infantry began infiltrating the woods surrounding our positions. At about this time it was reported that a German tank was approaching battalion HQ. This was the one danger we particularly feared. We knew that if an enemy tank got close enough to the brow of the hill to be able to direct its fire down to our location we could be in considerable difficulty. Sure enough, shortly after this message was received, a large self-propelled gun began to blast off in our direction. But fortunately it wasn't sufficiently far over the brow of the hill to be able to aim directly at the house and we could hear the shells whistling close overhead. At the same time we could see the blast and smoke of the gun as it fired through the trees in front of our position.

This was the moment that Dickie Quinn, our antitank platoon commander, had been waiting for. He had sited one of his guns close to the rear of battalion HQ and he immediately approached the CO, who happened to be nearby, and asked for permission to open fire. Although he couldn't see the enemy gun he felt he could at least estimate its location sufficiently well to make it clear that we had very adequate antitank defences.

Just about this time I came out of the dining room into the passage which ran along the rear of the house and was standing

229

talking to Rifleman Lickfold, one of the intelligence section. Fortunately, I had my back to a wall between two high windows overlooking the garden. Suddenly Lickfold appeared to lift off and to be pushed back against the wall on the other side of the passageway as if by some unseen hand, and immediately followed a tremendous blast and the tinkle of shattered glass. I immediately dropped to the floor, thinking we had been bit by an 88mm shell, but looking out saw that the blast had simply been caused by Dickie firing his antitank gun. He had used what was known as sabot ammunition, which had a high armour-piercing capability, and this had cleared a narrow pathway through the woods like an enormous scythe. How near he came to hitting the German SP gun we don't know, but there was no doubt the Germans got the message because it immediately withdrew. Fortunately Rifleman Lickfold only suffered a few minor cuts and Dickie Quinn was, of course, delighted at the first opportunity to fire his gun in anger.

Despite the withdrawal of their armoured support, the Germans continued to infiltrate and at one stage they reached the low wall overlooking the château-like house in which Dai Rees had his RAP and where, at that time, a number of wounded were being treated in front of the house; several stretcher cases were already loaded on jeeps ready to be moved down to the towpath and back to the casualty clearing station at Ranville. Despite the fact that the house was clearly marked with Red Cross signs, the Germans continued to shoot up not only the medical staff but also the casualties. Bob Hynds, the company commander of C Company, happened to be on the spot at the time and, with great courage, he seized a Red Cross flag and walked out of the building, waving it in front of the Germans. To his intense relief he heard a German shout of command and the firing stopped, and at the same time a German NCO stood up and waved the laden vehicles down the driveway. As soon as the vehicles had gone and the remaining wounded moved back into the house, firing started again. At least the incident demonstrated that some Germans paid attention to the rules of war governing the Red Cross. Strictly, Bob Hynds was not entitled to claim protection under the Red Cross flag, as he was armed, and as the jeeps drove off he smartly withdrew to the house and returned to his Company HQ via the back door. Eventually, a strong patrol under Jack Chapman moved up into the woods behind and the Germans withdrew, leaving a number of dead in their wake.

Later that day, John Drummond, who was usually moving around the company locations giving encouragement and support, came into battalion HQ and we briefly discussed how things were going. John was a quiet man who didn't issue orders in a peremptory or authoritarian way but simply made 'suggestions', which amounted to the same thing, I suppose, because one knew that John's suggestions had to be put into effect. Whilst we were talking he mentioned that there were several dead Germans — four or five he thought — lying in a ditch on the other side of the roadway at the top of the hill and in front of A Company's position and he 'suggested' that I might take a group from battalion HQ and go up and bring the bodies down for burial.

My natural inclination was to make a counter suggestion that if some Germans had been stupid enough to be killed in what, in effect, was No Man's Land, they should be left where they were. However, I didn't want to leave John with the impression that either I or any of my staff were unwilling to undertake such a hazardous operation, so I simply replied, 'OK John, just leave it to me.' Later that day during a lull in the seemingly endless mortaring and after sending out a message to both of the forward companies that a patrol from battalion HQ would be moving along their front, I collected my batman, Gillanders, a jeep and driver and two stretcher bearers and set forth up the laneway alongside our location.

Gillanders and I were walking about twenty yards in front of the jeep, and just before we reached the roadway at the top of the hill I signalled to the jeep to stop and cautiously went forward to peer around the corner to ensure that all was clear. This was probably quite unnecessary because there was no firing going on at the time, which would certainly have been the case if any German patrols had been in the vicinity. However, just as I was doing this a voice from the hedge on my right said, 'What do you think you are up to?' Somewhat startled I turned and there, peering at me through the hedge, was Lieutenant Windebank who commanded our pioneer platoon. Windy was a schoolmaster by profession and not given to caustic language. However, when I explained the object of my mission he made a very rude comment on the manner in which he thought dead

Germans should be treated. He then went on to tell me that my jeep driver should be extremely careful because his platoon had laid anti-tank mines at the side of the road along which we were about to proceed. Provided we kept well to the left hand side of the road we would probably be OK, but if he heard a loud explosion he would arrange to collect our remains! With these encouraging words in my ears, I waved the jeep forward and warned the driver of the position. He cheerfully acknowledged my warning and turning right we set off once again.

The roadway on which we were moving ran along the crest of the hill separating Longueval from St Honorine, but fortunately there was a thick hedge on the left hand side which gave us some protection from view from the St Honorine direction, and we carried on for about 200 yards without any incident. I turned from time to time to check that the jeep was keeping well to the side of the road. I could make out quite clearly where the gravel surface had been disturbed by Windy's men and it didn't give me much encouragement to notice that from time to time the wheels of the jeep were not more than twelve inches or so from these danger signs.

After about 200 yards, I saw just ahead of me the gateway which John Drummond had mentioned as the spot where the German bodies were located. At this point, the protective hedge at the side of the road became considerably less dense, so signalling the rest of the party to stay where they were, I crawled forward on my hands and knees to the gate and peered into the adjoining field. Just beyond the gate was another hedge at right angles to the road and alongside this hedge I could see two recumbent figures in field grey uniforms sprawled half in and half out of the ditch, with their arms and legs splayed out in a very ungainly fashion. The next question was to decide how to get them out and onto the jeep without being unduly conspicuous and, more particularly, how to turn the jeep around on this narrow road, half of which, so far as I was aware, was littered with mines. Because of the mines I did not relish the idea of telling the driver that we would return from where we had come, in reverse.

Raising my arm, I lifted the large wooden latch-like bar which held the gate closed and it obligingly swung away from me into the field until it came to rest against a German jackboot. I then crawled back to the jeep and told the driver and the stretcher bearers what they were to do. After the jeep had been turned the stretcher bearers would crawl through the gateway with their stretchers and with Gillanders and me to collect the bodies and bring them back to the jeep. I warned them to listen intently for the sound of mortar fire, in which case they were to abandon Germans, stretchers and jeep and to put as much distance between the gateway and themselves in the ten or twelve seconds or so it would take for mortar bombs to arrive. I had no illusions about the accuracy of German mortar fire, particularly when they could observe where their bombs were landing and that if they decided to interfere with our mission they would do so with deadly accuracy. Aided by the instinct for survival I had little doubt that we could probably cover a hundred yards or so before diving into the nearest ditch and hoping for the best.

We squatted in the ditch and watched with some apprehension as the driver turned the jeep with great dexterity, and there was no explosion from mine or German mortar. When this was completed, Gillanders and I and the two stretcher bears crawled through the gateway and began to lift the first body onto a stretcher. Only those who have attempted to load dead German soldiers in an advanced state of rigour mortis onto a narrow stretcher will understand the difficulty that this can cause. Whichever way we put the bodies, an arm or a leg would be extended at right angles and cause the whole to tip off. However, we managed the first two bodies, by which time I had noticed two more lying a little further along the ditch in the long grass. I quietly cursed John Drummond for his accuracy, but had no alternative but to carry on with our task until we had two bodies on stretchers on the bonnet of the jeep and two more lying in the rear, and we were able to start our return journey. Back along the road we went, keeping well to the right hand ditch to where Windy was still standing on the corner and expressing disappointment that we hadn't blown ourselves up, thus proving the effectiveness of his mine defences.

I later reflected that the Germans in St Honorine must have seen what was going on because immediately after we turned into the driveway up to battalion HQ and the driver had switched off the engine of the jeep there were cries of 'Mortar!' Without thought for the safety of our disinterested passengers we all dived for the nearest slit trench and, sure enough, in a few seconds there was the usual sound of whoosh crash as the salvo of mortar bombs dropped immediately to the rear of our position. After a couple of salvos the mortaring ceased and I visualized some German commander down in St Honorine turning to his men and saying, in German of course, 'That will teach those damned Irishmen to treat our dead with respect.' We did. The bodies were carried up to our temporary mortuary until graves could be dug and Jim Taylor could carry out the committal rites the next day. I won't go into detail as to the difficulty of burying dead Germans whose arms and legs are rigidly extended in what could be interpreted as a form of salute or gesture of defiance.

That night I mentioned to John Drummond, casually, that we had brought in the German bodies he had mentioned earlier. As might be expected from John, he simply replied, 'Oh, have you,' and went about his business. I thought that at least we might have received a commendation for the award of an Iron Cross, even if of a very low class!

10-11 June, 1940

At first light the following morning, 10 June, I was making the round of battalion HQ positions. After a disturbed night, the early morning was strangely peaceful with the birds singing and a clear sky lighting up from the east and promising a beautiful day. Without warning, a heavy artillery barrage opened up beyond the river and the canal; the area over which we had been expecting and hoping the 3rd Division to advance on D-Day plus 1, 7 June. I walked across the road to the low wall which overlooked the towpath and the country beyond, and with two or three others had a grandstand panoramic view of an infantry attack taking place across open country. The situation was strangely unreal. We had frequently been spectators at and taken part in similar set pattern attacks, but this was for real. There were no umpires.

We sat on our wall in the warm morning sun, smoking cigarettes as we watched the artillery barrage moving slowly up the slope to our left, towards Colombelles and Caen. Behind the fountains of earth and black smoke thrown up by the bursting artillery shells, the infantry appeared, emerging in small groups from behind hedges, ditches, woods and whatever places of concealment they had moved into while it was still dark, then spreading out into open formation as they slowly advanced through waist-high corn, with Bren gun carriers scurrying around on the flanks like sheep dogs keeping their flock on the move. We were about 500 yards from the nearest troops on the left flank of the attack and although initially there didn't appear to be much resistance, we were greatly impressed with the disciplined way in which they maintained their section and platoon formations, despite having to scramble through and over hedges and ditches as they progressed steadily forward behind the protective barrage.

All seemed to be going well until the leading troops approached the crest of the rising ground, when the very distinctive rapid fire of the German Spandau machine guns and the bursts of defensive mortar fire increased in intensity, and the lines of advancing infantry thinned out as figures dropped out of sight in the deep corn. Still the remainder kept moving ahead until we lost sight of them in the smoke and confusion of whatever was taking place amongst the trees and hedges at the crest of the hill.

Whether and to what extent that particular attack achieved its objectives we never knew, although it soon became common knowledge that the capture of Caen was proving to be more difficult than the planners had originally envisaged, which meant that the presence of the 6th Airborne Division to secure the eastern flank of the invasion force was likely to be prolonged, and there would be no early pull-out to prepare for whatever subsequent airborne operations might be necessary. However, we were now comforted with the knowledge that the country to the rear of our position was in friendly hands and that Longueval was no longer isolated.

While we were watching the progress of the battle across the river, my attention was drawn to a lone figure about half a mile away in the direction of Colombelles, making its way towards us along the narrow strip of land between the river and the canal. Whoever it was appeared to be anxious to avoid being seen, as he was dodging between whatever cover was available. Suddenly a shout rang out as someone recognized the rifleman reported missing from the patrol to Colombelles the previous day. It later transpired that when the ambush was set up, he was ordered to take up a position alongside the road in the direction of St Honorine from where the enemy were expected. When our patrol had been ordered to withdraw he hadn't heard the order and, as a result, had lain concealed in a ditch only a few yards from where a number of very angry German troops were collecting their dead and wounded, and threatening to shoot a group of the local French people. He was under no illusion as to what would happen to him if he was captured, so had remained concealed until late in the night, when he had cautiously made his way back to Longueval.

13 June, 1940

During the night of 12 June we learned that there was to be another attempt to capture St Honorine. Our initial attack on 7 June by two companies had failed, but this time the assault would be carried out by a battalion of the 51st Highland Division which had achieved considerable success in battles in Africa, and which had now arrived in Normandy. The attack would be carried out on the morning of 13 June from a start-line secured by one of our companies along the line of the road in front of our location, overlooking St Honorine. I remember the sense of anticipation with which we awaited the arrival of these battle-experienced troops, and the relief we felt as the leading units came down the towpath towards us in the early hours of the morning. At least, after six days of almost complete isolation and continuous enemy attack, we would get some respite from continuous enemy infantry, mortar and artillery attack. The troops of the 51st Highland Division were indeed a splendid sight. Having landed after the initial assault divisions, they were well turned out, with many wearing their Africa Star and other decoration ribbons. Our troops, after living for several days in and out of slit trenches, were looking more than a little shabby in comparison.

After a short delay the Highlanders were led forward to their forming up positions, after which a tremendous artillery barrage was brought to bear on St Honorine.

From reports received at our HQ, the initial phase of the attack appeared to go well and units of the Highland regiment were seen to penetrate into the village. However, the Germans

236

repeated the tactic with which we were familiar. In the face of the artillery barrage and infantry assault, they had withdrawn from the village and shown only token resistance to the assault. Then, before the Highlanders had time to consolidate their positions, the Germans put in a series of strong counter attacks supported by self-propelled guns and tanks, to which the Highlanders could offer little or no response. They withdrew as rapidly as they could, back to the woods around Longueval where they had started.

I was at battalion HQ at the time, with Colonel Carson, and we received a message that the Highlanders were withdrawing and at the same time shouting to our men to pull back, as a major German assault was impending. The CO immediately instructed me to send out a message to each of our companies to the effect that in no circumstances would any of our men leave their positions. After the Germans had re-occupied St Honorine they followed up with a strong attack directed towards Ranville, but by-passing us, in Longueval.

During our seven days at Longueval we were never attacked by enemy aircraft. The air activity we saw consisted solely of German planes streaking inland from the direction of the coast with a Hurricane or Spitfire on its tail, guns blazing, and on several occasions we saw enemy aircraft burst into flames, zoom up in the sky and turn over, when the pilot would drop out and parachute to the ground. I have clear recollections of two cases when the parachutes failed to open and the unfortunate pilots dropped out of sight, presumably to a sudden death.

A strange occurrence, which was repeated over several nights, was when a German radio transmitter cut in on our wave lengths and a voice, in perfect English, suggested that it would be in our best interests to seize the first opportunity to lay down our arms and surrender. Needless to say this advice was received by our radio operators and men with derisive laughter but it was even more strange when the voice told us that the enemy not only knew we were the 1st Battalion Royal Ulster Rifles but also knew, and quoted, the names of our officers.

Another interesting incident was when the Germans fired mortar bombs which exploded in the air and scattered paper leaflets over our area. These leaflets were addressed 'To British and Canadian Soldiers,' and asked the question, 'Do you know what's going on in England?' The leaflets then informed us that since 15 June, Germany's new weapons had been in action against London and southern England and that London was in flames. They exhorted us to go to the nearest hills and see for ourselves. Something seemed to have gone wrong with the German timing, because we received these leaflets on 13 June, two days before the VI bombardment of London was stated to have begun. At that time we didn't know about the VI pilotless bomber, although it was reported that one had been seen over the division area, apparently heading in the wrong direction. Anyway, the leaflets were received with the same derision as the German broadcasts, and it was the unanimous feeling that because of the shortage of toilet paper, the German leaflets would serve a useful purpose.

British and Canadian Soldiers!

Do you know what's going on in England?

Since June 15th Germany's new terrific weapons are in action against London and Southern Engle... London is in flames for days now. If you don't believe go on the hills nearby and look for yourselves. At night you can observe the great fire. Or ask your people at home. They can tell you in their letters, that is if your Government will permit them which we doubt. They have belittled our decisive action but at the same time they have put in force a new and stricter censorship on outgoing letters and reports.

They don't want you to know the truth.

Just before we left Longueval we received our first supply of bread, which was extremely welcome as a supplement to our diet of dog biscuits, solid porridge and solid meat. However, despite our somewhat limited diet, morale continued to be extremely high due, to a large extent, to the fact that we never seemed to run short of tea, which reflected very well on the efforts of our quartermaster's department. After the first three or four days we had received a supply of slightly larger and more sophisticated compo packs, which had run the gauntlet of the towpath from Ranville. These included extra chocolate and little packs of jam, which at least added some flavour to the biscuits which had been the basis of our meals. But throughout that period, provided we had plenty of tea, solid food seemed of somewhat secondary importance. The main thing we were lacking, of course, was sleep.

On the evening of 13 June orders were received that first thing the following morning we would hand over Longueval to the battalion of the Cameron Highlanders and move to the village of Breville.

Breville

Breville is a small village about a mile or so east of Ranville. It is located on high ground with a commanding view of most of the surrounding countryside, including the wide plain east of the River Orne in the direction of Caen and Troarne, and to the west towards Ranville.

Breville had not been secured during the initial phase of the 6th Division landing, and had become a weak link in the chain of perimeter defences around the bridges. Several attempts had been made to secure the village, but these had been unsuccessful until a very bloody battle on the night of 12 June. The Germans had then been driven out and the village captured but with very heavy casualties on both sides. On the evening of 13 June one of our companies had moved to Breville to assist in holding the village against the possibility of counter attack.

In the early hours of 14 June, after we had handed over our positions in Longueval to the Cameron Highlanders, we set out on the march to Breville, or what remained of the village. The attack which led to its capture had been preceded by a massive artillery barrage to which the Germans had responded, with the result that, with very few exceptions, every house had been badly damaged or destroyed and many were still burning when we arrived. Strangely enough, in one of the very few houses where the upper storey was more or less intact, our troops found a girl in bed and very ill, who in some miraculous way had

239

survived the onslaught. She was quickly evacuated but whether she lived I don't know. The carnage was appalling. Most of the British dead had been removed but the village, or what remained of it, was littered with the bodies and partial bodies of dead German troops.

The object of our move to Breville was to secure the village against counter attack by the Germans, and the first priority was for our rifle companies to take up positions for that purpose. A and D Companies, with antitank gun support, were to the north and north east; B Company on the east side of the village with C Company in reserve in the village itself. Battalion headquarters was set up in a fairly modern two storey house overlooking the village crossroads. The roof and upper floor had been badly damaged but the ground floor was more or less wind and water tight, and although fully furnished, everything was a shambles. There was no sign of any inhabitants.

The older parts of the village had been laid out or developed in the form of a triangle, the base being the road along which we had entered from Amfreville and the other two sides consisting of a number of small houses and the broken down walls of old farm buildings. In the centre of the triangle was a large grassy area which, in better times, had probably been a sort of village green, dotted with pleasant trees and seats and used for village functions and as a children's playground but which now consisted of little more than gaping shell holes, slit trenches, shattered and burnt out vehicles and littered with dead German troops, discarded equipment and arms of all types.

I remember walking around that area with the RSM after we had moved in and seeing a German soldier who appeared to be standing in a slit trench and leaning forward over the parapet with his rifle in his hand, as if on guard duty. I leaned forward and pushed his shoulder, and as the torso rolled over, realized that it was only half a body. Where the lower half of his torso and his legs were I didn't see. It was obviously important that all these human remains should be buried without delay, so, despite the possibility of a German attack, we requested the help of a small bulldozer, which soon arrived and dug a long trench in a field and adjoining the crossroads. It then took all the battalion stretcher bearers several hours to collect the shattered bodies of German troops and to carry them to the mass grave we had prepared.

240

In the hot sun the stench was appalling and the men involved were urinating on their handkerchiefs and tying them across their faces to provide some protection from the nauseating smells. Again I appreciated the true quality of our padre, Jim MacMurray Taylor. Going down on his hands and knees and despite the gruesome nature of his task, he went through the tattered and bloodstained clothing of each body to remove identity discs and personal possessions, which he placed separately in small bags which he then labelled, where identification was possible, for consignment to the Red Cross authorities and, hopefully, for return to the relatives. The bodies were then wrapped in blankets and placed in the communal grave and after the padre had recited a brief burial service the grave was filled in and a number of crosses placed in position to mark the spot. A couple of years later I visited Breville and looked into that field, but there were no signs indicating that it was where a number of Germans had been buried. No doubt the remains had been removed to an official war cemetery.

A very sad sight in a field just below the Breville crossroads was a line of about twenty bodies of Scottish troops who had been wiped out as they advanced up the hill in an attempt to capture Breville on 11 June. Why they hadn't been removed by the time we arrived, I wasn't sure, but presumably because the field where they lay was under German observation. They were lying face down in what we called open formation, which might have been appropriate in the wide open spaces of North Africa but which, without adequate covering fire, would have been suicidal in the close country of Normandy.

The countryside around our position at Breville consisted of small open fields and orchards, separated by thick hedges and wooded areas which limited fields of fire, and extensive patrolling was necessary. In many places the forward positions of ourselves and the Germans were separated only by the width of a field or two, and it was quickly recognized that the side which could seize and hold certain vantage points could make life very uncomfortable for the others by sniping and observed control of mortar activity. Extensive patrolling was also necessary to gain precise information about enemy locations, activities and intentions. One day Lieutenant Micky Archdale a platoon commander from A Company came to see me at battalion headquarters. He explained that he was taking out a patrol that night into the area in front of A Company to capture a prisoner or two and to confirm the identity of the German troops facing our positions. When he had been fully briefed on the known locations of enemy positions in his area, he departed, apparently well satisfied with the information he had received.

His took his patrol out that night and although the patrol came back, Micky was missing. The NCO of the patrol explained they had been moving very slowly and cautiously along the line of a hedge when they had suddenly heard German voices and movement a few yards ahead. Micky had whispered to the NCO to stop while he went slowly forward to find out what was going on ahead of them. He had disappeared in the darkness and the patrol knelt down to await his return. Suddenly, from about twenty yards ahead, there was an explosion as if a hand grenade had been thrown, a few shouts in German and then silence. After waiting for approximately fifteen minutes there was no sign of Micky and the patrol withdrew to A Company lines.

Charles Vickery, the company commander, immediately made arrangements for a larger patrol to go out at first light in the morning under cover of a considerable mortar barrage to try and find Micky or discover what had happened to him. Nothing was found and Micky Archdale was reported missing. Several weeks later, after the German withdrawal, a group was sent back to make a thorough search of the area, including the German positions where he might have been buried if he had been killed. Nothing was found. We hoped, of course, that Micky would turn up as a prisoner of war but such was not to be. I was told many years later that his mother had never accepted that he had been killed and until her death lived in hope that one day he would turn up.

This was a period of considerable sniping activity. Both our own selected sharpshooters and those of the enemy would vie with one another to occupy vantage points from which they had would hope to increase their respective 'bags'. This frequently involved crawling out at night time to a preselected spot up a tree, or in a hedge, where the sniper would have to conceal himself from view or maybe secure himself from falling out of the tree during a prolonged stay, possibly a complete day. Needless to say this was a task which was only undertaken by men of very considerable courage and endurance but nevertheless there was no shortage of volunteers. One of the hazards was to secure an ideal spot before daybreak and then find an enemy sniper a few yards away.

We had a number of casualties from enemy sniping, one of whom was Lieutenant Dickie Quinn, one of our most popular young officers. He was in charge of a section of our antitank platoon, and one morning, as was his regular custom, he paid each of his gun crews a quick visit. The guns were well concealed but as dawn was breaking, Dickie stood up with his binoculars raised to see what he could see. A sniper's bullet hit him in the head and killed him instantly.

Although we were still living, officially, on compo rations at this time, the men were becoming more and more adept at scrounging the local fields for unharvested fresh vegetables. It was also reported that Huw Wheldon of C Company had organized a programme of patrols to a farmyard in front of C Company's area for the purpose of collecting fresh eggs laid by the abandoned chickens. Huw was extremely annoyed one morning when he and his patrol arrived at the farmhouse to find that the Germans had beaten him to it and removed all the eggs. He therefore decided that the only course open to him was to take some of the chickens back to C Company area so that their production and use could be effectively controlled.

One day, when returning from a visit to brigade headquarters, John Drummond noticed a number of our men digging potatoes in a field adjoining the landing zone where our gliders still littered the area. As on a previous occasion he 'suggested' to me that Billie Beattie, our QM and therefore responsible for our supplies, might take out a patrol to this area to dig a supply of potatoes for battalion headquarters before they were all removed by the men of the rifle companies. The field in question was behind our forward positions, but was still the object of periodic mortaring, so when I passed on this 'suggestion' to Billie Beattie he was not amused. However, like me at Longueval, he acceded to John Drummond's 'suggestion' and for a few days thereafter we feasted on delicious new potatoes.

On another trip to brigade HQ John's eagle eye spotted considerable quantities of that delicious Normandy speciality, Camembert cheese. Naturally, this was followed by a further suggestion that I should take a jeep back over the bridges to Ouistreham on the coast to see what I could find in the way of 'luxuries' which might further relieve the monotony of our compo pack rations. Naturally, I jumped at the opportunity and after collecting as much 'invasion money' as I could, I set off on what was a most fascinating trip. On the road from Ranville to Ouistreham there was a constant stream of supply vehicles moving up to the forward lines, and Ouistreham itself was as busy as Piccadilly Circus at rush hour. All the shops seemed to be open and, although with a somewhat limited variety, they had plenty of fruit, vegetables and cheese and were doing a roaring trade with British and Canadian troops. By visiting several shops I managed to load the jeep up with dozens of small round boxes of cheese together with a supply of fresh vegetables and fruit and, last but not least, a few bottles of Calvados. The French shopkeepers didn't seem all that keen on 'invasion money' but nevertheless they were willing to take it, but no doubt charged exorbitant prices in the process.

Before returning I took the opportunity of driving along the seafront where the British and Canadian forces had landed over the beaches and I was staggered at the volume of traffic still coming in from the hundreds of ships out in the bay. The cargoes from these ships were being transported to the beaches in landing craft of all shapes and sizes, the bigger craft disgorging tanks and fully laden trucks from their black interiors, while other amphibious vehicles ground their way out of the water and up the beaches along wide metal articulated tracks which had been laid across the soft sand up to the roadway. On my return my goodies were distributed among all the troops and although maybe each man didn't get very much, what they did get was more than welcome.

Our stay at Breville lasted about two weeks, during which time the expected German counter-attack failed to materialize, and confined itself to sniping, mortaring and shell fire on our positions. Our patrols brought in a number of prisoners and two enemy patrols, or at least some of the men in these patrols gave themselves up to our forward positions. From these we learned that the morale of the German troops was at a low ebb.

On 27 June the battalion was relieved by another battalion from our brigade and we moved to what was classified as a 'rest area' just behind Breville. The description 'rest area' is somewhat of a misnomer because we were, in fact, filling a gap between two other battalions and were in reserve to support them or any other battalion of the division should the need arise. There were no houses or farm buildings in the area where some of us might have been able to make ourselves comfortable and we had to make do with the slit trenches dug by our predecessors for protection from enemy activity and from the weather, which had turned very wet at the time. Over all, this location was most uncomfortable, the only advantage being that most of us could enjoy a reasonable night's rest at the bottom of a six foot grave-like trench, and groups could be dispatched in small numbers every few hours by truck to the rear areas for their first bath or shower since our arrival three weeks earlier. I have often heard it said that lice are endemic amongst troops in the field but I can recollect no instance amongst our men when lice were even suspected.

One of the benefits of serving with an experienced regular battalion became apparent when battalion HQ staff produced a small tent which was erected in the corner of the field where we were now located. How they had fitted the tent into the small trolley which contained all the other equipment I don't know, but apparently it had always been an essential item of equipment when operating on the north west frontier of India. To some extent, no doubt, they were motivated by their own personal interests of setting up battalion headquarters in a dry tent in preference to a very wet slit trench. The tent was about six feet high by twelve feet long and about six feet wide. A table and a few chairs had also been procured from somewhere or other and the tent soon became the centre of administration, conference centre and dining hall!

One evening, shortly after relocating to the rest area, we received a visit from about six or seven officers from the 2nd Battalion of the regiment who were also in a rest area on the other side of the Orne. They brought with them a couple of bottles of Calvados and wine and we had an interesting and convivial hour or so in our tent, exchanging news about mutual friends and activities. As the evening light was fading our friends from the 2nd Battalion decided to take their leave and we were all standing around the gateway leading to the road where their vehicle was parked. Suddenly and without any warning, a German fighter came over the hill from the direction of Breville, flying at tree top height, and down the line of the roadway where we were standing with machine guns and cannon blazing out bullets and shells along the line of the road. Instinctively, everyone dived for cover, probably too late to be of any value, but by a miracle no-one was badly hurt other than from the splinters of cannon shell exploding along the road and in the trees.

As we sent them on their way, one of our visitors called out, 'You'd better watch out. Jerry will probably do exactly the same tomorrow night.'

These were wise words which we took note of. The following morning one of battalion headquarters staff drew my attention to a small hole in the roof of the tent and we then saw a small hole in the seat of the chair in which Robin Rigby had been sitting when chatting with the officers of 2nd Battalion the previous evening. Further examination showed a hole in the ground which, after investigation, revealed a dud cannon shell. It was fortunate for Robin that our friends from the 2nd Battalion had decided to leave when they did.

Remembering the words of advice the previous evening, RSM Griffiths rounded up every Bren gun he would find, together with their tripods, and had these mounted so that they could cover the line the aircraft had taken the night before. That evening, as the light began to fail, every Bren gun operator was beside his gun with his finger on the trigger ready for any repeat of the event. In sighting the guns, care had been taken to ensure that if they were fired they would not shoot up any of our own troops. Sure enough, at exactly the same time, the German fighter pilot made his reappearance, except that on this occasion he was met by a curtain of Bren gun fire with tracer bullets that made the area look like Guy Fawkes night. How the plane got through this barrage apparently unscathed is impossible to say, although the following day we did receive a report that a German fighter had crashed on the outskirts of Caen about the time in question, and needless to say every Bren gunner in the battalion claimed a kill. The same reception arrangements were laid down for subsequent nights but the German fighter did not return.

Throughout most nights during our stay in this so-called rest area spasmodic firing was heard in the areas of the two forward battalions, but only on two occasions were we alerted when it was reported that enemy patrols had penetrated the forward areas and that our counter action was required. With the weather at this time having badly deteriorated through long periods of heavy rain, conditions were very unpleasant. Slit trenches became flooded and everyone soaked to the skin as we waited for orders as to what was required, until dawn broke over this muddy and slushy resting place. Both occasions turned out to be false alarms. Despite all this stress and discomfort, our troops remained incredibly cheerful, not only the men from Ulster, and Belfast in particular, and whether Protestant or Catholic, but also the many London cockneys now amongst our ranks. Whether due to the very harsh conditions under which these men had been raised I don't know, but to me their cheerful resilience and their resolute determination to continue to accept whatever hardships they were asked to endure, was truly remarkable.

Le Mesnil

Our stay in the rest area lasted for about a week until, on 4 July, we moved to another position about two miles away known as Le Mesnil, where we relieved the 12th Parachute Battalion, by this time about half its original strength. The move, so far as we were concerned, was a jump out of the frying pan into the fire. The area we were required to occupy was centred on a farmhouse with extensive farm buildings and was reached by a fairly long driveway off the road from St Honorine to Cabourg. The farm buildings were surrounded by typical Normandy orchards, and where there were no apple trees there were other trees, so that the environment was close and oppressive. Our companies were grouped around the farm area with forward positions literally about a stone's throw from similar positions occupied by the Germans, so it was incumbent on anyone who wanted to live more than an hour or so to keep his head down and make maximum use of the cover provided by the trees and high hedges.

As at Longueval and Breville the order of the day so far as we were concerned, and no doubt also of the other battalions of our flanks, was to control the forward areas between us and the German positions by extensive and aggressive patrolling. We wanted to know what German troops were in front of us — their order of battle — what they were doing, and where, and then to stop them doing it; to find out whether the Germans were building up their strength at any particular point which might indicate an intention to force a break through in our front, and to take prisoners who might provide us with information and evidence of enemy morale. No doubt the Germans were under orders to do much the same thing, with the result that there were frequent clashes between patrols with casualties on both sides, but we certainly felt that we had command of the situation.

Both sides also seemed to get irritable with one another. If we mortared their positions, they responded by mortaring ours, to such extent that Lieutenant John Hanna, who was in charge of our mortar platoon, was looked upon as a sort of harbinger of gloom. Whenever he appeared, German mortar bombs would soon follow, so it was made clear to him that the further away he stayed the better. However, John was a very cheerful chap and took the jibes thrown at him in good part. He always took the line that he could invariably pinpoint the exact location of German mortars and hit back at them with great accuracy as soon as they were fired. I don't think he accepted that the Germans could do exactly the same thing. The Germans also had machine guns on fixed mountings so that if at any time, and whether during the day or night, they became alarmed at anything we were doing, they could bring heavy fire to bear on our positions, whether they could see us or not. The result of this was that at times the air seemed to be full of the snap of bullets and the crack of mortar bombs.

When we moved into the Le Mesnil area there was no sign of the occupants of the farm, except for a mentally retarded boy of about fourteen who either lived or had taken shelter in a small stone building in one corner of the farmyard. Who he was or how he came to be there we had no idea but he became very friendly with our troops and was allowed to say. It was a very harrowing experience one day when he was caught in the open during an enemy 'stonk' and was badly wounded. Dai Rees sent him back to the casualty section but we later heard that the poor boy had died.

Getting casualties back to the division casualty station was a major problem. They were normally carried on jeeps out of the farm and on to the road and then had to pass a crossroads which was looked upon as a deathtrap; 'Hell Fire Crossroads.' The Germans had registered their mortars on this crossroads and could hit it with unerring accuracy. They had also established listening posts which gave them warning of any vehicle movement, when mortar bombs would rain down within a matter of seconds. There were two alternatives open to drivers having to get past the crossroads. They could either wait a hundred yards or so away and then rev their engines like mad to give the impression that they were driving up the road, then wait until the stonk arrived and then go like hell in the hope that another one didn't come immediately afterwards. The other course was to proceed very slowly and quietly in the hope that the vehicle wouldn't be heard. This latter course was more nerve racking and a greater strain but on the whole more successful. Just before we arrived, a Red Cross ambulance laden with wounded had received almost a direct hit at the crossroads and lay on its side beside the road, burnt out, as a reminder of what could happen to the unwary.

However, like all locations, life had its brighter moments. As in most farmyards, there was a flock of about twenty ducks which, from time to time and led by the drake, waddled their way through the farmyard quacking their resentment at our intrusion on their peaceful domestic domain. They were quickly christened the 'O' Group because of their resemblance to the commanding officer leading his officers out on a reconnaissance. It soon became apparent that the number of ducks in 'O' Group was declining each day until only the drake was left in solitary and despondent isolation.

There was also the problem of the pigs. In the pigsty when we arrived there were about twenty medium size pigs, all apparently in a good state of health, and it may well be that these had been the responsibility of the mentally retarded boy I have mentioned. Anyway, after the views of all involved had been sought, it was resolved unanimously that, as there was no-one to look after the pigs and no foodstuffs available to feed them, they should be slaughtered. Furthermore, that as we had no means for delivering the carcasses to the rightful owners they should be used to supplement our rations. I had often seen my uncles slaughtering pigs on their farms in Ireland, the technique being to string the pig up by the hind legs and then cut its throat with a sharp knife so that all the blood ran out into a receptacle below which would result not only in good white pork meat but also the main ingredient for black sausage. The responsibility for slaughtering the pigs was given to one of our cooks, a butcher in civilian life, but whether he adopted my techniques or some other I don't know, but for a number of days we were able to provide the troops with a hot meal of pork meat. A week or two later we heard that a staff officer who didn't get on with General Montgomery had privately reported to the War Office that the general was turning a blind eye on the illegal slaughter of farm livestock to feed the troops, contrary to some rule or other. Apparently the staff officer also disappeared at about the same time!

During a lull in activity one day I suggested to Dai Rees that we might take a walk and visit C Company area. He agreed, so after telling one of our signallers to tell C Company on the field telephone that we were on the way, we set off. We walked to the end of the farmyard, then through a gateway which led onto a narrow track running through a thick copse of over-hanging trees for about fifty yards, where there were two gateways at right angles to one another, the one on the left heading into an orchard and the one on the right into an open field, with a high hedge dividing the two fields.

We were just opening the gate on the left when I noticed two men in a slit trench well dug-in under the dividing hedge. Before I had time to speak to them one of them said, 'You'd best be advised to go up the right hand side, sir.'

'Why is that?' I asked him.

'Well, there's a lot of sniper activity from that side,' he replied pointing over towards the orchard. As we retreated through the gate the rifleman called out, 'And keep your heads down, sir.'

Taking the right hand gate we made our way up a track alongside the hedge, keeping well doubled up in accordance with the advice we had just received. The ground in front of us was a gentle upwards slope so we couldn't see what lay on the far side of the field but away to the left the countryside was thickly wooded and I couldn't help but wonder whether that area was held by 'us' or 'them.'

When we reached the crest of the hill, we saw in the dip ahead a cluster of solid but dilapidated farm buildings, which I assumed were intended to provide shelter for farm animals during the winter. When we reached these buildings the track led us into a small courtyard where I saw a rifleman standing over a horse-trough with a towel wrapped round his neck, busily shaving himself in front of a small mirror hung on a nail in the wall of one of the buildings. I asked, 'Where's company HQ?'

Without taking his gaze from the mirror he pointed over his shoulder with a soapy looking razor to a stable-like building on the far side of the courtyard and replied, 'Over there, sir.'

As we walked across, Killer Johnson, the company commander, came out of the stable door. 'Hello,' he said, 'how nice to see you. You're just in time for elevenses.'

'We didn't come up here for elevenses,' replied Dai in his lilting Welsh voice. 'We came up to see what you buggers are doing about winning this bloody war.'

Just then Huw Wheldon appeared in the doorway, unshaven and with his battledress jacket flapping open. It occurred to me that we had woken him up from a much needed sleep. However, Huw wasn't the sort of person to be taken by surprise. He held up his arms in a gesture of welcome and said with an air of exaggerated surprise, 'Two gentlemen from the War Office, I presume. You would like to know how the war is progressing? Do come into our operational headquarters,' and he stood aside and, with a mock bow, gestured us to enter the shed.

Inside, the shed wasn't quite as dark as it appeared from the outside, with shafts of daylight showing through gaping holes in the roof above open rafters. It was about ten feet square with a cobbled stone floor and a feeding trough and hayrack along one end. Alongside the wall opposite the door a ground sheet was spread over a layer of straw, which obviously provided Killer and Huw, in turn, with somewhere to sleep when circumstances permitted. In the centre of the shed was a small very broken down looking table with two upholstered chairs that had obviously seen much better days, and on the table was a bottle of Calvados which I could see was about half full.

'Now,' said Huw, as if welcoming us to a cocktail party, 'What would you gentlemen like to drink?'

'Well, I don't suppose you've got any champagne?' I replied, 'but I don't think Calvados would do us any harm.'

Killer's batman had appeared on the scene with four enamel mugs, and also pushed up to the table an inverted wooden tub and a milking stool. Huw carefully poured out four small measures of Calvados and with mock solemnity Dai and I toasted the continued success of C Company. Killer's batman was still standing beside the table. He was an old soldier who I knew very well and who was very friendly with my own batman,

251

Gillanders. They were probably two of the best soldiers in the battalion but both were prone to get blind drunk from time to time when circumstances permitted, with the result that they were taken off batman's duties on such occasions until they had completed whatever sentence was pronounced for these periodic misdemeanours.

'Will Captain Sheridan and Captain Rees be staying to lunch, sorr?' he inquired of Killer.

'Yes, of course,' replied Killer, 'and you can bring it along as soon as it's ready.'

'Very good, sorr,' said his batman and disappeared.

Neither Dai nor I wanted to appear in any way anxious about getting back to battalion headquarters, which might suggest a reluctance to expose ourselves to the danger of the forward positions occupied by the rifle companies — probably no more dangerous than battalion headquarters anyway — but Dai did remonstrate about not wishing to deprive Killer and Huw of their ration entitlement. However, they were quite adamant that we wouldn't be depriving them of anything, and in any event, there was still a little more Calvados in the bottle. They both seemed to be more than normally cheerful, which somehow or other sparked off a thought in my mind that something was going on, but as it was obviously their wish that we should share their meal we agreed to accept their hospitality.

After a few minutes, back came Killer's batman carrying four china plates, on each of which there were two pork chops, boiled potatoes and carrots. Both Dai and I looked at this in amazement. I realized that the pork had almost certainly originated with the pigs killed at battalion headquarters, but the thought of sitting down to eat these chops, well cooked and with fresh vegetables, in a cow shed approximately 200 yards from where the enemy was undoubtedly scheming to blow us all to smithereens, was difficult to appreciate. However, there were more surprises to come.

We were about halfway through our meal when there was a sound of footsteps and the large frame of Mike Gann, one of C Company's platoon commanders, appeared in the doorway. He saluted Killer and then said, 'Just to let you know, sir, that the Germans are reinforcing their forward positions, which could suggest that they are going to put in an attack.'

Killer finished chewing whatever was in his mouth and looking up at Mike replied, 'Whereabouts Mike?'

'In front of both 14 and 15 platoon areas,' said Mike.

'OK, thanks for letting me know and keep me informed,' said Killer and went on eating. Mike saluted again, and disappeared.

I looked at Dai and Dai looked at me. Neither Killer or Huw made any reference to the impending threat of German attack and carried on the conversation as if we had been sitting in a Piccadilly restaurant. We had all finished our food when Mike appeared in the doorway once again, saluting as before. 'The Germans are forming up in front of 14 platoon, sir,' he said, 'and it's pretty obvious they are going to attack very soon.'

Killer looked up at him and paused for a few moments. 'Thank you, Mike,' he said, 'keep me informed if you would.' Again Mike saluted and disappeared. I looked again at Dai and Dai again looked at me while Huw remarked how well the pork had been cooked.

I'm sure the same thoughts were going through Dai's mind as were going through mine. If a German attack was imminent, our place was back at battalion headquarters. On the other hand, with Killer and Huw showing such complete composure in the face of what seemed to be imminent danger, how could we withdraw without creating an impression of cowardice in the face of the enemy?

It then dawned on me that we were being 'set up' and Dai realized this at the same moment. He pushed his empty plate away with a grunt of satisfaction and sitting back said, 'Well, that was damned good. What about some pudding?'

At that moment, there was a sudden burst of machine gun fire immediately outside the door, which came as a shock despite the realization that it certainly wasn't the Germans who were creating the rumpus. Dai and I stood up, certainly startled, whilst Killer and Huw burst out laughing. Looking out of the door we saw Mike Gann still standing with a Sten gun in his hand, pumping bullets into the heavy plaster work of the adjoining building.

The German troops a couple of hundred yards away must have heard this racket and wondered whether the long awaited mutiny of British troops was at last taking place, but my immediate concern was that they might respond with a few salvos of mortar bombs. Anyway, after thanking Killer and Huw for their generous hospitality and entertainment, we made our way back to our farm buildings without further incident, although highly exaggerated versions soon spread around the battalion. These were not entirely unkind. It was considered that, for battalion HQ officers, we had conducted ourselves reasonably well under the circumstances.

It was always a matter of considerable concern to our CO, Hank Carson, when an officer or NCO or a rifleman was reported missing following a patrol or an attack of an enemy position. If someone was killed we could be definite in our report so that the next of kin could be informed. Similarly, if someone was wounded this could be properly reported and the individual evacuated for medical attention. To have to report somebody as missing seemed to carry with it an attitude of don't know or don't care which was far from the truth, as when this happened, as it did quite frequently, every effort was made by subsequent patrols and searches to try and pin down exactly what had happened to the individual concerned. It was therefore with relief, when we were all at Le Mesnil, to hear that St Honorine had at last been captured, and we could send back a small group to try and ascertain the fate of about twenty members of the battalion who were still missing after our operation against that village on D + 1.

Having obtained the necessary clearance from brigade HQ I took a jeep with a driver and two men and set off to St Honorine for this purpose. We had to follow a fairly circuitous route which took us through Ranville, then along the road above Longueval and after parking our jeep, a walk down the slope into St Honorine across the fields where A and B Companies had put in their attack on the morning of 7 June. The Scottish battalion occupying St Honorine were most helpful, and directed us to an area in a field on the outskirts of the village where the Germans had buried those killed in the desperate fighting which had taken place around the village earlier in the campaign.

Unlike our practice of putting small wooden crosses at the head of each grave, the Germans had simply stuck in a short piece of wood on which, in some cases, they had placed the helmet and the identity tags of the individual buried on that spot. By this means we were able to identify the graves of eleven of our missing comrades, including Reggie Morgan. Unfortunately, a number of graves bore no specific identification marks and it could well have been that some other members of the battalion were buried in the area. On the other hand it was always possible that some had been taken prisoner and might still be alive. It wasn't appropriate for us to make any attempt to identify the bodies lying in the unmarked graves, this being the responsibility of the war graves experts who, in due course, would be moving all the remains to official war cemeteries. We had always hoped that Reggie and some of the others whose graves we had found might have been wounded and taken prisoner, so we were feeling somewhat depressed as we made our way back to report our findings. A week or two later, a further visit was made to St Honorine for a more extensive search of the area but no other graves of our men were uncovered. Our deep sense of loss on confirmation of Reggie's death was accentuated a day or so later when George Maginnis was killed. George, Reggie and Harry Morgan had been close friends in civilian life, and in addition to playing cricket and other games together, had all joined the regiment in Belfast on the same day. George and Reggie were now dead and Harry in hospital having had his foot amputated.

On my way back from St Honorine I couldn't help but notice a considerable increase in activity within the bridgehead which we had secured on the eastern bank of the Orne river. Vehicles of every description, both with and without heavy camouflage nets, were parked in farmyards, in ditches, in woods, in fact in almost any place which would not cause obstruction of the narrow roads and laneways. I noticed in particular that tanks were parked under the shade of the enormous wings of the gliders which still remained on the landing zones where we had arrived. Obviously something was brewing! We were soon to find out. One evening a few days later, a message was received that particular attention should be paid to ensuring that all personnel were well and properly dug-in. No reason was given for this strange instruction and it was generally assumed that information had been received about an impending major German attack.

As dawn broke in the eastern sky the following morning, about 18 July, it was accompanied by a distant hum which gradually increased in intensity until literally hundreds of allied bombers appeared high up in the sky, coming in over the coast like an enormous armada. Needless to say everybody immediately realized what was happening and needed no encouragement to clamber into their slit trenches. From our position we could look out over the undulating plain to the south and after passing over our heads the massed aircraft released cascades of bombs on the enemy positions north of Caen. It didn't need much imagination to realize what would happen to the positions we occupied if a stream of aircraft dropped bombs a little short of their intended targets. This did in fact happen in one area, resulting in the death of many members of the 3rd Canadian Division and other allied troops who were in close contact with the German positions outside Caen. There was no sign of any enemy aircraft, but the Germans did put up a considerable anti-aircraft barrage with some success, and we saw a number of allied aircraft literally explode and disintegrate in the air, with bits and pieces of flaming wreckage amongst which, presumably, were members of the crew, tumbling slowly to the earth below. However, the enemy barrage had little apparent effect on these massed formations of bombers as the countryside in front of us became completely obscured with dust thrown up by the mass of bombs dropped during the operation.

The successive waves of bombers seemed to be endless but how long the raid lasted was difficult to say. Gradually, however, the explosions ceased and when the dust began to settle we could make out numerous allied tanks edging their way forward towards the strong points the enemy had constructed to prevent any break-out from the eastern flank of the invasion. An hour or so after the massed air raid, heavy rain resulted in the battle area becoming so water-logged that the attack was brought to an early conclusion.

We were subsequently told that the operation had not been intended as a break-out from this flank but was intended rather to draw enemy armoured forces on to the British and Canadian flank around Caen and away from the western end of the allied bridgehead, to assist the American forces in their preparatory moves before the break-out which eventually forced a general German retreat.

The apparent failure of this effort to break through the German defences east of Caen, despite the large number of armoured units taking part and the enormous air support given at the commencement of the assault, gave rise to the first signs of frustration among our men, and no doubt those of the other battalions in the division, although it was realized that the heavy rains must have had a serious adverse effect on armoured operations. By that time we had been in close proximity to the enemy for more than six weeks and subjected to almost constant mortar and shell fire, and it would be an understatement to say that we were heartily sick of the Le Mesnil location we occupied at that time. We suffered a constant stream of casualties with more than fifty officers and men in that area killed or wounded during that spell, and there was a very obvious feeling amongst all ranks that it was time we were 'up and at 'em' rather than constantly clambering in and out of muddy slit trenches.

It was obvious to everyone that the planned break-out from the Normandy beach-head was far behind schedule, but even making allowances for the occasional adverse weather conditions which had prevailed since D-Day, we were beginning to wonder how much longer we would have to go living like moles in the Normandy orchards. As airborne troops, we were neither equipped, supplied or trained for the unpleasant form of damp trench warfare which seemed to be developing. Nevertheless, our men never lost their sense of humour, even in the muddy and hazardous conditions of Le Mesnil, but comments would often be heard about how much longer those 'bloody Americans' were going to take to start the threatened break-out at the western end of the perimeter. There was no doubt that senior staff of 21 Army Group recognized the predicament in which the division found itself and we had frequent visits up to our forward positions not only by our own brigade commander, and the divisional commander, General Gale, but also from senior staff including, on one occasion, Field Marshal Montgomery himself. One could not help comparing this with conditions in the First World War when it was well known that general staff officers made a point of never getting within many miles of the front line.

We were well supplied with information through a division newspaper — *Pegasus Goes To It* — which was circulated every few weeks, giving up-to-date information as to how things were progressing, but to some extent the benefit of this was offset by English newspapers which arrived from time to time and which seemed to take a gloomy and critical view of the progress of the campaign. These views were largely those of people who had little, if any, knowledge of the enormity of the operation or of the conditions which the allied armies were facing. By this time we were well aware of the devastation being caused in London and the South East of England by the German V1 rockets, and there was undoubted anxiety that we should get moving along the coast towards the launching sites of these weapons before they and any other surprises which Hitler might come up with could have an impact on the eventual outcome of the war. Fortunately, mail from home was now coming through regularly, which went a long way towards maintaining morale and relieving anxiety as to what was happening on the home front.

Château St Come

It was with considerable relief that on 21 July we moved out of Le Mesnil, which was taken over by another battalion in the brigade, the 12th Devonshire Regiment, although the move was not without its problems. The Germans seemed to get wind of what was happening and at regular intervals fired several salvos of mortar bombs into the area, which made the move in by the Devons and out by us very hazardous, but which would have been more so if the Germans hadn't been so regular in the time lapse between their salvos.

After getting clear of Le Mesnil we moved back to the same brigade reserve position we had occupied previously. The area was in a terrible condition with slit trenches half full of water, which, for a day or so, made life very uncomfortable, but fortunately the rains stopped and the hot sun appeared, which had a great uplifting effect on everyone's spirits. On the same day a draft of reinforcements arrived, some of whom were former members of the battalion who had been evacuated as casualties. With this draft was a young officer, Lieutenant Cranston, full of enthusiasm and with great leadership potential who had joined us at Bulford shortly before the move to the transit camp and who was greatly upset and disappointed at being left behind with our reserve company. When he arrived with the draft he was obviously delighted to be with the battalion again and in particular to be posted to B Company, to which he had been attached in England and where he had made a number of friends. Despite all the other losses we had incurred we were greatly saddened when this young and enthusiastic boy was killed

258

the following morning before he had had any opportunity to demonstrate his courage and ability. As always, when adding his name to the casualty lists, I couldn't help but think of his parents back home who would shortly receive that dreaded telegram.

Around the end of July we relieved the Ox and Bucks in the area of Château St Come between Breville and Le Mesnil. Once again, the area was in close proximity to the enemy, with only a field or two separating our forward locations. The Ox and Bucks had left the area in excellent condition, with well constructed and well-sited slit trenches and other defensive positions, and this, together with the continued fine weather, was a great help to our overall morale. Periodic mortar fire and shelling continued but probably the worst hazard in this area was enemy sniping, particularly from two orchards on the left of our front. However, our snipers responded to the German challenge, and so far as we could estimate the enemy losses, honours were about even. It was in the Château St Come area that we could hear quite clearly the Germans bringing up supplies to their forward areas by horse-drawn transport. This always took place at night time, which couldn't have made the task very easy, in addition to which our mortars would fire off a periodic salvo, assisted, when available, by our artillery support, all of which must have added considerably to their discomfiture.

One important and interesting feature of our life in Normandy was the slit trench or foxhole as the Americans called it. This was simply a hole dug in the ground as quickly as possible whenever one stopped anywhere to enable the digger to get below ground level and thereby reduce the risk of death or injury from the inevitable enemy mortar and shell fire. For this purpose, everybody was provided with an entrenching tool — a wicked looking implement rather like a miniature pickaxe and shovel combined on the end of an eighteen inch wooden shaft — which was immediately brought into use whenever we stopped within range of enemy fire and regardless of how long the stop was likely to be. These tools were designed to be carried hanging from the belt and during training they were considered an irritating encumbrance. When it came to the 'real thing' they were invaluable.

When time and circumstances permitted, a slit trench could

259

be made quite habitable — if that description can be applied to a hole in the ground which was identical in almost every way to a grave, although perhaps not so deep. For example, in the many slit trenches which I occupied from time to time, my batman Gillanders was very adept in digging out little shelves on which I could put my morning cup of tea and my glasses and any other items which I had to keep close at hand. Again, when circumstances permitted, some form of cover was set up over slit trenches as protection against rain and, in theory anyway, against shrapnel from mortars or shells bursting overhead. This was frowned on in some quarters on the grounds that it tended to encourage men to 'hide' underground and there was much opposition to anything which might militate against mobility and accentuate a trench warfare mentality of the First World War. However, slit trenches were, of necessity, sited tactically in positions from which men could best defend themselves as well as move into attack, and during static periods such as we experienced these positions would be developed into defensive strong points with fire steps, shallow connecting ditches and camouflage. The required level of mobility was maintained by active patrolling.

Another interesting aspect of the conditions we experienced was the provision of that essential facility, the latrine. On training exercises in England the first priority on arriving at any location would be that of digging latrines, and it was simple enough, in those conditions, to select a more remote spot, hopefully obscured from general view, at which to dig a few holes where men could relieve themselves. Holes for officers were of course separate from the holes for the troops. In the situation in which we now found ourselves, the problem wasn't quite so easily solved. We quickly learned that latrines dug in what might seem to be the best places for such a private and necessary function could be death traps because of the danger of getting there and back and of survival when, as it were, *in situ*. Men were very reluctant to remove their equipment and lower their trousers in situations where, with little warning, they would be required to dive for cover from approaching mortar bombs. However, this difficulty was quickly overcome by siting latrines in the bottom of slit trenches close at hand where men could relieve themselves with less anxiety. This became quite a joke in the battalion when, after a diet of dried porridge, dried meat and

260

dog biscuits it was frequently suggested that a couple of mortar bombs in the vicinity would help to relieve any sign of constipation.

One feature of active service which we were quick to recognize was the importance of the disciplines which had been developed during our training in the UK and which had not always been readily appreciated in circumstances when enemy action was purely imaginary. 'Stand to' shortly before day-break every morning involved every member of the battalion being alert, fully clothed and armed, and in position to meet any situation which might develop. It wasn't always easy to ensure that every man was fully alert, particularly after several days without regular sleep and under considerable stress, but there could be no exceptions, and the troops responded well to the need. Military operations over the years have always shown that it is first thing in the morning that troops are at their lowest ebb and when they are most vulnerable to surprise. The Germans were well aware of this but soon learned that we were not to be taken by surprise.

As soon as daylight permitted adequate surveillance of the forward areas, and it was apparent that enemy action was not imminent, troops would 'stand down,' sentries and forward outposts would be relieved, and those not on duty would set about their daily routine. The men would usually pair off in twos and threes to prepare their breakfast, sharing their mess tins for making tea and converting their blocks of solid porridge into a hot, gooey, sweet concoction which was very satisfying. One popular culinary practice was to break up our hard biscuits into the porridge and then add some flavour with bits of broken chocolate.

After breakfast every man would wash and attend to his personal hygiene; then to a thorough cleaning of the weapons for which he was responsible. After this was completed under the scrutiny of officers and NCOs, the men would get as much rest as they could. Frequently, strict compliance with this routine was not possible because of enemy action but so far as it was, it did ensure that all concerned were ready to meet whatever eventually might occur.

During the early days after the invasion, printed cards were provided for each man to send home, simply indicating, by striking out the alternatives, that he was either well or wounded in hospital, as appropriate. Later on, when circumstances permitted letter writing, all letters had to be read and censored by an officer to prevent the disclosure of information which might be detrimental to the war effort.

So far as I was concerned, as adjutant, there were many duties which had to be attended to, and for tea and porridge I was very much dependent upon my batman, Rifleman Gillanders, who considered it a matter of personal pride that I was adequately fed and watered. The commanding officer, Colonel Carson, had to be relieved of any concern about administrative details so that he could devote his attention to the operational needs of the battalion. The CO would frequently be required to visit brigade or divisional headquarters to be informed as to what was happening on other fronts and what was to be expected of us. When he returned, company commanders would be called in to be informed as to enemy dispositions and anticipated activity and to receive their orders as regards patrols and impending action. The CO was also expected to write a personal letter to the next of kin of all men killed, to provide them with some details and solace.

Throughout our time in the bridgehead area from 6 June until the middle of August, it was the policy, presumably of General Gale, that the battalions would interchange their positions within the division area as circumstances permitted. Some of these areas were much more hazardous and uncomfortable than others, and it was obviously appropriate that each battalion should have its share of the less desirable locations. Longueval, for example, where we spent the first twelve days, was largely isolated from the division bridgehead and was open to attack from all sides. Furthermore, the area was thickly wooded and gave the Germans ample cover to infiltrate patrols into the location. This meant that a high state of readiness had to be maintained by everybody at all times, which was a considerable strain. The area was under observation from the tall factory chimneys at Colombelles to the south and with ample cover for enemy attacks from that direction. Our only line of communication for evacuating wounded and bringing up supplies was along the river towpath, which was frequently cut-off, thereby adding to our difficulties.

Breville, on the other hand, after it had been cleaned up and defensive positions established, was much more secure from enemy penetration.

Le Mesnil, to my mind, was the worst location of all, aggravated by the fact that while we were in occupation the weather was generally wet, accentuating the mud and slush and general discomfort. In addition it was ideal country for sniper activity which meant that any form of movement in the battalion area was extremely hazardous. Enemy mortars also seemed to have every hedgerow and gateway pinpointed for their periodic stonks.

Taking over another battalion's location involved taking over their defensive layout, and we were able to assess the state of morale and discipline of the units we replaced from the condition of the areas we occupied. In this connection the discipline of the three regular army battalions of the Air Landing Brigade which still had a strong nucleus of regular officers and NCOs was very apparent, and we were inclined to be critical of the somewhat easy-going attitude of the parachute battalions, although when it came to tenacity and courage and general fighting qualities they were second to none. We were also very conscious of the fact that before reinforcements arrived, they were very much below strength following heavy losses during the landings and initial fighting.

Return to A Company

At the beginning of August, I handed over the duties of adjutant to Robin Rigby and replaced Dickie Martin as second in command to Charles Vickery of A Company. This was quite a change for me, because I had been adjutant since 1942, holding the office for more than two years.

When I joined A Company it was occupying a position near to the Château St Come, standing in extensive grounds between Breville and Le Mesnil. Up to D-Day I think it had been a horse stud farm, but by now the main house and outbuildings had been badly battered. Once again, our forward posts in the surrounding hedges were only a hundred yards or so away from the nearest German locations. However, despite our close proximity and the usual sniper activity, our stay in the vicinity of the château was fairly peaceful, although made unpleasant by the stench from the rotting carcasses of dead horses and cattle lying around the adjoining fields and killed by mortar and shell fire weeks earlier.

We gained the impression at this time that the Germans facing our position had given up any idea of breaking through our lines and there were rumours that because of the threatened American break-out at the western end of the beach-head and the fear of encirclement, they were preparing to pull out from their positions and back towards the River Seine.

After about ten days at the château we were relieved by the Free Dutch Brigade which had been formed in the UK and which, after arrival in Normandy, was placed under command of our division. We were not only greatly impressed by the smartness and enthusiasm of these Dutch troops but also somewhat overwhelmed by the specialist support services with which they were provided. We then moved back to a division rest area west of the River Orne where we were able to spend several days in complete relaxation and in glorious weather, well out of range of enemy bullets or mortar bombs for the first time since 6 June.

8

Operation Paddle

Our move to the rest area at Colleville-Sur-Mer took place on 12 August, and as the days passed there was a growing feeling of excitement and- anticipation that our confinement to the Normandy *bocage* would soon end. Rumours circulated that the Germans had started to pull back on their western flank facing the American armies and there was much speculation that we would soon be on the move.

As the days passed and there was no confirmation of these rumours, the sense of frustration increased and was not alleviated by a visit by our division commander, General Gale, who congratulated the battalion on the important contribution it had made to the success of the invasion campaign. There was some comfort in the knowledge that plans had been prepared for the part the battalion would play when the 'breakout' did take place, to be initiated by the code word 'Paddle', but the order received on 16 August that the battalion would relieve the 12th Devons at Amfreville the following day wasn't viewed with much enthusiasm.

As dawn was breaking on the morning of 17 August the battalion was ready to move back to the bridgehead east of the river. All the usual inspections had been carried out and the men had been 'fallen out' to await the arrival of transport, and were sitting around in their platoon areas smoking and chatting. Suddenly, word arrived from somewhere, I don't know how or by whom, that Operation Paddle was underway.

As the news spread, a cheer went up and officers and men alike scrambled to their feet, laughing and shaking hands as if the end of the war had been announced. Sadly, the occasion was marked by an unfortunate incident just as the transport vehicles arrived and the leading troops were moving forward to embus. A single shot rang out from the ranks of one of the platoons about twenty yards in front of where we were standing. For a few minutes there was confusion, with shouts from the head of the column to 'Get a move on' conflicting with cries for 'Stretcher bearer!' It transpired that a man armed with a Bren gun had carelessly banged the butt of the weapon on the ground and it had gone off, hitting another rifleman standing a few yards away in the head and killing him instantly. The dead man was Rifleman Topping, a quiet purposeful man and a first class soldier who I knew well and who, a few seconds earlier, had been expressing his delight at the thought of the breakout from the bridgehead. No longer adjutant, I wasn't involved, but I understood that there was no time for an investigation as to exactly what had happened. Leaving medical orderlies to remove the body, the battalion moved off with, no doubt, an addition to the casualty return: 'Rifleman Topping — Killed in Action.' I remembered Robin Crockett's remark to me at the time. 'There are times and places where one expects to get killed, but standing around a rest area isn't one of them.'

On arrival at Amfreville, we were put in the picture. The badly battered Germans had begun to pull back along their entire front with the apparent intention of securing the eastern bank of the River Seine. The allied armies intended to destroy the enemy, or as much of it as they could, before they could cross the river. The task of the 6th Airborne Division was to follow up the retreating enemy on our front, causing as much damage and harassment as possible thereby delaying their 'escape' and facilitating the encircling efforts of the powerful allied armies moving up from the south. Our division was to move on two fronts; the main body, including the two parachute brigades, taking the main inland roads, and our brigade the coastal road through Cabourg and Deauville.

When the operation got underway, we were following the Devons and Ox and Bucks, and had the opportunity to see the defensive positions which the Germans had established in front of the areas we had occupied, and we could not but admire their handiwork. Slit trenches and gun positions were well located, constructed and camouflaged, which was a compliment to us I suppose, reflecting their recognition of the ability of our patrols to penetrate into their areas. At intervals of about a hundred yards along either side of the narrow roadway were slit trenches marked with long poles to which foliage had been tied, resembling a sort of twig broom used for sweeping up leaves. Apparently, these slit trenches were provided by the Germans to enable drivers and escorts of horse-drawn supply vehicles to find quick cover when subjected to our mortar fire. In such circumstances, presumably, the horses were left to fend for themselves.

As we approached Merville, location of the coastal battery which the 9th Parachute Battalion had destroyed during the night of 5-6 June, the roadway and adjoining countryside took on a lunar-type appearance due to the hundreds of craters caused by RAF bombing. However, the battery itself was located some distance away from the centre of this bombed area and showed little evidence of having suffered from air attack. Although I didn't see it, I understand that the Germans had constructed a dummy battery on which the RAF bombers had concentrated their efforts, and at the time, no doubt, the German camouflage experts must have been rubbing their hands with glee at the success of their subterfuge. To my mind this made the success of the 9th Parachute Battalion even more commendable and explained their heavy losses when the assault on the battery was made.

After passing Merville, we passed through the other battalions and led the brigade towards Cabourg, each company taking it in turns to lead the eastward advance. Movement was particularly difficult on the coast road because of the thoroughness with which the Germans had laid mines and, in particular, by the considerable number of small antipersonnel mines hidden in the verges and sand dunes, from which we suffered a number of casualties. Furthermore, on the southern side of the road, the low lying country had been flooded, in some places to a depth of several feet, by the opening of sluice gates in the nearby rivers, making it virtually impossible to leave the road and move across country. In addition, the flooded countryside had provided a very fertile breeding ground for mosquitoes, which added considerably to our discomfort.

Another problem experienced all the way to the Seine was the extensive use by the Germans of snipers, knowing, as they did, that because of the mines and flooding, we were forced to remain on or alongside the roadway. One or two snipers, well concealed in buildings or other vantage points, could easily delay a numerically superior force unless courageously led and very determined. When a sniper's bullet thuds into a nearby comrade the natural tendency is to dive for cover, and it takes a lot of courage in those circumstances to keep moving ahead to locate and destroy the hidden enemy. The sniper knows that immediately he has fired a shot, successfully or otherwise, numerous pairs of binoculars will be searching the nearby trees and buildings in order to pinpoint his location, in which case he can also be very brave and stay where he is in the hope of causing further damage, or get out while the going is good. He realizes that he can only kill one at a time, and if a number of determined soldiers are pressing on in his direction, the odds are very much against him, in which case he can either follow a predetermined line of departure or attempt to surrender — a course of action not recommended in such circumstances. The major problem for us was to ensure that we kept on the move despite the frequent sniper's bullet and not to let the leading troops go to ground with the attendant problem of getting them on the move again and thereby delaying the movement of the entire column.

The Germans were also very adept at blowing up every bridge or culvert which crossed our line of advance — sometimes when our leading troops were only a short distance away — and although this didn't cause much hindrance to troops on foot, it certainly caused considerable delay for the vehicles.

Just after we had turned on to the Cabourg road at a place called Le Homme there was a large crater extending right across the road which had to be partially filled in before any vehicles could proceed, and our pioneer platoon set to with their picks and shovels, the only tools available to them. It was at about this time that the battalion linked up with the Free Belgian Brigade who again, like the Dutch, were well equipped with Bren gun carriers and other heavy vehicles. In the meantime, A Company, which was leading the battalion, pressed on down the road towards the outskirts of Cabourg. We hadn't gone very far when we heard a large explosion to our rear and were later to find out that one of a section of tanks which the Belgian Brigade had sent up from somewhere in the rear to assist us getting into Cabourg, had attempted to cross the crater and had set off a large mine and had been put out of action. Later that day our battalion water truck was also blown up while attempting to cross the same crater, completely blocking our supply route and adding to our difficulties.

That night on the outskirts of Cabourg was extremely uncomfortable, confined as we were to a narrow roadway and unable to move forward or back, and although we were shelled spasmodically we were thankful that the German artillery on the high ground beyond Cabourg didn't appear to be able to take full advantage of our very exposed situation.

The following day, 20 August 1944, was my twenty-eighth birthday, and a very uncomfortable birthday it turned out to be. As dawn broke we became more and more exposed to enemy observation and any movement immediately attracted enemy shell and mortar fire, but there was little we could do other than huddle in the shallow trenches we had scraped in the stony ground on either side of the roadway. Up ahead our recce platoon continued their valiant efforts to press on down the road into Cabourg but fire from a German 88mm self-propelled gun and machine gun fire from strong points at the road junction made movement impossible. In the meantime our pioneer platoon was endeavouring to find a route through the mine fields in the gardens of pleasant holiday villas on the sea front, but again the position was too exposed to permit progress. Another patrol attempted to find a way through behind the villas on the right hand side of the road but came under heavy fire and it became obvious that we were not going to get very far without the assistance of the tanks which were held up to our rear, or of artillery support, which wasn't available.

Despite these difficulties Gillanders was still able to produce a mug of hot sweet tea to celebrate the occasion. I was enjoying this beside my slit trench when suddenly there was a whoosh followed by a thud and a shell landed in the field about ten yards from where I was sitting. As the arrival of the shell had not been accompanied by a violent explosion, of which I doubt whether I would have heard very much, I thought for an instant that it must have been a dud, or possibly with a delayed action fuse. The explanation quickly became apparent when a cloud of white smoke began to billow up in the air from the point where the shell had landed. During the next few minutes a series of similar shells landed close to our position, each sending up its tell-tale plume of smoke, and it was apparent that the German gunners were ranging their guns on our location from the high ground to the east of Cabourg from where they could observe the precise landing points of the smoke shells. We then had little doubt that these 'sighters' would quickly be followed by high explosive.

There was nothing that we could do about our predicament. We couldn't get forward and we couldn't go back, and it was impossible to get off the narrow road because of mines on the one side and flooding on the other. The best we could do was to crouch in our shallow slit trenches, scraping away with our entrenching tools and to get another inch or so of cover in the stony ground, and hope for the best. Strangely, nothing happened. Whether the Germans had run out of high explosive shells or had their attention directed elsewhere, or what, we never knew. Gradually, the tension eased, but later on that day we were not sorry to be pulled back from the outskirts of Cabourg. Having neither artillery nor tank support it was decided that there was little likelihood of progress against the determined German resistance in the town, and that we should be moved to another sector of the advancing allied front, and that our positions would be taken over by the Free Belgian Brigade. That night we were transported to Troarne and the following day, in pouring rain, moved on foot along narrow country roads in the general direction of Deauville, our next objective.

By this time, I had settled in as second in command of A Company, but I was finding life very different to that of adjutant. When on the move, one or two of the rifle companies were in the lead, and usually in contact with the rear elements of the retreating Germans whose delaying tactics continued to consist of blowing up bridges or culverts, and by leaving small groups of snipers, who were extremely difficult to locate, hidden in woods and hedges. The Germans were fighting hard for time to get the remnants of their armies back across the Seine further south, while we were being pressurized to get to the river as quickly as possible to cut the remaining routes available to them. It was usually my job to be with company HQ towards the rear of the company, but frequently Charles Vickery was called to battalion HQ for some reason or other, when I would take his place with the leading platoon.

We were fully aware by this time that the best protection against enemy delaying tactics was for us to keep on the move and thereby keep him on the move. This required a lot of courage and determination, particularly on the part of the leading riflemen, and acceptance of the risk of some casualties, but fewer than if we allowed ourselves to be pinned down and subjected to artillery and mortar fire. This was where we reaped the benefit of years of training in the leap-frogging techniques of 'fire and movement' — sections alternately giving covering fire, often indiscriminately into woods, hedges and houses where snipers or machine guns might be concealed, and thus forcing the enemy to keep their heads down, whilst others moved forward, keeping the momentum going and depriving the enemy of time to organize defensive locations. Our troops, both NCOs and men, responded magnificently to the demands made on them at this time. The situation was very different from the static warfare of the Normandy bridgehead, and they soon recognized that when it came to cat and mouse skirmishing in open country they were the masters. From the increasing numbers of German troops giving themselves up it seemed that they also recognized their inferiority, but from time to time I suspected that enemy troops who thought that they could suddenly switch from sniping at our men to becoming prisoners of war were never given the opportunity. In this type of close combat, when a split second decision could be a matter of life or death, no man could be criticized for shooting first and asking questions later.

Fortunately, the weather was fine during the week or so of our move up to the Seine and we were no longer hemmed in by flooded fields and anti-personnel mines. There appeared to have been little cultivation of the surrounding fields and orchards and the unmown grass and overgrown hedges were more to our advantage in getting to close quarters than our opposing numbers. As dusk descended each evening, we would hope to find ourselves near some old farm buildings or cattle sheds where some of us might find shelter not only from the occasional shower of rain, but also where we could light a fire to make tea and have a cigarette without the risk of enemy detection. If there were no convenient buildings, we would make do with a ditch or dyke, and provide our own cover with groundsheets and foliage. When a location was selected, whether suitable or not, the platoons of the company would close up and select their own bivouac areas, and sentries and standing patrols would be posted, after which, food, drink and rest were the priorities for those

271

not otherwise engaged. Whilst our men could always find a time and a place to brew tea, the provision of a hot meal once a day was not so easy when on the move and in close contact with the enemy. However, this was largely overcome by centralizing all cooking facilities at the rear and carrying hot food forward up narrow roads and tracks at night, by no means an easy task.

One particular night stands out in my memory. The battalion was moving into the outskirts of Deauville with one company, C Company, on the left on the main road from Cabourg and my company, A Company on a narrow road further south from Vauville. Our company objective was a small bridge over the River Touques, just west of the village of Bonneville. Charles Vickery had been called back to battalion HQ, so I was moving with the leading platoon.

We had been making good progress, and about four o'clock in the afternoon had reached the crest of the high ground running down to the wide flat plain where the River Touques winds its way between Deauville and Pont L'Evêque. There were a few small cottages scattered around, but no sign of any local inhabitants. Near the summit of this slope was a minor crossroads with a small pill box sited on the right hand corner, presumably part of the German defence system against the possibility of allied landings in the Deauville area. It was a lovely, peaceful, sunny afternoon, with no obvious enemy opposition and I stopped for a minute to admire the beautiful scenery. Away to the left I could see the buildings of Deauville, and to the right the wide flat valley of the Touques river. It was later I realized that I should have appreciated that we were almost certainly under observation from the high ground on the far side of the river, and I regretted not studying the line of the river more carefully.

The leading section continued on its way down the hill towards another crossroads. I was walking with the leading platoon commander about a hundred yards behind the leading section when we saw that the leading men were waving to the section to stop. We cautiously walked on down the hill, and suddenly, very much to our surprise, we saw a Bren gun carrier in the middle of the crossroads with several khaki clad figures talking to some civilians. I assumed that the khaki clad figures were on our side so I joined them and found that they were from the reconnaissance company of the Belgian Brigade. They had made

272

their way into Deauville and, finding the main river bridge blown up, had continued along the western side of the river towards the bridge at Touques, which was our objective. On reaching the bridge they had come under fire from the far bank and had withdrawn up to the crossroads, leaving one man missing and believed killed or wounded at the railway crossing beside the bridge. The civilians, who had appeared from somewhere, were all wearing Free French armbands bearing the Cross of Lorraine, but as they neither understood nor spoke a word of English, and insisted on all talking at the same time, they weren't able to provide any useful information.

At the time, I had little or no idea as to what was happening to the left or right of our position other than the assurance from the Belgians that they had come along the road from Deauville without meeting any opposition, or without meeting any of our battalion who, so far as I knew, were moving towards Deauville along the coast road. This all seemed to be a bit of a mystery. To the right, along the road to Pont L'Evêque, I had no idea what was happening. However, as the bridge over the Touques was our objective, I decided to leave two platoons to secure the crossroads and to move forward, with the other platoon, over the crossroads towards the river to find out what was going on there, and at the same time to see what we could do about the missing Belgian.

Having issued some brief orders to the senior platoon commander to take charge during my absence until Charles Vickery returned and telling him what I proposed to do, I set off down the narrow road leading to the bridge, taking with me the Belgian NCO in charge of the carrier section, who told me that he knew exactly where his comrade had been hit by German small arms fire. The road was little more than a lane, with extensive overgrown verges and hedges on each side cutting out any view of the neighbouring fields. I was following behind the leading section of eight men staggered on either side and keeping close to the hedges so as to be able to take cover quickly should the need arise. They were well drilled, moving cautiously but quickly from one bend in the road to the next, then pausing and, if necessary, crawling to a position from which to scan the stretch of road ahead for any signs of enemy activity.

All went well until we were about thirty yards from the railway crossing, just before the river bridge, when, from directly ahead, there were several short burst of machine gun fire. We all flattened ourselves in the undergrowth at the side of the road, but instinctively I realized that we had not been the target as there was no crack of passing bullets or whine of ricochets from the road or trees. Keeping as close as I could to the hedge, I ran forward to the leading man who was then only twenty yards or so from the crossing gateway. He thought that the firing had come from the far bank of the river and slightly to the right, but had seen nothing. A few yards further on our right was a wooden gateway leading into a field and beyond the gateway the end wall of a small house, presumably the home of the crossing keeper.

Very cautiously I crawled up to the gate from where I could see the river and the far bank, which was heavily overgrown with bushes and weeds and with dense woods to left and right. Suddenly there was another short burst of firing, and I ducked back from the gate, but again neither I nor the others on the road appeared to be the target. It was then that I saw the wounded Belgian. He was lying in the ditch just short of the crossing gate and waving his arm to attract our attention. The problem was how to get him out. There were obviously enemy troops on the far bank who could see the crossing and anyone who approached to help the wounded man would be exposed to their view, so I decided that the only course was to blot out the view with smoke for long enough to enable stretcher bearers to get to the man and carry him out of enemy view.

As usual, Gillanders was close at hand, so I sent him back to bring up the Belgian NCO and stretcher bearers, also a supply of '69' smoke grenades. Fortunately there was very little wind, and a few minutes later I was able to toss several grenades over the gate into the field and down to the railway. These quickly obscured any view from the river, and the stretcher bearers were able to lift the injured man and carry him off up the road without enemy interference.

While this was going on, I went forward to the cottage and found the doorway open. Very carefully, and with Gillanders behind me, I went in. The room I entered was small, but well furnished and appeared to have been only recently used with crockery and cutlery on the rectangular table. Leaving Gillanders to watch the front of the house I climbed the stairs to one of the two bedrooms where from the window I had a clear view

274

of the river bank. Standing well back to ensure that I wouldn't be seen, I scanned the far bank through my binoculars. Suddenly I saw what I had been looking for: three German soldiers standing well back from the river bank and largely obscured by the thick undergrowth, but clearly distinguishable by their square helmets.

As I watched, one of them pointed downstream towards the bridge and then moved off quickly in that direction. The other two were then joined by another man from the right and all three bent down as if examining something and disappeared from my sight. Although I couldn't be sure, I assumed that this was a defensive position covering the bridge about thirty or forty yards downstream. Moving slowly back from the window I went to the front bedroom of the cottage, which had a window facing the road. From there I had a clear view of the railway crossing and a somewhat restricted view of the road bridge over the river, and I could see that it had been only partially demolished. The road surface at the centre of the bridge had been blown up, but the girders and rails on the right were still intact, so although vehicles couldn't pass, it would be possible for troops on foot to scramble across. In the face of resistance, however, supporting covering fire would be essential. The thought did occur to me that I could bring up the platoon waiting down the road and force a crossing under cover of whatever smoke we could master, but it didn't take me long to decide that the best course would be to report back to Charles Vickery and find out whether a crossing at this particular point was justified. The light was also beginning to fade, which would have made a crossing in any strength particularly hazardous, so I rejoined Gillanders at the entrance to the cottage and with him returned to the crossroads to find Charles or await his return.

The company sergeant major had set up our company HQ in a massive German pill box or bunker located in one corner of the crossroads. 'Pill box' is probably the wrong description because although quite small, about twenty feet square I suppose, the walls were about four feet thick and the roof even thicker. What it had been designed and built for, I couldn't imagine because there were no apertures in the walls to permit defensive fire, and I could only think that it must have been intended for a communications centre or perhaps to carry an anti-aircraft gun. By comparison, the many small strong points

275

built around the English countryside to help repel the threatened German invasion in 1940 were like match boxes.

Many years later I happened to be driving around the area of the Trouville crossroads and had some difficulty in locating the position, as the roads have been widened and improved. The German concrete construction was nowhere to be seen until I suddenly realized that a row of poplar trees had been grown along two sides of the crossroads, completely hiding the building from view. But on investigation, there it was, as we had left it many years earlier, and I have little doubt that it is still there today.

After checking our platoon locations I returned to the bunker, hoping not only for some hot tea, which I had no doubt Gillanders would have ready for me, and for some rest. As usual on such occasions, a hot meal arrived from somewhere; steaming hot stew of meat and vegetables prepared in large oval 'kettles' and carried forward by jeep and on foot more often than not in conditions of extreme difficulty by cooks, drivers, batmen, sanitation orderlies and other rear HQ personnel whose cheerful dedication to their task of keeping everybody well fed was a moral tonic as well as a very necessary physical boost.

I was sound asleep when Charles Vickery arrived back at company HQ, but I was soon wide awake. As I yawned myself back into a state of consciousness, I had the impression that Charles was in a somewhat sombre mood. He was never particularly loquacious, but I suspected that he was either irritated at me being asleep or that the place I had selected as company HQ didn't meet with his unqualified approval. I had thought it ideal, but Charles never believed in permitting himself any comforts or advantages which could not be extended to all the men in his company. If the prevailing circumstances didn't permit any man in his company to have a roof over his head, then Charles would need a lot of persuasion not to spend the night in the open himself. I suppose that this was a reflection of his many pre-war years in the ranks, when the day-to-day running of the battalion was largely in the hands of the warrant and non-commissioned officers, while an officer's life consisted largely of polo matches, sandwiched between cocktail parties and mess dinners for the entertainment of local dignitaries.

Charles had sent for the platoon commanders as soon as he had arrived and we were soon all squatting on the concrete floor of the inner room of the bunker in the dim glow of a hurricane lamp with maps, pencils and paper ready to learn what was going on and what we would be doing next.

The first news he gave us was that Killer Johnson had been killed a few hours earlier. Killer commanded C Company, which had been moving along the road nearer the coast. A shell had landed on or near his company jeep, killing him and badly wounding his sergeant major and other members of his company HQ. This was a great blow for us all. Killer was a regular officer who had been commissioned into the regiment from Sandhurst a few years before the outbreak of war. He had joined the battalion in Palestine and had made a name for himself as a courageous and resourceful leader during the difficult period of the British mandate in that country. I had shared accommodation with him at Bulford and was probably more aware than most of his anxieties about the young wife he had married shortly before D'Day; a girl he had met during our stay in Harpenden some years earlier. As usual on such occasions I immediately thought of the telegram she would be receiving in a day or so — and how she would react. (Killer and the others killed near Deauville are buried in the military cemetery at Trouville.)

My reflections were cut short when Charles asked for a summary of what had been happening during his absence. I outlined the position at the bridge — that it was partially blown up, but could probably be crossed on foot if the enemy elements on the far bank of the river could be contained in some way. He asked me why I hadn't made some attempt to get across and seemed irritated when I told him that I hadn't thought the risks worthwhile. He then went on to explain that the division was now largely up to the line of the river, as far south as Pont L'Evêque. Crossings would be forced the following day, after which the division would continue the advance towards the River Seine as fast as possible. At that point, I was anticipating the possibility of continuing the sleep from which I had been suddenly interrupted, but it was not to be.

Battalion HQ, said Charles, wanted a patrol to cross the river immediately, with the object of finding out whether the Germans were holding the line of the railway on our front, and if so, in what strength; also, if possible to bring in a prisoner or prisoners from whom information about enemy strength and dispositions could be extracted. I knew instinctively that I would take out the patrol, and that when he had mentioned battalion HQ he had meant John Drummond, who was in charge of the battalion patrol activity. I was beginning to wonder whether being friendly with John was a good thing or a bad thing. Anyway, Charles went on to say that battalion HQ was sending up a section of Royal Engineers with a collapsible boat, and two Free Frenchmen who were familiar with the local countryside and who would act as guides.

'You should aim to be back by daylight,' said Charles. I looked at my watch; it was just after midnight, so time was short.

Telling Charles that I didn't like the idea of being guided by two unknown Frenchmen, Free or otherwise, I took my leave and with the company sergeant major, moved into the entrance area of the bunker. Night patrols were difficult and hazardous enough at the best of times, but particularly so when one hadn't the opportunity, beforehand of studying the countryside in daylight. In the thickly wooded Normandy *bocage* it was necessarily very slow work, moving along hedges and from tree to tree, stopping every few yards and straining one's ears to pick up the sound of voices or the clink of equipment from enemy activity a few yards ahead and knowing that a lapse in concentration would probably have only one result.

I told the sergeant major that I would take Sergeant McCully and the section from 7 Platoon commanded by Corporal Ayres. This was the platoon I had commanded several years earlier. Sergeant McCully, or 'the Brown Bomber' as he was known for his boxing prowess, and Corporal Ayres were regular soldiers and first class NCOs. (Many years later on a Normandy reunion, I met Sergeant McCully's widow who told me that after leaving the army he had joined the prison service in Northern Ireland, and had been murdered at his front door in Belfast by the IRA.) Each man would be armed with a Sten gun and would carry only spare magazines and two '36' grenades, and the patrol should be ready to move off in fifteen minutes, by which time I hoped that the boating section and the guides would have arrived.

During the short time available to me, I took another close look at my map. Facing east, the direction in which we were moving, the railway which I had to reconnoitre lay on our side of the river to the north towards Deauville, whilst to the south towards Pont L'Evêque it lay on the far side of the river. Obviously our crossing would be to the south. I could see that after crossing the river, we would have to traverse at least 500 yards or so of open, flat country before reaching the railway line. The area was criss-crossed with dykes and ditches, and in the darkness progress would undoubtedly be slow, which presented a problem if we were to return by daylight. However, my major concern was to know where we would cross the river, a problem accentuated by the fact that it wound its way from Pont L'Evêque in enormous loops and bends, which meant that unless we could identify our crossing point clearly we would be confronted by the river two or even three times before reaching the railway line. I offered up a brief prayer that our guides really had a sound knowledge of the countryside. As I checked my own equipment, Sergeant McCully came into the bunker and reported that the patrol was ready to move off. Despite the time problem, I told him to bring them all into the bunker, where I gave them a very brief explanation of what we were to do. After we had crossed the river, we would proceed in single file with me in the lead and Sergeant McCully in the rear. If we ran into trouble, no man would fire a shot without my order. I could afford to be brief, as they all had more experience of night patrolling than me.

We moved out of the bunker where I found a jeep parked on the road with a small group standing around talking quietly. One of the figures moved towards me and identified himself as a corporal from the Royal Engineers, explaining that he had the boat on the jeep and two men to assist in ferrying us across the river. He then pointed to two shadowy figures standing nearby, saying that they were Free French guides.

'Only one of them speaks a little English,' he said, 'but they have been instructed by brigade headquarters as to what they have to do.'

I replied, somewhat brusquely, 'What's that?'

'To guide us to a suitable point for crossing the river,' he replied.

When I spoke to the two Frenchmen I quickly realized that there was no point in trying to converse with them, but simply said, 'OK, let's go.'

As I had anticipated they headed off down the road to the right with the patrol following in single file and with the jeep bringing up the rear. I allowed the two Frenchmen to lead the way, and they had no apparent hesitation in doing so, which suggested that they knew where we were going and that they were confident that there were no enemy troops in the area. Despite the information given to me by Charles Vickery I wasn't quite so confident. However, I had to accept that the guides were reliable, and time was important.

After about 200 yards they stopped and spoke to one another rapidly in French, and then turned down a narrow laneway to the left which, by my reckoning, would lead us nearer to the river. The hedges on either side were high and heavily overgrown and combined with high trees to accentuate the darkness, and I was concerned about the jeep following on behind with no lights, so dropped back to check with the driver that all was well and that the boat wasn't going to be dumped in the ditch due to some mishap. I needn't have worried. He assured me that he could see his way perfectly well.

Catching up with the guides I could hear them talking animatedly to one another but without slackening their pace, from which I assumed that we were still on course for whatever crossing point they had selected. Suddenly they stopped, and I could make out a gateway on the left and a few yards beyond it, the outline of a small two storey house. Without saying anything to me they opened the gate and walked up towards the house which was in complete darkness. The patrol had closed up behind me so I turned to Corporal Ayres and told him to wait, and then followed the two Frenchmen up to the house, catching them up just as one of them bent down and gathered a handful of dirt from the ground and flung it up against one of the small upstairs windows. I watched and waited, but nothing happened. He repeated his effort and suddenly I could just make out an opening window and a head peering down at us. Then followed a rapid conversation between all three which I didn't understand, although I heard the word 'Boche' repeated on several occasions. Then the head withdrew, the window silently closed and all was again quiet.

Turning to me one of the guides said, quietly, 'Zees is ze point.' He then took my arm and steered me around the end of the house and pointed into the darkness. I couldn't see anything other than a sort of misty blackness.

'*Où est le fleuve?*' I said.

'*Quinze metres,*' he replied. We had arrived at our crossing point, but I was still unable to pinpoint the precise spot on my map which would have enabled me to decide on the direction we should take after crossing the river, nor could I distinguish any landmarks on the far side which would have enabled me to follow a compass bearing. However, I knew that the railway line I had to reconnoitre was up to 1,000 yards due east of the river so I decided to go ahead with the crossing and head due east until we met the railway, whether that was the shortest route or not.

The four Royal Engineers quietly lifted the boat off the jeep, and guided by our French companions we made our way down a narrow path at the side of the house, through a gateway into what appeared to be a grass field and in a short time reached the river bank. I could just make out the far bank, about ten yards away, and I could see that the river was fast flowing and appeared to be very deep, certainly deep and fast enough to cause serious problems for any fully clothed and equipped soldier who might be unfortunate enough to fall in. Knowing that a flat bottomed collapsible boat was not the most stable of craft I decided that we would cross with three of the patrol at a time, which meant five in the boat with two of the RE boatmen handling the paddles. This mean four crossings, including one of the Free French guides, but when I explained that they would go on '*la deuxième fois*' they both made it very clear that neither of them had any intention of crossing the river. I couldn't translate exactly what they were saying, but from their references to 'les Boches' and their gesticulations of drawing their hands across their throats I gathered that they were not going to risk being taken prisoner because they would be shot out of hand.

I decided to go first with the RE corporal and Gillanders. Very gingerly the boat was pushed off the bank into the water, and with the front paddle man in the lead and the rear paddle man lying on his stomach holding the flat stern of the boat against the bank to prevent it swinging downstream with the fast flowing current, one by one we stepped on board. In the darkness and with the need to avoid any noise, this was quite a tricky operation. As each man stepped into the boat it was important that he did so in the middle so that his weight didn't tip the craft too much to one side. He then had to edge forward, keeping to the centre until the next man stepped down, when both would edge out to make room for one another and maintain an even keel — if there had been a keel. With the five men on board the sides — or gunwales, I suppose you'd call them — were only an inch or so above the water, so there was very little margin for error. Fortunately, all went well, and in a few minutes we were across and the front paddle man jumped out and let the boat swing round against the bank for us to step out. I noticed that in addition to crossing the river we had also drifted about ten yards downstream.

Telling Gillanders to keep his eyes skinned 'inland' I turned to watch the remainder of the patrol brought across. All went well, and in about fifteen minutes we were all kneeling on the bank ready to move off. All was very quiet, still and dark. I had decided that we would move straight ahead at right angles to the river and keep as straight a course as we could until we came to the railway. I was on the point of standing up when there was what seemed to me at the time an almighty bang and I sensed a bullet missing my head by inches, or less. I turned in amazement, and immediately a quiet Ulster voice said, 'Sorry sorr, my Sten just went off!'

I knew of the propensity of the Sten gun to fire if the stock was banged on the ground with the safety catch off, so I said nothing. There didn't seem much point, and the shot had at least missed. I simply reflected that the sound of a shot from the darkness at two thirty in the morning was hardly likely to cause any panic amongst enemy troops within earshot, and set off. I had instructed the RE corporal to remain at the point where we had crossed the river and to be on the look-out for our return and for the possibility of enemy activity in the vicinity.

Although there was no moon, the visibility seemed to have improved, possibly because there were no trees around us, and I could make out small dark shapes which turned out to be bushes or clumps of overgrown grass and bullrushes. We were moving in single file, each man a yard or so behind the man in front, lifting our feet high with each step to reduce the rustle of boots on the undergrowth; stopping every fifty yards or so to listen; mouth open to make hearing more sensitive. On such occasions I always thought of what the enemy would be doing. If out on a patrol like us, probably much the same, possibly less cautious and moving more quickly. If in some static position, fidgeting around, talking or maybe smoking. That was what we had to look and listen for. Several times I narrowly escaped falling into a ditch or stream and we would have to search for a way round or where we could jump across.

Our first surprise was when we were suddenly confronted by a river — obviously the River Touques over which we had already been transported, but at this spot the river was flowing in the opposite direction. It was equally obvious that we had crossed on the outside of one of the many convex loops, and the question was whether we turn left or right to get out of the 'loop'. My hunch was left, which turned out to be correct, and after a hundred yards or so along the bank, the river looped back on itself again, and we were back in open country to pursue our eastward course.

From the river to the railway took about forty minutes, I suppose, and we had neither seen or heard anything which might suggest that there were any German troops in the vicinity. We were obstructed by a wire and post fence, on the other side of which I could make out an embankment which, I assumed, carried the railway lines, and beyond which, I recollected, from my earlier study of my map, was a small cluster of houses at a spot called Le Forge with a road running parallel to the railway; to the left up towards Trouville and to the right, to Pont L'Evêque. It took us only a few minutes to locate a suitable spot for getting through the fence without noise, and together with Sergeant McCully I clambered up the sloping embankment to take a look. We could see very little, although we could just make out the shapes of small houses, but there were no lights or any sign of movement. I decided to move up along the line of the railway towards the rail and river crossing where I had been earlier in the day.

We had only covered about a hundred yards when I heard the noise of a vehicle. I stopped and listened. Sure enough, it was a vehicle of some sort travelling towards us from the direction of Pont L'Evêque; maybe two vehicles. This was our opportunity if we could get down to the road in time and find a suitable position for an ambush, and maybe we would get the prisoners we were after. The patrol closed up and I quickly told them that we would get down to the road as quickly as possible. That was when our troubles started. We had been walking along a narrow pathway alongside the railway, having left the embankment behind us, and on our right was a ditch about four or five feet across. To jump this from a standing position wasn't easy. I flung myself forward, managed to land on the slope of the bank on the far side and grabbing the grass with my free hand, crawled and hauled myself up. I looked round to see half the patrol in the ditch and the other half helping to drag them out. We were then confronted with another fence and a thick hedge, so ran along this to find a way through. We came to a gateway and burst our way through into what, I suppose, was a back garden. We went down the garden through trees and bushes until, when I was about ten yards from the roadway, I saw two grey trucks, one close behind the other, passing along the road. I was tempted to open fire from where I was, but as I hesitated, they were gone, and we were left, panting with our exertions and disappointed at the opportunity we had missed.

In the hope that the trucks we had seen would return or that there might be other enemy traffic, we took up positions on either side of the road and waited, but nothing happened, and after twenty minutes or so I noticed a lightening of the sky in the east and decided that if we were to get back by daylight we should be on our way. We made our way back to the railway and then struck out across the flat valley on the far side back towards the river. We reached the river bank without incident and turned upstream along the bank to where we knew the boating group would be waiting. The light was still very dim with a dark background of trees on the far side of the river, and suddenly I saw two figures walking towards us wearing, I thought, the square German steel helmets. Instantly I sank down on one knee, keeping motionless, and with the patrol behind me doing the same. Was this to be the opportunity we had been looking to take prisoners back with us? I could hear them talking quietly to one another and so confident was I that they were Germans that I thought I could hear their guttural accents. They were only about five yards away from us and with my finger on the trigger of my Sten I was about to lunge forward with a shout of 'Handes hoch!' — which I understood to mean 'hands up' — when I realized they were speaking English and were the RE corporal and his boatman. My disappointment aggravated my annoyance that they should have disregarded my orders to stay with the boat, and I used no uncertain terms in telling them that they would never be nearer death than they had been at that minute without experiencing the real thing. As it happened, the boat was only about fifty yards further on, and soon we were back on the west bank and with the boat back on the jeep, were on our way back to company HQ. Our two Free French friends had disappeared and we didn't see them again.

It was daylight by the time we got back and just in time to hear the warning shout of 'Mortars!' and to dive for cover before a stick of bombs landed in the vicinity. The Germans had begun mortaring the area a little early, and had also fired a periodic high velocity shell at the crossroads at the top of the hill, which they had pin-pointed with great accuracy from their own positions on the high ground on the far side of the river. This was the crossroads where I had noticed the pill-box the previous afternoon and where I had spent a few moments admiring the view over the Touques Valley and listening to the birds singing in the warm sunshine. The crossroads, which were under visual observation by the Germans, had become somewhat of a death trap as we were to discover later in the day.

As soon as I was able to dismiss the patrol, after commending them for their efforts, I went into the bunker to see Charles Vickery. He was having a well earned sleep so, as was the practice whenever possible after a patrol, I set off for battalion HQ to report to John Drummond, taking Sergeant McCully with me. Fortunately the Royal Engineers jeep was still available so we were able to get a lift and to locate HQ in a hotel on the outskirts of Deauville.

I have never been in the dock of a court charged with an heinous crime and interrogated by leading counsel, but I imagine it would be somewhat similar to being questioned by John Drummond after a patrol. After recounting in considerable detail what had happened and my conclusion that the enemy were still occupying positions on the far side of the river but not in very great strength, he wanted to know why hadn't we done this; why hadn't we done that? Why hadn't we penetrated as far as Benouville? Why hadn't we crossed the road? And so forth. Why did I think that the trucks we had seen were German trucks? Why hadn't we shot them up? Robin Rigby, who had taken over from me as adjutant, and who knew John as well as I did, was hovering in the background and smiling broadly at me over John's shoulder. I think it was he who supplied Sergeant McCully and me with a very welcome cup of tea, of which I am sure John disapproved. Eventually, we were 'released,' not with any expression of sympathy that we should have been sent out on a difficult mission in the middle of the night, but a curt suggestion that we should get back to company HQ as quickly as possible, as the battalion would shortly be moving out.

Sure enough, soon after we returned to the company area, Charles summoned his O Group and told us that we would be pulling back and moving to another position further upstream where, it was anticipated, a crossing of the river could be achieved. The reason given was that the railway opposite our present position was held by the enemy in some strength!

Charles pointed out that our pull-out would have to be staggered because of enemy mortaring, with the men well spread out, and doubling across the crossroads at the top of the hill because of enemy shelling. Corporal Southam, the company driver had been killed at the crossroads early in the morning. He had taken two wounded men to the regimental aid post and was on his way back when for some reason he had stopped at the crossroads and tried to get into the pill-box. A shell had hit the pill-box at the same moment and he had been killed instantly. Southam, a regular soldier with strong family connections in the regiment, was a sad loss. A very courageous young man, always willing to take his jeep wherever required at whatever time and regardless of whatever hazards were involved.

It was my task to bring up the rear, and all went well until the last platoon, Number 7, had begun to move up the hill. I was standing at the entrance to the bunker, ready to take cover if I heard the unpleasant thump of German mortar fire, when a man ran over to me from the far side of the road and said something about a man refusing to get out of his slit trench. I didn't grasp for a minute why anyone should refuse to get out of his trench, but being in a hurry to get everyone away, I picked up my Sten and followed him back across the road, through a gateway to the area where 7 Platoon had been located and along the hedge where I saw Sergeant McCully and Corporal Ayres kneeling on either side of a slit trench trying to lift something out. The 'something' I then saw was Rifleman Martin. He was lying in the trench as if in a grave, shaking like a leaf and apparently quite incapable of doing anything to help himself. I had never come across a previous case, but I realized he was 'bomb happy', a condition which we had often talked and joked about, but never experienced. When under prolonged stress a man's nervous system somehow packs up and to all intents and purposes, he becomes paralysed.

It wasn't a question of cowardice. I had known Rifleman Martin for several years and he was in no way cowardly. I remembered the occasion several years earlier when we had been training with mules in the Welsh mountains. One of the mules carrying boxes of ammunition on its side had run amok and one of the boxes had struck Martin in the mouth, snapping off the bottoms of all his front teeth, which must have been agonizing. He had continued on the exercise for three days and didn't report sick until we arrived back in camp at Hereford.

'We'll have to carry him,' I said, and sliding into the trench with a foot on either side of Martin's shoulders I seized him under the armpits and with McCully doing the same at his feet and Gillanders and Ayres pulling his arms, we lifted Martin out of the trench and laid him on the grass alongside. Then, with his arms over the shoulders of a man on either side, we dragged him out to the road and taking it in turns made our way up the hill. Fortunately, the German mortars had gone quiet, but we still had to get over the crossroads.

When we were about fifteen yards or so short of the crossroads but still had the protection of a high hedge on our right, we stopped to get our breath. Martin appeared to have recovered a little and sat up, but he was obviously still very weak, and quite incapable of getting over the crossroads on his own. As I sat there, with sweat streaming down my face, I had a mental vision of some German artillery officer sitting behind a powerful pair of field glasses in his observation post waiting for any signs of movement, so that with the flick of a firing pin he could send a high velocity shell in our direction in much less time than the fifteen seconds or so it would take us to reach the safety of the ditch on the far side. I thought about sending one man across with all our Stens and rifles to draw fire, as it were, and then to dash across with Martin, but I knew there were too many 'ifs' and 'buts,' and we just had to go. With Gillanders carrying our weapons and loose gear, McCully and Ayres at Martin's shoulders and the rifleman and me with a leg each, we crouched like sprinters at the starting blocks in the Olympics. It occurred to me afterwards that we must have looked a bit like the start of a wheelbarrow race at a parish fete. Anyway, on the word 'Go' from me, we were off and it seemed as if my feet hardly touched the ground until we flung ourselves into the ditch on the far side of the crossroads. And we were indeed lucky. Even as we dived for cover there was a whoosh and crash as a shell hit the side of the pill-box. But fortunately the angle of the wall protected us against flying splinters. Immediately we were up again and in no time, fifty yards up the road and away from that problem. Sending the riflemen on to catch up with the platoon ahead, we still had to carry Martin between us, but in a short time he was in a jeep and on his way back to the RAP.

After a march of an hour or so, we joined up with the rest of the battalion in the area between two small villages, La Poterie and Glatigny, upstream two miles or so from our previous position. A Company was near La Poterie and located in an orchard on the side of a hill overlooking the river valley. We were probably out of range of enemy mortars, and had plenty of cover from visual observation but nevertheless set to work digging our slit trenches, followed by the usual routine of foot repair, cleaning up and eating whatever was remaining in our ration packs.

Again it was a glorious summer day, and I was catching up on my sleep when Gillanders woke me to say that from the forward edge of our position we could see a patrol from C Company heading over towards the railway where we had been the night before. Someone had located a narrow foot-bridge across the river, which had been only partially destroyed by the Germans and Colin O'Hara Murray had taken a patrol over to determine the enemy strength in Bonneville. Making my way down to the edge of the trees I found that quite a crowd had gathered to watch Colin's progress. Through my field glasses I could see him and his men making their way around the ditches and dykes which had bothered us the night before, and they seemed to be approaching the line of the railway without any opposition. Suddenly, I heard the rapid RRRRRRRRRUP RRRRRRRRRUP RRRRRRRRRUP of a German machine gun and the small figures of the patrol all disappeared from view. It was a very tense moment. Somebody, somewhere, I thought, should have been ready for such an eventuality and to put down protective mortar fire or smoke so that Colin and his patrol could extricate themselves. We waited anxiously and a cheer went up when figures appeared, running back towards the river, bent double to obtain whatever protection they could from dykes and undulations in the ground. Bursts of enemy machine gun fire from the line of the railway followed them. Suddenly one or other of the small figures I could see through my field glasses would fall or disappear as if hit, but then in a second or so would be up again, until they all reached the shelter of the river bank from where they made their way along to the foot bridge and across to the battalion area.

It is characteristic of the army, I suppose, that accurate information seldom permeates down to the men in the forward positions, who therefore became reconciled to doing whatever is required of them without really knowing why or how their task fits into the wider picture of events. That particular night, after a Battalion O Group conference, we were told that the line of the railway was held by the Germans in considerable strength — up to 2,000 men was the figure mentioned. Having been to the railway in the early hours of the morning and not seen any enemy troops, this sounded somewhat doubtful. However, we were ordered to remain very much on the alert overnight, and understood that we would be moving upstream in the morning to Pont L'Evêque, where the 5th Parachute Battalion had secured a crossing.

The following morning, at first light, we moved off, not towards Pont L'Evêque but across the foot-bridge in single file and up to the railway, without a shot being fired. An hour or so later, we were in Benouville and heading towards St Phillibert. We heard later that during the night, the Belgian Brigade on our left had managed to cross the river at Trouville, whereupon the Germans had pulled back and were in full retreat for the Seine.

That was 26 August, I think, and the next two or three days were spent pressing as fast as we could towards the Seine east of Honfleur. Except for the usual snipers and isolated machine gun positions, enemy opposition was slight, and German troops were giving themselves up in ever increasing numbers. We were using minor roads and laneways from St Phillibert to Manneville, and on to Berville on the southern bank of the Seine and about four miles downstream from Tancarville, the site of the new bridge constructed after the war. As we trudged through hamlets and villages the local inhabitants emerged from their houses with wine and Calvados to clap us on our way, although we were too tired to fully appreciate their enthusiasm.

After a short stop at Berville, where we witnessed the unpleasant sight of young girls having their hair shaved off for consorting with the departed Germans, we moved on to a beautiful spot overlooking the river. A Company was directed to a farm which, surprisingly perhaps, had an appearance of considerable affluence. The farm buildings surrounded what I suppose would be called the farmyard, but it was unlike any farmyard I had known, being more like a pleasant, well-mown grass paddock about the size of a football pitch. On one side was a row of enormous barns and sheds, obviously built many years ago, with heavy black timbers outlined against the yellowing plaster of the walls. At the end was a row of stables and loose boxes, sufficient to hold at least a dozen horses, and on the other side, the farmhouse, a large, solid, timber and plaster building with heavy wooden shutters on either side of the small windows, and with the entire front of the building covered in a dense growth of multicoloured ivy. The 'open' end of the farmyard or paddock led down to a small orchard, which the Germans had partially cut down and replaced with an outdoor gymnasium with horizontal bars, climbing nets and ropes, vaulting horses and many other forms of keep-fit apparatus. All this, we learned later, had been used extensively by the German troops billeted in the area, the last of whom had only departed a few hours before our arrival.

With our move into this location came the news that the division had been officially 'stood down,' which meant, I suppose, that we were no longer 'in action,' despite the fact that from a vantage point nearby and with the aid of our binoculars we could clearly see German troops going about their business around Le Havre docks on the far side of the river. It was also rumoured that the division was being moved back to the UK to prepare for another airborne operation. These rumours usually started with the arrival of our rear echelon trucks with cooks, quartermaster's staff and other support personnel, whose duties brought them into contact with their counterparts from brigade and division headquarters: officers' batmen, signallers, sanitation men and the like, were always the most reliable source of information about future plans.

Strangely enough, the rumoured return to England and Bulford, with the likelihood of home leave, didn't result in the elation which one might have expected. Despite the very strenuous training programme we had undergone in England and Wales during the years before invasion, we had been well aware that the real test would only come when live bullets were substituted for blanks and when death or maiming wouldn't be a question for decision by the nearest umpire. Now, however, in company with the other battalions in the division, we were undoubtedly a mature, effective and confident fighting unit.

When we clambered on board our gliders on 6 June very few of us had been under enemy fire, and despite all our strenuous training there was always a doubt as to how we would react when put to the test. Fortunately, the actual glider landing operations had been more successful than we could have hoped. For more than two months we had been in defensive positions in contact with the enemy and subjected to persistent mortar and shell fire and infantry attack, sometimes supported by tanks. Constant patrolling by day and night was essential. At times, the weather had been kind; at other times, unkind, resulting in muddy slit trenches and wet clothes. We had lost many friends, some killed, some missing and others wounded and evacuated. Although we were well aware that the division was holding a very long front from the coast to the north of Caen, and was very thin on the ground, I don't think it even occurred to us that if the Germans had made a concentrated effort to wipe out our bridgehead with all the resources available to them, the odds must have been that we would have been over-run, particularly during the early days following our landing. Each of the attacks they did make on us were repulsed with considerable losses and they may well have formed the impression that we were stronger than was the case, but as the days passed and the bridgehead was reinforced, and pressures east of the Orne towards Caen became more intense, pulling in German forces which might otherwise have been directed against us, our self-confidence grew and we were never in any doubt as to the final outcome of the operation.

When the breakout from the bridgehead started in the early hours of 17 August there was a feeling of great relief amongst all ranks. Despite much criticism by politicians and the press about Monty's slow progress, we had known that his strategy was to draw as much as possible of the Germans resistance to our end of the bridgehead and that the breakout would take place in the west when the American build up was ready. However, we had understood, correctly or otherwise, that this would be

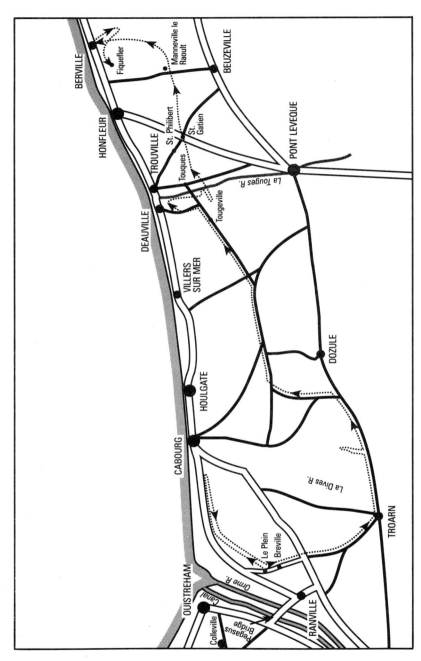

Operation 'PADDLE' 17 August — 1 September 1944
- - - - - - - - - - route of 1st BN. RUR

292

in a matter of weeks, not months, so affected by weariness I suppose, we were beginning to wonder if it would ever happen. When it ultimately did, the news was doubly welcome. There was some anxiety as to the effect which over two months' 'static warfare' had had on our fitness, particularly our feet, but as it turned out, those fears were groundless, a reflection on the high standard of personal hygiene which had been maintained despite the difficult conditions.

So, here we were now, the first battalion of the allied armies to reach the River Seine, and if it had been put to the vote I'm sure that the majority would have been in favour of remaining in France to help finish off the job which we had helped to start. The Germans were in full retreat, and we were hearing of the hammering they were taking around Falaise. If the pressure could be kept up, the war would be over by Christmas, when we could all go home. No doubt the welcome we received from the French people also boosted our morale.

After the platoons had been allotted barns and sheds so that all men would be under cover, and with company HQ in a shed adjoining the farmhouse, I was enjoying the usual cup of tea when Gillanders came in and told me that there was someone outside who wanted to talk to me. I asked him who it was and he said he thought it was the farmer. Going out, I met a very large Frenchman who shook my hand vigorously.

'Bienvenu msieu, bienvenu, Bienvenu.'

I took this to mean that he was glad to see me. He was very tall and very broad; about forty years of age, I thought. Clean shaven but with a dark skin and jowls, and in shirt sleeves and half dungarees with cross braces over his shoulders. His English was about as good as my French, but I had no difficulty understanding the reason for his call. First to let it be known how pleased he was to see us, and second, to ask the company officers to come and have a meal with him and his wife. In the absence of Charles Vickery, I thanked him for his welcome and accepted the invitation. I was by no means certain that Charles would agree to the dinner invitation, and on his return he did so with some reluctance after stipulating that one of the platoon commanders would have to remain at company HQ.

So, sharp at six pm, Charles, Robin Crockett, John Gardner and I presented ourselves at the front door of the farmhouse. We had no need to knock. They had been looking out for us, and we were greeted with hugs and kisses on both cheeks, not only by the farmer and his wife but also by their several young children. When we had arrived at the farm I had noted the apparent absence of members of the family who ran what was obviously a large farm, but during the evening it was explained that during the four years the Germans had been in the vicinity the farmer and his wife discouraged their family from fraternizing with them in any way, even to the extent of keeping them in the house if German soldiers were in and around the farmyard. They just hated all Germans. It was not that they had been maltreated in any way. They had simply been told that they must continued to farm the land as it had been farmed for generations. All the produce would be made available to the Germans but provided the farm was run to their satisfaction, the farmer and his wife could retain sufficient for the needs of themselves and their family.

Bearing in mind that the Germans had only just departed it appeared that the farmer hadn't done too badly, as we had a meal that I would remember all my life. We had, I think, four or five different meat dishes, each served up separately, and interspersed with beautifully prepared fresh vegetables, again served up individually so that one could savour all the delicious flavours. Only the farmer himself sat at the scrubbed wooden topped table with us. The wife spent all her time beside the large Aga type cooker, carving, dishing up and preparing the many sauces to accompany both meats and vegetables. The older children acted as waiters or waitresses, clearing away the used plates and dishes and providing their mother with an endless supply of clean plates. The two or three young children just stood apart and looked on. We had white meat, brown meat, pink meat and red meat, with delicious wines, but the pièce de resistance of the entire meal was the small glass of Calvados between each serving and of every flavour one could have imagined. Fortunately, time was not a factor, and as the evening passed, language became less and less of a barrier.

We had started our meal soon after six o'clock and by ten o'clock we had sung *God Save the King* and *the Marseillaise* at least six times each. Our host and hostess had been taught *the Sash*, *Mother Machree* and *The Mountains of Mourne* and we could all give a harmonious rendering of *Sur la Pont d'Avignon*.

The entente cordiale was at least partially restored that night, and even Charles was persuaded to give us his party piece — *I knocked 'em in the Old Kent Road*, but all good things come to an end. There was a knock on the door and one young subaltern duty officer appeared.

'There's a message just in from Brigade,' he said, looking at Charles. 'We have to be ready to move by 0600 hours.'

Before even Charles had time to react, Robin had raised his arms in the air and pointing to his wrist watch announced to the world that there was no problem. 'That gives us another six hours,' he said.

After more hugs and kisses we made our way back to our ground sheets and straw beds. The cup of hot sweet tea that Gillanders brought me at five am just as dawn was breaking was a life saver.

'Youse all had a great night last night sorr,' he said, and I nodded my agreement. I couldn't speak. By six o'clock we were formed up on the adjoining road ready to move to the RV where we knew our transport would be waiting. I was standing at the end of the column, not feeling very strong, when Robin suddenly appeared from further up the road. He was obviously in some distress and walking in a strange manner. 'I must have a xxxx,' he said to me grimly.

'You'd better get a move on,' I replied, 'we're just about to moved off.'

Only a person who has had to hurriedly divest himself of army equipment, an airborne smock plus a battledress jacket in such circumstances will understand Robin's predicament as he disappeared behind the nearby hedge just as the troops in front stepped off.

We didn't have very far to go and as we rounded a bend I glanced around but could see no sign of Robin. I was becoming a little anxious as I didn't want to send a message forward to Charles Vickery to the effect that one of his platoon commanders was missing. So far as Charles was concerned, he wouldn't object to a convivial evening, whether he was participating or not, but one thing he always insisted upon was that officers and men should be on parade and fit for duty in all respects at the stipulated time. Strictly speaking, I suppose, to be otherwise because of self-indulgence, was an offence under King's Regulations. The last men were clambering aboard their TCV when, much to my relief and no doubt also to his, Robin appeared, clutching his equipment in one hand and doing up the buttons of his battledress jacket with the other. With encouraging cheers from the men in his platoon, I pushed him up into the truck, signalled to the vehicles in front that we were all aboard, climbed up beside the driver and we were off.

Even at that late stage there had been no official information that we were returning to the UK. However, everyone accepted that such was the case and there seemed to be little doubt about it as we drove back along the coast, partly following the route we had taken during our advance a few days earlier. Back over the Caen canal and the bridge over the river — already signposted Pegasus Bridge. Shattered buildings and defensive pillboxes and strong points lined the road behind the British and Canadian invasion beaches, but these seemed strangely deserted with few signs of military activity. The reason for this became apparent when we climbed up a slight incline before Arromanche and looked down on what must have been one of the astonishing sights of the campaign: Mulberry Harbour.

We had, of course, heard of the artificial harbour that had been secretly built and towed across the Channel to permit the off-loading of military personnel and supplies regardless of weather and tidal complications, but I don't think any of us had imagined it to be so vast and comprehensive as now appeared before us. From where we sat, on high ground about two miles or so away, it was difficult to realize that a few months earlier, this had been simply a long stretch of sandy beach, ideal for children and their parents in the holiday months but deserted at other times during the year. Now it resembled Dover Harbour on a bank holiday weekend. The obvious major difference was that the main sea wall which enclosed the harbour area consisted of ships which had been sunk onto the sea bed but which nevertheless remained upright with their funnels, masts and superstructure clearly visible, and partly of enormous, concrete, rectangular, box-like structures resembling, what they were, harbour walls. How these could have been constructed in places as far away as Scotland and towed and sunk in the right positions was impossible to imagine, but there they were. Jutting out from the beach into the deep water of the harbour were several long finger-like jetties or pontoons which were designed to float up and down so that large ships could be loaded and unloaded whatever the state of the tide.

The whole scene was a hive of activity. The harbour was full of ships, large and small; some anchored, some on the move and other tied up to the jetties. Some small landing craft were discharging their cargoes direct onto the sandy shore. Vehicles of all shapes and sized were driving along the jetties and across the beach whilst others were coming from inland down onto the beach and out to the ships. Some kind of metal lattice work had been laid on the sand to provide firm surfaces for all this traffic between the beach areas to the roads inland. The most intriguing sight of all, however, from where we watched, was the long column of ant-like figures moving across the sand dunes and down across the beach and then disappearing into the black cavernous mouth of an enormous tank loading craft. These were thousands of German prisoners on their way into captivity. When we drove on and found ourselves alongside these columns of prisoners, they looked dishevelled and untidy, which was to be expected, but seemed cheerful enough that, for them, the war was over, giving us a cheery wave as we drove past. I noticed that the officers walked in groups together and did not appear to be so happy with their lot.

It was explained that we were to embark straight away onto a large troop ship which was anchored in the harbour near the entrance, and that we would be ferried out to the troop carrier in two small landing craft which were moored alongside one of the floating jetties. Each craft could take about fifty men at a time and all went well for the first few trips. The landing craft would pull up alongside the high side of the troop carrier down which rope ladders had been hung. The men would then take it in turn to step from the side of the landing craft, seize the rope ladder and clamber up to where sailors were ready to give a helping hand over the side and onto the solid deck of the larger vessel.

With a rifle or Sten gun or heavier weapon slung over the shoulder this wasn't all that easy, even while the rise and fall of the smaller craft was only a few feet. Unfortunately, the swell on the sea was increasing, even in the harbour and the rise and fall of the landing craft was making the operation of judging the right second to step onto the rope ladders increasingly hazardous. If anyone had slipped and fallen between the two vessels there would have been very little hope of surviving. About half of the battalion had been transferred when someone on the troop ship decided that it was too dangerous to continue until the sea had gone down. I was one of the last to get on board and after an excellent meal spent the most comfortable night I had enjoyed since 5 June at Broadwell. The following morning the remainder of the battalion came aboard, having spent the night in a village hall at Arromanche, very well looked after by the local inhabitants.

At around midday we set sail for Southampton.

9

The Last Grip

At some point during the Battalion's travels around England and Wales, the officers' mess acquired a painting which we understood was entitled 'The Last Grip,' but whether this was the correct name or who the artist was, I don't know. The scene appeared to be some remote, desolate outpost of the Empire, and portrayed two survivors of some British military force calmly awaiting death at the hands of the approaching 'infidels' or 'mujadeen' or whatever, who can be seen in the distance galloping up for the kill. One of the two survivors, with bandaged head, is recumbent on the ground resting against the body of his dead horse, whilst the other, standing alongside with pistol in one hand, gripping the hand of his companion with the other, is calmly and defiantly awaiting the end, determined to die with honour in the best tradition of his regiment.

At some stage, presumably after the war, the regimental badge of the RUR was added, together with the Airborne Forces' 'Flying Horse', the Glider Badge and the Battalion Battle honours.

Wherever battalion HQ officers' mess was set up, whether in country mansion, château, schloss or tent, 'The Last Grip' would be hung in some prominent place, and it became a ritual when circumstances permitted, at the end of all mess gatherings, both formal and informal, for all the officers present to gather around the picture and to toast 'The Last Grip' with the vocal ditty which had become the party piece of the 1st Battalion officers:

'Beer, beer, beer for the old RUR
Drink up your whisky, there's more in the bar.
Send the corporal out for gin,
Don't let a sober rifleman in.
We never stagger, we never fall,
We sober up on wood alcohol,
Mother if your son returns,
Don't blame the RUR.'

What happened to 'The Last Grip' I don't know, but it would be a valuable addition to the Regimental Museum. I was given a photograph by Ronnie Wilson many years later, but whatever became of the original, or who the girl is in the photograph I have no idea.

10

Return to England and Ireland

We arrived back in England, at Southampton Docks, on 4 September — my mother's birthday — and there was quite a reception for us on the quayside: the band of the Hampshire Regiment; a number of local city dignitaries and a group from our reinforcement company at Bulford, and, needless to say, the good ladies of the WVS with their supplies of tea and sandwiches. As the long column of trucks carrying our brigade made their way through the towns and villages of Hampshire, the cheers and waves we received from the local people indicated that they realized who we were, the 6th Airborne Division, or what was left of the division of which they had heard so much, coming back from Normandy. Strangely enough, there was a lack of jubilation amongst our men, despite the fact that for some weeks anyway they would be sleeping in comfortable beds and not worrying about snipers and mortar bombs, and even enjoying a short period of leave. There was, perhaps, a strange sense of guilt that we were coming away from the battle to enjoy some home comforts while thousands were still slogging away in France, and, above all, that about a hundred others, who had set out with us on D-Day in such high spirits would not be coming back at all.

Shortly after arriving back in Bulford, the entire battalion was sent off on ten days' leave with a reminder that the war was far from over and that on our return from leave further operations would be expected. A number of us agreed that if possible we would meet for at least a day or so in Dublin. At that time we had no idea that the following weekend the 1st Division would be setting out for Arnhem.

I had decided that I would first go up to Beckenham to see my brothers, Harry and Jack and their families who, I understood, were still in their homes at West Wickham and Beckenham. We all knew, of course, that London was being subjected to the V1 bombardment but had little idea of exactly what this meant and were not inclined to consider it of much consequence compared to the mortaring and shelling to which we had been subjected.

I arrived in London late in the afternoon and decided to make my way to Victoria Station, where I could catch a train for Beckenham Junction, which was close to our home in Beckenham Place Park; I wanted to look in there and telephone my brothers to let them know that I was back in one piece. By the time I got to Victoria it was almost dark and with the blackout still in operation it wasn't easy to find one's way around. However, I remembered that the Beckenham trains left from Platform 4, and as I clambered aboard a train standing at the platform, I was relieved to find that even Hitler hadn't been able to interrupt that arrangement. The blackout also applied to trains and the only lighting in each compartment was a small blue bulb which just about permitted the occupants to see whether a seat was occupied. All the windows had been painted over with black paint, except for a small square which enabled passengers to identify the names of the stations at which the train stopped.

When I got in the compartment was empty, but as I settled myself in a corner seat alongside the platform others followed until all the seats were occupied and one or two passengers were standing. There was no corridor to permit passengers to look for seats in other compartments, so, with the surge of travellers along the platform all anxious to get aboard, once a dark compartment was entered there was no escape, whether there was a seat available or not.

Everyone sat in complete silence waiting for the train to pull out of the station when suddenly the air raid warning started, first with a low groan as if reluctant to disturb the peace, then increasing to a crescendo, then dying away, then rising — on and on it went. Immediately the silence in our compartment was broken.

'Here they come again,' said a voice.

'Thought we'd miss 'em tonight,' said another.

Then, above the sound of the siren, I became aware of a strange noise rather like a small motor cycle engine, faint at first, but quickly increasing in intensity until it was immediately overhead. And then it stopped.

I realized that this was a V1 pilotless bomb, and my immediate inclination when I heard the engine cut out was to duck down below the level of the windows to avoid the blast which I knew would follow, and I assumed that the others in the compartment would do the same. To my surprise, they did nothing, although the silence returned. Suddenly there was a flash and a loud 'crump' from what seemed to me only a short distance from where we were sitting. I had a mental picture of demolished buildings and dead people but this was quickly cut short by the noise of another engine — this time I sensed, not heading directly for Victoria Station and sure enough, after the agonizing silence, the crump came from further away. By this time, the occupants of the compartment were becoming quite chatty.

We continued to sit in almost complete darkness while another three V1s could be heard in the vicinity. The pattern was the same on each occasion; first, the distant but very distinct and rapid pop-pop-pop-pop . . . gradually increasing in intensity and then the cut-out . . . followed by the silence as the small flying bomb dipped its nose and planed down on its path to death and destruction. On the train there was no sign of panic or, indeed of much concern, except during the brief periods after an engine cut-out when there was a tense silence as we waited for the explosion which we knew would follow. Then the sudden relief as the steady note of the sirens signalled the all-clear and almost immediately the train began to move out of the station.

I had been in London on a number of occasions when raids by normal piloted aircraft had been in progress, but this seemed very different. On those occasions, the period of warning before the arrival of the enemy aircraft overhead was longer, and gave people time to make their way to whatever shelter was in their vicinity, assisted by air raid wardens and the many direction signs set up in the streets. Once in a public shelter one just had to sit it out until the all clear sounded, guessing at the intensity of the raid from the racket of the anti-aircraft fire and the thump of bombs in the vicinity, always wondering if you would hear the next one or whether that would be 'it'. When the all clear had sounded everyone would stream out onto the streets and go about their business.

From this short initial experience of the V1s it seemed to me that the attitude of the public was now very different. The pilotless planes arrived almost as soon as the warning so there was little time to bother about shelter, and everyone carried on with whatever he or she was doing at the time, without any sign of confusion or panic. The same applied, even more so perhaps, with the V2 rockets which were just beginning to appear on the scene at that time, and for which there was no warning. In a strange way, the anxiety and nervous tension caused by the V1s and V2s was much less than in the case of the earlier bomber raids when hundreds of bombers would be arriving in waves and the alarm would often last for several hours and, with short intervals, repeated for days on end, thus giving rise to stress and tension for long periods. With the V1s and V2s, however, the attitude of the civilian population seemed to be that if you were unlucky enough to be where one landed you wouldn't know much about it. If you weren't, then all well and good, so why worry? In any event, this was Hitler's last fling and with allied troops rapidly approaching the launching sites, it wouldn't last too long.

As we accelerated out of Victoria station the atmosphere was certainly much more relaxed. Contrary to the usual practice of the London commuter to keep his thoughts entirely to himself, even when he cannot read his newspaper, everyone seemed anxious to exchange experiences about V1s and V2s and parachute mines; about near misses and freakish results. The V1 that had appeared overhead, then turned and gone back the way it had come. The V1 that had crash landed without exploding. The lumps of ice found in the crater of a V2 rocket. From the inner gloom, someone mentioned the strange blast effect of the parachute mine. Up to that time, I had never heard of the parachute mine, but I was shortly to see evidence of the strange effects the blast from this German adaptation of the sea mine could have. I was the only person in the compartment in uniform, and the only one who couldn't join in with this cheerful chattiness about activity on the Home Front. But listening to the terse comments of my fellow travellers about their experiences — as air raid wardens, fire wardens, rescue services, civic helpers, etc. — in addition to the hazards involved in going about their daily routine, confirmed my realization that a Service uniform or badge of rank was of itself no indication of exposure to risk or contribution to the objective of winning the war. By this time, with the German armies in Europe in full retreat, winning the war in Europe was now a matter of accepting the risk of being killed or maimed by a flying bomb or rocket plus the continued strain of the blackout and shortage of everything. How long this would last was anybody's guess, but with the allied armies fast approaching the Rhine and the launching sites, there was at last room for optimism, although there was an uneasy thought that maybe Hitler had some other horror up his sleeve. It was fortunate perhaps that at the time very few people had ever heard of an atomic bomb.

Each time the train stopped someone would call out the name of the station and with a cheerful 'Good night all,' passengers would stumble across feet and knees and clamber down onto the blacked-out platform. I noticed that on one or two occasions when the train stopped away from a platform, the person opposite to me beside the door made sure that no-one opened the door to get out and find himself falling onto the adjoining rail.

Brixton, West Dulwich, Sydenham Hill . . . on we went until it was Beckenham Junction and my turn to get out. Although I hadn't joined in the conversation along the way, I thought it appropriate to half turn and call out 'Good night' as I waited for the train to stop, and felt pleased that the few people left in the compartment responded.

Despite the complete lack of any form of lighting other than the tiny lights permitted on the few passing vehicles, I was soon entering the gates of Monalee, Beckenham Place Park, which, as I had assumed, was in complete darkness. I knew that my mother had returned to the house several months earlier when the bombing had almost ceased but that she had again been taken to my brother-in-law's farm at Marsh Gibbon to escape the flying bombs, of which the area around Beckenham received far more than its fair share, being in 'Bomb Alley' — the flight path from one particular launching site, into London. However, I always carried a set of keys to the house and was able to let myself in, and with the aid of my cigarette lighter began to stumble around the house to adjust the blackout curtains before switching on the electric lights. It was then that I found something which I couldn't understand.

After adjusting the blackout curtains in the downstairs rooms,

I went up to the room at the back of the house overlooking the garden which was my bedroom, and by the flickering light of my cigarette lighter I saw that the curtains only reached halfway down the windows and appeared to have been torn off in a very ragged way. On investigating the other room at the back, my mother's bedroom, I found the same unusual situation. Obviously those two rooms couldn't be used with the light on, but as the rest of the house appeared to be in reasonable order I couldn't understand why the curtains in the two back bedrooms had been cut or torn in this strange way. I found out the answer when I spoke to my brother Jack the next day.

Fortunately, mother had left a good supply of tinned food in the larder, together with powdered eggs and milk, and I was able to get myself an adequate meal, after which as the air raid warning had sounded I crawled into the bed in the strong metal shelter under our very large dining room table and soon fell fast asleep. How long that particularly air raid lasted, or whether any doodle bugs came over, I have no idea. The next thing I remember is banging my head on the metal roof of the shelter as I sat up, startled by loud banging on the front door and confused by the impenetrable darkness. Still in a sleepy haze, I fumbled my way to the front door where I discovered it was broad daylight, and a somewhat frustrated Jack standing on the threshold having been unable to get in because I had bolted the door on the inside, and he had spent about half an hour banging on the door trying to wake me up. It was then that the mystery of the curtains was explained.

Shortly before the advent of the flying bombs, the Germans had introduced the parachute bomb, a weapon intended solely for the demoralization of the civilian population. It consisted, I understand, of a large container like a sea mine, full of explosive, which was dropped indiscriminately from an aircraft. It was suspended from a parachute and detonated immediately it came into contact with anything solid such as a house, or tree, or the ground. It came down quite slowly, and on detonation none of its destructive power was dissipated in the usual crater formed by a conventional bomb. If, as intended, it landed in an urban area, the resulting destruction of houses and other buildings was very considerable.

A short time before I had arrived home, one of these devices had landed on the tennis courts at the end of our garden and the effects of the blast had been extraordinary. In addition to blowing off the tiles of the near side of the roof the entire roof had been lifted up at the level of the eaves, the curtains on the inside of the windows of the rooms at the back of the house had been sucked out through the gap in the brickwork, resulting from the lifting of the roof, which had fallen back into place, trapping several inches of the curtains which could be seen hanging from the brickwork on the outside. In addition, although none of the window glazing had been broken, the metal window frames had been bent and distorted — and so far as I know, remain bent and distorted to this day — and several inside doors had been sucked off their hinges. First aid repairs had been carried out a few days later to keep the house wind and rain proof, but the only thing that could be done with the curtains was to cut them off at ceiling level. They then hung down like three quarter length curtains, which was the way I found them. On the outside they were trimmed off to be level with the brickwork, which, I imagine, is the way they still are.

After giving me all the news about the family and friends, Jack dropped me off in his car at Beckenham Junction Station from where I could catch a bus for West Wickham, to visit my elder brother, Harry and his family. I was shocked to see the extent of the damage around the station area. The Station Hotel and much of the surrounding housing had been flattened, and any property left standing, including the shops, were boarded up, and it was impossible to know whether they were operating. I heard later that a V1 had landed on the town mortuary which adjoined the graveyard beside St George's Church, and bodies and grave stones had been scattered around the area.

Except for a short spell during the height of the London bombing, Harry and family had stayed at their house in The Grove, preferring the familiarity of their own home to the inconvenience of evacuation. Many of their friends in the neighbourhood had also stayed put or returned to their homes after the intensive bombing of London in 1940. They had an air raid shelter constructed in the garage, which provided reasonable shelter from the occasional stray bomb which might land in the vicinity.

Harry had joined the LDF — Local Defence Force — which had been formed early in the war, and which subsequently became the Home Guard, and in addition to his normal daily work was frequently called out at night for rescue and fire watching duties. I stayed with them for two nights, one of which happened to coincide with a Home Guard meeting, and I was persuaded to talk to the local company about the D-Day operation. Amongst the audience that night were a number of men wearing First World War medal ribbons on their chests, and from the questions and discussion which followed my talk, I was left in no doubt that we had been fortunate not to become involved in the static type of trench warfare which they had experienced, involving long periods in deep and often flooded trenches and with the prospect of going over the top as the only route to a change of surroundings. I was left with the impression that going into action by glider or parachute was a bit cushy compared to the long approach march through muddy lanes and fields which many of them had experienced. However, the beer I was offered after my talk made it very clear how much they had appreciated my visit.

I left West Wickham by car with Jack, who had procured enough petrol for a visit to Marsh Gibbon, where we found my Mother and others in good form, but all very anxious to know when it would be safe for them to return to Beckenham. I did my best to assure them that it wouldn't be too long, and much would depend on the outcome of the Arnhem battle which was still in progress. Unfortunately, as it turned out, this attempt by the allied armies to break out across the Rhine and into the German hinterland and end the war in 1944, ended in failure. However, as British and Canadian troops moved up into Belgium and Holland, the launching sites for the V1s and V2s were gradually over-run and the threat of these weapons declined.

After a few days at Marsh Gibbon I decided to take a quick trip to Dublin and Enniscorthy. Dublin was still a city of well lit streets and delicious steaks; a great contrast with the blackout and austerity of England at the time, and despite having been born and bred in London, I have always had, and still have, a strong sense of nostalgia for the towns and villages of County Wexford and the surrounding countryside, and the many relations and friends I had grown to love during the many holidays I had spent at my mother's birth place, Monalee Ballindaggin, about six miles from Enniscorthy. Expenses were no problem, as my leave travel warrant extended to Enniscorthy and back to Bulford; so donning my civilian trousers and jacket, and with my uniform in my suitcase, I made my way by train across England to Holyhead, a somewhat tedious journey, and on by boat to Kingstown — or Dun Longhaire — as it had then become known.

At the Hibernian Hotel in Dawson Street, where we always stayed when on these short trips to Dublin, I was warmly greeted by the hotel porter who added that he was delighted that 'we had thim Jerries on the run.' It had been quite obvious to him and indeed to all the rest of the staff in the hotel that we were British army officers on leave, but despite the so-called neutrality of Southern Ireland, they made no secret of their support for the allied cause. Undoubtedly there were many extremists in Southern Ireland who would genuinely have welcomed a German victory in the belief that not only would this result in the removal of partition of the six counties, but, in addition, the victorious Nazis would then permit a united Ireland to govern itself without external interference; a vain hope in the light of the experience of other 'neutrals' such as Holland and Belgium. I remember someone saying — maybe it was Winston Churchill — that the great mistake that De Valera made when he was Prime Minister of Eire, was not to join with the Allies in fighting Hitler, particularly after the Americans entered the war. If he had done so, his reward could well have been the reunification of Ireland when the war had been won.

When I entered the Hibernian, my friend the porter also told me that some of my friends had already arrived and were down in the Buttery — the small bar which seemed to be a favourite meeting place for everyone in Dublin. With a smile he also reminded me to keep my hands in my pockets; a reminder of the occasion with Hoppy Cassidy, when I had had my wallet stolen.

After checking-in and leaving my bag in my room, I went down to the Buttery to find Ronnie Wilson, Robin Crockett, Ken Donnelly and Tom Fitzgerald sitting in a corner, laughing and chatting with two youngish men who were strangers to me. As I approached them, Ronnie stood up and said in a loud voice, 'Hallo Bob, come and meet a couple of prisoners of war.'

Being well used to Ronnie's capacity for leg pulling and therefore somewhat cautious about how I should respond to such an unusual introduction, I simply shook hands with the others, including the two strangers, and suggested that we should all have another bottle of Guinness. At the same time, I was wondering what Ronnie could have meant, as the last people I would have expected to meet in the Buttery at the Hibernian were two prisoners of war.

'Didn't you hear what I said?' repeated Ronnie. 'These two fellas are prisoners of war,' and everyone burst into roars of laughter.

I looked around and saw that everyone else in the bar seemed to be listening and enjoying the joke. Gradually, and despite many interruptions and much laughter, I heard the following extraordinary story.

The two strangers were, in fact, members of the air crew of a Coastal Command plane that had developed engine trouble when on a flight over the Western Approaches, and had made a forced landing in the south of Ireland. Fortunately, they had landed in an Irish bog, and they and their three companions had survived with only superficial injuries. They could not speak highly enough of the local farmer and his young son who had helped them from the wreckage of their plane, despite the very real risk of fire, and who had sustained them with the offer of either poteen or butter milk. Not really knowing what it was, they had chosen the poteen, after which they had decided to make a forced landing in Southern Ireland at every available opportunity. Their arrival was soon followed by the arrival of the local police sergeant together with a constable, both of whom also required sustenance from the farmer's bottle. Much to his disgust, the constable was sent off on his bicycle to telephone 'the Military' whilst the crew sat in the farmhouse parlour imbibing their poteen and listening to the farmer and the police sergeant become more and more vehement in their condemnation of the Irish Government for not 'joining in with the British and Americans in fightin' them Nazi blackguards.'

Over the next hour, the level of poteen in the farmer's bottle receded while he and the police sergeant waxed more and more eloquent in their resolution of Ireland's problems: partition, the churches, Catholic and Protestant, neutrality in the war, and the prices of pigs, potatoes and milk, turning from time to time for support from the air crew who understood little of the conversation and between yawns and with drooping eyelids could do no more than nod their heads in agreement to whatever proposition was put to them. From time to time the door would open and a bare-footed, poorly dressed child would sidle in to stand behind their father's chair and gaze with wide eyes at the five strangers who had suddenly appeared in their midst and in an aeroplane, the like of which they may have heard about but never expected to see at such close quarters.

The sound of a vehicle approaching the house and the squeal of brakes as it stopped outside, drew the attention of the children away from the airmen, and they scuttled out through the door to find out what further strange events were taking place. There were shouts from outside, followed by a loud voice from the hallway, presumably addressed to anyone within earshot, and demanding to know 'Where are the prisoners?'

The door of the parlour then swung open and a young officer in the green uniform of the Irish army entered the room with a large revolver in his hand, apparently anticipating resistance from the air crew he had been sent to apprehend. The scene which confronted him was not what he had expected; five young men of about his own age sprawled out on a couch and armchairs, two of whom were sound asleep, and none showing any signs of belligerence or animosity to him or anyone else.

The local police sergeant had been feeling very contented as he leaned forward to have his glass recharged. The fact that the crew of the British aircraft had turned out to be a very decent and cooperative bunch in no way lessened the drama he would incorporate in his report on the incident and for which he would undoubtedly receive a commendation from his superintendent. The arrival of 'the Military' was not unexpected but was nevertheless an irritation. He turned his head to look at the young officer and said, 'Put that damn thing away, Lieutenant, it might go off and then we'll all be in trouble.'

Just at that moment, the pilot of the plane stood up and took a step towards the army officer, who stepped back a pace and swung the revolver in the pilot's direction. 'Stay where you are,' he ordered. He looked at the police sergeant. 'Have these men been searched?' he asked.

'Searched?' replied the sergeant with a snort. 'Sure, haven't we been searching and questioning them for the past hour, until we're all exhausted? Isn't that right?' And he turned to the farmer for corroboration.

'Begob it is,' nodded the farmer. 'Can't you see by the look

311

of them how exhausted we all are.'

By this time the two sleeping airmen were stretching their arms as they woke up and began to show some interest in what was happening.

The officer reflected for a moment and then appeared to relax. He placed his revolver into the holster at his waistband, then said that he had orders to take the British airmen direct to a military camp at the Curragh, and as it was a long journey, the sooner they got started the better. Collecting together their flying jackets, they filed out to the truck where the farmer, together with his wife and children were gathered, and with hand shakes and thanks for their kindness and hospitality, they clambered aboard. To the pilot's enquiry as to what would happen about the aircraft, the Irish lieutenant explained that a team would be arriving to dismantle it and take it to Baldonnel airport, to which the police sergeant added, 'Don't you worry about the aeroplane sir, I'll look after it for you!'

After a long and uncomfortable drive through winding country roads they arrived tired and hungry at an army camp. They were all directed into the office of an Irish army major who turned out to be the camp commandant and who greeted them in a very friendly way. After congratulating them on their 'escape' he explained that the neutrality of the Irish Free State and the presence of a German Embassy in Dublin required that they should be interned, but that as the Irish Government had no wish to detain them indefinitely, provided they were willing to give an undertaking for 'good behaviour,' after a short time arrangements would be made for them to 'stray' across the border into Northern Ireland, from where they could return to their squadron. The alternative was that they would have to be locked up, which would be a bit of a nuisance.

Although all this was very unofficial, it appeared to be a reasonable arrangement, and they all agreed to give the required undertaking, although with some anxiety as to what the reaction of the Royal Air Force would be if their decision became known by 'Higher Authority'. They were also told, again very unofficially, that during their 'voluntary' internment, if there was a vehicle going to Dublin at any time there was no reason why they shouldn't take advantage of a lift, provided that they wore civilian clothes, which could, of course, be provided. Hence their meeting with us in the Buttery at the Hibernian Hotel.

312

Despite their shortage of ready cash, we made sure that they enjoyed the evening until the departure of their transport back to internment.

Later the same evening we were joined by Robin Rigby, Huw Wheldon and Dai Rees, but that visit to Dublin was very subdued compared with earlier trips. We were all very conscious of the absence of George Maginnis, Reggie and Harry Morgan and Dickie Quinn, and our thoughts were with Dan Woods, John McFaddon, Peter Barry and many other friends in the thick of the battle at Arnhem, and despite the support of the Bourkes, themselves greatly saddened by the gaps in our ranks, it was apparent that our Dublin shenanigans would never be the same.

After a couple of days, and despite advice from my Dublin friends that 'it would be quicker to walk,' I decided to catch a train to Enniscorthy to see all my relations down there. I didn't take their advice too seriously as I assumed that it was simply based on the normal reputation of Irish trains, which certainly weren't renowned for their speed or time-keeping. What I didn't appreciate at the time, however, was that the Great Southern Railway had run completely out of coal, and the only means of keeping the trains on the move at all was by burning wood and peat, and for this purpose, enormous dumps of wood and peat had been established about every ten miles along the railway lines. The distance from Dublin to Enniscorthy is about eighty miles and in normal times the journey would take about four hours, allowing for mechanical defects and the social needs of the train driver, his mate, and the guard, to jump off and visit contacts living near the line to pursue conversations about politics or the weather initiated on earlier journeys. If, at any of these unscheduled stops, any passenger had the temerity to descend and enquire as to the time the train would arrive at its destination, he would receive the comforting information — 'Ah, sure we'll be there time enuff.'

This meant that instead of the Dublin Express only calling at — and I seem to remember — Bray, Wicklow, Avoca, Arklow, Gorey, MacMine Junction, and maybe one or two other places — it also stopped at every 'fuel dump,' whereupon the driver would rake out his boiler, while his mate plus any volunteer labour which might be in the vicinity, would throw up sufficient wood and peat to enable the train to continue its progress to the next 'dump.' These delays were prolonged to enable the crew to build up sufficient head of steam to get the engine on the move again, if only at a slow walking pace.

However, in making my decision to travel on the Enniscorthy express, there was something I knew with which my Dublin consultants were possibly not familiar, or on which they did not place the same degree of importance. I was confident that the train to Enniscorthy would not run out of eggs and bacon! I had travelled on that train many times, both before and during the war, and on every occasion I had a meal, sometimes twice, of eggs and bacon, supplemented with freshly baked wholemeal bread laced with lovely farm butter, jam and tea, and notwithstanding many expensive meals in expensive restaurants in many places, in my humble opinion, no meal compares with eggs and bacon in general, and eggs and bacon in the train from Dublin to Enniscorthy — and back — in particular. The recollection of cleaning the succulent bacon fat and egg yolk from my plate with wholemeal bread covered with farm butter fills me with nostalgia. Admittedly, the tea on this particular occasion was not up to normal Irish standards, being necessarily supplemented with dried grated carrot — to give the reused 'tay' leaves a bit more colour — but in war time one cannot have everything, and if it's a choice between speed and eggs, bacon and tea, give me eggs, bacon and tea every time!

The train journey from Dublin to Enniscorthy on this occasion took a little over eight hours, during the course of which I had three excellent meals.

At Westland Row I had no difficulty finding what was, I think, the only first class compartment; a little tatty perhaps, but clean and comfortable, and I settled myself down with a sense of warm anticipation of the journey ahead and without any concern as to whether it took four hours or forty. I have always enjoyed travelling by train, and this train journey in particular. Out through the Dublin suburbs, the Ballsbridge Show Grounds, Lansdown Road Rugger ground, the Dublin mountains grouped around the bare and aptly named Sugar Loaf. On through the beautiful countryside of Glendalough and Avoca, Wicklow and the distant blue haze of Mount Leinster, Arklow with Tara Hill sheltering Courtown Harbour with all its happy memories of many family gatherings on 15 August each year. Gorey, with its very wide main street, planned, I always imagined, to double-up as a market place to accommodate the many sheep and cattle brought in from the surrounding countryside on fair days. The level crossing at Clough leading to my uncle's farm, Moneycross, and where a few years later, my cousin, Jimmy Steacy, had a miraculous escape from death when his car was hit by a passing train and carried for a mile down the track.

And so to Enniscorthy, easily identified by the prominent spires of the Roman Catholic and Church of Ireland 'cathedrals' and the gentle contours of Vinegar Hill with the old castle ruins on one sloping side; the scene of so much murder and mayhem during the rebellion of 1798. As a child, I always associated the horror stories about the Battle of Vinegar Hill with the stream of blood and guts which used to pour into the River Slaney from the animal slaughter house adjoining the station — now no longer permitted of course.

There were no other passengers in my compartment, nor, so far as I could estimate from the activity or lack of it on the platform, were there many others on the train. Shortly after we jerked our way out of the station, the sliding door of my compartment opened, and a plump, ruddy-faced, genial looking man entered and bidding me good morning, held out his hand, presumably for my ticket. He was dressed in a somewhat soiled and baggy blue suit, the only indication of his status being a peaked cap bearing a large badge marked GUARD. I saw no need to question his authority for also acting as ticket collector, and handed him my ticket, which had been issued in Bicester. He studied this closely for a few moments before giving it a clip with the small gadget he had in his hand, and returning it to me saying, 'You'll be coming home on leave, sorr?'

I nodded in agreement.

'Well, tings are going better now, although the lads at Arnhem are having a tough time,' he continued.

This took me by surprise, as it hadn't occurred to me that either the guard or ticket collector on the early morning train from Dublin to Enniscorthy in neutral Ireland would have been concerned with what was happening at Arnhem, and I felt a tinge of guilt that I hadn't opened the front page of the newspaper I had bought at the station to find out the latest news of the battle in which many of my friends were involved. As the guard turned to leave he said, 'Will you be having some breakfast, sorr?' He didn't wait for my answer. 'Come on along to the dining car in a few minutes and we'll see what we can do for you,' he said as he closed the sliding door.

The dining car bore very little resemblance to the railway dining cars to which I was accustomed. It consisted of half of a normal carriage, redesigned on an open plan basis, with two four-seater foldaway wooden tables on one side, and two two-seaters on the other, all supported by wooden, free-standing chairs of a design one would normally associate with a kitchen or schoolroom rather than a restaurant. It occurred to me at the time that the speed at which we were moving obviated the necessity for the dining car furniture to be anchored to the floor in the manner usually adopted on boats and trains.

There was no-one else present when I entered, so I sat down at one of the small, bare, wooden tables and opened my paper to catch up with the latest news. After about five minutes, the swing door leading to the front of the train opened, and my friendly guard-cum-ticket collector came up to me with the advice that 'You'll be liking a plate of bacon and eggs, sorr, with a pot of tea.'

I suppose I could have had eggs in some other form, or perhaps just bread and jam, but he offered no alternative and in any event he was quite right. Taking my agreement for granted, he said that he'd get it for me as quickly as possible, as 'We'll be stopping shortly to refuel,' and disappeared hurriedly through the swing door into what I now assumed was the galley. I also gathered that, in addition to his duties as guard and ticket collector, he was also the dining car attendant, and it occurred to me that in view of his remark about stopping to refuel, he might also be the train driver! In next to no time, he was backing through the swing door with a large tray bearing my breakfast, the centre piece of which was a large plate of delicious rashers with two eggs, soft fried to perfection. There was no table cloth, but otherwise everything of importance, including a bottle of HP sauce, which I would never think of using with eggs and bacon.

As I settled down to enjoy my meal I noticed that the train had slowed to almost walking pace, and very soon, it clanked to a halt; then rolled back a few yards and stopped with a squeal of brakes. I decided to take a look, and getting up from my table I walked up to a window. Dropping it down, I looked up the line towards the engine. Sure enough, beside the track was an enormous stack of peat turves, about fifteen feet high and twenty yards or more in length, much as I had been told in Dublin. Several figures were already busy transferring the turves from the stack to the engine tender, one of whom I thought I recognized as the guard ticket collector/dining car attendant, although he had removed his jacket and cap of office. There was obviously nothing I could do, so I returned to continue enjoying my breakfast and the columns of the *Irish Times*. But not without reflection on the comfort of my situation and that of the 1st Airborne Division, the remnants of which, I read, were fighting their way back across the Rhine.

I was back in the comfort of my compartment having a quiet doze when a somewhat half-hearted whistle from the engine signalled that steam was up once again and we began to chug slowly ahead. I hadn't paid my bill for breakfast, so I wasn't surprised to receive another visit from a hot and sweaty guard who now appeared to have added a fourth qualification, that of stoker, to his other duties. He was delighted to hear that I had thoroughly enjoyed my breakfast. 'Dat's grand, Dat's grand,' he repeated several times, and assured me of a warm welcome back at the dining car whenever I felt in need of further refreshment. When I asked how much I owed him, he was both embarrassed and confused. 'I 'tink about tirty shillings 'll cover it,' he said, 'if dats ahlright wid you, sorr,' and invoked the blessing of the Holy Mother on me and all my next of kin when I handed him £2 and told him to keep the change.

It was then that he explained how it was that he, as guard, was also looking after the dining car. The reason was very simple. On the journey up to Dublin the night before there had been very few passengers, and Liam O'Leary, the dining car attendant, had dropped off at Wicklow to visit his mother who was in poor health. Liam was a very reliable young man, I was assured, and would be back on board at Wicklow to cope with the needs of the passengers. He explained all this to me in a very matter-of-fact way, and without any apparent thought of irregularity or breach of the rules. What could be more appropriate than for the dining car attendant to take the opportunity of visiting his sick mother when there was no pressing need for his presence on the train, which, in any event, would be adequately covered by a colleague? A strange way to run a railway, I thought, but how pleasant, and indicative of the kindness and humanitarian instincts of the vast majority of Irish people.

By the time we reached Wicklow I had read every column in my copy of the *Irish Times* and at one of our frequent halts had followed the lead of the few other passengers on the train and clambered down beside the track to walk along and view the refuelling process. Whether the members of the viewing group knew one another or the men heaving baskets of turf up to the engine, I don't know, but there was no shortage of friendly banter, largely related to the quality of the turf, the weather, and what dogs were going to win at the Wicklow dog track that evening.

'Gemorra Paddy,' said a burly man in the front of the 'gallery'. One of the two loaders looked up.

'Hallo, Mick,' he replied, 'howa tings wid you?'

'Great,' came the reply. 'Dat's very wet looking turf you've got there.'

'Divil a bit wet,' replied Paddy, 'dats what'll get you to Wexford on time.'

This caused a laugh amongst the spectators.

'On time for what?' someone shouted.

There appeared to be no quick answer to that question, and the impromptu debate switched to the weather; if it was a 'grand' day or a 'soft' day; whether rain could be expected or not expected. I recollected the local legend that if you could see a blue mist on the slopes of Mount Leinster it would rain, and if you couldn't it was already raining, and decided to return to the comfort of my compartment, satisfied that I could make no contribution to the debate or to the refuelling procedure.

At Wicklow, I decided it was time for a bottle of Guinness, and made my way back to the dining car, where I made the acquaintance of Liam O'Leary. He was a younger man than his stand-in, but equally friendly and forthcoming, and seemed most gratified when I addressed him by name and enquired about the health of his mother. 'Ah to be sure she's not too well at all,' he replied and then proceeded to give me a lengthy explanation of his family circumstances.

He was the youngest of twelve children all of whom had left home with the exception of himself, the youngest, and one sister who looked after his mother at their home near Wicklow town. His father, who had also been employed on the railway, had been dead for some years — which didn't surprise me — but, Liam went on, 'he was too fond of the drink and was worn out, God rest his soul.' Of his brothers and sisters, he confided in me, two brothers were in the British Army and one in the Royal Air Force. Two other brothers were priests, one in England and one in America, and two sisters were nuns. Then he had to think for a moment as if confused as to the whereabouts of the rest of the family. 'Ah yes,' he continued, 'Another sister is a nurse, again in England, Mary is a teacher, and Josephine is married and living in the West of Ireland.' He quoted other names as he went along, Michael, Joseph, Patrick, Sean, Kathleen, Elizabeth and Maggie, the youngest, at home looking after her mother. I felt sorry for Maggie, apparently the Cinderella of the family, and he may have sensed this by going on to assure me that they were all very thoughtful about their mother, and made sure that she didn't want for anything. I still thought, 'Poor Maggie,' and was tempted to ask whether he had many nephews and nieces, but decided against it.

By this time we were on the move again, and picking up my empty glass and bottle, he announced that he was sure I could do with a plate of eggs and bacon and a bottle of Guinness to keep it company. Without offering any alternative or waiting for my reply he was away through the swing door, returning almost immediately with another bottle, 'to keep me going,' he said, and shortly afterwards with my eggs and bacon, brown bread and butter and a pot of jam. 'If there's anything else you want,' he said, 'just give me a shout,' and turned his attention to two other passengers who had entered the dining car.

It was early in the evening when we at last crawled slowly into Enniscorthy station, but not before I had made a final sortie to the dining car for a cup of tea which Liam insisted should be accompanied by boiled eggs and which I hadn't the heart to refuse, particularly on receiving his assurance that it would do me good and after all, it might be the last meal I would have for some time. Why he should have thought that, I didn't enquire. As I stepped down from the train he wished me good luck and, in the Irish fashion, invoked the blessing of the Almighty on all my goings and comings. The thought did occur to me that if the personal attention I had received during my journey was attributable in any way to the few extra shillings I handed over when settling my accounts, I should perhaps have added a few more.

In accordance with my usual practice when arriving at Enniscorthy, not having told any of my relations of my impending appearance, I left my bag at the ticket office, mentioning that I would be back later to pick it up, and set off to walk to Greenville, an uncle's farm a mile or so outside the town. From there, I knew from past experience that some means would be found of transporting me to Monalee, Ballindaggin, another farm some seven miles distant, my ultimate destination. Monalee, Ballindaggin was a kind of Mecca for all our family returning to Ireland for whatever reason, and although we had many relatives and friends throughout County Wexford and beyond, there was never any suggestion of 'why not stay here or there' but always ready acceptance of the simple fact that the place we were heading for was Monalee. We would, of course, always visit as many other family homes as circumstances permitted, but the base had to be Monalee.

When I arrived at Greenville only Aunt Tillie and my cousin Violet, about my age, were at home, and after a warm welcome it was suggested by Violet that I might like a plate of bacon and eggs, which I thankfully declined, assuring them that I was well fed and quite happy to wait for Uncle Harry and Jimmy, another cousin of about my age, to return from their labours on the farm. Dudley, the youngest of the family, was at that time in Africa with the RAF.

It wasn't until Jimmy came home that I was told of their predicament as regards transport. Petrol for private use in Southern Ireland at that time was for all intents and purposes non-existent. Farmers were allowed a small ration which was only to be used for essential purposes in connection with their farming activities, such as taking vital pieces of machinery to a forge for repair. There was no allowance for motor cars for social and non-farming domestic driving.

For farm equipment, a product called Tractor Vaporizing Oil had been introduced and this was also strictly rationed according to the number of tractors registered in the farmer's name. The farmers had soon discovered, of course, that TVO could be used in a motor car, either neat or mixed with petrol, if one was prepared to put up with the clouds of black exhaust smoke which this created. However, the authorities soon put a stop to this practice by making it illegal and by introducing severe penalties for those caught in the act. Furthermore, a coloured dye was incorporated into the TVO which made it simple for the police to detect.

As always in such circumstances, car owners had little difficulty convincing their consciences that the occasional use of their cars for some purpose which might not be in strict accordance with the law was nevertheless in the national interest. This, of course, required subterfuge of some kind or another against the possibility of being stopped by the police and asked to explain the reason for the journey. To that end all vehicles on what might be considered 'questionable business' carried an item of farm equipment alleged to be in urgent need of repair and ostensibly en route to some place where this could be carried out, so that essential production of food for the Irish people should continue without interruption. An alternative ruse was the transportation of someone in urgent need of medical care. This would necessitate the inclusion of a passenger who had no objection to having a heavily bandaged arm in a sling, or having pieces of wood strapped on either side of an imaginary broken leg. On all occasions, of course, the phoney patient had to be someone who could act the part by giving vent to cries of pain and anguish should the situation require. As time passed, the police became adept at seeing through these charades and identifying the phoneys, after which anyone who had suffered a genuine accident could more or less command his own price for participating in an irregular car journey. It was rumoured at one time that some astute person spent his time outside the exit of the local hospital casualty department approaching emerging 'walking wounded' with a proposition for them to join a 'rent-a-casualty' business, but whether that was true or not I don't know.

Greyhound breeding and racing was a popular sideline and an attractive alternative source of tax free income for farmers and others around Enniscorthy at that time, and as motor transport was the only suitable means of transporting the animals to race tracks, the regulations limiting the use of petrol presented a serious problem. Dispensations from the regulations had been granted by the authorities for race horse owners because of the importance of that industry for the Irish economy, but this was considered most unfair by the greyhound fraternity who therefore had no compunction about devising ways and means for getting around the rules. A simple method of doing so was to use the 'essential piece of machinery' or 'accident victim' ploy with the dog or dogs in the back of the car under a blanket. If an inquisitive policeman happened to notice the dog or dogs he would be assured that they had simply been 'brought along for the ride!' But this wasn't very convincing, particularly if the enquiry took place in the vicinity of a greyhound track on a race night. Dogs could also be given sleeping pills to lessen the possibility of them being noticed, but this was somewhat inconvenient because the dogs would have to be taken to the vicinity of the track in sufficient time to allow the effects of the drugs to wear off before presentation to the presiding veterinary officer. Fortunately, some local police superintendents were not entirely unsympathetic to the plight of the dog owners, and although the law was the law, and had to be enforced, a little persuasion could result in officers who might be checking vehicles on certain roads near dog tracks at certain times finding themselves otherwise engaged in fighting crime at some other locations, with beneficial results for all concerned, particularly those who were inclined to have a flutter on the dogs.

However, the immediate question was how I was to be transported from Greenville to Monalee without the somewhat dreary night drive in a pony and trap. Jimmy had already exploited the 'broken machinery' ploy a few days earlier, and was reluctant to try his luck so soon again. We discussed the possibility of me being an 'accident victim' en route to O'Neal the Bonesetter near Newtownbarry — a dispenser of fringe medicine much favoured by the inhabitants of the Counties Wexford and Wicklow at that time — but decided against it because my accent, if questioned as I surely would be, might give rise to further interrogation and investigation. Jimmy eventually decided that it would have to be 'broken machinery in urgent need of repair' — he already had a tractor half-shaft in the boot of his car — but that he would follow a different route, somewhat longer, but avoiding the outskirts of the town. Then I remembered something: my bag was at the railway station. Fortunately, Jimmy again had the answer. He had to visit the guards barracks in Enniscorthy to renew his gun licence — which he was sure was legitimate business for car driving purposes. He would drop me at the end of Enniscorthy Bridge from where I could quickly walk to the station and collect my bag, and he would pick me up again at the same point on his way back to Greenville after a detour to Monalee by way of a quieter route through Ballycarney.

All went according to plan, and in less than an hour I was walking into the embrace of Aunt Lizzie in the warm kitchen of Monalee.

Although my stay was short, just three nights and two full days, it was, as always, well worth whatever effort had been involved, little enough on this particular trip. My uncle Thomas, who being the eldest son had inherited the farm from his father, had died a couple of years before the war, leaving Aunt Lizzie with a viable farm, no cash, and six children: one daughter and five sons, one of whom, Fred, was my particular buddy.

My two days in Monalee on this occasion were largely spent meandering around the farm buildings and fields, where every corner held nostalgic memories of wonderful carefree times during my summer holidays each year; joining the farm workers in the fields as they built hay cocks and stacked the ripe corn sheaves, riding on the hay cocks as they were brought into the enormous barn, carting in the ripened barley, wheat and oats, and all culminating in the annual threshing day when the gleaming steam engine driving the mill and pitchers would be set up alongside the corn ricks, and the farm yard would be alive with the puffing and clanking of the engine and the bustle of the many helping hands from all the other farms in the neighbourhood. What a marvellous day that always was, now largely supplanted by the combine harvester and other modern machinery.

One afternoon I borrowed a bicycle, and rode the two or so miles to Ballindaggin to see my old friend Willie Jordan, who, with his sister Mary Anne, ran a general store in the village with, of course, the usual 'back bar,' where, as a boy, Willie would always insist on giving me a large bottle of Letts lemonade. The questions flowed, thick and fast. On this occasion, Willie decided that as a young man back from the war I deserved something stronger than lemonade, and insisted on giving me a 'glass' of Irish whiskey which, if I had drunk it all, would have rendered a bicycle ride back to Monalee impossible.

Then, on down the hill to visit Mary Doyle who ran the combined post office and sweet shop, and who, with many others in the village had been schoolgirl friends of my mother. All these people were, of course, devout Roman Catholics, unlike ourselves and indeed most well-to-do farmers in the area, who were mainly Protestant, but never did I hear or see any signs of friction or animosity between the religious groups, the only apparent difference being the locations where they attended services on Sunday. On the many occasions when we were in Ballindaggin, Fred and I used to be more than pleased to meet the local priest. Father Mearns, I think his name was, would invariably enquire into the well-being of our respective families and hand us sweets to help us on our way.

Keeping one eye closed to offset the effect of Willie's whiskey, I rode on through Templeshanbo, past the Protestant church and on to Shroughmore, the home of the Jacobs, neighbours and close friends of the Hattons of Monalee, several generations of both families having been born, reared, educated and, indeed buried alongside one another in the graveyard at Templeshanbo. Once again a warm welcome, many questions, followed by tea and apple cake — no alcoholic drinks while Mrs Jacob was in command! The Jacobs were also a large family. One of the four boys, Sam, being the same age as Fred Hatton and me, had been a regular participant in our youthful exploits.

As in most country farm houses the 'parlour,' with its carpeted floor, settee, armchairs, tables, ornaments, family pictures and piano, was used mainly for entertaining 'non-family' guests such as the vicar, doctor, solicitor, and maybe the bank manager. The spot where the family and close friends always gathered was around the open hearth in the large stone flagged kitchen, with an enormous dresser at one end, and with the large, bare wooden table around which the many workmen would gather for their midday and evening meals, pushed to one side to make room for as many chairs as were necessary around the blazing log fire.

When the day's work was over, the kitchen at Monalee was open house for anyone who cared to call, and it was very seldom that there weren't a number of callers. Ned Watkins, an elderly bachelor, who farmed a few acres around the cluster of tiny, mud-walled cottages a couple of fields away from Monalee, seemed to be a permanent evening fixture. He never took off his wide brimmed felt hat except when saying 'Good night, mam,' to Aunt Lizzie, and sat smoking his pipe and from time to time and to Aunt Lizzie's disgust, ejecting a large spit with unerring accuracy into the heart of the open fire where it would sizzle away to extinction. Other regulars were Har Clare and Eddie Warren, neighbouring farmers, and John Sheil, a somewhat backward offspring of blood-related parents who sat with his hands tucked between his knees and said nothing.

Word had got around that I was 'home' and each evening there were many other callers. Jim Leech, John and Sam Jacob, and one evening, much to my delight, Henry Nolan, then well over seventy, who had worked at Monalee all his life and who was overflowing with reminiscences about my mother and her many brothers and sisters, as well as of my grandparents.

There was, of course, no TV, and entertainment had to be self-generated, but there was never any shortage of talent. Eddie Warren, with a fine baritone voice, was always happy to sing Irish ballads as long as the applause required. Ned Watkins could always be persuaded to recount stories of his many confrontations with the 'little people,' with whom he claimed to be on very friendly terms during his nocturnal strolls to and from Monalee and across the surrounding fields. Ned, it appeared, was also a firm believer in the Irish folklore that the wail of a banshee foreshadowed the death of some local person, and would quote chapter and verse of the many occasions when this had occurred, including, naturally, the demise of many well known to this audience. Ned would embellish his stories by explaining that the 'little people' lived in 'raheens', small areas of scrubby bushes and trees about twenty yards or so across, which farmers leave uncultivated in their fields and which are a common sight in the Irish countryside. It would be a foolish farmer indeed who ploughed up a raheen and risked the wrath of the little people, and I can well remember when, as a child, my cousins would warn me against encroaching upon a raheen. Not that the little people were necessarily antagonistic towards their human neighbours, but being endowed with special powers, they could cause problems if their way of life was interfered with. Why risk a plough breaking against a submerged rock or a horse going lame or sheep and cattle developing coughs or milk turning sour, all for the sake of a little give and take? I never discovered exactly what a banshee was supposed to be or whether it had any connection with the little people but it was generally accepted by sceptics to be a vixen seeking her mate, any foresight of approaching death being purely coincidental.

Henry Nolan lived at Monbeg, a small farm two or three miles from Monalee, also owned by the Hattons and where the family lived before acquiring Monalee. Henry was also a great raconteur, and that night told of a most exciting event which had taken place a few days earlier.

A German bomber had crashed on Mount Leinster a few miles north of Ballindaggin, and the following evening Henry, with two of his local friends, Tom Doyle and Eugene Stephens, had decided to cycle to the scene. At that time, very few country folk around Wexford had ever seen an aeroplane in the sky, much less on the ground. After reaching Kiltealy they were directed to the location of the crash, which meant leaving their cycles beside the road and tramping for an hour or more through the deep heather up the side of the mountain to where the wreckage was scattered over a wide area.

'Begob,' said Henry, 'there were injuns here and wings a mile away, you never saw the loike, and weren't the troops and police just standing around looking; sure there could have been bombs and bullets and petrol exploding any time.'

Another onlooker told Henry that the bodies of the crew of three had all been found in the wreckage and taken away. 'Ah, 'twas a shokin' sight,' said Henry, 'but sure in England you must be seeing them wherever you go.'

They had wandered on, peering into the interior of the broken fuselage, when suddenly Tom Doyle had bent down and picked something up from the deep heather. He looked at what he had found for a moment and said, 'If I could find the pair of that I'd be made up.'

It was a leather flying boot, which he quickly stuffed inside his jacket.

'Well,' continued Henry, 'we walked around the wreckage half a dozen times, looking for the pair of the boot Tom had found, but divil another one could we find, so we came on back to Tom's place with Tom carrying the boot inside his coat. When he walked into the kitchen and showed the boot to his missus, she asked him what was the good of one boot, and told him to throw it out, but Tom wouldn't have any of it. 'You never know,' he said, 'sure if I wear out one of my boots I can use this as a replacement,' and sat down to try it on. 'Be the 'pissin mice,' said Henry — a favourite expression of his when he wanted to emphasize the importance of what was coming next — 'it was only then that Tom discovered there was already a foot in it!'

'What happened then?' asked Fred from the corner.

'I dunno,' said Henry, 'but when Eugene and I left, Tom and his missus were arguing as to whether they should take the foot to the priest to find out whether it should be given a proper burial!'

11

The Parachute Regiment

A shock was awaiting me on my return to Bulford; I had been transferred to the Parachute Regiment. No reason or explanation was given in the message I collected from the letter rack in the officers' mess, but when I enquired from John Drummond the following morning, it was explained that following the considerable losses incurred by the 1st Airborne Division at Arnhem, and because of the urgent need to reform that division, officers and other ranks who were trained parachutists were required as quickly as possible. The main source for these requirements was the 6th Air Landing Brigade. Those transferred could, of course, decline, as parachutists had to be volunteers, but this was unlikely as we had all volunteered for the short parachute course, although not for service in the Parachute Regiment.

Although I was very sorry to be leaving the battalion in which I had served for more than four years and in which I had made many very good friends, the possibility of doing more parachuting appealed to me, and I was also told that promotion to company commander was possible.

So, late in September 1944, with a sense of sadness tinged with keen anticipation for what lay ahead, I set off once again for Hardwick Hall near Chesterfield, the Airborne Forces Depot. From there, I was posted to the 2nd Battalion, located in a very large baronial house south of Grantham in Lincolnshire. The battalion at that time consisted of only a handful of officers and other ranks who had not taken part in the Arnhem operation or who had managed to get back with the remnants of the division. The battalion had reached the Arnhem bridge and had fought tenaciously for six days, hoping for relief by ground forces which never arrived, until every man was dead, wounded or out of ammunition. A new commanding officer had been appointed, John Marshall, one of the original parachutists, who had been second in command in Africa. Maybe I didn't respond with much enthusiasm when he asked me to take over as adjutant, but he pointed out that this would only be until such time as other officers arrived, when he would be in a position to decide who would be appointed adjutant on a permanent basis.

The first thing I had to do was to get across to Ringway and bring myself up-to-date on parachuting techniques and to make some more jumps to qualify for full parachute wings. This was quickly arranged, and the following day I explained to the officer in charge of the Parachute Training Centre what was urgently required. Two days later I was on my way back to Grantham with four more jumps under my belt, all from a door instead of a hole in the floor, and the proud possessor, in my pocket, of the coveted parachute wings, and without a batman to sew them on my sleeve. I was also sadly conscious of the need to replace the black Royal Ulster Rifles buttons on my service dress with the brass buttons and badges of rank of my new regiment.

The atmosphere amongst the half dozen or so officers in the 2nd Battalion mess was naturally somewhat subdued. Despite the success of the 2nd Battalion in securing its objective, Arnhem Bridge, and the outstanding courage shown in holding out against far superior odds, the operation had failed, and hundreds of close friends were either dead or prisoners of war. I was particularly mindful of Dan Woods, John McFadden and Peter Barry, all of whom had previously served with the RUR and were later reported to have died of wounds.

However, the newly appointed commanding officer, John Marshall, was not one to sit around bewailing the events of the past. A regular soldier in his early thirties, cheerful and full of energy, an early volunteer for parachuting, he set about the task of restoring the battalion to its former greatness as the elite of the regiment. All he needed was a full complement of officers, NCOs and men, and over the next few weeks, these began to arrive. Several officers rejoined who had previously served with the battalion: Tony Franks who took over from me as adjutant, Dennis Rendell, who had been taken prisoner in Africa.

After his capture Dennis had been shipped back to a prisoner of war camp in Italy from where he had escaped and made his way to Rome where he had lived for several months as an Italian with an Italian family until Rome had been liberated. One day he showed me some snapshots of himself surrounded by a group of German troops at a rifle range in a Rome funfair. There a 'bullseye' had triggered an automatic camera which photographed the 'customers' who, on that occasion, were Dennis and some admiring Germans, all in uniform. The fact that he looked like an Italian, with his dark skin and large bushy moustache, no doubt helped him to pass himself off as one, although he also told me that he thought some of his German 'pals' suspected that he was an escaped prisoner, but for some reason did nothing about it.

Another welcome 'escapee' was Digby Tatham-Warter, who, as the only surviving company commander, had assumed command of the battalion for the final hours on the Arnhem Bridge. He had somehow managed to avoid capture, and together with members of the Dutch Resistance, had been instrumental in organizing the escape of a number of other survivors through the German lines across the River Rhine and back to allied lines. He became second in command of the battalion.

In November, with the arrival of reinforcements, we moved from the baronial hall near Grantham to a hutted camp a couple of miles outside Oakham in what was then the county of Rutland. I was appointed company commander of C Company and promoted to acting major. The camp was located on a secondary road near the village of Cottesmore. It was not large enough to accommodate the entire battalion, so my company was billeted at the Cottesmore Kennels, a group of solid, well constructed stable-like buildings where a pack of fox hounds and a number of hunters were kept. The hounds and hunters were still 'in residence,' and we were allocated about half of the available space, using the lofts as the men's sleeping quarters, and the ground level stables for stores and company headquarters. The company officers, Dennis Rendell, Dennis Field, 'Boy' something or other — who gave his civilian occupation as 'an artiste', and another subaltern, whose name I forget — all had our sleeping quarters in the main camp a couple of hundred yards down the road.

What was, to all intents and purposes, a new 2nd Battalion, soon began to take shape, and I was very conscious of the reputation we had to live up to. The quality of the men who joined us was first class. The average age was about twenty; they had all had their initial training at their regimental depots, and although mostly conscripts, they had all volunteered for parachuting, had survived the strenuous pre-jumping spell at Hardwick Hall, and had completed their seven jumps at Ringway and were very proud of the parachute emblems and their red beret headgear. The task now, as John Marshall made very clear, was to weld them into a fighting unit in the shortest possible time so that the division would again be ready to rejoin the battle in whatever task it might be called upon to carry out. The men were very different from the 'old sweats' with whom I was familiar in the Ulster Rifles. They were keen, intelligent and receptive and not tainted with the 'anti' and sometimes obstructive attitudes of the 'bolshies,' although there were one or two I tried to get rid of, without success.

From a small group of volunteers I selected as my batman a young Scot from Galashiels by the name of Eoin Clapperton. Unlike his predecessor, Goosey Gillanders of the Ulster Rifles, he was neither a boozer nor a womanizer, and turned out to be a very good choice, and I regretted not keeping in touch with him after the war.

The next few months passed very quickly, despite the very cold and miserable weather during the winter of 1944. My objective was to ensure that C Company retained the reputation it had earned as the most efficient company in the battalion, and if this could be measured by the enthusiasm and spirit of the officers and men we were soon well on our way to that end. In March, each company in turn spent two weeks at a commando training camp at Lochailort between Fort William and Mallaig in Scotland. Lochailort, at the end of the loch about three miles in from the open sea, consisted of a railway station, a few houses, a hotel and a small hutted camp behind the hotel, which was where we were accommodated. The scenery was superb, even at that time of the year, with high heather-covered mountains on either side of the loch and stretching away towards the sea.

Every day, and on several nights, we carried out platoon and company exercises designed and written up by someone — I don't know who — which involved walking, running, climbing and frequently crawling over these heather covered slopes. The camp was fully staffed so it was an added bonus when we set out in the early hours each day that every officer, NCO and man could take part without the usual need to leave behind cooks, clerks and guards to look after the camp. The spell at Lochailort, although short, helped to strengthen the feelings of comradeship and trust between all ranks which had developed during the relatively short period we had been together and which is so necessary amongst a body of men who may need to live and fight together in hostile country and when complete reliance on one another is vital.

A strange incident occurred one evening after we had announced the 'cease fire' following a strenuous twenty-four hour 'battle' which found us on the highest point of a mountain from where we could look down on the beautiful scenery surrounding the calm waters of the loch and see in the misty distance the Islands of 'Muck, Egg and Rum.'

All the men had been told to make their own way back to camp, and Dennis Rendell and I decided to follow a winding sheep track down the side of the mountain to the narrow road which ran alongside the loch, which would then give us a walk of about two miles, but on level ground. This road was dead straight for about a mile, and as we turned onto it, with some relief, I noticed in the distance a small speck of someone walking in our direction. In such a remote place, this seemed strange in itself, but more so as we gradually got closer, and could make out that the figure was that of a girl of about twenty, carrying a suitcase. Even more strange, she didn't have the look of a country girl, but was smartly dressed, as well as being very attractive. As we met, we stopped and said, 'Good evening.'

She stopped and said, 'Hallo,' resting her suitcase on the ground and flexing her fingers as if to relieve the strain on her hand and arm.

'Have you got far to go?' said Dennis.

'Oh no,' she replied in a soft Scottish accent, 'just around the bend and I'm home.'

We looked back up the road, and couldn't see any bend. 'Have you come very far?' I asked.

'From Glasgow,' was the reply, 'home for a long weekend.'

She didn't appear to resent our inquisitive questions in any way, and when Dennis asked whether we could assist her with her suitcase, she laughed as if highly amused at such a suggestion. 'Not at all,' she said, 'it's very kind of you but I shall be home in ten minutes.'

Picking up her suitcase and wishing us goodbye, she continued her way, and we agreed that it was a pity that we would be leaving Lochailort in a couple of days.

Forty-two years later, at my daughter Jill's wedding, I was chatting with her new mother-in-law, a Scotswoman who had received her nurse's training at a Glasgow hospital. I happened to mention my fleeting association with Lochailort, and the unusual incident when I had met a young girl carrying her suitcases from Lochailort station for three miles to her home at the mouth of the loch. She reflected for a moment and then said, 'That must have been . . . ' — and she mentioned the name of a girl who had also trained at the same hospital, and who lived with her parents at the croft overlooking the entrance to Lochailort. It's a small world!

The final event of our training spell at Lochailort was a practice assault-landing from the 'sea' on to a defended beach under conditions as near as possible to the 'real thing.' This involved an early morning bus ride to another loch used by the commandos for this type of field firing exercise and where the 'defenders' — staff at the training centre — had set up machine guns on fixed lines, planted imaginary remote-controlled mines incorporating explosives along the landing area, and were also well armed with thunderflashes to simulate hand grenades and mortar fire.

Just before daybreak we embarked in small assault boats propelled by paddle, and in line abreast paddled our way along the loch towards our objective, the defended beach from where, when we were about thirty yards out, all hell seemed to break loose. Simulated mines exploded a few yards ahead of the boats, throwing up fountains of water through which the boats had to plough their way. Live bullets, including tracer, snapped around our heads and into the water between the boats, all with a deluge of thunderflashes creating a picture comparable to anything we had experienced in Normandy, and despite its artificiality as good a test of the resolve and determination of our young troops as they could have experienced. When the boats slid to a stop they leapt out into eighteen inches of mud and scrambled their way up to relatively dry ground, from where they charged up the slope, shouting and urging one another on like true veterans and into the trenches where the imaginary enemy had to be destroyed. Despite the make believe and unlikely tactical aspects of these field firing exercises, they demonstrated that the men were strong, fit and determined, and when faced with the real thing they would give a good account of themselves. Before we left to return to our camp, the commando officer in charge told me that the need to create 'realism' meant that they were allowed a casualty rate of killed and wounded from 'accidental causes.' It was gratifying to hear him add that in his experience, no company had put on a better show than C Company.

On the two or three evenings we had 'free' during our stay, Dennis and I and our three platoon commanders would walk across to the hotel bar for a nightcap, where we met the lady who ran the hotel and her two teenage daughters. When we were catching the train for our return journey to Cottesmore, we noticed that the two girls were also travelling on the same train to Glasgow, so we invited them to join us in our reserved first class compartment. During the journey one of the girls slipped a piece of paper into my hand. I was a bit mystified and a little embarrassed by this, so didn't examine it until I found an opportunity to slip along the corridor to the toilet. On it was written, 'When will I see you again?' When I returned to the compartment I didn't say anything until we were saying goodbye at Glasgow, when I simply said to her, 'I'll be back sometime.'

Forty years later, my wife and I were on our way by car from Inverness to Stranraer to catch a boat to Larne when, on a very wet and windy day we found ourselves in Fort William. After paying our respects at the magnificent Commando Memorial beneath the slopes of Ben Nevis, I decided to digress and see if Lochailort had changed over the years since my previous visit. As we drove along the narrow bumpy Arisaig road past Glenfinnan and the Bonny Prince Charlie memorial, I described to Janet how the village had looked and wondered whether forty years had seen many changes. As we rounded the final bend, Janet said, 'It's exactly as you described.'

The railway station, the small houses, the hotel, and behind, the hutted camp and small barrack square — now, it appeared, a car park — and stretching away into the mist, the smooth, dark waters of Lochailort bounded on either side by the dark slopes of the surrounding mountains ascending into the mist and cloud. After parking the car, despite the heavy rain, we walked around the camp and down to the edge of the loch, from which I gathered that the only change had been the conversion of the camp into the offices of a fish farming company with a number of large circular contraptions just visible on the surface of the water, presumably where the fish were hatched and reared.

Because of the weather, shelter and refreshment in the hotel seemed a good idea, and when we entered the small bar the thought came to my mind that this was one place that hadn't changed over the past forty years. Even the used glasses sitting on the table in the corner could have been those used by us in 1945. I got the impression that there had been a late party the night before, and cleaning-up operations hadn't yet got underway. After a few minutes tapping on the bar a cheerful looking man of about thirty appeared in the doorway behind the small circular bar in the corner of the room. In next to no time, while ferreting around behind the bar for two clean glasses and pouring out a lager and a light ale, he made it clear that if we were interested in staying the night or several nights, or in shooting and fishing, or sides of fresh salmon, or trout or a side of venison, with or without the offal, we only had to say the word. He seemed genuinely disappointed when I explained that ours was only a fleeting visit, but he perked up when I added that my last visit was forty years earlier when the hotel had been in the hands of a lady and her two daughters.

'That was Mrs so and so,' he said, 'she only left here three or four years ago.'

I didn't get an opportunity to enquire as to the whereabouts of the two daughters because at that moment three other customers came into the bar, apparently a husband and wife and the mother of one of them, and known to our host, who immediately explained that this was my first visit since being billeted in the camp forty years earlier. They were obviously locals, and the man was soon discussing the availability of venison and insisting that he certainly required the offal. Meanwhile, the mother told me that she had lived in Lochailort all her life, and well remembered the visits of commandos and parachutists over the war years. As we shook hands and left on our way, I remarked that there hadn't been many changes in

Lochailort, to which she responded, 'Please God there never will be.'

When C Company arrived back at Cottesmore, we, together with the rest of the battalion, and no doubt the remainder of the re-formed 1st Parachute Brigade, were fit and ready to take on whatever task was required. But unfortunately, the next couple of months were to be a period of intense frustration. We arrived back just about the time of the allied assault across the Rhine in which we knew the 6th Airborne Division were taking part, and as news seeped back of considerable German resistance, thoughts of my friends in the 1st RUR were never far from my mind.

We were in a continual state of readiness, anticipating an operation ahead of the advancing allied armies, but after the breakout following the river crossing the advance became so rapid that possible objectives for an airborne operation were overrun without the necessity for airborne assistance. In the meantime, we continued with our training, despite the difficulty of maintaining enthusiasm for make believe, with the thought of the real thing in the back of everyone's mind. On one occasion we were actually at the airfield before being informed that the operation in Northern Germany was off. Another cause of disappointment and frustration was the usual shortage of aircraft for training jumps, which would at least have relieved the tension in young men keyed up in anticipation of going into action for the first time.

For one training exercise we were delighted to hear that American Air Force planes were available, and before take-off the officers had a joint briefing session with the pilots involved when they assured us of a 'pin-point' drop on the selected dropping zone.

After flying around the Lincolnshire countryside for an hour or so, the red 'action stations' warning light came on, and as Number 1 in the stick I was standing in the door of the aircraft with one eye on the light and the other on the passing countryside, and the thought came to my mind that I couldn't recognize any of the landmarks approaching the dropping zone. Suddenly, 'Go' and I was floating down to a landscape that bore no resemblance to the one I had anticipated. I landed in the corner of a small meadow, very close to a thick, prickly looking hedge which I was lucky to miss on my final oscillation. I wasn't

336

alone, and a number were less fortunate and found themselves swinging from the branches of tall trees from, which they could neither descend nor ascend and for whom we could do nothing other than extend the hope that help in the form of the nearest fire brigade would soon arrive.

As I studied my map and tried to identify features of the surrounding countryside which might give a clue as to where we were, I was joined by a number of others, including another company commander, and we agreed to head off in the direction our planes had taken, which was towards a cluster of buildings we could see a few hundred yards away. Fortunately, these included a small garage workshop where we were able to establish our location and persuade the proprietor to use his lorry to convey us to our proper dropping zone some three miles away, having first notified the local police by telephone of the predicament of our comrades still suspended in the trees nearby. It's an unfortunate fact that even the most intrepid parachutist is powerless when hanging some forty feet above the ground from a parachute which is itself caught up in the branches of a tree. To release the parachute harness and drop or attempt to climb up the rigging lines into the offending tree are options both fraught with considerable risk of serious injury, which would have to be accepted on active operations, but not on training.

When our greatly overladen lorry trundled into the dropping zone some forty minutes later than planned, we found a somewhat irate John Marshall making very rude remarks about American Air Force navigators. However, as he pointed out, we had to be prepared for the unexpected.

The news that Hitler was dead and that the war in Europe was over, was very much an anticlimax. There was, of course, profound relief that there would be no more air raids, no more doodle-bugs, no more rockets; an end of the blackout and, hopefully of rationing — a hope not to be fulfilled for a long time. On the other hand there was a great sense of disappointment amongst all ranks that we had been as it were on the touch line, and had not participated in the final 'kill,' despite all our efforts over the previous few weeks.

However, despite our dejection, we could not let VE day pass without some celebration, and that evening — I forgot whether it was 7 or 8 May, a truck load took off for Nottingham to participate in the festivities. I don't remember much of that evening except being invited with most of our party to join the city mayor and civic dignitaries on the balcony of the City Hall from where, accompanied by the local brass band, we made a brave attempt to entertain the dancing crowds below with our rendering of *Phil the Fluters Ball*. Whether anyone appreciated or even heard our contribution I very much doubt, but it certainly earned us liberal further entertainment at the city's expense.

Soon after the end of the war in Europe, the newspapers were full of speculation about demobilization of the armed services, and although all this appeared to be very uncertain, one thing was sure, and that was that it would be a slow and prolonged operation because of the need for troops to police the liberated and conquered countries, the requirements for the continuing war against Japan, and last but not least, to avoid flooding the home market with millions of unemployed before industry and commerce was ready to receive them back into civilian jobs: a gigantic switch from a wartime to a peacetime economy.

Shortly after VE Day, I heard from Robin Crockett of happenings with the 1st RUR. With the 6th Division, they had formed part of the vanguard for the crossing of the Rhine, with the glider landing zones near Hamminkeln, north of Wesel. There had been considerable and fanatical opposition on and near the landing zone, which, together with poor visibility caused by a smoke screen put down to cover the assault boat troops, resulted in many casualties, including Charles Vickery, Dickie Martin, Harry Croft, Mike Gann, John Robertson, Ken Donnelly, all killed. Although I had been disappointed not to be with the battalion, I couldn't but reflect that perhaps I had been fortunate.

It was about this time that we were told that the two airborne divisions were about to be amalgamated, and although it wasn't official, we gathered that the combined division would be going to the Far East. However, no officer with a 'demob category' of twenty-four or less would be involved. As I was in 'Demob twenty-four', I would not be joining the new division, but would be posted elsewhere. The 'demob categories' were decided on the basis of age and length of service, but there was uncertainty in my case, as I had applied for a regular commission but hadn't been informed as to whether this had been approved, so I was in a state of limbo, at least for the time being. The day approached when the majority would depart for Bulford, whilst the others, including myself, would set off on a short period of leave before reporting to the Airborne Forces Depot to await instructions as to where we went from there.

I then received another letter from Robin Crockett, now back at Bulford, telling me that he and Ronnie Wilson had 'arranged' to be attached to the Belgian Army in Northern Ireland as liaison officers and that if the idea appealed to me, he would 'arrange' for me to join them. I couldn't help wondering what the Belgian Army was doing in Northern Ireland, but because of the uncertainty as to my future I jumped at the possibility and sent off a letter to Robin telling him to include me in his 'arrangements.' I later discovered that after the liberation of Belgium, two brigades of the army had been reformed, a Walloon Brigade, and a Flemish Brigade, and had been sent to Northern Ireland for training. Liaison officers were required to assist the Belgians with their relationships and communications with the local population, police and civil authorities. According to Robin, the only qualification required by prospective liaison officers was reasonable conversational ability in French and/or Dutch. When I mentioned that my French was no better than matriculation level, he assured me that this would probably earn me immediate promotion, and in any event it wasn't likely that there was anyone on the North of Ireland HQ qualified to check my linguistic capability or form an opinion one way or another.

The day soon arrived for the departure of the main body of the battalion, and I shook hands with each man of C Company as they clambered aboard the trucks, wishing them good luck wherever they found themselves. I was particularly sorry to say goodbye to my batman, Eoin Clapperton, who had turned out to be such an excellent choice. He assured me that he would write and let me know how he got on, which he did for a year or so, after which we lost touch. I often wondered whether, in due course, he returned safe and sound to his native Galashiels.

After lunch that day with the few officers left at the camp, and as we were not due to depart for the station until the late afternoon, I decided to walk across to the kennels to check that everything had been left in order. After inspecting the troops' accommodation I was heading back to my office when I passed the stable which had been used as a company store, and hearing voices I looked inside, where Colour Sergeant Sharpe and his storeman appeared to be stacking a number of small tin cans on a table. In reply to my query, Sharpe assured me in his broad Scottish accent that everything was under control, so knowing that they would be staying until the camp and all the equipment were handed over to an incoming unit or properly secured, I wished them good luck and continued on my way, not going straight back to the main camp, but to my office where I sat down to sort through some papers that had been left on my table.

All was peace and quiet until suddenly I heard a very solid thump from somewhere in the vicinity. I didn't take too much notice until it was followed by a series of further thumps and the building appeared to shake, so I decided to investigate and walked out of the building and around to the hedge which separated the kennels area from the adjoining field. In this field, and running parallel to the roadway for about a hundred yards was what I had thought when I first saw it to be a disused canal, about ten yards wide, but which I subsequently learned to be a trout farm. As I peered through the hedge I realized immediately the cause of the thumps. The colour sergeant and his storeman were fishing. Not in the conventional manner with a line and rod, but with small explosive charges which, when thrown into the water had the effect of stunning the fish which floated to the surface, flapping feebly as they recovered from the effect of the concussion. Colour Sergeant Sharpe was already in the water up to his armpits and apparently stark naked, as he tossed the larger fish to his storeman on the bank. I remembered the small tins I had seen on the table in the store a little earlier, no doubt filled with plastic explosive with detonators, and ready for their fishing expedition.

I stood back. The first thought that came into my mind was that this was a serious offence, and they would have to be charged; then the implications came flooding into my mind. There was no commanding officer, no regimental sergeant major, in fact no-one around to handle the matter. Moreover, I was due to catch a train to London in about an hour. I decided to take the easy way out, and leave them to their ill-gotten gains, and turning made for the gateway from the kennels to the road. As I emerged through the gateway, I saw, to my consternation the unmistakable figure of the local police sergeant about 200 yards away, pushing his bicycle in my direction. Instinctively, I stepped back into the gateway, not knowing whether he had seen me. The last thing I wanted at that moment was to get involved with the civil police, which might involve a local magistrate who might even own the trout farm. Someone might have heard the explosions and phoned the police and he was coming to investigate. The instinct of self-preservation prompted me to take the coward's way out.

I knew there was a narrow track leading from the far end of the kennels around the area of the trout farm, and by a circuitous route back to the officers' quarters, where my packed bags were awaiting collection, and without even shouting a warning to Sharpe — something for which I had always had a sense of guilt, I skedaddled, and feeling hot and sweaty and not a little relieved, I was soon on my way to Northern Ireland — via Beckenham. Whether Sharpe and the storeman were caught in the act, I don't know, but I always comforted myself with the fact that even if they had been, Sharpe, an old soldier of many years experience, would have talked himself out of any difficulty, even if it meant handing over enough trout to feed the local police force and their families.

12

Liaison Officer with the Belgian Army

My spell as liaison officer with the re-formed Belgian Army was frustrating and disappointing. At NID HQ at Lisburn I heard that Robin Crockett was attached to the Walloon Brigade at Carrickfergus whilst Ronnie Wilson was based at Lisburn near his home at Portadown, which was where he was at the time. I was despatched by truck to join a battalion of the Flemish Brigade at Caledon near Armagh.

I arrived in Caledon on a glorious sunny Saturday evening to find the battalion HQ in the Dower House of the Caledon estate — owned by the Alexander family, and situated in the Caledon main street. However, finding the Dower House was one thing; finding someone who knew anything was another. My driver helped me dump my large metal trunk and bedroll in the hallway, and then disappeared whence he had come, leaving me to make contact with our Belgian allies of whom there was no sign. The front door was open, but there was no guard, no duty officer, no mess staff and so far as I could ascertain, no telephone or signals office.

The Dower House, a double fronted Victorian style house, reminded me of a four or five bedroom suburb residence in Ealing and it had undoubtedly seen better days, both outside and in. On the right from the hallway was a large room furnished only with several six foot wooden top tables and a number of chairs, which I assumed was the officers' mess dining room. On the left of the hall was another large room containing a number of very dilapidated armchairs. I was beginning to feel sorry for the Belgians. Presumably they had arrived from Belgium with nothing in the way of officers' mess equipment, nor had anything been provided by he local military establishment. I made a mental note. One of the first things I would do, if the Belgian CO agreed, was to chase up NID for some decent mess furniture.

When I did eventually meet the CO and mentioned the point, he flapped his hands a few times and told me not to bother. They would be moving to Germany before too long, and the Germans would provide all the comforts they required!

After stamping around the hallway for several minutes trying to attract the attention of anyone who might be in the building, a sleepy looking individual emerged through a doorway leading to the backstairs. He was about eighteen or nineteen, with red hair and dressed in battle dress trousers and a cardigan, and, I quickly discovered, spoke no English or my version of French. His only response to my question, as to the whereabouts of the adjutant was to emit a guttural noise which I took to be Dutch, and indicated that I should follow him down the passage from the hallway, out of the back of the house into what had at one time been a very attractive garden with a lovely lawn and flower beds, but which was now overgrown and untidy. I followed my guide down a well trodden track across the lawn, through a thick copse, until we emerged, to my surprise, into a cleared area where there were about six Nissen huts linked by narrow concrete paths, and all looking strangely uninhabited. My guide led me to the entrance into the nearest hut, opened the door and ushered me inside. With a narrow corridor down one side, the hut was divided into a number of cubicles, each with its own door. I opened the first door and went inside. The room I found myself in was a little larger than the cells in the Old Bailey we had occupied at the beginning of the war. A bare concrete floor, a brick wall on one side and breeze blocks on the other, a metal bed on which was a thick grubby looking mattress, a small table and a chair. In the sloping roof was a small window, the glass panes looking as if they hadn't been cleaned since the hut was put up. I looked at my Belgian friend who looked back at me with bright eyes and, I think, read my mind. He said something which I didn't understand but which I'm sure meant that this was to be my 'quarter' until the commanding officer and the other officers arrived back on Monday morning from an enjoyable trip to Belfast and if I didn't like it, that was too bad because there was nothing I could do about it.

343

My immediate thought was to find a telephone and ring NID and ask them to send a truck to carry me back to Lisburn, but decided against it with the thought that the corporal on duty would probably have gone off duty by now, and in any event the best thing I could do was to be patient and see what transpired on Monday morning. Having by sign and gesticulation persuaded my companion to assist me in carrying my box and bedroll to the room he had allotted to me and having located a very primitive latrine and washroom in one of the huts, I decided to have a wash and then to take a walk to find out what other delights Caledon had to offer a somewhat disillusioned liaison officer. My good fortune hadn't entirely deserted me.

About a hundred yards down the Main Street from the Dower House was a small unpretentious looking shop-front marked 'Café', and being in dire need of a cup of tea, if not something more substantial, I decided to investigate further with the thought in mind that there was no likelihood of getting a decent meal at the Dower House. I was most warmly received by a buxom, bustling, warm hearted Ulster woman, and within the hour I had not only consumed a superb plate of eggs and bacon, but had also learned much of her family history, the history of Caledon, her opinion, somewhat disparaging I thought, of American troops who had 'occupied' Caledon a year or so earlier, and of the current Belgian 'invaders.'

The great breakthrough, however, was when I told her that my parent regiment was the Royal Ulster Rifles in which her father had served — then the Royal Irish Rifles — in the First World War. From then on, I was as good as adopted as a member of the family and that small café became my home for the next several weeks, where I took most of my meals, ate like a fighting cock and quickly became one of the locals. A day or so later, when I described my sleeping accommodation, her great regret was that she hadn't got a spare room to put me up but offered to arrange something with neighbours, an offer which I declined with the thought that my Belgian 'hosts' might consider that I was deserting them, which, as it turned out, was the last thing they would have thought.

As I made my way back to the Dower House that first evening I was feeling much more at peace with the world until, in the dark, I had to make my way across the garden and through the trees to my room, and with the aid of a cigarette lighter, locate the electric light switch only to find that there was no bulb in the socket. However, I slept well and woke the following morning to the sound of a church bell, the birds singing and the sun's rays trying to penetrate the dirty window panes. Being a Sunday morning, my first inclination was to return to the café for breakfast but I wasn't sure at the time whether it would be open, and in any event it was only right and proper that I should see what the officers' mess had to offer.

When I entered the room I had identified the previous evening as the dining room, there was one other person present, a middle-aged man, in Belgian army service dress uniform, sitting at one of the tables. Wishing to appear friendly to this stranger from across the Channel, I murmured, 'Bon jour' which, to a Fleming, I subsequently thought, was a mistake. He simply looked at me for a second and returned to what he was doing. In front of him was a large pint mug of what I assumed was coffee. On the table was the remnant of a large piece of bread and on a saucer, a lump of butter. As I watched, fascinated, he would break off a piece of bread, smear it liberally with a coating of butter, dunk the whole into the coffee and then pop it into his mouth. Neither of us said a word. When the bread was finished, he picked up the mug, swallowed the contents, including the molten butter and the sodden bits of bread, belched with obvious satisfaction, got up and walked out. I tested the coffee and then decided to adjourn to my café, which fortunately was open and which I was to patronize from then on.

I met the officer commanding the Caledon Battalion the following afternoon, after kicking my heels around the Dower House during the morning and a chop and chips lunch at the café.

The officers arrived back in ones and twos from wherever they had spent the weekend. Some, on seeing me sitting in the anteroom, introduced themselves, enquiring as to the subject of my 'visit.' I was standing at the window watching Caledon going about its business when a large khaki staff car drew up and out of the passenger seat stepped a red-tabbed colonel who walked up the steps into the hallway followed by his driver, a young girl dressed in the Belgian equivalent of the ATS uniform. He was a youthful looking man of about forty and spoke very good English when he invited me to follow him up the stairs to his office — followed by his chauffeuse.

It was quickly apparent that he regarded my attachment to his unit as a simple military manoeuvre to enable me to have a few weeks' rest on full pay, doing whatever I wanted to do and going wherever I wanted to go. He appeared to assume that I had some connections in that part of Ireland, business or private, and that if my superiors were happy to set up some phoney arrangement to enable me to pursue my own affairs, then he was only too pleased to cooperate. Naively, I suppose, I mentioned my status as liaison officer and my wish to assist him in any difficulty he might have, which he brushed aside with a hunch of his shoulders and a wave of his hand, saying that he had no problems. Sensing that possibly I was a little more conscientious than he had anticipated, he went on to assure me that if any problem cropped up he wouldn't hesitate to ask for my assistance, and, in the meantime, if I was in need of transport for any reason, Marie was available when not otherwise engaged. He turned and looked at the ATS girl sitting to one side. She simply nodded and smiled. As it turned out, I could seldom find Marie when I needed her, although she did take me into Lisburn on a couple of occasions.

I left the colonel's office somewhat bemused, and over the next few weeks became more and more fed up with my situation. From time to time I would watch the Belgian troops whilst on various training activities, but it was more than obvious that with their country liberated and the war in Europe at an end there wasn't much motivation to improve their fighting skills and they had their eyes fixed on the more satisfying prospect of occupying a bit of Germany.

I met Ronnie Wilson and Robin Crockett in Belfast on several occasions, but didn't get much sympathy from them. Ronnie's home was in Portadown, and having qualified as a solicitor before the war and with an office also in that town, he was able to keep himself gainfully occupied. Robin, whose home was in Dublin, was also finding life both in and around Carrickfergus enjoyable, and in any event, being several years older than Ronnie or me, expected to be demobbed well before the year end. Finally, in desperation, I managed to arrange an interview with someone at NID, and my request for a transfer elsewhere was accepted. Shortly after, I said goodbye to my Belgian friends and departed for Beckenham on indefinite leave. If I had known that twenty years later I would be living in Brussels for about fifteen years, I would have cultivated those friendships more assiduously.

13

Germany and Demobilization

I think it was early in August 1945, just after I had arrived home on leave when, early one morning, my mother brought me cup of tea in bed with a copy of the daily newspaper. Banner headlines announced that a new type of bomb had been dropped on Hiroshima and that city and its occupants had to all intents and purposes been obliterated. The Americans had also announced that unless the Japanese surrendered unconditionally another city would be atomized, and Nagasaki followed a few days later. The war with Japan was then over, and I thought it highly unlikely that I would be heading in that direction. A few days later I received instructions to report to someone or other at Victoria station, en route for Germany.

The journey via Dover, Ostend and by rail to Hanover was tedious and uneventful except for an alert in mid-Channel when we all had to don life jackets and proceed to emergency stations because of mines reported to be floating in the vicinity. The devastation in Germany was undescribable; towns reduced to mile after mile of rubble with Hanover a complete shambles. Despite this, there appeared to be plenty of people around, but where they lived and what they did I couldn't imagine, as there didn't seem to be a house or building habitable. At Hanover I was informed that I was posted to the 4th Battalion, Somerset Light Infantry in 43rd Division, who were located at Celle, a small town about thirty miles north east from Hanover and which was largely undamaged.

It's not easy to describe life in the army of occupation of Germany at that time. The battalion was quartered in the Hohenzollern Barracks on the edge of the town and I was given command of C Company. But although there were about 120 troops in the company, there was never anyone to command as every day they were all employed on guards, fatigues and other military distractions, including, of course, home leave.

My daily routine after breakfast was to walk from the officers' mess to the company office where I would meet the company sergeant major. He would report the 'state' of the company — so many warrant officers, NCOs and men, so many on sick parade, home leave etc. He would then go on to outline the requirements of the quartermaster, the RSM and so on for other duties, finishing up by telling me that we might have one or two men for company duties. We would then chat about one thing or another until I felt it time to join some other officers to walk into town for a coffee at the White Elephant, a coffee shop for officers opened in the town by some organization from the UK, possibly with the object of providing officers with somewhere to go until the Officers Club established in the Celle Ratskellar opened its doors.

When sitting in the White Elephant drinking coffee one cold wet morning, I had a stroke of good fortune. In walked a tall figure I recognized instantly as Hemsley, my former fellow student at the Law Tutors, Gibson & Weldon when we were swotting for the Law Society Intermediate exam. He was now a staff captain at our brigade HQ. After swapping notes as to what we had been doing over the past six years, he told me that he had signed on with Gibson & Weldon for a final exam course, starting the following April with a view to taking the final exam in September. He was in the same demob group as me, and expected to get out of the army about March 1946 which meant, of course, foregoing any demob leave.

Hemsley was in a very different position to me in that he had been articled to his uncle, the senior partner in Halsey, Lightly and Hemsley, a large firm of solicitors in St James's, whilst I had no family connections with Robbins, Olivey & Lake, and as my articles had long expired, I didn't know whether I could return to the firm. I was still uncertain as to what my position was with regard to my application for a regular commission. I had decided some months earlier that my future did not lie with the post war regular army; any illusions I had had about life in the army in peacetime had long since evaporated and some months earlier I had sent off a letter asking that my application

349

be withdrawn, but I had had no response. However, after chatting with Hemsley, I decided that the best thing I could do was to follow his example and work for the Law Society final in September the following year, so I sent off an immediate letter to Gibson & Weldon to find out if there were sill vacancies on the April course. I also sent off a further letter which resulted in an interview with the brigade commander. He was somewhat shirty initially, accusing me of messing the army about, but then changed his tune and agreed that I was taking the right course and dismissed me with a handshake and his good wishes. A few days later I heard that a place had been reserved for me by Gibson & Weldon on their April course.

With few troops available for battalion activities, plus the fact that the vast majority were marking time until their return to civilian life, most days were spent doing nothing in particular. After an hour in the White Elephant we would adjourn to the Officers Club in the Ratskellar for a beer before lunch. Beer, at that time if I remember correctly, was free or a few pfennigs, and liqueurs cost a Mark, and as Marks were like confetti there was every encouragement to drink liqueurs if one was so inclined. Sadly perhaps, there were a number of officers who were so inclined.

There were many junior officers in the brigade who had come from all walks of life and done all kinds of jobs and who like me, had entered the army through either the TA or by conscription and who made no secret of their determination to avoid a return to their pre-war civilian life, hopefully by staying in the army. Some, like me, had applied for regular commissions and some were still hoping they would be granted. Others told of unsuccessful wartime marriages and unfaithful wives or just seemed unable to accept that the status and the life style that went with wartime commissioned rank was an interlude which had to end. In the meantime, they took refuge in cheap liqueurs. I was fortunate in that I had now firmed up on a target when I got out of the army, and in any event, in my case spirits of any sort resulted in a violent hangover and were therefore to be avoided.

The daily boredom was relieved from time to time by visits to local places of interest. These trips included the Belsen concentration camp where, although the surviving prisoners had long since been taken away, the full horror of the place was still apparent. It was almost a pleasure to watch the local Germans 'required' to move in and clear up the squalor and inhuman conditions in which the inmates had been forced to live and die. Another visit was to a large factory at Wolfsburg, built ostensibly before the war to produce the 'people's car' but in reality to mass produce military fighting vehicles; all designed with typical German thoroughness, with centralized communal services and facilities so that workers spent their time working, sleeping and exercising without any of the distractions which would be associated with normal daily existence such as household chores, shopping, cooking and taking the children to school. It was rumoured that near Celle had been what was described as an Aryan stud farm, where selected females were serviced by selected males for the mass production of perfect Aryan babies to supplement the Master Race, but understandably this had been closed down and the blonde beauties and their offspring despatched elsewhere.

We also visited Hanover once or twice, where an officers' shop had been opened in one of the few stores which remained watertight, and where I purchased some German 'officers' handkerchiefs', some of which I am still using forty-three years later. Another avenue of escape which I was quick to seize upon was the opportunity to go to a large German Army riding school located on the outskirts of Celle to assist in exercising the large number of horses there. Where all the normal stable workers had gone I have no idea, but the assistance which I and two or three other officers were able to give was greatly appreciated by the British army officer who had been put in charge of the establishment. Whilst it was a bit of an effort to climb out of bed at the crack of dawn on the cold and frosty mornings of that winter, once the effort had been made it was great fun riding those splendid animals around the enormous indoor riding arena, as well as an added means of keeping fit and an appetizer for a good breakfast.

Hunting parties were also organized from time to time around the flat wooded areas near Celle, with the promise of shooting deer, boar or hare, but after spending several hours stumbling across frozen ploughland and through spiky pine forests without seeing anything alive I decided that all wildlife had been exterminated before our arrival.

After the non-fraternization rule had been lifted, all ranks dances were organized to which German girls were invited, and they turned up in their hundreds; some, I was told, having to walk distances like ten miles through the snow-covered countryside and with the prospect of a similar walk home, all for the pleasure of consorting with British troops and a meal of hot coffee and buns. At those dances, which officers were expected to attend, these Fraüleins showed no signs of animosity towards the conquerors of their own menfolk — exactly the opposite in fact.

Although we had no particular occasion or desire to mix with the civilian population in Celle, greatly swollen with refugees from Hanover, Hamburg and Berlin and other heavily bombed cities, the impression I gained from the little contact I had, mainly with elderly men and women, was that they were numbed and stupefied at the catastrophic turn of events over the relatively short period between the achievements and aspirations of Hitler's heyday and the utter defeat and surrender of the German Army and the occupation of their country. I was told that when the 4th SLI moved into Celle after the surrender, and were looking for quarters for officers, they simply selected suitable looking houses, hammered on the doors and when they were opened, told the occupants to get out — now. Men and women, young and old, it didn't matter, and they were lucky to have time to pick up their hats and coats. If they asked where they should go, they were told that was their problem. The British soldier is not cruel or vicious by nature, but he knew what the Germans had been doing and was in no mood to sympathize with German discomfort. I don't think that many of the people of Celle and probably of other similar small towns knew of the extent of the atrocities committed in camps like Belsen. Many must have known of the existence of the camp only twenty or thirty miles away, used for imprisoning so called enemies of the state, but not that those 'enemies' were being systematically exterminated, and even if they had suspicions they closed their minds to the matter, knowing that there was nothing they could do about it.

And so the days and weeks passed, through Christmas 1945 with the usual church parade followed by the officers serving the men's dinners and joining in their festivities before returning to their mess for further refreshments, and on to March, when with no regrets, I said farewell to Celle and the SLI and set off on the long train journey to Ostend, Folkestone and Number 5 Military Dispersal Unit. Before I left, Colonel Lipscombe shook my hand and wished me good luck, saying that when the war with Russia started he would be happy to welcome me back to his battalion.

After a day and night at the MDU, filling up forms and handing over my pistol and other bits and pieces, I was issued with my civilian clothing, a suit, raincoat, shoes and hat, and set off by train to Beckenham on fifty-six days leave, which I was unable to enjoy, and the proud possessor of a war gratuity of £144.4s.0d,, plus a grant of £4.3s.4d. per month for maintenance whilst attending Gibson & Weldon classes to enable me to qualify as a solicitor — subject to satisfactory attendance reports.

As I sat in the Folkestone to Victoria train, rattling its way through the Kent countryside, I began to reflect on my situation. I was no longer a war substantive captain and temporary major, but a plain MR, about to pick up where I had left off, six years and six months earlier. How would I react to a normal civilian life living with my mother in suburban Beckenham? The thought of regular rugger and cricket matches on Saturday afternoons lifted my spirits a little.

No more officer status with men to command and to be cared for. No batman to clean my boots, make my bed and press my trousers — I thought of 'Goosey' Gillanders and Eoin Clapperton. No more mess conviviality and guest nights. No more route marches or nights in slit trenches. No more gliders or parachutes. I thought of the many friends I had made and with whom I hoped to keep in touch, and of those who would never be demobbed: Derek Boustead, George Maginnis, Reggie Morgan, Mickie Archdale, Dickey Quinn, Peter Fogt, Dickie Martin, Killer Johnson, Charles Vickery, Ken Donnelly, John McFadden, John McFaul, Dan Woods, Peter Barry, Harry Croft, Mike Gann, Mike Dowling, John Robertson, Bill Cunningham. They never had the opportunity given to me of deciding what to do when the war was over.

I thought of the LRB and the Old Bailey and 168 OCTU, Ballymena and the RUR Depot, Hereford and mules, Carmarthen, Newbury and the Chequers, Bulford Fields and Hotspur gliders, Chilton Foliat, Ilfracombe and Weston Super Mare, Bulford Kiwi Barracks, parties in Dublin, Broadwater

Farm and D-Day, Ranville and Longueval, Breville, Le Mesnil, Cabourg and Deauville, Touqueville, Mulberry Harbour, Cottesmore, Caledon and Celle. Had it all really happened? Six and a half years seemed to me then about ten minutes, and I pulled my thoughts back to reality.

In three days, on Monday morning, I would be walking down Park Road to New Beckenham Station to catch the eight twenty to Charing Cross with my briefcase in one hand and my umbrella in the other. I decided at that point that a bowler hat would not be appropriate. I would resume my pre-war daily practice of walking along the Strand to Number 218, at Temple Bar, the offices of Robbins, Olivey & Lake, knowing that my articles had long since expired, and then over to Gibson & Weldon's rooms in Chancery Lane. At that moment, I couldn't think of anything I had learned in passing the Law Society intermediate exam.

I was nearly thirty years of age, fit in body and reasonably so in mind, and single, which was probably a blessing. What course of action I would have taken if I had been married and possibly with a family I couldn't imagine. I had no attachments. The girl with whom I might possibly have become serious, Marjorie Rangecroft, had discontinued correspondence during the war, and was probably married anyway. Another, Emmeline Deacon, had abruptly terminated our friendship on the grounds that I hadn't confirmed my intentions by buying her an engagement ring after many months of 'walking out'.

I had no worries about board and lodging, assuming without a thought that my mother wouldn't charge me for accommodation and food. How I would manage on the £4.3s.4d. per month which the Government had promised me provided I attended all my lectures, I didn't know and it didn't really trouble me.

All I knew was that I had to get down to work and pass the Law Society final exam in September. After that, things would take care of themselves.